Formative Spirituality

Volume Five

TRADITIONAL FORMATION

Formative Spirituality

Volume Five

TRADITIONAL FORMATION

·ADRIAN VAN KAAM·

CROSSROAD • NEW YORK

1992

The Crossroad Publishing Company
370 Lexington Avenue, New York, NY 10017

Copyright © 1992 by Adrian van Kaam

Printed in the United States of America
Typesetting output: TₑXSource, Houston

Library of Congress Cataloging-in-Publication Data
Van Kaam, Adrian L., 1920–
    Traditional formation / Adrian van Kaam.
      p. cm. — (Formative spirituality ; v. 5)
    Includes bibliographical references and index.
    ISBN 0-8245-1183-2
    1. Spiritual life—Catholic authors. 2. Christianity—Psychology.
  3. Developmental psychology.   I. Title.   II. Series: Van Kaam,
  BX2350.2.V187 1992
  248.4'82—dc20   92-4179
                                                            CIP

Contents

Preface

V olume V of my series in Formative Spirituality is to be read as a bridge between formation science and one of its possible form traditional articulations, in this case the Christian. As I have tried to show in previous volumes of this series, formation science, its sustaining formation anthropology, and its theory of personality can be used for the dialectical articulation of a wide variety of ideological or religious faith and formation traditions. Formation science can function, moreover, as an auxiliary science to other arts, disciplines, and sciences, notably among them those that we class as human and social. Formation science, in turn, can use these other resources dialectically as auxiliary to its own investigations. In both instances formation science functions, so to speak, on its own feet.

In the previous four volumes of this series as well as in my provisional glossary of terminology to be found in the journal I edit, *Studies in Formative Spirituality,* I discussed the general function of form traditional articulation. When we reflect on the application of these general principles of articulation to specific formation traditions, new questions arise. Appropriate answers to these prepare the field for any specific articulation. Some of the questions to be considered in this volume are the following: What is the role of formation traditions in the formation of any human person or community? How can we integrate within our life the various formation traditions to which we are exposed in pluritraditional societies? How do the differences in formation traditions relate to their sustaining faith traditions or belief systems? Why and how are traditions of more influence on our life than their remnants in the cultures of pluritraditional societies?

Only after gaining sufficient insights into these and related questions will I be ready to reflect in a systematic fashion on the dialectical interaction of formation science with specific Christian formation traditions. I can then begin to appraise their effective or ineffective answers to these questions. This does not mean that I will neglect to do any Christian articulation before its academic and methodological treatment in upcoming volumes. To the contrary, I have been deeply engaged in Christian articulation as a lifelong preparation to culminate in the production of further volumes. My work in this regard can be found in numerous books and articles, in courses and conferences.

In dealing with the questions proposed for consideration in this volume, I still am moving in the realm of formation science, though admittedly

slowly progressing toward its borders. Here my answers will still be formulated in the light of natural empirical-experiential reason. Yet I keep
in mind their possible specific relevance for an articulation of Christian
formation traditions. It is my belief that in these traditions the light of the
Christian revelation plays a dominant role through the mediation of the
sustaining faith tradition in which the Christian formation tradition must
be rooted. It is also my persuasion that this role of reason as illumined by
faith does not eclipse the significant role of natural empirical-experiential
reason and its comprehensive expression in formation science.

A first semester seminarian exposed to four semesters of philosophy before being allowed to start the study of theology may naively ask why we
do not use the Bible or church doctrine to prove the assertions of natural
human reason. Likewise I have met students, clergy persons, or even people who teach in theology departments who ask why, in the preparatory
or ancillary study of general human transcendent formation in the light of
empirical-experiential human reason, Bible texts and doctrinal pronounce-
ments are not used? The answer is simple. Such insertions make sense only
in the second phase of study in transcendent formation. This second phase
is one of dialectical interaction between faith-reason and philosophical or
empirical-experiential reason, in this case between the science of general
human transcendence, a dynamic of formation observable by empirical-
experiential human reason, and this same dynamic as complemented by
the light of revelation and as empirically-experientially implemented in
Christian formation traditions.

In summary, this volume on traditional formation is thus a bridge between two basic coformants of the discipline of formative spirituality. The
first coformant, that of formation science, has been outlined in its main parameters in my introductory four volumes of this series. In these volumes I
referred also to the second coformant, which I described as the articulation
of the science of formation in various formation traditions. Among them I
have chosen as my special interest the articulation of Christian formation
traditions. Before I can treat the Christian form traditional articulation
more systematically, I must examine in this volume the general role of form
traditions in any human formation whatsoever.

Sheer observation, to say nothing of the research that went into this volume, assures me that we are all heirs to more than one tradition. These
traditions interform with one another. I, for instance, am a Christian, but
I inherited among others also a Dutch, an American, and a scientific form
tradition. As for everyone else, so too for me, it is a lifelong task to let these
traditions interact with one another. In the case of Christians I believe that
traditions should be harmonized in such a way that they become integrated
into their everyday existence in the light of their basic Christian tradition.
Then they can serve their Christian quest for consonance.

In this volume I will discuss the interformation of such traditions. The purpose of this volume as well as of subsequent volumes is to prepare us for the final volumes in this series in which I shall consider how scientific, esthetic, economic, or any other tradition affects our Christian formation tradition and vice-versa.

Acknowledgments

It is my pleasure and duty to express my gratefulness to Dr. Susan Annette Muto, executive director of the Epiphany Association, an ecumenical assembly for lay men and women devoted to research, publication, and resource development in the field of spiritual formation, inspired in great measure by my own and her efforts to serve church and world. Dr. Muto, a highly respected author and colleague, coedited this volume with me and selected the terms for its index. Through our conversations and her astute corrections, the book is much closer to what I envisioned it could be.

I also thank Ms. Marie Baird, a doctoral candidate in this field of study. She processed fast and efficiently the final manuscript, often pointing out details of language that led to important improvements.

Earlier drafts of most of the tentative chapters were typed and retyped by Eve Bauer. I am deeply grateful for her dedication, often under pressure, in initiating the work as a whole.

The able administrative secretary of the Epiphany Association, Marilyn Russell, coordinated these efforts and worked diligently with others on the production of the index. She knows how appreciative I am of her as well as of her staff members for their unwavering commitment to faith and formation.

I owe a special debt of gratitude also to outstanding, now deceased, colleagues in the social sciences who honored me with personal invitations to direct many fascinating dialogues with them concerning the differences between our personality theories. We had our polite disagreements. Most of these were rooted in the different nature of their pretranscendent sciences and my science of transcendent formation. I learned much from them that had to be reformulated in this volume in the light of transcendent formation. Some of what I did may sound like rejection, but it is really an elevation of their pretranscendent thoughts and observations to a higher transcendent level.

My friends and colleagues Carl Rogers and Abraham Maslow granted me a firsthand insight into their approach and ideas. Abraham Maslow and I argued amicably about our differences regarding the function of self-actualization in the pretranscendent sense. This did not deter him in his respect for my position. It led him to invite me to teach for an academic year in my own way his courses at Brandeis University when he went on sabbatical.

Another colleague, Professor Han Fortman, with whom I had argued in a series of articles in the Dutch journal *Dux* before I left for America, taught later the psychology of culture as a professor at the University of Nijmegen. During my visits to Holland he invited me to his apartment for days of discussion. He was an astute critic of the psychoanalytic tradition. Some of the quotes from people in that field, used in this book, were pointed out to me by him. I could confirm much of his critique and ideas during our hours of intense and pleasant conversation and note taking. He looked at all forms of psychoanalysis from the perspective of his own field, that of the psychology of culture. I researched the same movements insofar as they were also faith and form traditions.

As this volume will make clear, the perspective of formation science is not primordially that of culture but that of form traditions that underlie our pluritraditional cultures. Writing it compelled me to translate Professor Fortman's compatible ideas and those of others into the more comprehensive metalanguage of formation science.

Without the help of all these wonderful people this volume would not have attained the quality, breadth, accuracy, and lingual precision I believe it now has. I trust that what it says is the fruit of my own faith and formation journey, echoing especially what I have learned since the fateful years following the Second World War and my subsequent experiences of study, teaching, and research in Holland and in the United States.

CHAPTER 1

Exploring Traditions

There are many good reasons for an exploration of traditions. For one thing transcendent traditions focus our attention on effective ways to transcendence. They clarify, moreover, ways of transformation that may happen to resonate with certain aspects of our own unique-communal life call. Familiarity with traditions that emerge in our pluritraditional society helps us to understand and appreciate the adherents of such traditions whom we may teach as students, counsel as clients, or meet as colleagues, neighbors, employers or employees, buyers or sellers.

The ability to translate wisely the insights of other traditions while adapting them congenially to our own may widen and deepen the meaning of our formation journey. To the degree that we harmonize such insights with our own spiritual wisdom and experience, we expand our cohesive sense of the unique-communal call we are most deeply. For example, as an adherent of the Roman Catholic form tradition who is called to the solitude of scholarship, I find helpful insights into my own predicament in the solitary Christian form tradition lived uniquely by the Lutheran Søren Kierkegaard. Knowledge of his life expands my sense of how to appraise my own solitary creative endeavors. The sense of my life call is thereby enhanced.

When I engage in transcendence therapy and direction, teaching or practice, I should be willing to help adherents of all kinds of traditions who truly need my assistance. To reach out to them effectively requires a basic transcendent theory of personality and its applications, a theory that can make sense to those who live other styles of life. Such a multitraditional approach helps to universalize and enrich our theoretical insights as well as their practical applications.

As this volume proceeds, I will show that certain facets of different form traditions are consonant with one another. For example, there are significant similarities between certain aspects or methods of meditation as evolved in different traditions. Such points of agreement can be disclosed by means of dialogue between these traditions. I designate this as the "interformational dialogue of traditions." For instance, a dialogue between the ways of detachment in Christian, Hindu, and Buddhist traditions can

1

reveal commonalities that point to universal principles of the transcendent path for all of humanity.

On a uniquely personal level, we may assimilate elements of other traditions that are consonant with our own unfolding. Such a dialogue should be critical and creative, enabling us to keep our chosen traditions intact while enriching them. The dialogue between traditions that occurs within our interiority, where our own tradition reigns supreme, can be called an "intraformational tradition dialogue," distinguishing it from the interformational dialogue with traditions not yet or never to be internalized by us.

In both the intra- and intertraditional dialogue, we should take into account possible clarifications that come to us from arts, sciences, and other traditions. The result is, as I will show, that certain basic elements of different paths of transcendence come together at surprising levels of integration.

Form Traditions in the Social and Human Sciences

During my research I discovered that the main theories of the social and human sciences do not account sufficiently for the form traditional differences we can observe in daily life. These sciences seem inclined to reduce traditional layers of consciousness to something else, such as the influence of individual parent-child relationships, abstraction made of transindividual parental traditions. Such preapprehensions and preappreciations are dependent on implicit faith and formation traditions of the sciences. These incline the perception and the theory formation of social scientists and practitioners in a specific way. Of course, we are all exposed to the same danger. I introduced, therefore, as one of the basic principles of formation science, that we should consciously try to detect and avoid any insufficiently checked traditional preapprehensions and preappreciations we may have nurtured in regard to traditions unfamiliar to us. We must realize that each transcendent form tradition is embedded in religious or ideological faith traditions or belief systems that are fundamentally distinct. Moreover, the actual fields of everyday presence and action in which adherents implement their belief systems are distinct too. Adaptation to these different fields generates different social patterns in child formation. These may lead in turn to the assimilation of particular formation patterns that may guide people for a lifetime.

What Is a Form Tradition?

We must try to apprehend and appraise our own form traditions and those of other people. But what is a form tradition? How would I describe it from the viewpoint of my formation anthropology? I would describe a formation tradition as a distinctive, overall pattern of receiving, expressing, and giving form in one's life and world. This pattern is coformed by structures and elements that have attained a sufficient degree of consistency and mutual cohesiveness so that the pattern can be seen as a distinct and meaningful whole of basic dispositions, attitudes, and directives. These structures may have assimilated elements of other traditions. Some of these borrowed forms may have reached full or partial consonance with our own basic tradition, others not yet. I have to add that the consistence and coherence of a form tradition implies that it has recognizable principles of organization. For example, a Christian may add to the Christian form tradition some empirical findings of Carl Jung while rendering them consonant by the application of recognizable principles of critical organization and coherence of the Christian form tradition, which in this case would protect one against contamination by the gnostic Jungian faith tradition.

One may try to enter empathically into other transcendent traditions. Often this effort leads to an inner confrontation with our own familiar traditions. The battleground of this confrontation is our actual life form, as described in volume 1 of this series. Questions raised are: Should my actual life be changed in the light of what I am learning in this encounter? Should I assimilate some of these foreign elements insofar as they can be made compatible with the traditions to which I am already committed?

Premature Universalization of Particular Form Traditions
I have observed that clinical theories of personality are always based on at least some presuppositions that are rooted in one or more form traditions, albeit often unwittingly. The ultimate ground of these presuppositions can be found in the tradition that is perhaps one of the unacknowledged bases of their particular approach. For instance, a faith and form tradition of atheism and libidinal determinism is one of the bases of Sigmund Freud's theoretical approach.

Unlike academic theories, clinical ones are more immediately related to data about the empirical forms of life of the people studied or treated. The clinically observed forms of life by which people live daily are, however, always already coformed by specific form traditions. Tradition plays a central role in each human existence from its beginning. Clinical theories tend to universalize the empirically manifested life of the majority of people whose daily existence has been guided for generations by specific dominant traditions. These patterns may then be universalized prematurely. They may assume that they are normative and directive for adherents of all traditions, even those in faraway countries and cultures. Life patterns that are incompatible with these so-called universally human directives, such as those of discriminated minorities or of immigrants from Asian or African countries, may be declared signs of human inferiority or even of psychopathological deficiencies. Psychoanalytically oriented anthropologists, for instance, may explain indigenous African religions as systems of reaction formation against inner anxieties projected outwardly as threats by the spirits of the ancestors.

The universalizing of only one specific formation tradition often leads to the tendency to level people who are not following the basic elements of this absolutized tradition. For it has been made the norm of human wholesomeness and maturity by such social or personality theories. Such depreciation may even take place if people who share the same faith tradition express that shared faith in varied expressions in numerous diverse form traditions. For example, Euro-American Christians may try to convince Afro-American Christians that they should conform to all elements of the former's form traditions. Or paternalistic male Christians may force females to follow their form tradition, which they confuse with the foundations of its sustaining faith tradition.

Different Focus of Formation Science and Other Human Sciences

The social and human sciences have chosen to focus on the pretranscendent data of human life. My formation science, on the contrary, has as its ultimate formal object the transcendent formation of human life. Hence the psychosocial categories in which, for instance, clinical experts do their thinking are different from transcendent categories of thought. Transcendent formative thinking is of necessity transcendent "field thinking." It made me consider things in terms of our whole field of life, as nurtured by a cosmic and radical mystery of formation and as permeated through and through by the traditions of the groups and individuals that give meaning to this field.

The transcendent field approach, which I initiated and on which all of my volumes are based, leads increasingly to a diminishing of the boundaries between field structures. I see them as permeating each other. I already alluded to the example of the permeation of the intrasphere of the field by form traditions that are communicated in and through the interformational sphere. Consequently, in my style of transcendent thinking, I see less of a split between pre-, intra-, inter-, and outer forms, or between the sociohistorical, vital, functional, functional-transcendent, transcendent, and transcendent-functional dimensions of life. I believe that such interformation is also typical of transcendent traditions constantly operative within each of these spheres and dimensions, all of which will become clearer as we move into this volume. For example, during my research in Japan I observed how Buddhist and Shinto form traditions are constantly interforming in the family sphere, public sphere, and worship sphere of the Japanese in the countryside.

We must become attentive to the relationship between traditions and the situations of our field that carry them symbolically. Japanese gardening, for instance, is definitely related to the Buddhistic form tradition. Likewise we should respect the link between the traditions alive within our inner sphere and its relation to our vision of the cosmic and environmental spheres. For example, a tradition that generates respect for nature can facilitate our formation in ecological concern. These traditions deepen our awe for the intertwining that exists between the transcendent and the pretranscendent, between the divine and the profane. In fact, as we shall see, intrinsic relationships exist between any traditional assumptions about human formation and the actual lifestyle to which they give form. This makes us wonder about our own actual form of life and its relation to the manifold forms of personal and group traditions of formation that emerge within our field.

Individual and Transindividual Traditions

Clinical psychologies are overwhelmingly oriented toward phenomena of individualization. They ask, for instance, what happens in the individual relations between parents and children. They generally pay less attention to how transindividual, form traditional patterns shape first of all the interformational sphere between parents and children. On the pretranscendent level, they pay attention to the role of "the" culture on the formation of the pretranscendent ego ideal and superego. The latter are comparable but not fully identical with the executive, functional, managing, or lower "I" that I speak about in my formation theory of personality, to say nothing of the higher transcendent "I." Such a stress on ego and superego exemplifies the influence of pretranscendent individualistic form traditions of the West on the theories of the social, educational, and human sciences.

The prevailing psychological maps and norms of clinically and sociologically researched populations are often assumed to be universal. I do not believe that they can be in their present state. They are too onesidedly centered in individualistic pretranscendent traditions that emerged during the age of the Enlightenment. The unique approach I offer in this new science of transcendent life formation may, therefore, suggest a significant reorientation and restructuring of clinical, developmental, and personality theories.

To be sure I gratefully utilize formationally relevant concepts and constructs of the social and human sciences. But I release them from the limited field observations out of which they emerge and enter into the vocabulary of these sciences. Only in this way am I able to insert them in the wider context of my science and of transcendent form traditions, reformulating them in the process.

Some social scientists may apprehend and appraise pejoratively the life formation and functioning of Afro-American, Hispanic, Celtic, East European, or Mediterranean people; the same for Chinese, Japanese, Indians, Koreans, Indonesians, or Africans. These populations are in some way coformed by transcendence-oriented form traditions. Even those among them who lost or rejected these traditions are still marked by their remnants. There is little room in the theories of the social, educational, and human sciences for the transcendent formation wisdom of these traditions.

To complement the findings of the sciences about the pretranscendent life, I recommend that theorists and practitioners of my science of transcendent formation should not start out with constructs such as ego, superego, libido, collective unconsciousness, archetype, self-esteem, ego identity, or self-actualization. They should identify and elaborate the deeper universal categories of distinctively human formation — categories I have tentatively called: formation, reformation, transformation, formation field, transcendence dynamic, embodiment or implementation dynamic, founding life form, transcendent I and pretranscendent I, field spheres, dimensions, regions, and ranges, integrating core, current, apparent, and actual forms of life. Only after establishing such universals should we observe and describe how these aspects of distinctively human formation function within the unique-communal traditions of people, how they affect and are affected by pretranscendent conditions that are researched by other social, educational, and human sciences.

I realize, of course, that transcendence therapists, directors, counselors, and teachers themselves are a part of their own form-traditional field. Their sets of traditions color their basic preapprehension and preappraisal of those who come to them for counseling. Unwittingly, they may relate to other traditions in terms of the symbolic systems and meanings of their own personally modulated tradition sets. They, as all others, are always in danger of subtly imposing their own tradition directives on the lives of others.

In our fast-changing pluritraditional world, many crises and conflicts emerge in the tradition sets of a significant number of people. Their intrasphere is expanding and differentiating by leaps and bounds. For many this is the unavoidable result of their encounter with religious and ideological form traditions less known to former generations. We cannot know a priori what form traditional conflicts may emerge in groups and individuals as a result of this confrontation. To facilitate the resolution of such crises, we must encourage people to express as fully as possible whatever comes to mind in relation to the implicit or explicit form traditions with which they are coping. We should focus gently on the resistances and resonances they experience in relation to their own traditions as a result of the encounter with other traditions. In the ensuing dialogue they may discover that they can possibly profit from certain selected readings that are relevant to these problems of transition. We should make it possible for them, should they so desire, to work through resistances and resonances evoked by such selected texts. The same applies to lectures, sermons, talk shows, movies, videos, and articles that have given rise to formational questions related to their own tradition set and its infiltration by other traditions.

Distinctions between Form Traditions

In studying and dealing with form traditional conflicts, we will distinguish in this volume between:

1. Form traditions that are merely apparent as distinguished from those that really affect the inner core of people's lives. For example, dress traditions among large crowds of teenagers are for many of them more an imitation of peer appearances that are popular than expressions of deep changes in inner dispositions and attitudes.

2. Form traditions that are consonant in principle with transcendent traditions, at least in their main assumptions, and those that are basically dissonant. For instance, antiminority traditions are dissonant, transcendent democratic traditions are consonant with transcendent traditions.

3. Traditions that are respectful and nonviolent in their communication and propagation and those that are aggressively intruding, giving rise to severe conflicts and crisis experiences. An example of the latter are the colonial European form traditions of the past in the Third World; an example of the former are the present-day Western "volunteer-movement" traditions for social and medical assistance in the same countries.

At the end of these considerations I will take unto account the distinctions that emerge between the various degrees of intensity of each of these three types of form traditions. The intensity of anti-Semitism in the National Socialist and the Stalinist-Communist faith and form traditions is obviously greater and more terrifying than the petty anti-Semitic envy of bourgeois form traditions.

In formation therapy, counseling, teaching, and direction, these considerations about form traditions are not primarily based on philosophical or theological argumentation about the merits of the faith traditions that support these form traditions. They are about the experiential, formational, and transformational reverberations of interiorized facets of such traditions in the intrasphere of one's life and the consequences in one's inter- and outerspheres of life. One can abstractly share the theological principles of the same faith tradition yet inwardly deform them into a shared form tradition of hate and war against form traditions of adherents of the same faith tradition. This has been exemplified in the wars between different Christian form traditions in Lebanon.

Central in the process of healing of inner tradition dissonance is the disciplined or trained empathy of a transcendence therapist, counselor, director, or teacher. If helpful and possible, they should consult with experts of the form tradition with which the person-in-conflict has difficulty.

It is also important to distinguish between what is form traditional for a significant segment of a population and what is characteristic only of this person, family, or subgroup. We should, moreover, appraise how far a person's basic form tradition has been affected by other form traditions. Formation science tries to cast as large a net as possible to catch the many form traditional influences that are operative in the actual lives of people today.

I will thus use a pluritraditional approach. It is only by means of an approach of this sort that I can do justice to the formationally relevant insights and data of other sciences and traditions. I order such insights and data in the light of the formal object of my science. One possible descriptive definition of this object is: foundational transcendent life formation in its very movement of implementation in the various interforming facets of people's fields of presence and action.

The formation scientist or practitioner should be aware that the original viewpoints that I present can be misrepresented by themselves or by others. My formulations can be used by students or readers in either a reductionistic or an integrative manner. The breadth of this formational viewpoint is no absolute guarantee for avoiding reductionism. My foundational concepts and constructs of transcendent life formation can easily be reduced once one begins to focus exclusively on their articulation in one or the other particular way within a specific ideological or religious form tradition. The task of articulation is not to reduce one way of thinking to the other, but to integrate them in each other without distorting them. For instance, my principle of reasonable, realistic, relaxed compatibility can be distorted to defend a levelling or homogenizing of formation traditions that are basically different. This abuse can be facilitated by underemphasizing my corresponding principle of congeniality with one's own tradition.

Tradition Phase Transposition

In other social and human silences, especially in clinical theories, a construct often used is that of *transference*. In terms of my science it refers to the *transposition* of the form dispositions, attitudes, and directives of a past interformational relationship to a present one. For example, in the life history of some people, there may have been a period in childhood of overdependency on the father figure. This dependency developed as a result of the kind of interforming relationship that was fostered between the father and the children. This type of dependency has become part of the ongoing history of the now grown-up children. Every time they find themselves in an interforming relationship with somebody who reminds them of their father, the old dependency relationship repeats itself routinely, for it is deeply programmed in their autonomous nervous system, which is a part of what in my theory constitutes the neuroform of one's life.

In this volume on formation traditions I shall question past over-dependent relations to form traditions as well as present ways of relating to them. At the same time I will investigate how this overdependent relationship of people is related to the traditions of their parents or their substitutes. I will carefully appraise such coercive repetitions due to child-hood overdependencies on the modulated form traditions of the parents. Do they interfere with the real here-and-now relationships between this person and significant others, especially with the transcendence therapist, director, or teacher? I try to establish how family-modulated form tra-ditions were the deeper cause of excessive dependency. My question is then whether present modulations of one's form traditions changed the disposition to overdependency for better or worse.

Therefore, instead of using the term *transference* I introduce the term *tradition phase transposition* or briefly *transposition*. I indicate by this term that we transpose a former phase of interformational relationships with parental traditions to a later phase. These principles are essential for our flexibility in dealing with a great variety of sets of formation traditions in different people.

Universal Human Nature and Varying Form Traditions

The great question for transcendence thinking about traditions is: To what extent is human nature universal? And to what extent is it a change-able manifestation of varying form traditions? A response to these ques-tions can be approached by observation and reflection on the various interformative relationships we observe between people.

To facilitate such observations and reflections on comparative particu-lars, I teach formation theorists and practitioners how to be emphatically in touch with potentially universal threads of distinctively human or transcen-dent formation. They must be alert to the manifestation of such common threads in people and in the traditions they may encounter in persons or may study by means of informational documents. I developed and will fur-ther expand here the structures as well as the metalanguage of formation anthropology and formation science to direct our attention to possible uni-versal aspects of transcendent human formation. Initially some of these basic categories may be mixed in the minds of students and readers with the specific and particular categories that are implicit in their own pre-apprehensions and preappraisals. For our appraisal capacity as a whole is modulated by the specifics and particulars of our own traditions. Hence I stress the need for constant self-critique during our formation study and practice.

We have to go deeper into our own preapprehensions and appraisals. If we are willing to go deep enough, they may become like mines where the ore of universal human life directives lies buried under layers of particular prejudices that feed and strengthen our attitudes of social injustice and discrimination. Neither should we forget that there are profound variations on the sets of traditions that direct the lives of different individuals. This fact demands that we adaptively articulate the findings of common formation, making them compatible with such variations in those who come to us for teaching or counsel.

This introduction to the traditional search for transcendence, its impact on the generation of a wide variety of form traditions and subsequent problems and conflicts, clarifies the necessity to consider in depth our traditional formation in this volume.

CHAPTER 2

Formation Anthropology and Formation Tradition

Formation tradition is a seminal concept in my science of formation. In my anthropology, too, it takes a central place. In formation science, as well as in its underlying anthropology, the idea of formation tradition is interwoven with other basic concepts and constructs. These came to me at the time of my first intuitions of a new paradigm in the human sciences. Among these concepts the idea of formation tradition played a major role in my gradually unfolding anthropology and in the beginnings of a formation science built on its assumptions.

I designed formation tradition as a comprehensive concept embracing all of formation in light of transcendent transformation. All chapters of the story of our life are interlaced with traditions or systems of customs that influenced us along the way. To understand our life implies that we take into account the traditions by which we have been touched through parents, other family members, peers, neighborhoods, towns, country, schools, churches, places of labor, and leisure.

This insight grew in me when I was interacting with people of many different locations, backgrounds, ideologies, and religions during the last year of the Second World War. Some of the groups I helped to hide from the enemy shared a similar ideological or religious faith tradition, yet the ways in which they gave form to their shared faith varied considerably. It became clear to me that traditions of how to receive and give form in life had a more direct impact on their everyday dispositions and comportment than the theological or ideological statements of their belief systems. I found that I ought never to underestimate the essential links of their form traditions with their sustaining faith traditions. I soon realized, however, that these connections were often implicit. Such tenets of belief are the object of research by ideological philosophies or theologies; they are taught to others in catechisms or ideological manuals such as the so-called Little Red Book by Chairman Mao. Some of the people hiding with me were well instructed in theologies or ideological philosophies; they could talk about theories at length, at times eloquently. This sophistication had been an advantage in their formation. But in the affairs of everyday life they

11

were guided more immediately by their specific formation traditions. Often lacking was a basic insight into their own formation traditions and the distinction between these and their faith traditions. They did not fully appreciate the weighty influence of form traditions in their own life. Neither did they suspect how distortions and contaminations by their own or other particular form traditions could have affected the basic faith and formation tradition to which they were committed primarily.

Limited Effectiveness of Theologies and Ideological Philosophies

Theologies and ideological philosophies, while of tremendous value for people's understanding of their faith, cannot assist them sufficiently in all details of the everyday implementation of their belief systems. Beyond helpful pastoral guidelines of a general practical and ethical nature, theologies and philosophies in themselves do not have the tools for a minute scrutiny of the practical art of dealing with daily formation dynamics, crises, conflicts, affects, and images.

How to live compatibly together with others coming from different form traditional communities became an acute problem in our situation of hiding. A number of people had earlier sought guidance in the social, therapeutic, and educational sciences. This had helped them considerably but not sufficiently for coping with a life-and-death situation. Some of the practical, helpful insights of these sciences are rooted in their own underlying anthropologies, with their implicit faith and form traditions. Certain concepts of these anthropologies were at odds with the anthropologies sustaining the formation traditions to which people had committed themselves — traditions that became now crucial for them. This led to an inner split in their lives. Their need inspired me to initiate a formation science with an explicit, more universal and fundamental anthropology that would be compatible with a significant number of faith and form traditions and complement the pretranscendent counseling they had received. Such a science would be a protection against contamination and confusion while highlighting and complementing the relevant contributions of arts, sciences, and other traditions. Clinical and pastoral counseling courses, too, could be enlightened by such a new discipline. A frame of reference could be developed that would prevent the borrowing of concepts from the social and human sciences without sufficient appraisal of possible contaminations by alien anthropologies and their sustaining implicit faith and form traditions.

In this volume I shall try to show how any distinctively human tradition is related to the age-old wisdom of transcendent formation. I hope to awaken a new appreciation of the form traditional element in all of human life, love, labor, and leisure. The examination of this element will complement the contributions that the social and educational sciences can make to our understanding of the pretranscendent aspect of our life.

In this and the immediately following chapters on my anthropology, I limit myself to the relation of this formation anthropology to the function of formation traditions. In subsequent chapters of this volume the role of formation traditions will be considered more closely. We will ask ourselves what their empirical implications are for the formation of their adherents.

At the end of my next volume in the series I shall give an overall view of my formation anthropology, integrating in a general frame of reference the various anthropological aspects discussed in these five earlier volumes.

Human Life and Formation Tradition

Our life is distinctively human because of our powers of insight and freedom in regard to what is congenial with our nature and compatible with our environmental situation. As all other forms of life, so, too, human life can survive only by being compatible with its surroundings. Without compatibility no life can maintain itself and prosper. The form reception and donation of subhuman forms of life is directed by instinctive formation dispositions. Subhuman and human forms of life have in common that they must somehow appraise which aspects of their surroundings are either relevant and beneficial or irrelevant and detrimental to their congenial unfolding. But there is an essential difference between their modes of appraisal. Subhuman forms live by an instinctive appraisal that can be called appraisal only in an analogical sense. From this innate type of instinctive appraisal, directives for formation flow forth instantly and automatically. These directives and their underlying instinctive dispositions organize spontaneously the surroundings of subhuman life forms into useful environments for instinctive formation. As a result of this instantaneous process, subhuman life forms find themselves from the beginning in an environment that is formationally relevant to them. They fit smoothly into surrounding nature like a glove fits a hand and its fingers. Therefore, animals do not have to appraise mentally or imaginatively how they can reform their surroundings into well-organized fields of presence and action as humans must do continuously.

Human Appraisal is Appraisal in the Proper Sense

We are far less endowed with formational instincts than animals are. We make up for this lack by our powers of insight and freedom. Subhuman sentient forms of life disclose instantly and automatically aspects of their surroundings that are relevant for their growth and survival. They translate these instinctively into predictable fields of formation and action. To humans, however, the cosmos appears initially as chaos. The first striving of instinct-poor but insightful human life is to turn this chaos into fields that are meaningfully ordered and predictable. This striving for the constitution of predictable environments, while typical of each human life, marks also humanity as a whole. In principle people search together for increasingly predictable, meaningful fields of presence and action that are congenial with human nature. They embody the results of their search in formation traditions so that others today as well as future generations may profit from them.

Horizontal and Vertical Interformation

People living today try to survive and grow by interforming with each other in this search of mind, heart, and senses. I name this aspect *horizontal interformation* because it happens between individuals and populations, scientists and practitioners, scholars and teachers, laborers and entrepreneurs, who share here and now the task of implementation of their common faith in their niche of society. I try to comprehend in the expression *faith implementation* the ways in which people of varied times and places attempt to live their faith compatibly and compassionately within an endless variety of situations. I try to find out how they stay faithful to their basic convictions as well as compatible with the ever-changing demands of their successive environments and societies. I distinguish this horizontal interformation from *vertical interformation*. I call the latter vertical insofar as it represents an interformation between individuals and populations who live today and those of the past or of the future.

Vertical interformation with past generations is made possible through communication with their form traditions, rites, symbols, and writings. Vertical interformation with future generations takes place through what we think or imagine will be their needs and how we allow these imagined needs to give form to our life here and now. For example, our concern at the present with nuclear waste storage and with the destruction of the environment may be motivated by our concern for our children, grandchildren, and their offspring.

Formation traditions develop by means of prefocal, sometimes focal, dialogue between adherents of specific faith traditions who are compelled by history to share a somewhat similar journey within the same life situations. Traditions contain records of dissension and consensus, of tentative integrations and failures, of mutual understanding and respect, of wars, depreciative discriminations, and persecutions.

Human life *is* traditional. The effectiveness of its journey depends on interformation with others. We must take into account past and present attempts by others to give form to life in response to challenges that are similar to those we are facing. Therefore, human life cannot be understood by an analysis of its vital strivings alone or by an exploration of merely the minimal remnants of traditions reflected in shared general cultures or social surroundings. Many facets of influential particular traditions are mirrored in cultural directives, symbols, and social institutions. To understand them in depth, we must dive below them. We must explore the underlying traditions themselves. We must not be deterred by the fact that they may be hidden deeply in our nonfocal consciousness.

During the war I observed firsthand how various traditions led to different lifestyles of Dutch people, who evidently shared the minimum of a general Dutch culture. This growing insight led me to a consideration of the difference between the concept of general culture and that of specific formation traditions.

General Culture and Specific Formation Tradition

Out of these observations arose my concept of *vormings traditie*, or formation tradition. I saw it as one of the core concepts of formation science (*vormings wetenschap*). During this period I engaged in many conversations with university students and Dutch professionals with whom I was hiding from the Nazis. Our lively debates made me aware of the differences between their views and my concept of tradition and its planned role in my anthropology. Trained in the social sciences, they were familiar with the standard idea of culture and its role in life's unfolding. Their wonder about the new idea that I proposed compelled me to ask myself: Why did not someone before me come upon the idea of formation tradition as distinguished from "faith tradition" as well as from "nature" and "culture"? To explain to them the "why" of this lack of awareness, I told them the fictitious story of a Dutch herring already familiar to some of them. By some miracle of nature this herring was able to reflect on its own existence and its conditions. As the tale goes, only at the end of its life was even this smart herring able to discover the nature of water and its everyday necessity for its survival. Only after being caught and gasping for air on the deck of a fishing vessel did the fish realize what it means to be a water creature. Before that moment water had been so much taken for granted, was so natural for the everyday life experience of even this perceptive resident of the sea that it escaped its awareness.

Similarly we should not be surprised that social sciences only emerge late in the history of human thought, enabling us to discover how we are formed daily by the sea of the culture in which we are immersed by history. My own observations in that fateful year of war compelled me to go deeper than this influence of culture. I began to realize how we are formed continuously by a power beyond or below culture. We are coconstituted first of all by selected formation traditions. Only remnants of them find a place in our pluralistic cultures. These cultures are only significant indicators, mirrors, shells, shadows, and compromises of the various specific traditions by which people live. Traditions are like unique streams and rivers that discharge some of their contents into the homogeneous sea of the culture.

Social scientists may have been reluctant to acknowledge this all-pervasive, primary power of traditions. They may have been inhibited by their assumptions about the "unscientific" status of religious and ideological traditions. They may have felt uneasy with the concern of the latter for the transcendent dimension of reality. To them the concepts of nature and culture may have seemed more objective and manageable.

Seeing the impact on people around me of their traditions, I began to realize that the exploration of formation traditions should be a basic feature of the science I had in mind and its anthropology. In my discussions with the students in hiding I did not deny that social sciences, such as information science or *informatica*, psychiatry, psychoanalysis, sociology, cultural anthropology, history of culture, political science, economy, and education science could add significant insights and findings to our explorations of transcendent formation traditions. These sciences of the pretranscendent life may consider similar events from their own viewpoints. Their vision usually restricts itself to the role of nature, culture, and society in the pretranscendent formation of human life and its environment. The discipline of transcendent formation can profit from their findings. Conversely, they may gain from the insights generated by formation science on the formational role of traditions in human life in its transcendent dimension. For this dimension affects indirectly the pretranscendent facet of life that is the formal object of the research and theorizing of the sciences and disciplines of the pretranscendent life.

CHAPTER 3

Human Nature and
Specific Formation Traditions

I t had become clear to me that the influence of general culture on formation had been overrated at the expense of the deeper effects of specific formation traditions. But what about nature? Is nature not more powerful than formation tradition? How are nature and tradition related to each other? The more I saw the impact of traditions on people hiding with me, the more I asked myself if this influence was basically due to human nature itself. Was the forming power of tradition simply added to our inherent formation potencies? Or did it in some way enhance and orient these potencies? What share did human nature have in the formation of our life?

I became fascinated by these questions. Before the role of culture in formation was raised by the emergence of the social sciences and before I myself had raised the question of the more basic role of traditions, the existence of both seems to have been taken for granted. Therefore, in the beginning of our civilization nobody focused on the question. For the prescientific mind there was no question to begin with. How much more astute, however, was their interest in human nature! From the beginning of our Western culture, thinkers have been concerned with the part that nature played in their lives. Philosophical anthropology spoke already since Aristotle and Plato about *nature* (*fysis, natura*) while saying little about general culture or specific form traditions. From the beginning of humanity's history of reflective thought, there arose a need to speculate on what was the essential and inalienable form of human life as basically different from plant and animal life.

The Greek word *fysis* (from *fuomai* = to be born) and the Latin *natura* (from *nascor* = to be born) refer to what comes into existence by birth. According to ancient philosophers both words point to the principle of the vital movements of living beings. From this meaning it was only one step to the subsequent idea of essence. (See, for example, Thomas Aquinas, *S. Theol.* 1, 29, 1 ad 4.) Our nature is our very human essence out of which emerge some unchangeable form potencies with which human life is basically endowed. Every person is responsible for his or her own ac-

17

tualization and orientation of these potencies. However, at that time not much was said about the empirical-experimental role that either general culture or specific form traditions play in this process. It was probably not only the lack of empirical interest that made for this neglect. One cause of this inattentiveness may have been the absence of a highly diversified pluritraditional society. When a general culture and a specific tradition coincide, the unfolding of most people's life falls into one and the same undisputed groove. The course of one's life unfolding seems natural. The homogeneous dominant way of understanding and doing things looks unquestionable. They seem without beginnings that are freely initiated at some point in time. Hence few felt the need to ponder how specific formation traditions influenced the general cultural way of life. It simply was there; it was always there, will always be there for everyone to follow like driftwood follows the stream of a river without questioning.

Complication of Nature by Form Traditions

The moment I introduced the concept of form traditions and perceived their variety in pluritraditional societies, things became more complicated. We are no longer faced with only the unchangeable nature or essence, the basic form potencies of people, or with a homogeneous general culture naively conceived as natural, self-evident, and necessary. These are no longer for us a sufficient explanation of how people in our pluriform societies will receive and give form in their lives. The availability of a variety of specific form traditions sets up a tension between the human essence and the way in which people choose to actualize their essential potencies. People adhere to varied form traditions. These enable them to actualize their form potencies in many different directions. Such directions are exemplified and favored by the traditions they prefer. Obviously the directions proposed by form traditions should not deny or neglect what we essentially are. In some way they must be in tune with the essence of our life. There must be some relationship of congeniality between these directions and our nature as humans. To deny this would lead to an existentialistic, absolutely self-actualizing, view of formation.

Faced with so many form traditions in people hiding with me during the war raised in my mind the question of whether every one of these traditions, lived by my cooperators and protegées, was in all facets congenial with our human nature or essence. I kept asking myself what is natural or consonant with nature, and what is unnatural or dissonant? Is every way of life I observed in them in all its directives congenial with human nature?

I myself had to integrate with my own basic tradition the time-honored form traditions of resistance against a common enemy. I experienced that such a modulation of my lifestyle and dispositions felt initially somewhat artificial. Later on when I had absorbed this accommodation in my everyday life, it became a "second nature." This very expression made me aware again how easily we identify our basic nature and form traditional ways of living. What became more and more clear to me in all of this was how many of our personal core dispositions are taken unwittingly from our form traditions.

For example, it seems natural to Shiite Muslims of Iran to be disposed in the core of their being to religious martyrdom. Many of the young country boys, who marched proudly off to certain death, may have been unaware to what degree this disposition was an effect of their tradition, assimilated by early formation in their family and community life. To take this example one step further, we may ask ourselves again, where and how does this martyr disposition of the Iranians tie in with human nature? As such it is surely not prescribed in detail by the basic nature all humans share. However, there is in that nature a predisposition for transcendence of self-centered gain and for dedication, for surrender, even of one's life for a perceived noble cause. How one gives direction to this dynamism, disposes one's self or lets oneself be disposed by it, depends on the basic tradition in which one has been formed initially or which one has later chosen. Neither is it a result of only a foundational faith tradition. To return to our example of the Iranian Muslim tradition, other Muslims with other formation traditions, while adhering to the same Islamic faith tradition, may not be disposed in the same enthusiastic way to religious martyrdom.

Typically and Distinctively Human Traditions

Toward the end of the war, I had come to the conclusion that the form traditions of people give rise to life directives that in their particulars are more than what human nature in general prescribes. Nevertheless they are rooted in human nature insofar as they give a certain form to dynamic potencies and predispositions inherent in nature. Such directives can and are often inspired by the traditions to which people have been exposed. Their directives and those of their form traditions are not necessarily in all facets consonant with the distinctive form of human nature. If not, I call them still *typically* human insofar as only the human type of life could give form to and execute such directives. Animal types of life could not organize concentration camps to extinguish methodically their real or imagined opponents, as I observed in the Nazis that occupied my country. To distinguish such inhuman directives and deeds of human types from consonant human directives and deeds, I called the latter *distinctively* human dispositions, attitudes, acts, and directives.

Both the *typical human* and the *distinctively human* are linked to human nature but in different ways. The typical human is linked to human vital-functional possibilities of thought and action. These possibilities are inherent in human nature. The actualization of such possibilities can be vitally-functionally congenial without being necessarily humanly congenial. The distinctively human is linked to human nature as called to be primarily spiritual or as guided by the human potential for loving appreciation of the good, the true, and the beautiful as epiphanies of a higher mystery. The war had taught me, as nothing else did, the distinction between the typical human technical potencies and the distinctively human higher possibilities. I observed in horror those who destroyed the life of my fellow citizens, in awe those who gave their life to save humanness. Deeply etched in my wounded war consciousness, these memories would be another guide on the way to my gradual establishment of a distinctively human science of formation.

Mystery of Formation

The variety of traditional ways of form reception and donation I saw among the people with whom I lived kept bringing me back to the human nature and essence we must somehow all have in common. Otherwise how could we distinguish humanity as a unique species from other species on earth? Where did this basic sameness of our shared humanity come from? My question concerned the mystery of our ultimate origin. Speaking with my new companions, I realized that the answers to this ultimate question were influenced by each one's faith and form tradition. People have responded to this question in a variety of religious or ideological ways. The same diversity of response holds for the prescientific anthropologies that are the hidden fundaments of the social and human sciences. The question of our beginnings raises many other questions. Our origin is a mystery for us. Can we know anything about this mystery? Are we somehow preformed in this all-embracing ground? Does this mystery in some way accompany us during our journey on earth? Are we responsible to that mysterious source for the form we give to our life and world? Is that nameless spring of our life and its formation personal or impersonal? Different answers are given by different traditions.

Human Essence and Existence

As I have already indicated, I make a distinction in my own anthropology between the essence of our human life form and its ongoing formation in and through the very act of living or existing. As all empirical-experiential sciences, so, too, formation science cannot focus its main research on a speculative study of essences. This is not to deny that formation science, as all human sciences, has philosophical underpinnings. It must clarify for itself and for others how it views the nature or essence of the human life it proposes to study in its empirical manifestations. But such unavoidable philosophical prolegomena do not make the social and human sciences professional philosophies or theologies. Empirical sciences are not primarily about essences and ultimate causes. Formation science, as one of them, is first of all about the form we receive from and give to our everyday human process of living or existing. It asks how we can appraise and improve the daily form reception, donation, and expression in our life. How can we *give* empirical form effectively and elegantly, yet congenially and compatibly? We cannot apprehend and appraise how we should live or exist without referring to our basic nature or essence and its mysterious source. These prescientific presuppositions, as in all other social and human sciences, function as an ultimate guiding light.

Prescientific Presuppositions

All scientists follow, at least implicitly, certain prescientific conceptions. These cannot be proven nor disproven in their universality by empirical research. They are too comprehensive to be taken apart in a test tube. They are so universal that they comprehend everything, including all the ways in which we do science. This is even more true of the human sciences. These deal with human events and the observable manifestations of the experiences to which they give rise. Such events and experiences are more directly influenced by the philosophical outlook of people than the material objects examined by the physical sciences. It became clear to me from the university students and professional people hiding with me that almost all people, including scientists, form these anthropological concepts under the influence of religious or ideological faith and form traditions in which they have been reared at home, in school, in the workplace, through recreation or by the media.

I saw the possibility of a continuing reverse impact of these traditions, even in students who were rebelling against their early upbringing. Their choice of new prescientific universals was a "contraform," a going against the traditional form of their parents. I realized soon that the choice of what they held on to was in a reverse way dependent on their initial form tradition. They were so intense about it because they had to ward off, perhaps for a lifetime, their adherence to an earlier tradition. Especially the war threat to their life, their isolation from the university in the attics and haylofts of lonely farms, tended to evoke past traditions, such as that of a religious Judaism. The influence of a formation tradition, once embraced, never seems to wear off totally. It keeps coforming in reverse even the elaborate contraforms we erect against it. Our life is too short, our experience too small, to disclose by ourselves alone the wisdom of consonant living. If we give up a tradition, we always seem compelled to fall back on some other tradition, or on a syncretism of aspects of various traditions. These replace the original one we assimilated at home.

Existential and Existentialistic Assumptions

Persistent reflection on the prescientific assumptions regarding the role of the concepts of essence and existence in the various sciences gave me a new insight. I became aware of a basic difference between the existing social and human sciences and my projected human science of formation.

Formation science like other human sciences would be necessarily existential. This means it would be life- and praxis-oriented. Human sciences ask how people live or exist instead of mainly or exclusively concentrating on the speculative study of their essences and essential properties. I could not escape the impression that the social and human sciences, as they came to me in our discussions, were not only *existential*, as they should be. They were also for many of their representatives what I began to call *existentialistic*. This means that for them human nature is not a lasting essence receiving its unchangeable primordial meaning and direction from a higher power. For many of them it seems more to be a totally changeable self-project, a mere becoming. In their view we make ourselves by existing; we are our own creation. They believe that we are absolutely independent self-actualizers, that we give form to our own life merely by our own inventive and adventurous existing.

The mistaken assumption of the psychological existentialists is that self-actualizing existence precedes essence instead of the other way around. For them human nature is totally changeable. There is no enduring essence that escapes in any way the *hubris* of human self-creation. This assumption of many social scientists is usually implicit or, to use my term, prefocal. I sensed that this assumption and its popularization could undermine the classical religious formation traditions. My mounting concern in this regard was another reason that inspired me to initiate at the appropriate time a distinctively human formation science. I hoped that this would help people not to fall into the existentialistic trap. Such entrapment is by no means necessary as can be seen in many outstanding social scientists who are necessarily existentially or empirically oriented without being existentialistic. My science, too, would be a practical science of life based on concrete observable existence. Hence it would be existential by its very nature. This implied that it would be occupied mainly not with speculations on the essence of life but with empirical-experiential life formation. By the same token its students would be prepared not to be existentialistic as a number of representatives of other social sciences had become unwittingly. Students of distinctively human formation would not exclude the human essence as the normative ground of human existence. At the same time they would complement, correct, and integrate any findings of the existentialistic social scientists that would be compatible with the formal object and the anthropological presuppositions of formation science.

Instead of being existentialistic implicitly or explicitly, formation science would be explicitly existential or implemental. Its ultimate criterion would be the consonance of human existing with human essence as rooted in a preforming mystery that called it forth. Continuing the same course of thought, I asked myself what could be the bridge between essence in its generic, specific, and unique coformants, on the one hand, and the practical striving for its everyday implementation in our empirical existence on the other? In answer to this question, I developed the construct of a foundational or founding life form.

Founding Life Form

The founding life form is not identical with either our abstract essence or our empirical existence. It is a bridge between the two, partaking of both in a fundamental way. From our abstract essence it takes the specifically and uniquely transcendent nature of our life and its ultimate calling. From our empirical existence it takes our genetic-vital and our primordial socio-historical context in time and space. This first, most basic incarnation of our essence will always be with us. The transcendent-essential, the vital-genetic, and the basic sociohistorical-functional context together are the fundament on which we have to build our life. The three coform in intimate interwovenness a foundation of our uniquely individual-communal formation in time and space. We have to take them into account as the basic givens, the point of departure, that we cannot totally escape. We must increasingly disclose them to ourselves if we want to attain consonance instead of conflict. Our formation must be in fundamental congeniality with this ground floor of our existence as with our inmost reality. It is an expression of the unique meaning the mystery gives to our life.

Here again we see the inseparability of essence and existence. Early on in Holland I appraised critically the existentialistic foundations of some representatives of psychology and other social and educational sciences. My critical notes on psychology's existential, instead of existentialistic, foundations were the beginning of the first book I wrote after I was appointed an assistant professor of psychology in the United States. I entitled it *Existential Foundations of Psychology*.

My lectures as a psychology professor given in that department — before I was able to return full time to my formation science in a newly established, separate institute — were for a great part dedicated to the countering of an existentialistic psychology of mere self-actualization and individuation. I neither denied the contribution of this psychology and the other social and human sciences nor did I belittle their empirical researches, insights, and theories. My disagreement was mainly with any of the existentialistic assumptions some representatives of these views seemed to harbor. Their assumptions threatened to contaminate the formulation of their theories and findings. Mine was a concern for the true classical meaning of existential as basically different from the absolute meaning given to it implicitly by some existentialistic psychologists, psychiatrists, and sociologists, and soon enough by a number of pastoral counselors and therapists. The latter lacked at times sufficient formation in theoretical critique and appraisal of the form traditional assumptions hidden in the formulations of these scientists from which they borrowed so heavily.

CHAPTER 4

Disclosure of Formation Traditions

Observations of the influence of form traditions on people around me disclosed to me the role of traditions in my own life. The last year of the war I was ejected out of the homogeneous milieu of a theological seminary. I felt like a pilot catapulted out of a downed plane. I became acquainted on a day-to-day basis with men and women in crisis who had grown up in environments different from my own. Many of them shared my faith tradition, but how different were their ways of giving form to this common foundation!

In helping all kinds of other stragglers to hide and survive, I was faced not only with different form traditions but also with faith traditions, with people of various denominations and ideologies. In their case, too, I discovered that adherents of the same Jewish, Protestant, Freudian, Jungian, Adlerian, humanistic, Marxist, or existentialistic belief systems developed different formation traditions. They gave form to their life in accordance with their own faith and personality while trying to be compatible with the particular situations in which they had to live and express their basic convictions. It soon became clear to me that there must be an essential difference between a faith and a formation tradition.

Another thing I observed in my growing empathy with them was that these people of diverse background had still some things in common. Certain facets of their divergent traditions manifested some basic similarities. This alerted me to the possibility of a formation science and anthropology that could examine such similarities. I had ample time to reflect on these observations in my hiding place or in my leisurely walks along the lush, watery meadows, or *polders* in the lowlands that surrounded the farm that had given me in its hayloft a refuge from deportation to Germany and a hidden center from which to start an underground newspaper. My reflections made me aware of my own form tradition, its difference from that of others who shared the same faith or were of other persuasions. I saw room for its enrichment. I pondered its limits and possibilities, above all its impact on my life, an impact I had taken for granted.

The confrontation with other traditions compelled me to compare them to one another. Steady comparison disposed my mind and perception in a new fashion. It gifted me, first of all, with a new understanding of myself as coformed by a limited set of form traditional dispositions and directives. I realized increasingly that my directives in many ways differed from those of others, even if they were rooted in the same faith foundations as I was. For the first time I began to understand that formation directives went beyond the basic directives of my faith, even if they were congenial with its foundations. What went beyond or expanded these faith directives were the directives of the empirical-experiential implementations of my faith in my own concrete life and in the situations I shared with others within a specific environment. This made clear to me why they could not be minutely explored in *all* their empirical details by the scholarly disciplines of theology or philosophy.

I sensed almost from the start that empirical-experiential methods would be needed within a new science that would serve the formational implementation of basic belief systems. Suddenly the answer to a question that had bothered me for some time dawned on me. I had been asking myself for many years why classical spiritual masters like Teresa of Avila, John of the Cross, Thérèse of Lisieux, Francis Libermann, Hadewych, the author of the *Cloud of Unknowing*, and others engaged so little in theological discussion in their writings. They did not analyze the nature of grace, of the sacraments, of angels, of dogmatic and moral issues. In the writings of each of them one could put the theology they implicitly espoused on a few sheets of paper. Only now did the why of their lack of extensive theological analysis become evident to me. They were dealing with the empirical-experiential expression of their faith in the concrete situations of their own inner and outer life or in the lives of their directees. I saw at once how formation science could be nourished by continual dialogue with these intuitive predecessors.

I became sensitive to the fact that my own personal schemes of formation perception and appraisal, my form-giving categories of thought, affects, and images, my familiar language forms by themselves alone would not be sufficient to help me understand the form traditions of people of other religions, denominations, and ideologies and their impact on their lives. I realized for the first time how impossible it would be to establish an unprejudiced science of formation and its anthropology without attention to this language problem. I had to give form to a language that would not exclusively point to the everyday language of people of my own tradition alone.

The observation of other form traditions became for me a mirror of the endless possibilities of human life to give form to its transcendent faith and commitment. The exploration of formation traditions shows us as in a magnifying glass the inexhaustible variety of human expressions of form reception and donation within always changing life situations.

Reflection on the myriad ways in which people create their form traditions enhances awareness of our own formational identity and therewith of our field of self-control. Insofar as we are not conscious of the impressions of form traditions on our life, we are not in control of their influence. Prefocally dominated by them, we lack the power to give direction to this mighty stream that carries us continuously.

Disclosure of Form Traditions and Missionary Sensitivity

The seminary where I received my philosophical and theological training was a seminary for missionaries. One facet of missionary preparation was that of a preferential interest in people who did not belong to one's own tradition. This missionary sensitivity played a role in my discovery of the distinction between faith and form tradition.

Historically a number of missionaries have shown a serious interest in the form traditions of others without knowing this new concept explicitly. They did not formulate the rationale of this concept, its distinction (not separation) from the concept of faith tradition and its many ramifications. Hence they often confused form tradition with an underlying faith tradition.

A remarkable sign of such openness was the adaptation to Chinese form traditions in Peking by the missionary Matteo Ricci (1553–1610). His attempts became the occasion for the so-called battle of rites, which Rome decided against Ricci. Similarly in India the missionary Roberto de Nobili (1577–1656) tried to make Christianity compatible with the form traditions of that country. He took on the formation customs of the Brahmas.

The second founder of my own missionary society, Francis Libermann, was the son of an Orthodox rabbi and himself a rabbinical student. Formed himself first in a Jewish and later in a Catholic tradition, he was sensitive to the traditions of others. He was convinced that his missionaries should adapt themselves to the traditions of those they encountered. "Be Black with the Blacks," he used to say. "Do not judge by first impressions. Do not judge according to what you have seen in Europe, according to what you have been used to in Europe. Rid yourselves of Europe, of its customs and spirit. Become Black with the Blacks, and you will judge them appropriately; become Black with the Blacks, to form them appropriately, not in the European fashion, but leaving them what belongs to them" (N. D., 9 [330], 1847; Gilbert 1983).

Once I had initiated the distinction between these two kinds of tradition, I gained a better understanding of the initial hesitancy of Roman church authorities in adopting too readily alien rites. In that period of history the distinction was not yet clearly defined and carefully elaborated. That was what I was trying to do. Neither was there yet a science that could facilitate the prevention of confusion between traditions of faith and formation, between doctrine and its formational implementation, between professional theology and the scientific exploration of empirical-experiential adaptations of faith directives to field directives. Those responsible in the church were cautious, understandably so. They sensed intuitively the danger that the adoption of a foreign form tradition could mistakenly be confused by people with the faith that was at the root of that tradition. Such indistinctiveness could compromise a person's own faith tradition.

A similar concern can be found in the adherents of ideological faith traditions. I observed this caution in Marxist members of the Dutch underground. They would betray their vigilance for the purity of their ideological doctrine in the word *revisionism*. They feared the contamination of their Marxist faith tradition by an insufficiently appraised adoption of alien form traditions by their adherents during our shared battle against foreign invaders. Revisionists among their own comrades were those who in their appraisal seemed insufficiently critical in their attempts to foster form traditional compatibility with freedom fighters motivated by other persuasions.

More recently the chaplain corps of the United States Navy enabled me with my colleagues to test my initial intuition. During two and a half years (1986–89), we could observe the responses of eleven hundred chaplains of eighty-six different denominations to a foundational formation theory I proposed to them as compatible with their basic belief systems. These chaplains had been exposed not only to each other's formation traditions but also to the specific form tradition of the Navy. We observed that the dialogue with the Navy tradition had led to modulations in the way they lived the rich variety of their own form traditions. Yet these modulations and the basic paradigm of transcendent formation that I proposed did not compromise the basics of their respective faith traditions.

Formation Tradition: Bridge between Culture and Faith Tradition

In the preceding chapters on formation anthropology as related to traditions, I made a distinction between the general culture of a population and its variety of lived formation traditions. I ventured that the form traditions are far more significant for a formational understanding of populations and persons than the resulting multicolored quilt of culture. I believe that the form traditions of a population can function as a link between their faith traditions and their pluriform culture. For example, the Catholic, Protestant, democratic, capitalistic, and individualistic form traditions of the U.S.A. can give us more understanding of the American way of life than a sheer inventory of "The American Culture."

Faith Tradition

Deep down most people tend to live their life on the basis of their belief in some ultimate source of meaning and direction of their existence and the world at large. This implicit faith is given explicit form in a faith tradition.

A faith tradition, as well as its many corresponding form traditions, can be free-floating or institutionalized, focally explicit or prefocally implicit, religious or ideological. For example, a nonfocal faith tradition that pleasure alone is the ultimate source of meaning in life can be part of a larger free-floating hedonistic faith tradition expressed in corresponding free-floating formation traditions. To see an example of the opposite, an institutionalized tradition, we can observe the Islamic religious faith tradition. Islam has been thoroughly institutionalized over the centuries in its basic assumptions, doctrines, and prescriptions. Marxism, National Socialism, and existentialism are in their anthropological assumptions examples of focal, explicit, institutionalized *ideological* faith traditions. Orthodox Freudianism, Jungianism, and behaviorism are in their prescientific assumptions examples of focal, explicit *scientific ideological* faith traditions.

Compatibility in Pluralistic Formation Fields

We want our faith assumptions to become effective and livable in daily situations. Therefore, we look for ways to implement them in dispositions, attitudes, directives, and customs that are at least somewhat compatible with the reasonable demands of our everyday coexistence with others. This becomes complex in an environment or country with a plurality of faith and formation traditions. These tend to give rise to a pluralistic field of traditional influences. I observed this pluralistic process at short range in the shared field of presence and action of the Dutch resistance and their charges. This observation is one of the reasons why I initiated the construct of formational compatibility. It gained a prominent position in my formation anthropology and subsequent personality theory and transcendence therapy. Everyday life in an ever-changing pluriform formation field poses a challenge to believers of all kinds of ideological and religious faith traditions. It compels them to develop ways of compatibility between their particular faith commitment and their effective presence in a world to be managed with people of other persuasions.

This attempt to *compatibility without compromise* gives rise to an empirical-experiential tradition of formation. It complements and it concretizes one's faith tradition. This added tradition comprehends theoretical-practical ways of apprehension, appraisal, and application. Such paths are devised in a fashion that renders them both congenial with one's faith tradition and compatible with one's life situation. For example, the way in which a banker or military commander gives form to the Christian command of love for one's employees or soldiers differs from the way in which an abbess of a monastery of Poor Clares implements the same commandment in her situation.

The pluralistic formation efforts of adherents of various significant faith traditions in any shared field of presence and action are reflected in the common elements of the general culture of the population in that field. Beginning with my war observations in Holland, I was able to observe again and again on my world travels that there is no culture in a pluritraditional society that is not coformed to some degree by the significant traditions of the participants in that culture. Followers of such traditions try continuously, often prefocally, to attain some compatibility with the reality of the life situations they share with others. This implies, among other things, the attempt to come to terms with the practical formational adaptations made by adherents of other formation traditions. For these are made in response to similar reasonable and realistic demands that issue from the same field of presence and action.

For example, in a country faced with a severely threatened ecology, participants in different traditions may find within their own traditions special means and motivations to respond to the challenge with which all are confronted. In this and countless other ways the various traditions in a field give form together to a common culture. From the perspective of formation anthropology, a pluralistic culture is the result of an ever-progressing attempt by adherents of significant faith and form traditions to foster their shared symbolic and pragmatic coformation of a culture. They coform a culture in response to the realistic challenges they face in the same field they share. The adherents of the various significant faith traditions, in turn, will modulate in some measure their own formation traditions in accordance with the already existing culture. We observe, for instance, that Italian, Dutch, Scottish, Mexican, and Asian adherents of the same Roman Catholic faith tradition differ in their respective form traditions.

A cross-fertilization goes on continuously between culture and faith traditions. In pluritraditional societies the process of interformation between a culture and its manifold underlying faith traditions is not directly observable. It is a hidden process of implicit selectivity. This process is mediated by formation traditions alive within the culture. For example, the social security directives of a culture are the outcome of the interactions of traditions of entrepreneurs, labor unions, church groups, and ideological associations, to name only a few.

The adherents of culturally significant form traditions spark this selective modulation of their pluralistic culture in two ways. The first of these involves constant new form-giving to their own adaptive formation traditions. The second entails interformation with the already existing culture and with relevant facets of the formation traditions of others. As a result, the culture is a mirror of its underlying faith and formation traditions. It is, however, a distorting mirror because of the nature of the complex selective processes that went into its formation, including the shifting power positions of the traditions involved within the culture as a whole.

Transcendence Dynamic and Faith Tradition
A variety of transcendent form traditions is continuously operative in a pluralistic culture. Because they seem so different the question arises: what do they have in common? What is the criterion that allows one to call any

one of them a transcendent formation tradition? The answer to this question can be found by recourse to one of my descriptions of transcendent formation traditions. These traditions are about the empirical-experiential art and discipline of implementing the general human transcendence dynamic in our everyday concrete fields of human presence and action in the light of a specific faith tradition. For example, the Buddhist faith tradition orients the transcendence dynamic of its devotees to detach themselves from the delusions of materialism. Going beyond them, they try to give form to "compassion for all living beings" in their everyday style of life within the situations they encounter.

The transcendence dynamic can be described as the supreme potency and tendency to integrate transformationally all of human life in light of its rootedness in the mystery of formation. Such transformation happens in the light of a transcendent or quasi-transcendent meaning. Our transcendence dynamic moves us to adopt such a meaning as our ultimate direction. It elevates it above all other directions and points to a transcendent mystery as the source and end of all formation.

Transcendence means going beyond. This going beyond can be consonant or dissonant with our common, distinctively human as well as our uniquely human form of life. I call transcendence consonant when its movement is congenial with the primordial transcendent or spiritual dimension of the human life form. I call it dissonant when it is uncongenial with this dimension. For example, to persecute people simply because of the color of their skin is dissonant or uncongenial with the distinctively human qualities of what human life is meant to be; to approach all people with respect and justice is consonant or congenial with the transcendent dignity of the human form of life.

In the case of consonant transcendence, we live in harmony with our graced nature as it shines forth in the supreme dimension of our being. We are enlightened. We are less driven to make any striving of our functional-transcendent, functional, vital, or sociohistorical dimension of life into the ultimate meaning and direction of our existence. For example, while we may still strive zealously (if it is our call) to construct with our functional, logical, analytical rationality some excellent theological theory, we are less compelled to make this abstract construing the ultimate and exclusive meaning, love, and joy of our life.

On the transcendent level we may strive to meet in love the Transcendent Mystery in a cloud of unknowing and in a cloud of momentarily forgetting our theological constructions. Returning from the cloud of unknowing to the everyday functional-rational structuring of theologies, we may engage in this exercise of the mind even more devotedly. Our zeal is now deepened, directed, and inflamed by its subordination to the transcendent dimension. There we have met the mysterious Godhead of our constructions in a gentle stirring of graced love. Our rational functioning in this area is now integrated into our distinctively human transcendence dynamic. It is transformed in this integration.

I speak, therefore, about *transformational integration*. In this transforming harmony we rise above any ultimacy of direction that we may have ascribed to an articulation, meaning, or purpose of our functional-transcendent, functional, vital, and sociohistorical dimensions of life. Yet, while transcending such subordinate directions as ultimate, we take them wisely into account as relative directions with their own irreplaceable position and value in our human existence. For example, the diplomatic dealings of Teresa of Avila with benefactors, with secular and ecclesial authorities, with the representatives of the inquisition drew upon all of her functional, vital, and sociohistorical knowledge and power without ultimate attachment to their intended effects.

In the case of a dissonant or failed transcendence, I use the term *quasi transcendence*. This expression means that the striving of a lower dimension has been made ultimate. This insubordination causes a rift or a dissonance between the lower and the higher dimension. For example, the functional-transcendent ideal of individuation is not fully consonant with the absolute primacy of the Transcendent Mystery in and by itself. Mistakenly the functional-psychological manipulation of one's transcendent form potencies is forced to serve our individuation or self-actualization. Not the Transcendent Mystery, but our own spiritual self-enhancement is made ultimate.

The meaning, source, and direction of the transcendence dynamic is more specifically defined by one's faith tradition. This tradition also defines the means of fostering and maintaining one's faith direction. Our faith tradition, moreover, provides us with basic ethical dispositions. These enable us to establish core dispositions that are consonant with the basic direction of our faith tradition.

One of the main instruments used by institutionalized faith traditions to clarify and communicate the tradition are theological or ideological doctrines. These are usually connected with the founding writings of the faith tradition concerned. Such writings receive their authority from religious revelation or ideological intuitions. Examples are the Bible in Christianity; the Koran in Islam; the Hebrew scriptures and the Talmud in Judaism; the Sutras in Hinduism; *Das Kapital* in Marxism; *Mein Kampf* in National Socialism; and the "Little Red Book" in Maoism.

Formation Traditions and Culture

Formation traditions, as distinguished from faith traditions and their theological or ideological elaborations and commentaries, are about something quite different. As we have seen, they are about the everyday process of effective life and world formation within a pluritraditional field. They point to a compatible yet congenial implementation of the faith traditional ultimate direction of one's transcendence dynamic. This direction guides and inspires the graced journey of transformation remotely, not proximately. For example, the Christian faith tradition teaches us to love our neighbor as ourselves. Theology demonstrates increasingly by exegesis of scripture texts and texts from the tradition that and how we in general should love one another. Moral theology presents us with principles and general guidelines for the implementation of these principles. What it cannot teach us is the concrete proximate socio-vital-functional implementation in particular life situations. How does a nurse give effective form to this love in her care for terminally ill patients? What does Christlike love mean for one who is the mother of an autistic child, or the husband of a drug-addicted wife, or the teacher of children of dysfunctional families? In these practical situations of effective implementation of Christian love, special formation traditions can assist us.

Culture is nourished immensely by such rich and detailed formation traditions. They are its lifeline, its wellspring of renewal and restoration. Culture, however, especially one that is pluralistic, tends to emancipate itself from this, to use an analogy, "umbilical cord." Usually in the end it is the residues of formation traditions that keep a pluralistic culture alive. These residues in turn are kept intact by the commitment of adherents of the tradition concerned, by the true believers. For example, the Russian culture developed for seventy years under the absolute domination of the Marxist formation tradition. Yet it could not totally shake off the lingering residues of religious formation traditions in the hearts of many people. The reason was that many suppressed adherents of these traditions maintained their commitment and provided nourishment indirectly for the surviving elements of religious transcendence within the culture.

It is conceivable that no sufficient residues of traditions survive in a culture that has been initially coformed by them. The fact is that a culture as such may die, though remnants of it may be taken over and reshaped in a new culture formed by other traditions. Such may have been the fate of the Moorish culture in Spain nourished by the Islamic and partially by early and medieval Christian and Jewish traditions. The original Moorish culture is no longer alive; only certain facets and appearances have been taken over by later Christian and secular traditions.

Transcendent Formation and
Pretranscendent Development and Education

For me the terms *formation* and *transformation* point always to a *distinctively* human event, not only to a *typically* human process, as the terms *education* and *development* often do. While the latter are included in a subordinated fashion in a full-fledged process of formation, the term *formation*, as I use it goes beyond what the former words connote. It is primarily and ultimately oriented toward a transcendent or quasi-transcendent transformation of life and world. Formation is always rooted, usually pre-focally, in an underlying religious or ideological faith tradition. Such a tradition may be free-floating or institutionalized. In a culture it is always mediated by a fledgling or a well-seasoned formation tradition.

CHAPTER 5

Form Traditional Pyramids and Changing Fields of Life

I n this chapter I want to introduce my concept of the "form traditional pyramid." It expresses for me that we all live by personal and shared "pyramids" of form traditions, for we live in pluritraditional societies. Many of their directives affect in different intensities our daily existence. I diagrammed this difference in intensity by means of a pyramidal structure. At the base of my pyramid I situated the basic form tradition to which we are committed as a congenial and compatible expression of our faith tradition within our formation field. Above this base, I located ever smaller, less intensively influential form traditions. We try to integrate their form directives with our basic form tradition. One of the fundamental criteria of this integration is that they are consonant with our form as well as our faith tradition. The pointed top of the pyramid represents the actual penetration of our personal pyramid into the shared field of formation. It images a kind of lived synopsis of all our form traditions as more or less integrated into our basic tradition at the base of our pyramid. The top of the pyramid thus stands for our actual life form.

For example, the broad, all-sustaining base of my pyramid is my Catholic form tradition. Slightly above it on a less wide line are the compatible directives I can gather from other Christian formation traditions. Further beyond this line are those from other religious and ideological traditions. Then I drew the ever smaller lines of respectively my national, professional, and political form traditions.

Our form traditional pyramid should remain open to the reformations that may be demanded of it by our appraisals of changes in our field of life. This appraisal is related to my concepts of *compatibility* and *compatibility striving*. People want to be in harmony with their field of presence and action as shared with others insofar as this is possible without unfaithfulness to their basic tradition. The desire for compatibility will at times of change compel us to look beyond the boundaries of our own set of form traditions. We appraise them anew in light of the changes in the field in which we seek for compatibility.

34

For example, when deep concern for the ecology leads in our society to the emergence of free-floating or institutionalized ecological formation traditions, we may try to bend the ongoing unfolding of our own form tradition in such a way that it can integrate compatible ecological form directives. In service of such compatibility we look also for faith directives in our sustaining faith tradition, directives that were perhaps less emphasized in the past and less elaborated in the practical implementation directives of our many formation traditions.

Personal and Institutional Aspects of Form Traditions

Our form tradition is at the same time personal and more than personal. It is lived and made compatible with daily life by its personal followers, but it can also be systematized in more or less transpersonal enduring structures. We observe, moreover, that a common sensitivity is shared by many followers of a tradition. Often we see that different adherents in different places sense at the same time, independently of one another, that a new compatibility striving has to be tried out in answer to their changing field of presence and action. An example is the emergence in a number of adherents of the Leninist-Stalinist form tradition in Russia of a sense of the necessity of change in their economic and political traditions. Such shared sensitivity shows that more than merely one's own personal appraisal is at work in compatibility changes in form traditions. Traditional forms exude a power that surpasses that of their individual adherents. The health and sometimes the survival of a form tradition are based, among other things, on the right balance between the input of those followers who are creatively open to changing demands of the field and the reliability and endurance of its basic customs and shared fundamental sensitivities. The power of the structures of a form tradition should thus not become so overwhelming that the personal needs, aspirations, and insights of its followers cannot find a hearing. The structures of a tradition must be flexible enough to enable them to personalize their tradition in unique as well as individual ways. It must be possible for them to enrich their formation tradition creatively by newly disclosed ways of effective implementation of their faith in changing situations.

Sometimes people can be so awed by the claims of a tradition that they subject even their vital needs completely to its directives. A young lady wanting to look slender may refuse to eat a diet sufficiently balanced for her vital well-being. She is not motivated by reasonable compatibility. She may be moved by blind compliance with the directives of a contemporary free-floating form tradition for the "ideal" feminine figure.

The hold of form traditions on our lives explains why they can be looked at by people as if they were organisms with a life and power of their own, independent of historical events and dynamics and of the persons who try to live the tradition in dialogue with their daily, ever-changing surroundings. Such total independence is a myth. Form traditions in and by themselves do not do anything by their own power alone. If they seem to take on a new form, this phenomenon can be understood as arising out of preceding forms, out of reactions to these past forms and to new needs and aspirations, and out of responses by creative or innovative adherents of the tradition. For example, the Gothic form of the West European art tradition can be understood as emerging out of the Roman art tradition while the Renaissance form emerged out of the Gothic art tradition, as well as out of the critique of each preceding form by new generations of artists living in the orbit of newly emerging form traditions.

But what about personal formation needs and aspirations, dispositions and attitudes? Do they or do they not play a part in this unfolding of traditions? To some degree they do. Yet personal creativity never takes over totally the historical course of a tradition. No matter how brilliant it may be, personal insight can never be claimed as the exclusive explanation of profound changes in form traditions. Consider language traditions, for example. The formation and reformation of a language follows among other things also the law of sound. It is not merely or mainly personal-psychological forces that change a language.

Something similar can be said of all aspects of form traditions. This explains in part why we need a formation science that takes into account, among other things, sound personal and social aspects of formation as researched in the social, therapeutic, and educational disciplines. But these too must be transcended when we allocate their hierarchical place in the overall formation of human life. For example, the libidinal erotic dynamic as affecting in some pervasive way the formation of our life is researched in psychological, physiological, psychoanalytic, lingual, and medical sciences. Yet formation science must still locate the precise role of their findings in the overall transcendence-oriented process of formation, reformation, and transformation of human life and its traditions.

Two Basic Approaches to Traditional Life Formation

Formation science looks thus at traditional formation in two ways: from the viewpoint of the form directives inherent in the tradition itself, and from the viewpoint of the personal free carriers of a tradition. For example, the origin and centuries-long formation of the subtradition of monastic or conventual life in the West and in the religions of the Far East can be understood as arising from the objective needs and aspirations of successive religious and profane formation fields. But they are also coformed by the personal spiritual inspirations and aspirations, mindfulness and skills of initiators and reformers of the monastic or conventual life and their creative successors.

Epistemological Considerations

As a formation scientist and formation anthropologist, I am aware that each way of observation grants us insight into only a part of the total process that goes on. As in all sciences, so too in formation science, each observation can become the source of a theoretical abstraction. For example, my concept of "the" form tradition is an abstraction as are all concepts and constructs in my formation theory. It is the same with other scientific and scholarly disciplines. When I speak about formation tradition, I take the traditional facet of human formation out of its interforming context. The context I speak about is the formation field as a whole lived here and now by uniquely interacting persons. The abstraction from this totality gives rise to the abstract anonymous character of the theoretical reflections of formation scientists and, for that matter, of theories in all sciences. When, for the sake of sharper focus, I lift the forming power of tradition-as-an-institution out of the whole context of formation, I neglect necessarily to focus on the formation experience of the persons who implement the tradition. Neither can I with these concepts alone produce a vivid description of the formation field as a living interforming whole. This is one reason for my insistence that formation scientists should regularly return to the field as concretely lived not only theoretically but also experientially.

The empathic observation and full description of a life event within this field of always ongoing formation brings them back into life's concreteness. Such a return is obviously necessary in applied formation science, for instance, in transcendence therapy and formation counseling where one should never lose sight of the concrete here-and-now field of life of the counselee. But it is also required during scientific research in, for instance, the form traditional aspect of a field. Therefore, reintegration of the form traditional abstracted facet of life into its original living context is essential for formation science. Formation science aims to be a discipline that relativizes and reintegrates into the original field of life the formationally relevant partial insights that particular arts, disciplines, and sciences have already gained into cultures and formation traditions as lived by people. For instance, the important roles of conditioning and reinforcement in the formation of any human existence disclosed by various disciplines have to be relativized and reintegrated into the transcendent totality of distinctively human formation and formation traditions as a whole.

Objective and Subjective Aspects of Formation Traditions

The science of formation looks thus at tradition-as-formational in two ways. One main aspect of formation tradition is the tradition as objectified, structured, and institutionalized. The other aspect is the tradition as subjectively lived, responded to, and enriched by successive generations of groups and persons in formation. My search for the "abstracted" objectified marks of traditions made it possible for me to disclose hidden but objectively existing coherences of assumptions, dispositions, attitudes, and directives that basically structure formation traditions. This enabled me to make these structures understandable as well as to create a theoretical frame of reference that could be used as a tool of insight and critical integration of new compatible form directives disclosed by adherents of form traditions.

The view of the objectified coformants of the tradition should thus be complemented by a study of its subjective coformants. In everyday life it often escapes us how hidden subjective coformants of a tradition prepared the way for changes in its objectified structures that later become institutionalized. For example, Gorbachev could only change certain institutionalized forms of the Stalinist-Marxist form tradition of Russia because of already existing doubts in a number of Communist subjects about their economic viability, because of feelings of oppression, of desire for more freedom, of emerging aspirations for transcendent meanings. Such experiences of the subjects of the tradition had been undermining trust in the formation system as codified in form traditional Communist directives and customs.

Both the so-called subjective and the objectified coformants of a form tradition are reflected in the ways in which the followers of a tradition or tradition pyramid appraise their field. We should not underrate the power of change the subjects of a tradition can exercise, often unwittingly, in regard to institutional aspects of a form tradition.

Form Tradition of Functionalism

One tradition in the form traditional pyramid of many people in the West is that of functionalistic formation. A number of representatives of this tradition make it the basis of their pyramid of form traditions. Some of them, for instance Leslie A. White (1949), claim that functional technology is the ground of any relevant form tradition in modern society. According to them, social systems would only be a secondary set of layers in my pyramid. These would be nothing more than social implementations of what has been disclosed and structured by means of technological form traditions at the base of the pyramid. Finally in their view, the third set of layers in my pyramidal diagram would be composed of sets of general philosophical, ideological, theological, and spiritual traditions. These would merely express in a sophisticated manner the guiding discoveries and structures of the basic technological tradition. They would be merely a reflection of the functionally grounded layer of social traditions.

I have an opposite vision: human life and society constitute a field of mutual interformation. Our form traditions are operative in all dimensions of our life and in all structures of our field. Within our form traditional pyramids, functional-technical, social, philosophical, and spiritual form traditions interform constantly. For example, the philosophical form tradition of the Enlightenment had a rationalistic impact on all spheres of the formation field. It was followed by the reaction of the "unmasking" of faith and form traditions initiated by such thinkers as Freud, Marx, and Nietzsche. Their acknowledgment of the subrational facets of formation began to influence all spheres of the formation field. Then came the somewhat mystifying (not mystical) impact of the gnostic Jungian as well as of the cultic faith and form traditions. In some way all of these did enrich existing form traditions. They can be advantageous if complemented and corrected in their onesided emphases by the all-embracing vision of the human formation field as a whole with its covert and overt dynamics. I take into account and appreciate the technical and techno-social form traditions and their considerable influence on contemporary life formation. But it does not reduce for me the higher distinctively human facets of form traditions to mere outgrowths of these functional-technical traditions.

Objectified and Institutionalized Forms of Traditions

All form traditions, including the free-floating ones, have objectified forms. However, the objectified forms of institutional form traditions are institutionalized in a more systematic fashion. For example, the free-floating hedonistic form tradition in many Western countries is not institutionalized in a well-developed system, yet it has many objectified forms in the world of commercials, seductive symbols, and beguiling models of people who exemplify the hedonistic tradition. The Christian, Islamic, Marxist, Freudian form traditions, on the other hand, have institutionalized customs, symbols, arts, buildings, training centers, schools, libraries, and so on.

The objectified forms of a tradition should not be kept closed off from the responses and questions to them of the people who implement the tradition in the everyday world. The unfolding of these forms should profit moreover from the insights of other form traditions, arts, sciences, and disciplines. The essence of a form tradition is to be a bridge between its underlying faith tradition and its everyday compatible embodiment in the contemporary scenes of life. The adherents of a tradition as living in family life, in the school, the market place, the neighborhood are the antennae of a form tradition, warning it when new bridges of implementation have to be built.

The arts and sciences provide the tradition with another sort of insight based on artistic imaginative or scientific analysis of the state of the world. It would be a great disadvantage for any tradition if its followers would be nothing more than sponges soaking in passively the forms of compatibility developed by the tradition in the past.

The Christian tradition of formative spirituality, for instance, has been enriched recently by wise critical integration, after necessary reformulation, of certain form directives disclosed by confrontation with social injustice situations or by reflection on some compatible aspects of the spirituality of other religions.

Historical-Structural and Personal-Experiential Approach

Formation science should not limit itself to only the study of broad historical outlines and the main structures of a form tradition from a distance, as it were. Such a limitation would cause the finer nuances to drop out of the picture. To be sure, this broad historical approach has its advantages and should not be neglected. It aids us in apprehending and appraising the wider coherences and connections of a historical, relatively integrated form tradition that otherwise may escape us. Many past contributions to an unfolding tradition appear less important later. They were time- and situation-bound. They do not help our understanding of the overall process of the historical formation of a tradition. They are not as meaningful to us as they may have been to people who were close to particular phases of the process in its critical moments in the past.

The distance inherent in the broad historical approach also has its disadvantage. It tends to falsify the richness and complexity of a tradition. A person who studies only English grammar or the linguistic development of English pronunciation easily forgets that each person and each group speaks English somewhat differently. Similarly, when we study only the enduring, basic forms of a tradition, we do not see any longer that these forms can mean something different for everyone. Therefore, formation science complements its historical and basic structural approach with a person- and situation-oriented approach: the study of the interformation between a form tradition and the unique-individual, situated life forms of those who adhere to it. Hence I insist that my students begin the study of any facet of a formation tradition with a description and analysis of a formation event as lived experientially in a concrete formation field. For example, when a student proposes to research for her or his Ph.D. dissertation "The Formational Impact of a Coercive Attachment" in light of my formation theory of personality, I ask the researcher to start out with a description and analysis of a personal experience of coercive attachment in her or his own concrete life situation.

Form Traditions and Regions of Formation Consciousness

There is still another reason why I do not want my formation science to limit itself to an objectified historical or structural approach only. This rationale is rooted in my subtheory of the various regions of formational intra- and interconsciousness as explained in volume 1 of this series. The form directives of traditions as lived by their followers are intimately interwoven with their focal, prefocal, infrafocal, and transfocal dispositions and directives of consciousness. This gives rise to a continuous complex interformation between the focally conscious "objectified" directives of formation traditions and the focal, prefocal, infrafocal, and transfocal dynamics and aspirations of unique persons and groups who embody them in their daily living.

Therefore, as noted above, I ask formation scientists to start out from a description and a general articulation of a formation event as lived by a person or persons in a formation field. They then ask themselves how this event-as-lived is influenced by and influencing the formation tradition of a person or group and how it expresses related focal, prefocal, infrafocal, and transfocal dynamics.

Another cause of change in form traditions is the change in the formation attentiveness of consciousness in persons or groups, changes that can take place over the years. Formation attentiveness refers to our consciousness insofar as it directs our apprehension and appraisal of formation opportunities and how to use them. For example, in the Christian formation tradition the medieval formation consciousness would often direct medieval form attentiveness to the form reception of biblical words and stories in an allegorical way. Some of these formative allegories are foreign to contemporary Christian formation consciousness, at least in the scripturally sophisticated. This change in Christian formation attention changed in turn the attitudinal implementation of the form-receptive disposition of the tradition.

Formation Traditions and Formation Mystery

As I have shown in previous volumes, at the center of my construct of the formation field is neither the interforming form tradition nor the personal intraformational modulation of that tradition. At the center I put the experience (initially transfocal) of the uncanny, the mysterious, the "more than." This mystery is so foundational, all-embracing, and surpassing yet so all-penetrating that it transcends the tradition as well as its unique modulations by its followers. The hidden influence of the mystery of formation is shown by the fact that individual persons go beyond the limits laid upon them by form traditions. Form traditions put their stamp on their unique followers, but conversely unique followers change the form tradition, often inspired to do so by the formation mystery.

In some way there is always a modulation. Nobody who is truly alive repeats in perfect, robot-like fashion what has been taught traditionally. Some personal mark, no matter how slight, is left upon it. The more creative the person, the more this will be the case.

Form Traditions and Life Dimensions

In previous volumes in this series, I also addressed at length the socio-historical, vital, functional, functional-transcendent, transcendent, and transcendent-functional dimensions of human life. My reflections on tradition make it more and more clear that our life is form traditional through and through. This raises the question: how are form traditions changed by and how do they change these dimensions?

First the vital dimension: I include in this dimension of the human life form, among other things, all that we have received as the outcome of our formational biological evolution. In this respect our life is related to animal life, yet it goes far beyond it. The formation of our biochemical and nervous system is far more refined and complicated than that of animals; it shows more individual variation. We share with animals certain basic drives. But beyond that we are endowed with the biochemical and nervous conditions necessary for the unfolding of creative curiosity, insightful learning, and thinking. This enables us, among other things, to initiate, update, and live by formation traditions. They make up in us for the lack of instincts that direct animal life. Our vital biological richness empowers us to give form to new formational motives that expand immensely the drives we share with animal life. It makes possible our progress beyond animal life in the formation of our sense experience and neuromuscular motor expressions. Our physiological vital powers give rise to what I call our "neuro" form and our "temper" form or temperament, which in turn influences our core or character form. We conclude that our typically human vital dimension is the condition for our potency to give form to the inherent potential functional and functional-transcendent dimension.

Our vital potency entails the nervous conditions necessary for insightful learning. This makes it possible for us to project, functionally and transcendently, an amazing variety of human form traditions. Once these traditions have been initiated, our functional dimension develops and manages them. This implies the danger that functionalism takes over.

Functionalization of Form Traditions

When a form tradition is functionalized, it becomes a source of rigid behavior instead of a point of departure for creative appraisal, compatible, congenial accommodation, and renewal. A long-lived rigidified form tradition may seem to many "natural" in the sense of its being the only possible way of receiving and expressing form in life. People do not realize that both the life-giving vital dimension and the inspiring creative transcendent dimension are silenced when functionalism dominates in a tradition. The form tradition, if functionalized, loses its power of creatively bridging the gap between the faith tradition and the challenges posed by a changing field of affectively and effectively shared everyday life with others. The gap may become an abyss. Then creative adherents may feel tempted to discard the form tradition that has lost its relevance for them. No longer do they see how this tradition might aid them in implementing their faith concretely and creatively in their life. As a result they may become estranged from the faith itself. It ends as it began. For the faith tradition usually comes to us through the form tradition in our family; it may be lost through the failure of the same form tradition to uphold the faith later in life, congenially and compatibly.

To solve the problem of the functionalization of form traditions, I introduced the concept of a basic difference between the foundationals of a faith tradition and the great and changing variety of form traditions that try to implement one and the same faith tradition in different formations fields. Every form tradition leaves unused a great number of form potencies. It sacrifices a lot of them. Even if we would put together a vast variety of form traditions from the same faith tradition and combine with them those of other faith traditions, we would still not have a complete inventory of human form potencies in all their potential ramifications. We should thus not hesitate to appeal to other form potencies, highlighted perhaps in other form traditions, not yet sufficiently covered by our tradition pyramid, if changes in the field ask for such expansion or restructuring. It goes without saying that such reformation should always be faithful to the fundaments of the basic faith tradition to which we are freely committed.

The functionalization of essentially limited form traditions is the greatest handicap for creativity. It impedes free and open apprehension and appraisal of the field. Our appraisal of forms is directed by the dispositions of appraisal implanted in us by our pyramid of traditions. We may have been conditioned to dismiss as bad or absurd any form that does not fit immediately and ostensibly the appraisal dispositions of our traditions. Blind fascination with the directives of traditions leads to a stereotyping of our apprehensions and appraisals. To break out of this bind causes anxiety. For what does not fit into the traditions of a population is usually experienced as threatening.

For example, during his life Jesus of Nazareth tried not only to enrich and deepen the faith tradition of his people but, also even more directly, their form tradition, for example, by telling them in word and deed how to give form to the Sabbath. This was bitterly opposed by those who held tightly to a functionalized tradition. Gandhi was resisted when he introduced new forms of clothing, of passive resistance, of reconciliation with Muslims. And Buddha had to leave his father's house as a young prince. His unique search for ultimate transcendent truth could not fit the form traditions in his surroundings.

Form Traditions and Basic Strivings

Form traditions specify the basic strivings of humanity. All people share the same fundamental needs. But the forms of fulfillment of these needs differ considerably. The ways of gratification and satisfaction of similar needs are soon marked by specific preferences. Formation traditions play a role in this direction of need fulfillment. I call this the "form directive preference of need fulfillment." The way of fulfillment of our needs is in part

directed by certain traditionally preferred forms of gratification and satisfaction. For example, the fulfillment of the basic need for food is directed
by form traditions in certain regions of India to be gratified by rice and
spicy vegetables. The basic need for functional mastery is directed by Western form traditions to be satisfied by career and promotion as manifested
by higher income, company perks, and status symbols.

Original needs are given; their forms of fulfillment are acquired for
a great part under the influence of one's form traditions. Gradually the
acquired directives become independent from the original ways of need
fulfillment. They gain what I call *formational autonomy*. Our functional
reasonings and transcendent inspirations as well as our aspirations, in dialogue with our form traditional pyramid, begin to transform the ways of
need fulfillment in such a manner that we can no longer trace their characteristics to our original needs and their fulfillment alone. For example,
a highly stylized dinner for heads of state at a solemn celebration cannot
in all its refined forms be explained by the elementary need to still one's
hunger pangs.

Especially important for life formation is the form directive preference
for the way in which we satisfy our elementary need for self-appreciation.
Decisive is our early self-experience, combined with the appraisals of the
form traditions to which we are exposed. For instance, in Asiatic and pre-
literary form traditions, people are far less formed to appraise themselves
in the light of position, career, income, and social status than people in
the more individualistically oriented Western form traditions. The self-
esteem taught by humanistic formation traditions differs essentially from
the graced appreciation of the redeemed life form taught by Christian
formation traditions.

In all form traditions, however, the system of appraisal dispositions stays
on long after the formation field — in which this system is used — has
been changed. I call this phenomenon of delay of attunement *compatibility
lag*. Formation traditions tend to be slow in their search for new forms
of compatibility with changes in the formation field. We can observe this
lag in the delayed attunement of the Stalinist economic tradition to newly
introduced elements of the free market tradition.

The form directive preferences of our traditions specify not only which
forms we prefer for need gratification and satisfaction. They also determine in great measure how we appraise, perceive, think, feel, imagine,
move, speak, dress, and act. Our form traditional pyramid modulates to
some degree all our form receptions and expressions. A white American
of Scottish descent cannot sing and rhythmically move his or her body like
an Afro-American can. They cannot feel, think, or dream in the same way.
The human life form as actually lived in numerous different formation
fields the world over is endlessly differentiated by personal experiences
and by an inexhaustible variety of form traditions. To counteract the myth

of one fixed human way of being, I introduced the term *human life form*, for it connotes immediately the countless forms of life to which the same human essence can give form.

Language and Formation Tradition

Our traditional ways of need fulfillment are maintained for the most part by our use of language. Language is a direct or indirect product of the significant traditions that over the centuries have given form to a culture. Our use of language coforms what we experience. For example, the American expression "regular guy" is meant as a compliment; it forms us in an American form traditional way of fulfillment of our need for popular acceptance by our peers and easygoing conviviality. It also helps us to satisfy our need for success and advancement without paying the price of less popularity with other "regular guys." An entire facet of one American form tradition is contained in this language use.

We use language as a form traditional instrument to order our formation field. The danger is that language — if not constantly updated, revitalized, and appraised as always relative — can stereotype our thoughts and feelings and paralyze our creativity. Through use of language and other symbols, some form traditions can deform human life from infancy on. Consider the way in which totalitarian regimes use language. An example would be the 1989 official account of the Chinese government's slaughter of prodemocracy students in Tiananmen Square. All that occurred was couched and covered over in the language of the Communist Chinese form tradition.

The deformation by language use of form traditions is reinforced by our natural inclination to interpret and verbalize formation fields in terms of our own personal and collective needs, our egocentrism and ethnocentrism. It makes us realize how difficult it is to develop a style of formation that is consonant with the foundational directives of distinctively human life yet takes into account creatively the ever-changing demands of our fields of presence and action.

Ways that Foster Openness of Form Traditional Appraisal

Some ways that foster a reasonable openness of appraisal of our form traditional life are the following.

1. Search for, disclose, and examine more closely personal and form traditional prejudices. Am I, or is one of my form traditions, for instance, prejudiced against foreigners, certain nationalities, other religions or denominations?

2. Grow in awareness of how certain common thought forms fostered by traditions in our form traditional pyramid distort our perception of the field in which we live. For instance, does my health tradition make me perceive every obese person as a willful responsible glutton excluding the

perception of any other possible physiological or psychological cause of obesity?

3. Develop, as formation science does, a critical appraisal disposition in regard to the claims and discoveries of any particular scientific faith and formation tradition, especially those of the social and human sciences. How do they handle their data, particularly when they are formulated in terms of their own traditional theories?

4. Foster the formation of rational inquisitive minds. These must be able to balance wisely and reasonably form traditional imagery and feeling when they threaten to twist our appraisal of our field here and now.

5. Teach parents and their substitutes to prevent the formation of too great an attachment of their children to those who care for them. They must watch against the inclination of children to take over blindly their own form traditional pyramid. Parents or their substitutes communicate their form traditions to children in their own idiosyncratic fashion. Over-attachment to the parents or their substitutes hinders the child's playful exploration of her or his own formation field. This is not to deny the importance of normal attachment to and spontaneous assimilation of consonant parental traditions. These are a necessary part of the process of maturation of children. Overattachment, especially when linked with overdirection, adds to this normal and indispensable phase of formation an abnormal coercive anxiety and guilt about ever in the future under any circumstances changing any form of family traditions. For example, such change may later be required for compatibility with the person one marries. Another example, the form tradition of our family of origin may have made us appraise Afro-Americans as somehow inferior to whites. The college kids in our own family may teach us to change our prejudiced form donation in this regard.

6. To transcend one's form traditional pyramid, to make space for reflection on possible new demands in our field of life, we must create moments of silence, of observation, reflection, and contemplation. We have to give room to the human spirit to disclose its own unique life call. We need to ponder in the light of this call the deeper meanings of the forms that appear in our ever-changing formation field. For example, I may be touched by the need for social justice as it appears in our world. Before joining excitedly one of the countless particular ways in which one of the numerous aspects of social justice can be served, I must quietly reflect on what is the best way and aspect for the unique-individual me in tune with my faith and formation tradition.

7. Immerse heart and spirit often in the mystery at the root of our being, at the center of our formation field. This immersion will free us from form traditional paralysis. It will open us to the consonant hidden treasures of our form traditional pyramid, to its bridging function between our faith tradition and our field of life, to its inherent call for openness

and compatibility. If one's basic form tradition, at the base of the pyramid, is a transcendent one, it can teach us the means, symbols, doctrines, and disciplines that foster this liberating immersion.

8. Our heart needs to be challenged by the changes in our field here and now. We ought to become creative in finding new answers first in the traditions themselves of our pyramid. If they contain only partial answers, we need to try — preferably in dialogue with others — to expand this partial answer. If there is not yet an answer available, we can at least try out a response that may in due time enrich our form traditions.

In any case, it is always necessary to distinguish between faith and form traditions. If the foundationals of religious or ideological faith traditions are in question, other experts, such as theologians or ideological philosophers, may in due time propose new answers to the legitimate authorities of their faith tradition.

CHAPTER 6

The Structural Approach
to Formation Traditions

I n previous chapters I made the distinction between the objectified, structural aspect and the personally lived subjective aspect of form traditions. Both need exploration. In this chapter I shall focus on the structural, usually institutionalized, aspect, yet relate it to the personal aspect that I will discuss in more detail in a later chapter.

Necessary and Sufficient Structures of Any Formation Tradition

First of all, I can study theoretically what the necessary and sufficient structures of any formation tradition whatsoever are. In that case I do not ask what the particular structures are of some specific formation tradition. When I explore the basic structuring of any form tradition whatsoever, I ask such questions as: What is a formation tradition? Which sciences, arts, and disciplines can help me to clarify the essence and essential structures of any formation tradition? What theoretical concepts and constructs are most helpful for the formulation of what any form tradition basically is? What is the general role of any form tradition in any formation field? What is the general process of initiation and unfolding of a form tradition? How is every form tradition in some way linked to an underlying religious, ideological, scientific-ideological faith tradition or belief system? What role does a form tradition have in the formation of groups or persons? Can I make general distinctions between main groups of form traditions, such as between those that are prevalently transcendent and pretranscendent?

Structures and Symbols of Particular Formation Traditions

I can also study structurally the form tradition in a more limited sense. I can explore the structures of one particular form tradition. What I look for then are the structures and the interforming relationships between the structures of that particular form tradition. I ask what the form directive symbolic meaning is of everything I observe in that tradition and how these meanings hang together in its overall system of symbols. For example, the symbol of the cross in the Christian form tradition has a meaning that guides many other related meanings, such as the acceptance of suffering, crossing oneself, putting the sign of the cross on church steeples as well as in bedrooms and living rooms, compassion with those who have crosses to bear, and so on.

Only humans can create symbols. They alone can go beyond their sense-given observations and attach to them nonsensual meanings. Such meanings cannot be understood or perceived by means of our senses. They are transsensual. A good example is holy water in the Catholic faith and form tradition. The water can be seen, touched, and tasted. However, its symbolic form traditional meaning cannot be grasped by our senses.

Difference of Structural and Personal Approach

How does this structural approach differ from the personal formational approach to be considered later? During my structural approach, I do not necessarily relate the general structure of symbols to their particular formative influences on people. What I look first at is the relation between the different structures themselves and at their interformational interweaving within the totality of the form traditional system. In this regard, structural and personal approaches are not different in their overall object, which is the formation tradition itself. The difference lies in the context within which I consider this tradition. During the structural approach I may look, for instance, at the structure of the formation conscience of an Islamic form tradition. I study its relation to other structures, such as the symbols of the underlying Islamic faith tradition, its marriage customs, divorce conditions, the use or nonuse of alcoholic beverages. Or I research the position of Islamic women, war against the infidels, the words of the Koran. All of these contain "ought" directives for the formation of conscience in Islam.

Conversely, I can also focus on the personal aspect of the form tradition. Then I look at the Islamic formation conscience insofar as it affects the guilt feelings, needs, desires, hopes, repressions, fears, imagination, disposition formation, gratifications, satisfactions, and aspirations of Islamic persons and groups. How do they come to terms with their traditionally structured formation conscience in their everyday life within particular monolithic or pluralistic fields.

The principle behind this distinction seems clear. The structural formation approach concentrates on the interformational relationships between the symbolic structures themselves. The personal formation approach focuses on the interformational relationships between these structures and the groups or persons who try to live them. In the structural approach, however, I am not so much interested in the experience of the initiators, carriers, and implementers of these form traditional structures as in the structures themselves.

The distinction between the structural and the personal approach is not absolute. Often both approaches flow into one another. For example, the formational description of a married life of a particular Amish couple elucidates both the general structures of the Amish form tradition and its bearing on their relationship as this particular husband and wife.

Ideally each formation scientist should be involved in both approaches, for only then can one render a fuller understanding of the tradition and assess its concrete formational impact on people here and now. For example, a structural approach to the formational function of spiritual reading in a tradition should be complemented by a personal approach to those who try to give form to their unique life by such reading and by patient observation and analysis of how this approach concretely affects their life. Otherwise our understanding of this structure would be less adequate from a practical formational viewpoint than it could be.

Nonfocal Structures of Formation Traditions

My theory of consciousness emphasizes also its nonfocal regions. A better understanding of the forming influence of these hidden regions is of importance not only for therapy, counseling, and direction, but also for the structural approach to form traditions. Not only the subjects who carry the traditions but also the tradition itself, as a structural system, is coformed by hidden structures. To gain an understanding of what constitutes a tradition, we should not restrict ourselves to the study of structures that are immediately available to our focal consciousness and its observations.

Each tradition is a system of interrelated symbols. Certain directives as well as the structural ground — the dispositions and moods — from which they emerge are concealed from focal understanding. Also hidden is their meaning, power, and function in the totality of the symbolic system. This concealed ground must be explored. For only out of the totality of a symbol system, including its nonfocal grounds, can we gain a more adequate understanding of each symbol embedded within it.

Nonfocal Vital Infrastructure of Formation Traditions

Among the nonfocal structures of traditions, those rooted in the vital dimension of our life are crucial. To clarify their function in our personal formation, as well as in our form traditions, I have to recall briefly some facets of my formation theory explained in previous volumes of this series.

I introduced there my concept of six dimensions of human life formation. One of them I called the vital dimension. This dimension roots our formation in our physical-physiological-chemical-neurological bodiliness. Our life directives, formative or deformative, are programmed into the vital computer of our neuroform. For example, during childhood a little sensitive girl may not have dared to admit to herself the resentment she felt against her overdirective parents. Deformed by a distortedly communicated form tradition she dreaded what the unspeakable punishment might be for such unworthy feelings. While her mind banned such dangerously explosive emotions from her focal consciousness, her body chemistry, her neuroform, could not be deceived and kept reacting intensely any time the refused resentment was triggered. Her neuroform would lead her vital chemistry to translate its neurophysiological reactions in vague vital forms of physical distress or in a formless anxiety. We are no longer focally aware of such moods and feelings and of their permeation of our day-to-day existence. This compelled me from the beginning to conceive of a way of "focalization-through-centering" of these nonfocal vague forms insofar as they turn the vital dimension into a vital infrastructure of our core form or character. The concept of "focalization-through-centering" became so central in my thinking that it inspired me to a new way of thought about consciousness. I began to conceive formational consciousness as differentiated in various regions of availability to focal formation. I defined and named each region in relation to its availability or nonavailability to focalization — hence the terms *focal* and *nonfocal consciousness*. I diversified nonfocal consciousness in pre-, infra-, and transfocal consciousness. I applied the same focalization theory of consciousness to both intra- and interconsciousness, a distinction I made in relation to the intra- and interspheres of my diagrammatic conception of the formation field.

The "focalization-through-centering" of our focal attention in the vital infrastructure of our life is crucial for the transformation of the obstacles we put in our path to transcendent happiness. At the base of our formation style are core formation dispositions. Some of them are no longer focally conscious because of their profound embodiment in our vital infrastructure or neuroform of life. These dispositions dispose us to certain vital moods. These moods in turn give rise to a variety of vital feelings and form directives. These feelings and directives point back to aspects of the moods from which they emerged, but none of them can represent adequately a mood in its singularity and complexity. Some of these feelings and directives are focal or partially focal; others are not focal at all or what I call infrafocal. A vital mood is pervasive; it fills our whole inner sphere. It is more difficult to center our attentiveness, cognitively and empathically, on a mood than on the feelings this mood may generate. Therefore, the focalization of our vital moods through centering on them is a real challenge to our focal formation consciousness. Let me return to the example of the resentful girl. The refused resentment, festering in her neuroform, blocks her growth toward transcendent happiness. It keeps alive in her core form a nonfocal disposition of vague resentment whose original source is forgotten. It generates in her an all-pervasive floating moodiness of anger, displeasure, and unhappiness. Out of this basic moodiness emerges a host of belated more particular feelings such as touchiness, asperity, despondency, loneliness, bitterness, moroseness. The angry moodiness gives rise also to behaviors she does not understand or like such as flying suddenly into a rage, flaring up at the slightest provocation, grinding her teeth, chafing, fuming, losing her temper, quivering with rage. Each of these outbursts seems somehow related to that strange dark mood that more and more clouds her life. She has to come to an understanding and appraisal of that mood and its neuroformational ground. The work of prolonged, patient attention and appraisal is before her. She may need the assistance of formation counseling or transcendence therapy.

We can come to know from experience that we may live out of a low-grade basic vital mood that colors our everyday existence. Beyond that we are also disposed to the emergence of other current, shifting moods. They return again and again when triggered by some event in our field of life. In the language of formation science we are formationally disposed to let these moods take form vaguely in us and color our appraisals, feelings, and directives. These dispositions are engraved in our vital autonomic nervous system, becoming part of our neuroform.

Certain dispositions — as well as the moods, feelings, and directives they generate — are sources of dissonance. This may hide for us the fact that the vital dimension of life is by itself consonant, at ease, and natural. It is our insatiable need and greediness, rooted in our autarkic quasi-foundational form of life, that disturb the consonance of our vital life. Our functional dimension's craving for mastery, control, one-upmanship; our sociohistorical dimension's hunger for security, popularity, conviviality; our vital dimension's greediness for pleasure, sensation, and excitation make us program into our neurocomputer dissonant dispositions giving form to moods that darken, aggravate, cramp or agitate our life without our focal awareness of what is forming within us. Much depends on our assimilation of the wisdom of transcendent and pretranscendent formation traditions insofar as it touches on the formation, reformation, and transformation of our vital life and its various moods and related feelings.

Inherent Wisdom of Our Vital Dimension

Our vital dimension, when not deformed by our autarkic pride form, has the inherent wisdom to strive for the consonance of the vital dimension with all spheres and dimensions of our formation field in the light of the wisdom of classical transcendent traditions. The vital dimension by itself tends toward directives that put life at ease, that make it relaxed, healed, and whole. Our vital infrastructure is by itself a consonance-seeking system. Every time we experience vital dissonance we are faced with an opportunity to disclose a new way to vital consonance. We find that way by allowing our vital dimension to straighten itself out without undue interference from us or from the dissonant dispositions and moods we have programmed into the automatic computer of our vital infrastructure, our neuroform.

Vitally dissonant feelings are an outcry of the vital dimension. It tries to tell us that we do not listen to it when it generates directives for consonant living. Our vital dimension knows better than our functional dimension what is *vitally* good for us. This dimension has an innate sense of vital consonance. In the light of this sense, it appraises vitally the direction in which we are receiving and giving form to our lives. The vital computer of this dimension takes myriad bits of information in at any second of the day or night. Functional intelligence by itself alone could never gather that amount of information. Neither can words do justice to it. The vital dimension alone knows what are the vitally right directives for its consonance. I say *vitally* right directives. For our whole appraisal of directives includes not only vital but also functional, transcendent, and sociohistorical dimensions of appraisal. For example, transcendent directives about praying and fasting tell us what to do as adherents of a certain faith and form tradition, also how to do it in a manner that fosters our spiritual life as spiritual. But vital directives help us to appraise how we can do it in such a way that we do not harm our health and therewith indirectly our functional and transcendent wholeness.

When I use the phrase "vital dimension," I mean more than what is usually called the body. The term *dimension* means an aspect of our life that has its own function but that *as* dimension affects all our other dimensions and is affected by them in turn. For instance, when we think, any physical aspect that enters our thinking mind will touch our vital dimension and its appraisal implicitly.

When something deforms our life vitally, leading to dissonance, our vital infrastructure knows it and immediately tries to reform what is wrong. The vital dimension knows what its own consonant balance feels like; it is constantly appraising its own dynamics so as to remain as close to that balance as possible. Again how we apprehend and appraise the wisdom aspect generated by our vital dimension is profoundly influenced by our form traditions as well as by the personal way in which we assimilated them.

Mood and Form Tradition

I distinguished a basic mood in which we may be daily living and a variety of other shifting, current moods that are triggered by events in our field of life. What triggers these moods is for a great part dependent on the vital dispositions we have programmed in our vital life computer. This raises the question of the relationship between form traditions and moods. Can our basic mood be determined wholly or in part by a formation tradition?

Populations who have been formed by the Jansenistic tradition may show a basic mood of seriousness, of proneness to excessive guilt, of fear of damnation that are less pronounced in people formed in less rigorous traditions. Southern Italian people may develop a basic mood of warmth, joy, and lively self-expression typical of their form tradition. It makes them differ from Anglo-Saxon North Americans. The latter may have been formed in the same faith tradition but by a form tradition that is more one of lawfulness, of do's and don'ts, of friendly but somewhat less intimate relationships. This may color their basic moodiness.

Things are somewhat more complicated when we look at the fundamental formative moodiness of people from the viewpoint of their form traditional pyramid. For example, if I am a North American singer or dancer, the artistic formation tradition of successful performance and warm public relations may melt somewhat a more puritanical North American mood of emotional reserve, which may also be mine.

Something similar can be said of the various shifting moods that mark our form traditional personality. Take, for example, the artistically formed person who is no longer hemmed in by a basic form traditional style that was more anxious, less outgoing, less warm and open, more self-accusative because of an upbringing in a too restrictive form tradition. One of the recurrent moods in this person's life during periods of crisis may be one of falling away from a new, basic, everyday moodedness of joy, optimism, and appreciation to a former mood of restraint, mixed with excessive self-condemnation and depression. Seen from this angle, it is important to study what basic and shifting moods are fostered by formation traditions.

Apparent Form, Other Forms, and Moods Fostered by Form Traditions

Another coformant of human life that complicates the picture is that of the *apparent form*. My personality theory holds that human life is coformed not only by core and current but also by apparent forms. I want now to add to this that form traditions too are coformed by an apparent public form as well as shared core and current forms and vital moods. Take the difference between the professional form traditions of bartenders and undertakers, of clergy persons and vaudeville actors. Each of these traditions prescribes a style of public appearance that is quite different. Here again we must study the typical apparent form demanded by each form tradition and the mood that goes with it. I distinguish that public apparent form from the core form of basic moodedness as well as from the current, shifting moods of the same form tradition. For example, the basic moodedness of the Calvinist formation tradition differs from that of the Unitarian tradition. One of the objects of research of formation science are the dynamics of interformation between the different forms and moods instilled by the form tradition. The question of how far the vital life dimension of adherents is given form to by these basic, current, and apparent traditional forms is meaningful, especially for formation praxis, therapy, counseling, and direction. In later chapters dealing with the subject's approach to form traditions, I shall take up these questions again for more extensive consideration.

Another question raised by this reflection on the forming influence of form traditions on our life is that of the relationship between our unique founding life form or life call and the determinations by our form traditions. In what sense and to what degree are we determined by our form traditional pyramid and in what sense do we transcend our form traditions? These questions will be dealt with in the next chapter.

Focal and Nonfocal Meanings of Form Traditional Symbols

A formation tradition is a system of symbols. Its purpose is to promote forms and moods by means of which an ideological or religious faith tradition can express and maintain itself compatibly in pluralistic formation fields. The symbols point to what ought to be, to what is possible and not possible within the boundaries of congeniality with the foundations of the sustaining and inspiring faith tradition and of compatibility with the formation field. Symbols can carry different meanings. In exploring a form tradition, we are looking for the form directive meaning of symbols. This applies also to our search for the hidden symbolic infrastructure of a form tradition. This infrastructure is marked not only by form traditional moods but also by symbols. To understand more adequately the traditional rituals of an African religion, I must understand what each word and act means symbolically, even if the present adherents of that tradition can no longer tell me their meaning. They may not know it focally but sense it nonfocally in a sort of vague traditional sacred moodiness.

I make a distinction between the focal meaning of the form directive symbol here and now for its present adherents and its more ancient meaning that may escape present focal consciousness. For example, the original meaning for Christian life formation of the symbol of the immersion of the Easter candle in the baptismal waters eludes the average adherents of a Christian form tradition today, yet they may still be taken up in the religious mood of the symbolic ceremony, which may touch nonfocal regions of Christian consciousness.

Different Layers of Symbolic Meanings

Different layers of symbolic meanings develop during the history of a form tradition. Some of them may still be focal; others become nonfocal. For instance, in early medieval tradition, the symbol of the open handshake was meant to show that no weapon was hidden, that the hand would not be used for attack. Later it came also to mean a symbol of trust in closing a deal on the market. After that the handshake was a symbol of intimacy. Now it is often a symbol of merely polite greeting. None of these symbolic meanings has totally evaporated. They still play a vague analogical role in the form tradition of handshaking. The meaning of no attack is still there, though nonfocally. So is the meaning of the expression of trust, of dealing well with each other as in making a good market deal. There remains also some vague hint of intimacy.

The same symbol can carry different meanings in various form traditions. For instance, embracing and kissing between men carries different symbolic meanings in Mediterranean and Northern European traditions.

Structural and Personal Approach to Form Traditional Writings

A crucial aspect of a form tradition is its formational writings.These are mainly expressions of the overall symbolic system of a tradition. Therefore, the authors of these writings, their intentions, and their personal life histories, are less important than the function of the writings in the overall structure of the symbolic edifice they represent, enrich, and elaborate. This is true as long as we approach the works structurally. But the scene changes again if we complement the structural with the personal approach. For there is a difference between the structures as such of a form tradition and the personal meaning of these structures for the authors and readers.

Each form tradition and, therefore, each form traditional work of an author has a structural and a personal dimension. Each writer and reader can develop, as it were, a personal map of the meanings of the form traditional symbols offered to them. This subjective dimension is not necessarily identical with the objectively established structures represented by the work. The same process is possible in communities and groups of writers and readers. To deny this intra- or interformational dimension could lead to a mutilated view of the actual life of a form tradition.

It is for this reason that I always insist that both approaches are necessary in formation science. They should complement each other. The objective examination of the structure of a tradition remains incomplete without the knowledge of how the structure is lived as form directive by at least significant groups of adherents. One of the tasks of formation science is to make explicit and clarify the connections between the two.

Formation science should thus clarify the focal and nonfocal structures of a formation tradition as well as their mutual relationships. It should elucidate, moreover, how these structures are formationally appraised and implemented here and now by groups or by individuals who come for direction, consultation, or counseling. The search for the interforming relationships between these two clarifications and for the way in which they are implemented in formation praxis is one of the basic tasks of formation science.

Summary of Questions for Formation Science

I shall now summarize some of the questions that should be raised in the structural and personal approaches to form traditions:

1. What are the structures of the form directive symbol systems of form traditions? How should we complement the exploration of such structures with a study of their formational influence on particular groups, persons, and especially form traditional authors? For example, what is the structure of the Mass in the Catholic form tradition insofar as it may serve as a form

directive symbol for daily transcendent life formation? How does or can the Mass as also a form directive symbol serve the life formation of specific groups or individual adherents of that faith tradition?

2. What is the forming influence of groups, persons, and authors on the process of traditional formation? For example, how has a specific way of attending Mass, inwardly and/or externally, in a certain period of the history of the Catholic formation tradition given form to the style of Catholic life formation in and through the Mass as also a form directive symbol in this community of memory?

3. What are the ways in which groups and persons assimilate and implement their form traditions within their unique form traditional pyramids? How do they translate the objectified structures of these traditions in their formation of core, current, and apparent form dispositions and of their corresponding moods, feelings, attitudes, and form directives?

4. What are the formation processes along which one is formed by formation traditions? What about the formative imitation of form traditional prototypes, such as parents, teachers, clergy, saints, heroes, masters of formation, gurus? How do we grasp the formational process of the fulfillment of needs and aspirations?

5. In what way does a form tradition respond to the demands and desires of the sociohistorical, vital, functional, functional-transcendent, transcendent, and transcendent-functional dimensions of the human life form?

6. How does the form tradition touch upon the pre-, intra-, inter-, and outerspheres of the human formation field? How does the content of these spheres in a specific field influence the formation of a specific form tradition?

7. How does the form tradition influence and how is it influenced by the focal, prefocal, infrafocal, and transfocal regions of intra- and interconsciousness? How do these regions interform in a particular form tradition or in one's form traditional pyramid?

8. How does a form tradition or a form traditional pyramid affect the consonance and dissonance of the life of its adherents?

9. What are the criteria for the appraisal of the relative consonance-dissonance balance in a form tradition?

10. How far is a form tradition a source of unity in diversity or a paralyzing principle of leveling uniformity?

11. What is the interformational relationship between form tradition and human nature?

12. What is the interformational relationship between a form tradition and the characteristics that the adherents of the tradition have in common? Is there, for instance, a typical Amish, Charismatic, Southern Baptist, Buddhist, Islamic, socialist, capitalist personality form? To what degree is a common form traditional personality type affected in a pluralistic forma-

tion field by other form traditions as partially adopted in one's formation pyramid?

13. What is the interformational relationship between a formation tradition and the unique-individual adherent?

14. What is the interformational relationship between changes in one's basic form tradition and other changes in one's form traditional pyramid?

15. What is the relationship between a formation tradition or a form traditional pyramid and deformation in the human life form?

Some of these latter questions we shall try to answer in the following chapter.

CHAPTER 7

Congenial and Compatible Assimilation and Implementation of Form Traditions

The previous chapter dealt with the enduring structures of form traditions. This raises the question of how far life is determined by them. Each of us is unique. Yet we live our uniqueness in a life always already coformed by an internalized pyramid of traditional structures. We all assimilate various traditions. The question is: how congenial and compatible is our assimilation?

To answer these questions is the task of assimilation and implementation research. The examination of the structures of traditions must be complemented by an exploration of how people assimilate and implement them congenially and compatibly.

Special Sciences and Distinctively Human Traditions

Many researchers and theorists in social sciences look at people and their traditions in a mechanistic way. For them persons are not unfolding their life in relatively free interaction with their own deepest *I* and with a field of meaning. Human life is seen by them as determined by causes. If we apply this view to the tradition pyramid, what determines life would be a set of developmental causes. In my view it is not a set of causes but of directives that ultimately give form to a distinctively human life. These form traditional directives appeal to our free choice through motivations, even if it is true that we must repeatedly regain this freedom when lost. Instead of believing in the adventure of formation, many social scientists put their faith in a deterministic process of human development that strictly follows developmental stages.

I do not deny that human life is also determined. Physiological changes, for instance, are biologically determined; their influence on other facets of our life, which go beyond the mere physiological, is considerable. What I deny is that human life is totally determined. Distinctively human existence transcends absolute determinations while taking relative formational determinations wisely into account. We determine our determinants by adding to them our own human meanings symbolically. We do so in unique-communal coformation with the traditions to which we are committed.

59

I appreciate findings that result from scientific research in the conditioning of our lives. Academic social sciences about the pretranscendent life are oriented toward the study of determinants that are measurable. This research bears much fruit. One of my aims is to integrate its proven outcomes in my theory of distinctively human life formation as a whole. We should not resist but respect these scientific endeavors. It seems well-nigh impossible to change the original historical specialization of the well-established academic methodology of the social sciences. Those who try may end up on the fringes of these sciences where they may at most be tolerated.

I was asked to suspend for some time my exclusive study of formation. I had to obtain a Ph.D. in psychology. I was asked to introduce psychology as a human science in the university where I was employed. After accomplishing this goal, I was able to return to my own field of formation research. This interim experience taught me that we should not assume too lightly that we can change the basic historical orientations of the academic social sciences. We should appreciate their findings and integrate them into a wider new science of life as distinctively human. We should *compliment* and at the same time *complement* them. Neither should we neglect the findings of social scientists who work on the borders of the academic social sciences and strive to change their original historical direction. In this worthwhile attempt, they may create new insights that can be critically assimilated by formation science, even if they cannot significantly expand the traditional orientation of the social sciences as a whole. What we should not take over from some of these internal critics is a depreciative attitude toward the work done by the academic social, human, and educational sciences in their traditional ways. My aim as a formation scientist is to integrate, not to reject, to enrich, not to impoverish, the unfolding and emergence of the whole person. I want to celebrate any finding that expands our insight in any determined or nondetermined structure of our human field of presence and action.

Form Traditions as Motivational Form Directives

Form traditions do not act upon our life as mechanical causes. They appeal to our freedom as invitational form directives. We are challenged to decide freely for or against these directives, no matter how initially unfree our conformity to them may be and how limited our powers to transcend them.

Traditions give form to the traditional coformants of personality in those who are committed to them. We can decide to allow a model of traditional life to coform our personality. If we do so, in congeniality with our own uniqueness, our coformation with our tradition will not be the result of blind determination. It will be our here-and-now choice, or an affirmation, rejection, or reformation later in life of a choice made earlier for us in childhood. Through this personal choice, our unique life form will modulate our tradition pyramid. Freedom of choice enables us to assimilate formation structures in our own way, leaving their basic meanings intact, while not impinging on the fundamentals of their sustaining faith traditions. This brings us to the question: What is the relationship between our traditions and our unique form of life?

Unique Life Form and Form Tradition Are Not Identical

Our formation tradition does not take the place of our unique form of life. The individualization of our uniqueness in our empirical life implies more than a transcription of our tradition pyramid. Life form and form tradition are alike only in some of their facets; they are not identical.

When Princess Diana married Prince Charles, she added to her own tradition pyramid the royal tradition. She assimilated the style of Windsor without giving up her transcendent uniqueness or her individualization of this uniqueness in her pretranscendent empirical life. She merely expanded and modified accordingly the further individualization of her uniqueness. Conversely she modulated the royal tradition in her own fashion. Her royal disposition did not turn her into a copy of Queen Elizabeth or Princess Margaret. It is this always ongoing congenial and compatible modulation by new or creative adherents that directly or indirectly may also enrich the traditions themselves, keeping them alive.

Still, in the light of the previous chapter, we should not forget that tradition is always more than congenial and compatible assimilation by its adherents. Tradition is also an objective, institutionalized system. It is coformed by enduring structures that constitute the tradition as basically this one and not any other.

For example, the tradition of constitutional monarchy directs its adherents never to mix publicly in party politics. The gracious style in which one refuses to be drawn into political statements by journalists or interviewers will be modulated by one's uniqueness and its empirical individualization, but the basic enduring structure of this political impartiality of the constitutional royal tradition remains the same.

Tradition has traits that cannot be explained merely by the study of how its adherents assimilate its structures. Returning to our example, the tradition of constitutional monarchy — not to involve itself in partisan politics — cannot be fully understood without a study of the change from absolute to constitutional monarchy. Another example will clarify further what I mean. The traditional Islamic custom of a pilgrimage once in a lifetime to Mecca cannot be adequately explained from the observation of a pilgrim following this directive with ardent personal piety. One has to study the underlying faith tradition and its corresponding basic form tradition to understand how this could become an enduring basic coformant institutionalized in the Islamic tradition.

Fundamental Tradition Direction

Every tradition is always also an enduring system with its own traits that transcend those of its individual adherents. As a result of such traits, each tradition has its own inherent orientation and dynamism. I call this the *fundamental tradition direction*. For example, one basic trait of Roman Catholic, Eastern Orthodox, and Episcopalian faith traditions is the sacramental life and its liturgical celebration. Their corresponding formation traditions created over the centuries numerous forms by which to live and celebrate congenially and compatibly this sacramental direction. No matter what happens in new situations, no matter how much dissent individual adherents may express, the fundamental tradition direction will ultimately find new ways of sacramental celebration because this direction transcends the inclinations of individual adherents.

Formation scientists may study the general lines of a form tradition and of its direction. They put momentarily personal periodic and small group modifications of this tradition into brackets. This procedure will enable them to compare the basic distinguishing traits and general directions of different traditions.

Pluriformational Culture,
Tradition Pyramid, Personal Assimilation

Our personal life is not a literal translation of our tradition pyramid. An interformation takes place between traditions within this pyramid. This interformation happens in the light of our personal assimilation and implementation. This process tends to modulate every form tradition within our pyramid. Our choice itself of the traditions in our pyramid is influenced by our uniqueness and individuality.

As I have shown earlier, pluritraditional cultures are somewhat incoherent systems. They are collections of elements of significant traditions that gave form to a culture. We select usually prefocally from tradition elements that are available in our culture, those that will confirm and coform our own pyramid of form traditions. This does not mean that we are totally unlike each other. We share the same culture. Certain elements in our different tradition pyramids will be similar in many respects. Because we choose them from the same fund of directives, we will have certain traits in common. This makes it possible for observers to create an image of *the* American, *the* French, *the* German, *the* Baptist, *the* Roman Catholic. As long as it is clear that we are dealing here only with surface traits, there is no problem. When we have the illusion that these generalizing traits help us to understand people or their tradition pyramids in depth, we are mistaken.

The historical orientation of social sciences, such as anthropology, sociology, or education, prefers to do research with cultural determinants rather than with form traditional directives. Cultural determinants lend themselves to measurement, sharp definition, control, statistical treatment, and clear-cut comparisons. We can learn a great deal from their research. Its results can be integrated into our distinctively human frame of reference. Their strength rests in their limitation. Their rigorous focus on the measurable aspects of cultures makes them outstanding experts in traits that people in a culture have in common. Instead of trying to change their orientation and methodology, I opted for the initiation of a new complementary science and methodology that would focus on the study of the distinctively human dimension of life and its formation traditions. I would include the exploration of the transforming effect of both on all facets of the pretranscendent life. We should neither rob ourselves of the particular contributions of the positive sciences from which we can greatly profit nor confuse their constituting focus or formal object with that of this complementary science.

Ideal Instead of Common Tradition Form

Our study of form traditions and tradition pyramids contributes greatly to our understanding of the form people give to their life. It can help us in formation practice, in transcendence therapy, counseling, and direction. Already a simple conversation with counselees or directees tells us something about their formation pyramid. To understand them and empathize with them, it is not enough that we study the enduring basic structures of their traditions. We must ask about the bearing of these structures on the personal human formation of those who come to us with their problems. Without such knowledge about their assimilation and implementation in their personal lives, our knowledge of traditions remains incomplete and in part incorrect. For we bypass the sources of ongoing modulation to which every living tradition is constantly subjected when lived by people.

Already children begin to make traditions somewhat their own. They modify them at least slightly in small matters. We should thus be cautious in ascribing too easily identical characteristics to the followers of a tradition. I propose the term *ideal tradition form* instead of *common tradition form*. "Ideal" points to the fact that a tradition may suggest symbolically an ideal image of what its adherents might strive to be like. The way in which each adherent assimilates and implements that image concretely is different from the ideal. This assimilation is codependent on the demands of congeniality and compatibility, which are different for each person and each field. There is thus no absolute commonality between adherents of traditions, only a relative one. What committed adherents have basically in common is that they strive to live up in their own way to the ideal image of their tradition.

I conclude again that structural research gives us necessary insight into the fundamental structures of a tradition. This must be complemented by assimilation and implementation research. The study of structures alone would make it impossible for formation science to gain an adequate understanding of a traditional formation of people that is distinctively human. We should not mix up or confuse these two types of research and their outcomes. To keep our research and its findings clear and surveyable, we must distinguish between the fundamental traditional system as studied by structural research and human life as coformed by the assimilation and implementation of these structures. If we merge these two types of research uncritically, our findings will be falsified.

Motivations for Focusing on Structures or on Their Assimilation

Why do some people prefer to focus on structures of their tradition, others on personal assimilation of them? Even in everyday life these two types of attention alternate and complement each other.

In situations with which we are familiar, we are usually more attentive to the individual ways in which a tradition is lived out. During the war, I helped to hide people from German soldiers. Later in my life I was invited to teach as a guest professor in the psychology department of the University of Heidelberg. It struck me how different the focus of my attention was in each situation. Working every day with German colleagues and students, I was far more attentive to them as individual persons than I was to certain aspects of their German tradition. I realized how differently I had looked at the same Germans when they had been commanded to occupy my country, to abduct Jewish and other citizens, to suppress our resistance. I did not see them then as unique persons but as a gray mass of feared helmets and uniforms. I focused my attention on the rigid organizational facets of the German tradition and how that could harm or help our own strategies of resistance. Each German soldier seemed to us at that time not much more than a mechanical embodiment of a German authoritarian tradition.

The opposite can also happen. I may mistake an individual trait of an adherent of a tradition for an expression of the form tradition itself. For instance, when I meet a Jewish person who is avaricious, I may falsely conclude that this is an inherent quality of the Jewish tradition. Deadly persecutions of whole populations have been set in motion by such generalizations about the traditions of certain populations like Arabs, Jews, Afro-Americans, Catholics, Protestants, socialists, the rich and the poor.

It can also happen the other way around. An attractive traditional apparent form may be mistaken for a personal quality. For example, the tradition of effective selling includes an at least apparent form of friendliness for potential buyers. If we conclude that this friendly concern is in all salespersons a core quality of their personality, we may be disappointed some day. During the Hunger Winter in Holland, the sellers did not need us anymore. For sheer survival we were wholly dependent on them and the last supplies they had stocked away. People would beg from them, offering them their jewels and other possessions in exchange for food. Some of these shopkeepers — so friendly and polite before in keeping with the apparent form aspect of the tradition of effective selling — now allowed their personal arrogance and boorishness, their vindictiveness and resentment of formerly demanding clients to come out in force.

These are the conflicts and confusions that can arise in our everyday field of form traditional living. They can foment tensions or even wars between the adherents of different religious or ideological form traditions, no matter the splendid principles of brotherhood and sisterhood that they claim to foster in their faith traditions.

Nonfocal Sources of the Choice
of a Structural or Assimilative Approach

We may be inclined to take either a more structural or a more assimilative approach to our own traditions. A preoccupation with the structures of one's form tradition may be rooted in the need to lose oneself in the safety of a historically established set of forms. One feels complacent and secure in the conviction that one never has to doubt, question, amplify, or improve any of the established forms of one's form tradition. One mistakenly transfers to each of them the certitude of the underlying faith tradition itself. This may explain, for example, why a number of South American landowners hold on to the particular Christian form tradition of their divine election as a privileged class with absolute right to all their powers and possessions, even in the face of the poignant misery of abused *campesinos*.

On the other hand, a preoccupation with one's congenial and compatible assimilation and implementation of the form tradition can be related in many cases to the need and aspiration to distinguish oneself from the structural form tradition insofar as it could deteriorate into a tradition that could become collectivistic and oppressive.

In the end formation science always returns to the field of life as experienced by people. Scientific appraisals are useful abstractions from the field of life as a whole. When formation scientists return to the field, they look again at the structures they elucidated. They ask once more how these structures operate formationally within the context of life. Similarly they consider anew each trait of the personally assimilated form tradition that they have abstracted for research. Their question now is how does this personal traditional life form affect and how is it affected by the field of living as a whole? In this way we keep checking the outcome of our scientific approaches against the reality of our everyday field of presence and action.

Formation of Everyday Institutional and Assimilative Appraisals

So far I have dealt for the most part with scientific structure-oriented or assimilation-oriented approaches. We should be aware that each of us in daily life can be directed either more toward the structures of the traditions we try to live by or to our personal assimilation and implementation of them. One aspect of our formation is that of our appraisal dispositions in this regard. As children we are immersed in the tradition pyramids of our parents and families. We are not yet able to make a distinction between the structures of the family tradition and our own unique way of assimilating them. There may be a substantial difference between the pyramids of tradition of respectively our father and mother. Our assimilation of these antagonistic pyramids may lead to confusion, conflict, and crisis in the future. As children we cannot yet see that the traditional family pyramid presents us with only one possible path of formation among others. This insight comes later. For some it may never come.

The tradition pyramid at home is initially experienced as self-evident. The image of parental tradition changes slowly from an institutional unquestionable family tradition to one that demands personal critical assimilation and implementation. At first there is not a real assimilation of the family tradition, only a kind of blind absorption. Adolescence, with the discovery of one's uniqueness and individuality, gives rise to a *confrontational appraisal* that leads to a questioning of the parental form tradition. Confrontational appraisal is intensified for better or worse by further life experiences. An example can be found in the movie *Born on the Fourth of July*. The hero of the movie, a paralyzed and disillusioned Vietnam war veteran, is first shown in childhood in full conformity with parental tradition. Part of this family tradition is an unquestioning patriotism: my country right or wrong. Enthusiastically the young man volunteers for marine service in Vietnam. As he returns paralyzed for life, facing antiwar demonstrators, the movie takes us along the way of a slow and painful reformation of his parental absolutized patriotic tradition into an absolutized antiwar tradition.

We can be either more institutionally or more assimilatively oriented. Whether we prefer one or the other way depends in part on our vital neuroform, temperform, and subsequent core or character form.

Conservative people tend to feel uneasy when the emphasis is on the creative aspects of personal assimilation of the structures of a tradition. They fear that these structures or even their underlying faith traditions themselves may be threatened by this disposition. Persons of a more progressive disposition may find it difficult to bear with a mainly structural appraisal of the traditions to which they are subjected. If persons of one or the other extreme become formation scientists, they may be inclined to be too onesidedly focused on either the structural or assimilative approach in their studies. To grow in a mature scientific attitude, they must become aware of the basis of their onesidedness so that they may transcend either extreme.

Formation History and Form Tradition
A form tradition is a never-ending dynamic dialogue. It is an ongoing historical interaction between the structures of the form tradition and their

assimilation and implementation by a varied range of adherents faced with a great diversity of sociohistorical situations. Both assimilation and implementation are modulated by our needs for congeniality and compatibility. Structural form directives have to be lived by people in tune with their unique life calls and in harmony with their ever-changing fields of presence and action.

An example is the form given to the implementation of the Christian directive of justice. For a long time justice directives gave rise mainly to forms that guided the right distribution of personal possessions. Then the form tradition began to include forms of care for persons and groups suffering material destitution. More recently the form tradition has been expanded to forms of social justice, including the reform of economic and political structures that cause discrimination and destitution. For the anticipated future of the history of this aspect of the Christian form tradition, it seems safe to say that the forms of justice-as-lived may widen even more. They may include forms of promoting justice in marriage relationships, in child rearing, in education of the gifted as well as the less endowed, in attention to the aesthetic rights of every person, not only of artists, thinkers, and poets.

The historical nature of traditions is increasingly evident. This characteristic was not universally acknowledged until the nineteenth century. The notion of historical unfolding itself is an outcome of the formation history of humanity. The theory of biological evolution in the nineteenth century, and later the dialectical approach initiated by Hegel and Marx, made us also aware of the historical aspects of form traditions. The psychoanalytic mode of thought fostered this historical awareness as well. This background inclined me to introduce in my personality theory the notion of the sociohistorical dimension of human life as an all-pervading dimensional power of always ongoing formation, reformation, and transformation.

Only by the nineteenth century was the formation history of humanity ready to become form-receptive to the notion of the pervasiveness of the sociohistorical dimension of human formation. Most sciences started out from the assumption of an essentially fixed and unchangeable world in which we can discover mechanical causes and natural laws. There are some partial truths hidden in this sweeping presupposition but it does not cover the whole story of formation of cosmos and humanity. This story implies also unique formational changes. These changes can take a long time before they give observable new form to life or world. The notion of ongoing change is hardly two hundred years old. It took even more time before I could introduce a study of formation traditions that goes beyond a recording of facts and takes into account the formational dynamics of sociohistorical change.

Now that this awareness is emerging, I have introduced the sociohistorical dimension as essential to human formation and formation traditions. It enables us to understand how present directives of form traditions emerge as continuations of, modulations of, or reactions against past directives. Comparison with the past directives delineates more sharply for us what the present directives really entail. For example, the past directives in the Catholic form tradition against marital relations the night before receiving communion give us clearer insight into the progress toward less rigidity in this regard in present form directives.

Our growing awareness of the sociohistorical dimension increases our relaxed receptivity for reasonable and realistic changes of forms. These are evoked by humanity's need for congeniality and compatibility. We become less easily fixated on passing structures and forms of our form traditions. We are more aware of their distinction from faith traditions in this regard. The sociohistorical dimension enables us to view formation traditions as moving, dynamic forces in the history of the unfolding of humanity's form potencies. These are alternately changing that history and changed by it. My conclusion is that form traditions not only have a personal and transcendent genesis but also one that is sociohistorical.

Closed Mythological Model of Formation

The presence of the sociohistorical dimension cautions us from taking a closed mythical view of formation. This view dominated the Greek and Roman notions of formation at the spring of Western civilization. Aspects of it still reverberate in our history. In a closed mythological formation model, not enough attention is paid to the sociohistorical dimension. People are encouraged to give form to their life in the light of the same recurrent formation myths that guide the *implementation* of one's faith, as distinguished from the faith stories that communicate to us the *foundations* of the faith itself. Formation myths enshrine fixed ideal ways of giving and receiving practical form in everyday life. They do not take into account compatible sociohistorical changes.

In an approach that takes into account the facts of history, formation myths cannot be excluded. They play an indispensable role in the unfolding of form traditions as such. Formation myths are coformed by the sociohistorical dimension. We interpret old formation myths and create new ones in dialogue with the congenial and compatible responses we give to our historically changing formation fields. We elaborate what I call an *open* instead of a *closed* formation mythology. One that is closed presupposes an essentially fixed, unchangeable world. This is the opposite of my notion of a flexible, always changing formation field. For example, in the song "We Shall Overcome," there are many mythical images that give form to the sociohistorical aspiration not to accept repression as a lasting, divinely willed state for discriminated groups of the population but as a challenge to give form to a new life that resists unjust oppression.

Traditions that do not heed the sociohistorical dimension are often tempted by the remnants of closed mythological formation models. For example, medieval formation stories are mostly patterned after a stereotyped, mythical model of heroism and holiness. They seem to suggest that this model should be reenacted in every detail if one wants to realize the ideal form of one's tradition. Little is communicated in these stories of their fidelity to a unique life call or their struggle for reasonable compatibility with a particular sociohistorical field of life. As a result, the intraform of their life, as onesidedly reported and exalted, may seem rather bland and boring. A striking exception can be found in the experiential accounts of the spiritual journey by such people as Augustine, Francis of Assisi, Teresa of Avila, Catherine of Siena, Francis Libermann, Dietrich Bonhoeffer, Etty Hillesum, Corrie Ten Boom, and Søren Kierkegaard.

We do not have enough similar spiritual biographies written by or about common people. One of the reasons for this may be related to the cultivation of an almost exclusive interest in the "stars" in the firmament of spiritual formation. The supermodels are easily mythologized by popular authors. The influence of past closed mythological approaches to formation may still be operative in these attempts. This represents a formidable handicap in the traditional formation of the laity.

The sociohistorical approach helps us to disclose recurrent symbols and their meanings. These appear and reappear in the most diverse periods in the history of a tradition. The forms in which they appear may change, but an enduring ground meaning seems to survive. The disclosure of such permanent, fundamental structures of basic meaning helps us to bring to light structures that are not permanent or essential, even if we thought they were for a long time. For example, in the Catholic form tradition it was thought for some time by many common faithful that Latin was a permanent form of the Mass, almost a part of the faith tradition, not of the form tradition. The same for eating meat on Friday.

Sociohistorical Dimension
and Prefocal Form Traditional Influences

An aspect to be reckoned with in the sociohistorical approach is the fact of prefocal formational influences. A shocking formation event may be experienced focally at one point during the history of a form tradition. Its impact may keep reverberating, even prefocally, during the further history of the same tradition. For example, the slaughter more than a century ago of a million and a half adherents of the Armenian Christian formation tradition by Turks keeps reverberating in that tradition; it gives form to a certain alert militancy that affects even those who are less aware of the historical event at the source of this formational disposition.

No formation tradition should paralyze itself by the notion that *the unconscious* is a secret powerful agent that enslaves us against any exercise of freedom as adherents of the tradition. This is one of the reasons I chose my terminology of pre- and infrafocal consciousness. Many misunderstand *the unconscious* as a mechanism, an entity that does something to us, that, as such, totally escapes the free formation potency of the human life form and its traditions. The unconsciousness is not like a little person hidden within our larger person; it does not create lasting invincible forms in our life by its own anthropomorphic power. What has become unconscious or what is in my theory "infraconscious" is a side effect of the way in which we receive and give form to people, events, and things sociohistorically. This is the forgotten hidden power behind the infraconscious life. If we become aware of it, perhaps by psychotherapy, we will regain our potency to reform the side effects of our insufficiently focal options of the past. Formation traditions can be a great help in this reformation, once we have found again our potency in regard to this problem.

The either prefocal or infrafocal consciousness is formed differently by people in different periods of the history of their form tradition. In each of these periods, they spontaneously give form to their own dispositions of appraisal and to their own form directives in response to that period. For example, the average adherents of theistic Christian, Jewish, and Islamic formation traditions in the period of atheistic persecution in Russia and Eastern Europe formed prefocally a more cautious, subdued, retiring style of life, different from that of adherents of the same traditions in the same countries living in other periods. While their dispositions are fundamentally in tune with the form tradition as a whole, and especially with its sustaining and inspiring faith traditions, the compatibility demands of the period compel them to their own compatible expression. Initially this happens prefocally. It precedes focal appraisal and verbalization. Together such prefocal appraisals, dispositions, and directives coalesce into a general periodic disposition of the form tradition in that period. This periodic disposition gradually defines and colors a fundamental way of formation. It gives form to thought, affect, imagery, language habits, to a style of interformation, to attitudes and motives of a significant number of adherents of the tradition living in that period. For example, the style of formation of the early immigrant adherents of the Irish tradition to America differs from that of their Americanized heirs in the present period.

CHAPTER 8

Commonly and Individually Deformed Traditions

E ven the best traditions can be turned into protectionistic walls against our anxieties. We can use our traditions in this way as individuals as well as with groups with whom we share these traditions. In the course of time, such a shared protectionistic use of traditions can become institutionalized. In both instances the traditions are deformed. We have to ask, therefore, in what ways are commonly and individually deformed traditions alike? In what ways are they different?

Resemblances between
Commonly and Individually Deformed Traditions
At first sight we are struck by resemblances between deformation of traditions by individuals and by the deformation of a form tradition as a whole. Neurotically deformed individuals use traditions to protect themselves against their excessive fears; so do groups of people who share a deformed tradition. In both cases they use traditional directives and dispositions to develop contraformations to thoughts, images, symbols, memories, and anticipations that are felt to be threatening. Both try to overcome intolerable tensions. These tensions emerge from an inner conflict between expansion and contraction. Deformed traditionalists distrust the growth dynamic of an alive tradition, its thrust toward expansion. Their vital eros disposition and its dynamics fluctuate between two poles: contracting vital self-love and expanding vital love for what is not self. To mitigate the tension, they look for a source of stabilization, an anchor in the restless ocean of vital feelings. That anchor is tradition. If some form traditions themselves, however, have been turned into anxious walls of self-protection, they can no longer advance our creative congenial and compatible life formation.

Notice here my use of the notions of congeniality and compatibility. Overemphasis on congeniality — in an improper individualistic sense — leads to unreasonable self-contraction. It silences the call for compatible expansion. The less mature the life form of a group or individual is, the more it seems inclined to turn its traditions into shelters and barricades.

71

These being some of the resemblances between commonly and individually deformed traditions, what, then, are the differences?

Differences between
Commonly and Individually Deformed Traditions

Some representatives of the social sciences would say there are no differences, that religious traditions are merely shared neurotic systems. I have already made a distinction between original classic traditions and their unhealthy deformations. My question is: even if traditions have deteriorated into mere protectionistic systems, are the adherents of such deformed traditions neurotics in the same sense as individual, idiosyncratic distorters of classical traditions? If not, what are the differences?

Personal deformations of tradition are rooted in the past of an individual. Traumatic events of the past keep resonating in present-day appraisals, including the appraisal of one's traditions. For example, certain types of sexual impotence are linked with a maternal ambience that froze any warm expression of affection as erotically dangerous or demeaning for people in "our" tradition. The children of such deformed parental traditions may carry this conditioning with them for a lifetime. It may interfere with their friendships or marital love life, paralyze their spontaneity, isolate them inwardly, and put them at odds with other people who do not suffer the same deviation.

It is different for adherents of a deformed societal tradition. In their case the cause of deformation is not an individual experience. Living with the group that shares the same outlook on life, they do not necessarily experience the pain of personal estrangement that the individual neurotic suffers. From the beginning of their conscious life, they find themselves at home in an already existing protectionistic system. It unites them intimately with their fellow adherents, with their family, with shared organizations, ceremonies, myths, symbols, accounts of history, political and economic enterprises.

For example, the white Afrikaners, the Boers, in the Transvaal region of South Africa share the same agricultural history, life, and economy. They are bound together by their common protectionistic distortion of the biblical tradition. They feel that essential to this tradition and their community is preaching and maintaining "apartheid" at any price. They use this deformation of tradition as a bulwark against the threat of the emergent power of black Africans, who evoke in them a latent anxiety, sociohistorically related to the experiences of the first settlers with marauding tribes. Yet their immersion in communal thoughts, projects, and interests makes them different from individual sufferers of neurosis and their personal distortions of traditions.

It is my contention that the vital eros of people is affected differently by the two types of deformation of tradition. I have observed that the personal traumatic experiences in the vital-erotic facet of human love affect the development of the erotic life far more deeply than the impact of a shared deformative tradition. One's personal eros formation is not as directly wounded by a deformed tradition in which one shares by mere association. Therefore, in this case, the vital eros orientation may still be kept alive. It may yet grow into transcendent human love, or what I call "transeros" and make its contribution to this higher love. It may also vitally animate one's everyday dedication to family, work, and community.

Vital eros — as defined in my theory of personality — strives to express itself in all the animated enterprises in our field of life and of our service to others. It does so through our functional *I*. This *I*, if it does not deteriorate into a functionalistic *I* or if it is not sabotaged by individual neurosis, enables adherents of deformed traditions to function effectively. Through it, the vital eros can animate action and social life in business, entertainment, ecological concern, and community organization, while paying dues to what I call the apparent forms of a shared deformed tradition. We already gave the example of the economically and socially effective Boers of the Transvaal within their own closed-off white communities.

Persons who adhere to these deformed traditions have more possibilities than the individual neurotic does to escape their full negative impact on his or her personal vital animation and spiritual inspiration. For example, a famous adherent of the rigid Jansenistic tradition, Blaise Pascal, could allow his vital eros to animate his creative scientific research, profound philosophical reflections, and literary expressivity. In spite of his adherence to a partially deformed tradition, he could transcend it sufficiently to allow his transcendent inspirations and aspirations to penetrate and transform his vital animation.

Formational Shielding

A deformed tradition can even have some restricted healing effect. Some facets of insecurity are accessible to limited healing by what I have defined in my theory as *formational shielding*, which can be formative or deformative depending on its purpose, motivation, and situation. Take, for example, the pious conviction instilled by the form tradition of groups of South American landowners. This approach enables them to believe that God gave them wealth and privilege in order to maintain and expand them. God wants them, they believe, to protect what they own for the coming generations of their blessed family tree. This conviction, combined with popular devotions, prevents the emergence of intolerable guilt feelings about not sharing part of their lands with the destitute farmers exploited by them. Persistent nagging guilt, when not acted upon wisely and healingly, is bad for our health. It gnaws away inside of us. It generates enduring tensions as long as we keep refusing to acknowledge and remedy the cause of our guilt. This suppression may affect the immune system, thus exposing landowners to disease. The deformed tradition not only prevents awareness or acknowledgment of guilt; it also suppresses its incidental emergence, threatening the health of adherents.

I would see this as a limited pretranscendent healing effect that touches only the surface of life. It is a deformative use of formational shielding. In the meantime it aggravates the far deeper spiritual disease. It does not heal or "make whole" human life in its totality. To escape their social conscience, proponents of such deformed traditions must wall themselves up in self-righteousness. This imprisonment closes them off from liberation from the dungeon of family and group self-centeredness. The illusion of healing is due to partial relief of anxiety symptoms by the pretranscendent distortion of transcendent traditions. The tragedy is that people are blinded to the ultimate healing powers of transcendent and posttranscendent love or consonance that I have put at the summit of my structural design of the human personality. Vital eros is denied the fulfillment of its striving to be transformed by transcendent consonance into transeros.

Persistent Receptive Potency of Eros

In my personality theory, the inner receptive potency of eros, to be elevated by universal transcendent love, never dies. It keeps feeding secret longings, a hidden nostalgia for the "real thing." Victims of the illusion of fulfillment by pretranscendent eros alone are never fully satisfied. Many substitutes are sought in later life to calm the remnants of the hunger of the infant in us for the vital-erotic facet of love. None of them can still the deeper famine of the human heart.

Insofar as traditions are deformed, they make us regress instead of progress. They cannot fulfill our deepest longing. We regress in our search for the kingdom of joy and consonance. Unwittingly we begin to seek fulfillment in the real or imagined consolations of the maternal ambience we have lost. Everywhere we are looking for substitutes. A tradition deformed by personal fear of nearness to others is a source of ambivalence. It is laden with conflict. It may erode the vital-erotic striving itself. Erotic desires can be isolated from transcendent love. The erotic animation of life and relationships runs wild. This insulated striving of a pretranscendent eros implies for its gratification the necessity of some lower type of surrender. The people, events, and things one prefers as sources of consolation can be attained only by reaching out to them. The curtain of separation, drawn by fear of self-loss, can thicken. In the end, even the thought of a pretranscendent, merely vital-erotic surrender may become too threatening to consider.

Fallacy of a Merely Erotic
or Libidinal Explanation of Culture or Form Tradition

I want to underline what I see as the fallacy of speculations by some representatives of personality theories that are different from mine. They explain the formation of culture through early pretranscendent erotic factors, usually named and explained differently. For them the history of infantile erotic life is the only history of what they see as automatic human development, not as relatively free human formation. By implication this vital-erotic history of culture would apply also to tradition. For, as I have shown, traditions through their remnants are the mother of culture.

An example of their approach is the so-called swaddling-hypothesis of Geoffrey Gorer. This social scientist tries to explain the heavy pressure of vague feelings of guilt observed in the great Russian farmers of the past. He postulates its origin in the powerless rage felt by Russian babies. In accordance with Russian form tradition, the infant is so tightly wrapped that movement is barely possible (Honigmann 1954). Or take the contention of Roheim, quoted by Kroeber: "We see then, that the sexual practices of people are indeed prototypical and that from their posture in coitus their whole psychic attitude may be inferred" (Kroeber 1952, 308).

We can also think about the excessive formational influence Freud attributed to the Oedipus complex, which he considered to be universal, a claim refuted by eminent anthropologists such as Malinowski. Freud's bold speculations sometimes seem to be directed by onesided vital-biological assumptions. These assumptions underlie certain facets of the Freudian faith and formation tradition. Ultimately he does not seem to acknowledge a relatively autonomous reality to culture and by implication to its traditional sources. Following his train of thought, traditions would be mainly manifestations of libidinal strivings and of the history of their dynamics. Thinking in terms of my own formation science, I would say that the Freudian faith and formation tradition gave form to a libidinal epiphanic form structure; the Adlerian to an epiphanic structure of power strivings; the Jungian, Maslowian, Rogerian to a functional-transcendent epiphanic structure, namely, to "how we can functionally manipulate certain facets of our transcendent life dimension." I call them epiphanic — perhaps more correctly quasi-epiphanic — insofar as they are presented as the manifestation of our ultimate hidden ground, camouflaged in the apparent dynamic forms of our human life.

Because my formation science is comprehensive and integrational, I appreciate the partial truths in all of these theories without totalizing any of them. I integrate them into a higher epiphanic structure rooted in transcendent and subsequent posttranscendent life formation. In this regard the classic transcendent formation traditions too differ essentially from the epiphanies of only the pretranscendent dynamics of the human form of life. This does not mean that my theory downgrades or deludes the distinct powers and operations that were imprisoned by the walls of one's exclusively pretranscendent life orientation. On the contrary, the transcendent dimension awakens by posttranscendent transformation the pretranscendently encapsulated socio-vital-functional capacities and operations to their full unique potential.

Monoformational and Pluriformational Assumptions

In my theory of transcendent formation, I call pretranscendent faith presuppositions *monoformational* assumptions. They are typical of a number of social-scientific and educational faith and formation traditions reflected in their personality theories. As all basic assumptions of the sciences, including my formation science, they are prescientific. I contrast them with the *pluriformational* hierarchical assumptions of formation science that I formulated in Holland. These assumptions were rooted in my observation of the differentiated reality of each formation field as a whole for each of the people hiding with me in the countryside during the war. I saw the impact of all its directives on their human formation. I felt then that the construct "Lebenswelt," or "Life World," of Edmund Husserl, while useful in philosophy, was too undifferentiated for my empirical-experiential science. It could not account explicitly for the formation spheres and dimensions as well as for the particular form traditional pyramids that made these persons and their outlook distinct and different. Personalities are not forming their dispositions in dialogue with "the" world as a whole. They let themselves be formed by the world as defined for them by their unique and individual pyramid of formation traditions. My science is not concerned with all one's possible experiences of the world but only with those that are formational, that have a truly formational impact on the person. Each form traditional pyramid renders one receptive only for a limited field of world forms. Beyond this each formation field has its horizons that invite us to expand this field by taking in more of the world formatively. On the other hand, I realized also that the monoformational approach of many other personality theories was too onesided to take into account all spheres and dimensions of the formation field as I have done. An example of such onesidedness is the reduction of the whole of one's formation to vital-erotic experiences.

The life directives, dispositions, and affinities instilled by our form traditions cannot be traced exclusively to vital-erotic infancy experiences or to later personal experiences of their adherents. They are also the result of other dimensions and spheres of each one's limited field. Moreover, they are in great measure colored by the form traditions to which people are committed. They first assimilated these traditions via the familial tradition pyramid, later through their own focal appraisal and option. During the first assimilation, the personal modulations of the traditions by the parents play a significant role as does the affective or nonaffective way in which they communicated or imposed these personally modulated traditions. It is my observation that the early history of vital-erotic strivings, conflicts, and resistances can have a significant influence. The partial truth of social scientific and educational speculations should be taken into account in appraising the subsequent deformation of the original classic form traditions. I formulated as a general rule in my personality theory: *the more a formation tradition is assimilated and lived in a transcendent (not merely functional-transcendent) and subsequent posttranscendent way, the less its formational influence can be attributed to early vital-erotic experiences alone.*

Our traditions, transcendent and pretranscendent, determine in a significant way the formation of our vital strivings, dispositions, attitudes, and affinities. Yet we should never minimize in our life formation the leading role of the transcendent dimension of traditions. Its denial would make us more vulnerable to our hidden infantile vital-erotic desires. On the other hand, even if we are granting our spirit the leading position in life, we cannot reduce formation to the directives of the spirit alone. That would be another instance of a monoformational explanation. We are always also directed by other dimensions and spheres as well as by significant remnants of our formation pyramid and its early modulation by our parents. Not all of this pyramid can be reduced to childhood experiences. Nor is all of it perfectly integrated with our transcendent form tradition at the base of this pyramid. Neither should our awareness of the vital and spiritual directives blind us to the formative influences that affect us later in life. For example, success or failure in our projects of life can change our core dispositions and therewith their directives.

The story of our tradition and our field of formation as an interforming whole is the story of our life. For our field of life unfolds in the light of our tradition pyramid. It explains what happens with vital-erotic and aggressive strivings and how parents influence us by their tradition pyramids and their modes of modulating and communicating them to us.

A source of conflict in our life story is the loss of balance in the way we live our pyramid. Sometimes excessive congeniality strivings freeze our pyramid into a closed-off fortress. At other times extreme compatibility strivings reduce our pyramid to a kind of sieve. It lets the rivers of popular pulsations wildly flow in and out. Our tradition becomes spineless, hence unreliable as a stable guide of life.

I started this chapter with a discussion of the differences between commonly and individually deformed traditions. I conclude that the main difference is due to the fact that it is not primarily personal traumatic experiences that generate the core dispositions of the adherents of a deformed tradition. Their source is more external-sociohistorical, less immediately intimate and intraformational. Personally sound and balanced adherents may temper the warped directives taught by a deformed tradition. We should never judge the health of personal adherents only on the basis of the tradition to which they belong by birth and initial formation. Such persons may rediscover the original transcendent meanings of a distorted tradition, resource themselves in them, and become sources of transformation for the deformed tradition itself.

CHAPTER 9

Transcendent Ground
of Form Traditions

C lassical traditions of formation show a basic similarity. They point to
a power beyond themselves. Their initiators stood in awe of a mystery they believed at work at the origin of their style of life. They trusted
that this higher power would assure the continuation of their emerging
tradition. This claim appealed to a profound need in human nature. People are inclined to seek for the "more than," for an ultimate meaning of
the fleeting story of their existence. Certain traditions became classical
because they were considered by generations to hold a response to this
deepest desire.

Transcendence Dynamic and Transcendent Dimension

I came to call this tendency the dynamic of transcendence. It gives rise to
the supreme dimension of our life, which I subsequently designated as the
transcendent dimension. This dimension comprises in my theory both our
responses to this dynamic and their posttranscendent radiation into the
pretranscendent dimensions of our existence. In my theory lower dimensions by themselves alone are initially unaware of their inherent incipient
striving for consonance with the deepest direction of the human form of
life. They have to return home, as it were, to their country of origin, guided
by the light of posttranscendent radiation.

Why do I call this highest or deepest ground of our life a dimension
like the lower ones? Mainly to stress that it is an integral part of human
life, and by no means an extra addition. We should not think about our
spirit as something that unfolds somewhere within us in a sequestered compartment. Nor should we separate our spiritual life from other aspects
of our everyday existence. This would spawn a split, a dissonance, that
tears our life apart. Some edifying writers seem to conjure up a dualistic
mood and atmosphere. I came early to the decision that the anthropology of formation should avoid this trap. This concern was at the root of
my conception of primarily a *dimensional* theory of personality instead
of only a level or stage theory. In the end I came to the selection of
six basic dimensions of life, of which the transcendent is the highest. I

stressed that all of these dimensions interact with one another. In some way they give form to each other. To express this mutual form donation I coined the term *interformation*. Finally, my view developed into a six-dimensional interformation theory of human life. These dimensions are: the sociohistorical, the vital, the functional, the functional-transcendent, the transcendent, and the transcendent-functional or posttranscendent. All of these are interforming. Together they coform the tapestry of human life, its presence and action (see van Kaam, *Fundamental Formation*, 1982).

Functional-Transcendent;
Transcendent-Functional or Posttranscendent

In volume 1 of this series, I developed four dimensions. Recently I expanded these for the sake of accuracy with two more: the functional-transcendent and the transcendent-functional or posttranscendent. They are a response to the incomplete notions of transcendence, for example, in Carl Jung and his disciple Joseph Campbell. In his article "Joseph Campbell and the Power of Myth," Owen Jones says: "When Campbell uses the term transcendent he does not refer to a real transcendent reality. As in his use of the name God, he employs the term transcendent as a metaphor for the experience of one's psychic depths. Hence, *transcendent* has come to mean *immanent* in the gnostic lexicon. This is an example of the way gnostics *invert* spiritual language to achieve the ends of their system" (18). And further: "Joseph Campbell is an epigone of Carl Jung. He is a popularizer and romanticizer of Jung's gnostic theories concerning the ground of human consciousness. He offers a seductive system of salvation, without the cost of submitting one's mind to divine judgment, to a generation of America's middle class intellectual pleasure seekers who are spiritually adrift in a sea of opinions" (20). Something akin to this can be found in the idea of *self-actualization* as used by Carl Rogers, as well as by Abraham Maslow and the transpersonal psychology he inspired. The same self-actualization concept led to nondirective education and value clarification, which is the opposite of directive formation and form directive appreciation in the light of formation traditions that are at the heart of my science and theory.

Intrigued by this development, I studied for a while under both Carl Rogers and Abraham Maslow. I scrutinized their popular ideas as well as those of Carl Jung, the transpersonal psychologists, New Age spiritualities, and various pastoral counseling techniques and texts. In spite of my appreciation of these colleagues and their many creative insights, I could not escape the conclusion that their concepts on transcendence were flawed. They used certain ideas and facets of the transcendent life they may have taken over from classical traditions. But the way in which they explained them differs essentially from the meaning these ideas had in the traditions concerned. What was cultivated were a few minor potencies of transcendence. These would be developed by means of self-actualizing strategies that were, by definition, functional-manipulative in nature albeit in a most subtle and refined way. They represented psychological approaches to transcendence that may enable people to attain a feeling of psychic bliss. By itself alone this is not the path to a true and full transcendence. I relegate these experiences to a dimension that I interpose between the functional and the truly transcendent. I call this inbetween dimension in my theoretical structure of the human personality the functionally transcendent. If one comes to premature closure there, one may experience what I liken to an aborted, amphibious, or truncated transcendence. It may be helpful as a stage of transition in our journey toward full transcendence, but it is not, as some might think, the end of the story.

The functional dimension itself is essential for the transcendent life. Functional information, reasoning, and its ordering of the pretranscendent dimensions prepares us for transcendence. The transcendent life in turn is pregnant with a dynamism of incarnation. The transcendence event strives to incarnate, express, and implement itself in all dimensions of our life form as well as in all the spheres of our formation field. The functional dimension serves this posttranscendent implementation. Instead of mastering the transcendence dynamic, it allows itself to be mastered by it. It becomes the servant of spiritual incarnation in the light of transcendent formation traditions and their posttranscendent directives.

Grace and Nature

Religious formation traditions refer to either a divine or quasi-divine power. They profess that its help is necessary. Without its aid, we cannot reach a consonant disclosure and empirical-experiential implementation of our transcendent founding form. One of the words used by many traditions to point to this power is *grace*. Formation science as science can only observe that adherents of such traditions name and experience this power as coformational in their life. The way in which they explain it differs from tradition to tradition. Even within the same tradition, we may be faced with different interpretations.

Formation scientists can explore, without becoming involved in such theologies, how different types of faith modulate empirically and experientially the observable human formation of life and its fields of presence and action. They may also articulate one or more specific formation traditions encountered in their own life or in their studies. In that case, they may choose either to articulate such traditions merely in terms of their own scientific categories or to complement their scientific articulation with one that goes beyond science as science. They may expand scientific categories with transscientific ones of the formation tradition they are articulating. In that case they choose to articulate the tradition also from the inside out.

I define this in the methodology of my science as *reverse articulation*. In a scholarly fashion they use the results of the direct articulation as well as other concepts and constructs of the science insofar as they are applicable to the reverse articulation. Both types of articulation function as a dialectical articulation of the tradition under consideration.

In service of this dialectical articulation, I developed the method of comparative articulation or the consonance-dissonance articulation method. The consonances between the concepts of the science and those of the formation tradition are seldom fully consonant. It is a consonance within dissonances. To highlight consonances within dissonances is the aim of the critical comparison of articulated formation traditions. The disclosure of formational harmony serves the consonant formation of life as a whole while respecting the unique depth and identity of each articulated form tradition by acknowledging the identifying dissonances.

Formation science as a science of transcendent nature also explores the succession of dominant traditions in human formation history. Formation scientists can examine the numinous formation traditions in the beginnings of humanity, the institutionalized monotheistic formation traditions later on, and the deistic formation traditions of the eighteenth century. The last assumed a distant God not involved coformationally in our formation story. Finally, formation scientists can analyze the skeptic formation traditions of the twentieth century, such as the "God is dead" traditions and the emergent gnostic traditions of Jungian and New Age spiritualities.

Social Interformation

I introduced in my formation science the term *interformation* to highlight the interforming dynamic relationship between all spheres, dimensions, articulations, regions, ranges, and horizons of the formation field. *Social interformation* is a special mode that general interformation assumes in our formation field. It is in fact one of the most significant modes of interformation, for it takes place between formationally significant people — between husbands and wives, parents and children, friends and acquaintances, teachers and pupils, superiors and subjects, employers and employees. Therefore, I gave it a unique position in my diagram of the formation field. I put it horizontally on the same level as the intraformational sphere. For our intrasphere is constantly influenced by and influencing our interformational social relationships, starting at conception. For the sake of diagrammatic brevity, I wrote it into the diagram as "interformation," omitting momentarily the prefix "social" (see van Kaam, *Fundamental Formation*, 1982, chart 5).

Interformation of Human Nature and Formation Traditions

Let us now consider another mode of interformation, understood in its original wider sense. In the light of this construct, we can look at the interformation between the base of our intraform of life, our human nature, and form traditions.

In my formation anthropology I envision human nature as a more or less permanent basis of human formation. I consider this basic point of departure for all formation under its generic, specific, and individual facets. The generic facet is typical of all people, the specific facet specifies this generic essence. For instance, a specific racial facet may modify our DNA. The individual facet consists of individual form potencies that mark our DNA as individual. I added to this threesome the unique transcendent facet of our essence, calling it our transcendent identity or life call, affecting the forms we may choose for our generic, specific, and individual formation.

This formational essence is the foundation and criterion of the actualization of our form potencies. We have to listen to our nature wisely and respectfully. For example, our vital nature as a main facet of our founding life form directs us to eat and sleep in order to survive. All kinds of qualitative and quantitative variations are possible when we are in dialogue with our formation tradition and implement this vital form directive in our everyday formation.

Vital Nature and Formation Tradition

Our vital nature lacks the instinctual consonant directedness of animal life. Hence it demands the complement of formation traditions. These enable us to act in vital, functional, and sociohistorical ways that are congenial with the more basic transcendent dimension of our nature.

I see as part of the same human nature the tendency of people always and everywhere to give form to a formation tradition. The form tradition complements the vital facets of our nature. It is natural for people to give form to and to receive form from a formation tradition. Traditional formation belongs to human nature. Based on observation and research, I am convinced that this nature and its limited form potencies essentially demand and presuppose the assistance for formation traditions for its survival and consonant unfolding.

Representatives of the human sciences may object that certain formation traditions alienate people from their vital nature. From the viewpoint of my formation anthropology, the answer would be that it is not the formation tradition as such that deforms the human form of life. We can only say this or that specific or particular formation tradition is in opposition to the consonant unfolding of our essential humanity. For example, the Jansenistic, excessively rigorous, formation tradition within seventeenth-century Catholicism led to partial deformations of human life. Similarly the Iranian form of the Shiite Islamic formation tradition under Khomeini manifested directives dissonant with basic human nature. In the end many formation traditions may decay or collapse if they do not flexibly foster sufficient interformation, not only with their underlying faith tradition, but also with changing field demands and with emergent data and insights regarding human nature.

It is thus not the formation tradition as such that makes originally natural people unnatural. The only thing we can say responsibly is that one or the other specific formation tradition or some of its directives lead to a lack of appreciation of certain basic form directives of human nature. Such a depreciation may be lasting or only sustain itself during a certain period of a tradition. For example, there was a period of secular colonial domination by the West of Arab nations. This led to a period of overreaction on the part of resentful Arabs, which modulated the Islamic formation tradition in certain countries. The overreaction blinded some groups to the need of our nature to find compatibility with those who do not necessarily share our own tradition, but who can affect our human, political, social, or economic conditions.

CHAPTER 10

Stability and Adaptability
of Formation Traditions

We observe a great variety of form traditions. Many of them seem basically congenial with human nature. This variety tells us something about the founding form of our nature and its wealth of form potencies. Through the exuberance of our traditions of formation, human nature discloses to us its exceptional plasticity. Our nature is unbelievably flexible, endowed with an immense adaptability.

Equally remarkable is the stability and endurability of certain classic traditions, such as those of the great world religions. The permanence of their founding features depends in great measure on the institutionalization of their originating events and directives.

The human life form, unlike lower forms of life, is limited in vital-instinctual specialization. Animal forms of life, on the contrary, are highly specialized in their instinctual form direction. They fit into their natural environment like a hand fits a glove. They find themselves in an environment already adapted to their nature. The animal does not perceive in its environment anything that has no vital-instinctual relevance for its survival. Its senses are only elicited by stimuli that fall within the limited range of its instinctual preformation and subsequent form directives.

The human life form, however, is continuously exposed to an abundance of stimuli, which it can observe, appraise, elaborate mentally and imaginatively, and give meaning to uniquely. It can fit these into its own formation projects. Instinctually, the human life form is handicapped in comparison with animal life; yet spiritually humans are rich in creative form potencies. Without them we could not survive and prosper. Our nature does not fit automatically into the environment like ink in a pen. Therefore, we must create, as it were, a second nature. What I have defined as a secondary dispositional nature enables our weak instinctual nature to receive form from and express form in a human environment or humanized formation field. This secondary founding form of life is a dispositional form. It enriches our nature with dispositions that are congenial with our unique preempirical life form and compatible with our formation field as humanized by us in the light of form traditions (see volume 2 of this series).

85

Our instinct-deficient life finds itself in an environment that is chaotic. Hence, together with others, we give form over aeons of history to human fields of presence as well as to an increasingly humanized cosmos. This field is congenial with our limited organismic as well as with our mushrooming rational and spiritual potencies. The creation and maintenance of human formation fields over the generations, in a variety of cultures and civilizations, is mediated by the emergence of an abundance of form traditions. These help people to give form communally and personally to their secondary nature, made up as it is of basic core dispositions.

Traditions of human formation are unfolding in dialogue with underlying faith traditions or belief systems. They are in dialogue also with a chaotic world as a potential field of human meaning. Diverse traditions are the source of the grand compromises that comprise in the end our pluralistic cultures. They are partly consonant, partly dissonant reflections of influential elements of various significant traditions in our culture. In my theory such traditions erupt and unfold in interforming accord and disaccord within the pluralistic culture they in great part create and nourish. A pluralistic culture is a sociohistorical, more or less arbitrary collection of form directive fragments of various form traditions, fragments that somehow at some time happened to capture the collective imagination of a significant number of influential members of a society.

Human Consciousness

In this process of secondary nature and field formation, human consciousness as intra- and interconsciousness unfolds to great heights. Formational consciousness feeds on all regions of our spheric and dimensional attentiveness. *Spheric* consciousness unfolds in its coping with the challenges of the pre-, intra-, inter-, and outerspheres of the fashioning and unfolding of human formation fields in the light of formation traditions. *Dimensional* consciousness expands and deepens in its participation in the ongoing formation of the sociohistorical, vital, functional, functional-transcendent, transcendent, and posttranscendent dimensions of life in light again of formation traditions. Their varied availability to various regions of awareness differentiates this awareness into focal, prefocal, infrafocal, and transfocal consciousness in both intra- and interconsciousness.

At the heart of human consciousness is human intelligence, which of necessity complements our limited vital-organismic intelligence. It gives rise to critical-analytical appraisal, systematic observation, science, technique, and scholarship. Technical-intellectual form potencies complement, therefore, the human lack of specialized organismic potencies.

Distancing Consciousness

Human consciousness is a distancing consciousness. Any reflection implies a certain distancing. Instead of giving form instantly to vital pulsions of our formation energy, human intelligence makes us wait and ponder, apprehend more clearly and appraise more diligently. One result of such continual distancing is that we do not spend all the vital formation energy that wells up in us while facing various life situations. Such unspent formation energy accumulates within us. It may overload the intensity of vital strivings that are aroused by situations and not fully satisfied. For example, the vital-sexual striving is not instinctually specialized and immediately satisfied as it is in the animal form of life. Therefore, this vital unspent energy can usually be evoked in healthy human life by the appropriate stimuli. This explains why the sex life of humans is not instinctually specialized to operate only in mating seasons.

One of the central constants of formation anthropology is the interformational nature of human life formation. Animal forms of life do not manifest this typically human characteristic. They do not need a time of transition to shift from one instinctual form direction to another. For instance, an animal can shift at once from fighting to eating, from nest building to feather cleaning, from food searching to sexual pairing. Neither does it accumulate and store unspent energy. In the interdimensional and interspheric human life form, however, a variety of lower and higher apprehensions and appraisals, of higher and lower strivings, of various regions of consciousness and their shifting availabilities can be operational simultaneously and continuously. This explains why, for instance, the sexual form reception and expression of humans is penetrated by motivations from life dimensions and field spheres other than the sexual articulation of the vital sphere alone. Conversely these spheres and dimensions can be permeated by libidinal strivings.

The actualization of any vital form direction in animal life is provoked by exclusive stimuli. Such stimuli are relevant to one specialized latent form direction alone. In humans, however, the interdimensional and interspheric interformation of the relatively free human life form gives rise to a formation field in which almost everything can evoke any form directedness. Only few forms in this field operate automatically as form directive triggers of specialized reactions. One example of such automatic triggers are certain facial expressions. Another are the specific arousing forms of vital sex attraction. Yet even those do not often evoke much more than an initial vital impulse. This impulse of human vital life is not always and necessarily followed by corresponding form-giving as it is in animal life. For, as we have seen, human consciousness, intelligence, and freedom cause a gap between drive or impulse and the formational act.

Instinct Reduction and Form Traditions

The anthropological fact of instinct reduction in human existence is related to the emergence of form traditions. Human formation is penetrated through and through by institutionalized and free-floating form traditions as well as by the remnants and surface reflections of such traditions in pluralistic cultures. Our instinct reduction makes such omnipresent traditions necessary for our survival and unfolding. The human life form does not find itself in a congenial field of presence and action. Hence, it must give form to a more or less congenial and compatible formation field. By nature unstable, endlessly flexible, and compatible, this life form must find a way to give stability and direction to human life. It utilizes for this stabilization and direction the wisdom treasures of form traditions and their surface reflections in pluralistic cultures. In this utilization it is directed by the faith traditions that underlie such form traditions. At the same time its realization of modes of stability and direction is coformed by continual dialogue with the ever-changing formational events in our limited field of presence and action that are carved out by the steady blades of tradition from the world as a whole. This world remains always the "horizon of horizons" of all human fields. Each field and tradition pyramid can always take in more of this wider world; it can penetrate deeper into it. Such expansion usually happens first via what I have defined as the more immediate *affinity horizons* of the field. Such indefinitely extending affinity horizons are outside the immediate concerns that organize our field and pyramid as I have defined them. But they have potentially a certain affinity or an appealing, attention-evocative similarity with these dynamic field concerns. For instance, a mechanic specialized in his or her own field may not know about mechanics in numerous different fields of concern. Yet once awareness dawns about their existence as one part of the indeterminately stretching horizon of all mechanics it may evoke interest and curiosity because of the implicit affinity of any specific mechanic to all mechanics.

Each expansion of the field into any affinity horizon offers by necessity also an entrance into the wider world as a whole beyond one's own limited field. Through every extension into the affinity horizon also the world horizon recedes a little more.

For example, one facet of the field of a poet is poetry inspired by the events transpiring in the life of poets who share her formation field and tradition pyramid. The corresponding affinity horizon of poetry outside the field can evoke her interest in poetry written from experiences in other alien fields of life or from the viewpoint of other unfamiliar traditions. For instance, among them the field and tradition of Far Eastern populations may be a closed book to her. A discovery of Far Eastern poetry may somehow lift for her a tip of the veil of this foreign field and tradition. Such disclosure may lead to the assimilation of this extraneous poetry and the field to which it points. It becomes a coformant of the poet's own field of life and own tradition pyramid. It will be gradually modulated by the already existing field and tradition facets. This process of formational assimilation will only happen if she lets this foreign poetry really coform her heart, mind, imagination, and lingual dispositions.

The expansion of the field and pyramid of the poet through this specific affinity-horizon makes the "horizon of all field horizons" yield a little farther. Part of the unknown world beyond her field becomes now an apprehended and appreciated coformant of her own life and field.

Similarly many facets of the beyond-world out there become successively part of our own tradition pyramid and field of formation usually through the gates of our own specific affinity horizons. The world-as-a-whole, however, can never become identical with any human formation field or tradition pyramid no matter how profound, extensive and diversified. No human field can comprehend formatively the inexhaustible depth and richness of the world-as-a-whole.

Probably Edmund Husserl, in his concept of the life world, pointed in his own way to the same processes I have been pointing to in a formational empirical-experiential manner. His concept is brilliant from the broad philosophical-phenomenological perspective. From my formational perspective, however, his concept seems insufficient for the formational, empirical-experiential science and personality theory that I have been developing since 1945. The construct of the formation field was one of my first seminal intuitions during that year of first conception of my formation theory of personality.

Stability and Reduction of Form Receptive Openness

During the sudden displacements and unpredictable demands I observed in war time, I became acutely aware of the threat of destabilization and loss of direction in myself and others. Besieged by the problems of those I helped to hide, I began to ask myself how much instability human life can endure without falling apart. How can people maintain some integration when their customary formation field is ripped open? Where can they turn when their culture and its conditions are ruined? On what resources can they rely when the depths of their formation tradition are not yet probed, appraised, and expanded sufficiently to take new events into account?

The displaced people I met in that last year of war had been stabilized and directed in their past by a peaceful, well-to-do society. This society doted on centuries-old traditions. Now these people were threatened by famine, deportation, imprisonment, torture, execution, gas chambers. They were overexposed and overburdened by new constellations of stimuli.

I tried to help them by counseling them about what I called in my emerging theory *strategic attention reduction*. They should silence in themselves an exclusive attentiveness to any constellation of stimuli in present, past, or future that would depress them more than absolutely unavoidable. They should not allow such constellations of depreciative thoughts and feelings to interfere with the priorities of survival, of maintenance of human dignity, of prudent resistance here and now. This reduction of uncritical openness and of its subsequent dispersed unfocused attentiveness led correspondingly to a shrinking of their formation field to proportions they could handle. Those who implemented my advice experienced significant relief from the anxiety and despair engendered in them by the upheaval of their familiar surroundings. They were better able to withstand the forces of disintegration. It dawned on me that this experience could clarify one of the sources of the institutionalization of formation traditions.

My hypothesis was that not only displaced persons in hiding but all people to some degree experience periods of intensified focal or nonfocal anxiety. Everyone experiences changes in her or his formation field. A strikingly unexpected change may bring to consciousness, prefocally and focally, one's original incompatibility with an unpredictable world. The cause of this basic incompatibility is one's instinct-deficient human nature. This evokes one's latent formation anxiety: Can I survive in dignity? Am I still able to give some consonant form and direction to the chaos that threatens my existence? In the search for ways to cope with this anxiety, people may become aware of the strategy of *receptivity reformation*, the tactical selective reduction of one's openness and floating attentiveness to manageable constellations of stimuli. The discovery of this strategy, however, can expose the anxiety dynamic to a new threatening question. How can I reduce my form receptivity in the most effective fashion without deformative side effects? Looking around for guidance in this act of reductive reformation, people found many often conflicting answers in free-floating formation traditions. To diminish the conflicting directions and expressions, people began to stabilize free-floating formation traditions by turning them into institutionalized form traditions. By defining and carefully observing this process, writing down the results of my analysis, subjecting them to intersubjective confirmation, I came to my theory of one of the important causes of the origin and function of the classical institutional form traditions.

Classical Institutionalized Form Traditions

I began to see how institutionalized traditions facilitate the stabilization and wise directedness of life's journey. They help us to give an abiding form to our receptivity. They suggest wise receptivity reductions. These are necessary to prevent a falling back into postinstinctual, pretranscendent chaos. Our nature is not sufficiently specialized by innate instincts to grant us this stability and direction. As a matter of fact, the human life form is continually endangered. Initial instinctual formlessness exposes it to the constant threat of dysfunctionality because of its uncontrolled striving for an uncritical compatibility. This is one of the sources of the power of totalitarian movements over many fearful citizens already weakened by the loss of the form traditional coformant of their life form identity. A charismatic dictatorial leader, supported by the media he controls, can fascinate especially people who do not have a dominant basic tradition to guide their compatibility striving. He turns them into excited followers by offering them a new faith and form tradition or a new fundamentalistically distorted version of a classical tradition. Adolf Hitler created a large mass of blindly applauding followers in many central European countries, offering them a new National Socialist faith and formation tradition with which they could identify in blind compatibility. Saddam Hussein tried to do something similar for the Arab lands by espousing momentarily a fundamentalist version of the Islamic faith and formation tradition in his apparent public life form.

The prefocal human fear of inner and outer chaos, the search for absorption in an absolutized compatibility that fills the empty space of the lost form traditional coformant of identity predisposes people for identification with the prophetic strong man and his cunningly crafted faith and form tradition, be it new or fundamentalistic. His assurance that he will bring a new law and order that will prevent even the possibility of moments of chaos soothes the prefocal fear of any threat of chaotic inner or outer upheavals. His sacred pledge of creating a force that will bring victory over all enemies that try to produce chaos by their false belief systems and form traditions can bring followers to a frenzy of compatibility with the leader and with one another in the battle for the newly or the fundamentalistically distorted tradition.

It is a process of prefocal identification of one's own pretranscendent and/or functional-transcendent I (the gnostic I) with the similar real or perceived I of the strong prophetic superman or superwoman. The process is intensified by an increasing faith and trust in the prefocal illusion that one will find by this frenetic absorption in an absolutized compatibility full and final liberation of the very possibility of chaos. Hoped for also is a liberation from the burden of balancing in freedom any coformant of compatibility with the basic coformant of one's unique founding life form or life call in light of a freely chosen tradition pyramid.

I felt that culture was no longer a dependable source for the formation of a balanced receptivity that saves us from disintegration. Culture is increasingly pluralistic. For me culture is a faint shadow of only selected elements of institutional form traditions. These are interspersed arbitrarily with fragments of free-floating past or emergent traditions. It is pernicious to give in to an uncritical striving for compatibility with any elements of a pluralistic culture that strike our fancy. Without at least an indirect guidance by classical institutionalized form traditions, it is difficult to prevent disintegration. Our vitally preformed nature is too weak instinctually to protect a stable form or *gestalt* of our unique human dignity. Institutionalized formation traditions thus create some certainty of direction, which sheer natural-vital preformation can never give us by itself alone.

The innate receptivity of our outer and inner senses enables us to take in all forms appearing in our world. When this sense receptivity is not wisely curtailed and guided, we are overcome by a polyphony of impressions, which overwhelm our potency for rational order. They rob us of our freedom. An institutionalized form tradition can assist us in ordering this wide-open receptivity of our senses. Classical traditions of this sort or their consonant derivatives point us to some way of ordering our impressions. They give us the benefit of the experiences of generations. They teach us how to simplify our field so that we may not be drowned in the sea of cosmic reality or lost in the streams and rivulets of pluralistic cultures.

In this way a classic form tradition gives a certain stability and direction to our patterns of form reception and donation in an unpredictable world of impressions and directions. Classic traditions can relieve us from the burden of constant choices. Without form tradition each of us would have to appraise, affirm, and improvise a totally new answer to any problem or task facing us. Tradition grants us a general insight into what to do and how to do it in a way that is effective, yet congenial, compatible, and compassionate, without danger to our basic dignity and integrity. Because of the gift of tradition, our formation journey becomes more smooth, less filled with problems, more clear in its direction. We share in the basic formational dispositions of the tradition to which we happen to be committed. Implicitly we share also in the powerful directives of its underlying faith tradition or belief system.

Formation directives that are subjectivistic are increasingly replaced by more objective directives. Profoundly clear in this regard are revealed faith traditions like Christianity, which far surpass what human minds can grasp. These faith traditions are coformed by form traditional directives that have gained an objective existence in the institutions and symbols of the implementary form traditions.

The dispositions and patterns of our form reception and expression are thus coformed by a traditional formation power that transcends our subjectivity. This coformational power does not reside merely in the intraform of our life. Form traditions through their mighty symbols dwell as forming powers also in the inter- and outerspheres of our field and its horizons. For religious formation traditions, their coformational power is rooted in the ongoing preforming mystery of formation.

CHAPTER 11

The Ethos of Formation Traditions

Each tradition radiates a power of its own. It evokes in the conscience of its adherents an experience of obligation. It makes them aware of how they should feel, think, and act as its participants. For example, physicians committed to the professional tradition of medicine will feel obliged to adapt a certain style of presence to patients and the public. Such often unwritten *oughts* of form reception and expression coform together what I call the particular ethos of a form tradition. The ethos, for instance, of the medical profession differs from that of miners, clergy persons, or bartenders. What comes into play here is my earlier distinction between faith conscience and formation conscience. As a Christian believer, I feel obliged to try to be respectful of the dignity of my neighbors. As a participant in the ethos of the professional traditions of university teachers, I feel uneasy when I do not follow the unwritten guidelines for a typical university presentation to graduate students. I sense that such neglect goes against the ethos of the professional tradition to which I belong.

Ethics and ethos do not necessarily overlap in all circumstances. The ethics of many faith traditions may not say anything specific about attractive dressing in tune with professional or societal functions. The ethos of a particular formation tradition, for example, of ambassadors and diplomats, may point to a traditional dress code. Fidelity to such a code can be related indirectly to an ethical directive of a particular faith tradition that would, for instance, explicitly promote the ethics of fidelity to one's profession. Yet it does not directly teach us the particulars of this professional form tradition.

Something similar applies to religious form traditions. A certain style of meditation in a particular body posture may be part of the ethos of a particular formation tradition within a specific faith tradition while not necessarily made ethically obligatory for all the adherents who share this faith tradition and who may adhere to other form traditions emerging within the parameters of the same basic belief system.

Ethos and Affectivity

The ethos of a form tradition touches in some way the affective dispositions of its adherents. The gentle contemplative lifestyle of the Zen

93

or the Zazen tradition of Buddhism gives form not only to the thought of their followers but also to the way in which reality is sensed and felt by them. This embodiment of the ethos of a form tradition in the affective life of its participants is crucial for the survival of a tradition. To be effective, a form tradition must stay alive. It can only do so when it is embedded in the affectivity dispositions of its adherents.

We should not understand such affective adherence as mainly or only about eruptive excitement or emotional elation when one is exposed to the symbols of the tradition. This may or may not be the case. While such exalted feelings may be helpful, they are not indispensable for the form effectiveness of the tradition. They can even hinder the formation of deeper attachment, of quiet affective affinity to the tradition. Basic affective affinity or moodedness can remain constant even when sentiment is absent and the heart is dry as dust. The former feelings come and go. When they become the main or only criterion of formation, they may lead to instability of one's lived commitment. Life will move up and down with the rise and fall of sentiment.

Excessive emphasis on subjective emotional experience is something rather recent in the history of formation. One of its sources is a form of popularized existentialistic psychologism. Classical form traditions endured because they were able to foster the basic affinity of a stable affective commitment. It is transcendent not vital affectivity that keeps commitment alive. Its possible resonance in pretranscendent vital affectivity depends for its intensity on the vital temperamental constitution or *temperform* of each particular adherent. Basic commitment to a formation tradition is continually restored by an empathic reiteration in faith of its rites, readings, symbols, and directives with or without intense subjective feeling. Pretranscendent feeling, while important, is not crucial; transcendent affectivity is. If people happen to be affectionate temperamentally, it is imperative for their integrated life that this vital affectivity be joyfully affirmed, illumined, and penetrated by the light of their formation tradition. It should transform vital affectivity without denying, distorting, or silencing its dynamics.

When a population shares the same vital-temperamental affectivity, it becomes one of the coformants of its shared formation tradition. There is, for instance, a difference between the form tradition of Southern Italian and Scottish Catholics, between that of Saudi-Arabian Muslims and the emergent form tradition of New York converts to Islam. Yet the true believers share the same basic underlying faith tradition as well as the foundations of a general corresponding form tradition. They differ in their affinity to the ethos of their different special and personal form traditions. Their vital affectivity colors their choice of expression and gesture, devotion and prayer, child formation, and style of worship and asceticism.

Formation Conscience, Ethos of Form Traditions, Institutionalized Forms of Conservation

The ethos of a formation tradition perpetuates itself dynamically by formation, reformation, and transformation of dispositions and directives in response to the changes in the formation field as shared by its participants. Striving to conserve the ethos of each tradition leads to institutionalized forms of conservation. These are mirrored in the core conservation dispositions in the heart of the adherents. The latter affect their formation conscience; they give the ethos of the form tradition its ought-character. Without such conservation dispositions and their expression in institutional forms, no continuity of the tradition would be possible. An uncritical excessive striving for compatibility with other traditions or with what is in today, gone tomorrow would soon take over.

For example, a weakening of affective conservation dispositions in some European religious form traditions led to a history of newly emerging secular-functional form traditions to the detriment or even loss of the religious form traditions. Therewith, the underlying faith-tradition itself was in danger. We should never forget that the faith tradition does not give form directly to people's everyday existence. It is always in and through their formation traditions that their hearts are formed in their faith. They are initiated in these form traditions far earlier than in the theological, ideological, or catechetical statements of the faith tradition itself. The atmosphere of the formation tradition is breathed in daily with the faith that is represented in and through it concretely, affectively here and now. This happens long before they learn intellectually the precise definitions of what they are invited to believe in. Even after this learning, their now enriched and deepened formation tradition will continue to give form to their faithful heart in everyday living.

Peruvian peasants, poor in the intellectual grasp of the dogmas of their faith, may be rich in the commitment and affectivity of their believing hearts. The source is the living, colorful form tradition. This tradition, in turn, has to be continually purified, transformed, and updated by a critical understanding of its consonance and dissonance with the underlying faith tradition. This purification process will protect and enhance its crucial congeniality with the founding form of the tradition. Uncritical compatibility always takes place at the expense of wise congeniality.

Subtraditions

To simplify matters I mentioned mainly specific form traditions as a whole. In fact, however, within most specific form traditions subspecific or particular traditions emerge spontaneously. We witness a progressive differentiation in styles and even schools of form traditions. This is not surprising. A form tradition is the result of a process of interformation between a faith tradition and the daily demands of a specific or subspecific formation field shared by adherents of that tradition. When the formation field changes, the form tradition has to change with it. The field, moreover, is a differentiated field. Hence, various parts of the field may call for approaches that are more specialized than people's specific form tradition. Adherents engaged in such a differentiated facet may give form spontaneously to a subtradition that, while consonant with the specific form tradition, adds certain features to its ethos that are not felt as obligatory by all adherents of it.

Francis of Assisi, for instance, manifests in style and expression a typical Italian Catholic formation tradition. Nobody would mistake him for a typical Swede or Icelander. He experienced the call to engage himself and his followers in a specialized style of poverty to enhance the detachment aspect of his contemporary formation field. This gave rise to the Franciscan subtradition of formation. In the course of history, it gained a certain autonomy. No longer a subtradition of the Italian form tradition, it became a specific form tradition in its own right. This Franciscan form tradition in turn differentiated into various Franciscan subtraditions of form expressions in consonance with new shared formation fields. Francis would have been quite surprised to see the non-Italian lifestyle of his Northern or American counterparts.

Each subtradition or school gives form to its own ethos. As long as it claims commitment to the specific form tradition within which it arose, it should be congenial with the basics of that tradition. Moreover, the subtradition should remain congenial in its unfolding with the foundations of the underlying faith tradition as proclaimed by its legitimate custodians. An example of loss of such congeniality is the subtradition of Archbishop Marcel Lefebvre leading to a schism not only in the Catholic form but also in some tenets of the Catholic faith tradition.

In a wider sense we can say that all specific as well as all subspecific form traditions are subordinate traditions in relation to the foundational classic formation traditions of any faith traditions per se. In the course of formation history, the universally applicable insights of all form traditions are absorbed in a foundational formation tradition for all. For example, certain prayer and worship traditions that emerged in subtraditional groups of faithful became part of the universal foundational Catholic, Protestant, Jewish, or Islamic formation tradition. The now universal liturgical form of the Roman Catholic Mass was a combination of different early liturgical form traditions in different centers of early Christianity.

A striking example of the emergence of subordinated form traditions in Christianity is the formational spiritualities of the numerous religious communities and lay associations. These spiritualities are coformed by the particular ethos and projects of the groups concerned. The special character of their ministry, in dialogue with certain preferential facets of the formation field, necessitate a corresponding style of compatibility and availability.

Another example is the various Judaic and Islamic subtraditions that arose out of interformation with particular cultural formation fields and their compatibility pressures on the subgroup. For example, the Jewish formation traditions in America, the medieval Moorish tradition in Spain, the Shiite tradition in Iran, the Islamic subformation tradition in secularized Turkey all manifest the same basic features of subordinated traditional formation. There is always the possibility that a subtradition becomes autonomous. An example would be the form tradition of the Amish in central Pennsylvania and neighboring states.

To incarnate their ethos in the affective life of their participants, formation traditions give rise to symbols, the consideration of which shall occupy us in the following chapter.

CHAPTER 12

Form Traditional Symbols

A ll formation traditions, ideological as well as religious, mediate their message by formational symbols. Even dissonant ideological form traditions that did not become classical, such as that of German National Socialism, Italian Fascism, and the Stalinist Marxism of the Soviet Union, exemplify this institutionalizing of symbolic formation directives. Examples readily come to mind: the swastika, the hammer and sickle, the martial salutations, the symbolic red flags, the Nazi standards, the orchestrated mass spectacles. Such symbols and symbolic rituals exuded formational life directions to excited adherents.

Symbolic Formation of the Affective Life

The institutionalization of symbolic formation extends itself to the affective life of participants in the form tradition concerned. A reformation of the affective life of adherents by means of the symbolized dispositions and directives of a tradition is necessary for its vitality. Without such affective reformation, a tradition cannot be implanted in the intraformational life of its followers. A tradition that is not interiorized by a sufficient number of participants dies from paralysis. It cannot survive in the long run. Only when a tradition has given form to one's inner affectivity and basic moodedness can one be vividly faithful to its ethos. Only then can one communicate it convincingly to others, so much so that they become apostles, propagandists, persuaders, promoters, evangelizers, missionaries, converters, proselytizers, or revivalists of the ideological or religious tradition that touched them affectively via its symbols.

Intraformation by a tradition is effective when it gives form not only to their images, thoughts, and reflections but also to their corresponding affects. Symbols play a decisive role in affect formation. Therefore, institutionalized traditions use symbols to give intraformational direction to the thoughts and feelings of their participants. The ethos of a form tradition directs to some degree what we should and may feel.

We cannot escape the emotional impact of the symbols of the ethos of our traditions. They demand from us heartfelt conformation and coformation. Our affective life is coformed under continual pressure of the emotional directives of the ethos of traditions in which we share. For

98

example, the names and images of traditionally appreciated as well as depreciated emotions are chosen as symbols of our formation ethos. Even if we do not opt for a powerful tradition, we may absorb its symbolic affect direction indirectly through its implicit elemental reflections in the language of our pluralistic culture. For example, the expression "blood and soil," "Blut und Boden," in Germany received a whole new affective symbolic meaning for the adherents and sympathizers of the Nazi faith and form traditions.

That we share and express unwittingly the core affects of the ethos of our traditions does not necessarily mean that we as persons only pretend to do so. We feel what we truly believe we feel. The awareness itself of our feelings is formational. What we discover in our self-experience as moving us emotionally are really *our* feelings, no matter from whence they emerge. We should also realize that in the process of the formation of our affectivity the formational power of what is real cannot be separated from the form-giving power of our imagination as nourished by the image-laden symbols we pick up from our pluralistic culture, filled as it is with elemental symbolic remnants of numberless underlying formation traditions.

Faith Symbols and Formation Symbols

To give concrete form in one's life to one's faith directives may demand the working through of many empirical-experiential problems and minicoercions in one's pretranscendent life. Neither the doctrinal nor the professional-theological or ideological expression of basic faith directives seem by themselves alone or by their own methodologies to be sufficient. They cannot provide each individual group or person with the detailed empirical directives one needs for an effective solution of every possible empirical problem or coercion. The concrete implementation of faith in our everyday style of life in a pluralistic formation field demands complementary practical insights. Detailed empirical analysis falls outside doctrinal, theological, or ideological-philosophical methodologies. Belief systems can and should give us general directives for our experiential and ethical life based on a theological-practical, ideological-practical, or scientific ideological-practical analysis of experience.

I created formation science to do for us what theology or ideology cannot fully accomplish by itself alone. It is desirable that professional theologians or ideological philosophers of practical theologies or ideologies strive to integrate within their scholarly projects what formation science may offer them in this regard. On its part the science, in its articulation of its concepts and constructs into existing specific form traditions, can assist the attempts of these traditions to complement faith symbols with corresponding formation symbols. These should serve the implementation of faith by these form traditions in present-day formation fields. This may sometimes imply an enrichment, addition, or even substitution of the symbols created by the classics of formation and its acknowledged masters.

In this always ongoing process of compatible implementation in everyday pluralistic formation fields, we need to keep an eye not on nature alone, culture alone, or faith tradition alone and their symbols. We need to look at all three, asking ourselves if they, in spite of differences, may also have something in common. In other words, we look at our formation field as a whole, including all the influences of nature, culture, and faith traditions playing within it.

Within the field of formation, traditions occupy a central place. We can ask if a formation symbol of any one of them can also be used by another tradition without betraying the message of its own symbols. For example, the symbolic power of the song "We Shall Overcome" with its striking imagery and melody can give expression to both the hunger for freedom and justice we share with many contemporaries in our present-day formation field as a whole as well as in the field as warmed and illumined by our faith tradition. Thus an adherent of the Christian faith tradition lives in the faith that Christ is the ultimate source and example of freedom and justice in its fullness. Affectively touched by this symbol, Christians may share enthusiastically in consonant movements for social justice as these are awakened in contemporary life. Cultural formation symbols cannot replace for Christians such faith symbols as the liberation from Egypt. It can complement them, but to keep alive the faith aspect of a new traditional formation symbol, we have to relate it implicitly or explicitly to corresponding faith symbols.

Interformational Differentiation of Affective Ethos and Its Symbolism

Our affective dispositions and directives share in the ethos of an institutional form tradition. Every form tradition symbolizes binding directives and prohibitions in regard to the formational direction of the affective life of its participants. A living form tradition implies an inherent dynamic to differentiate and refine this ethos of affectivity. It does so always in interformational dialogue with the structures of one's specific formation field. This dialogue reforms the affective ethos of a tradition. Therefore, we can observe and report on the consonances and dissonances between affective directions and expressions within the same faith tradition as implemented concretely in different formation fields and as expressed in corresponding symbols. Compare, for instance, the formational feeling and expression of African, Mexican, British, and American Catholics or Protestants and their corresponding formation symbols.

Reformation of Form Traditional Symbols

Form traditions, in short, must express their directives in symbols, loaded with affective-cognitive power. In the course of history, the power of symbols may weaken. They can become merely ornamental, conventional signs. In the end their transformative vitality may be extinguished. Then the form tradition *as dynamic* is in need of renewal of its symbols. The reformation of symbols of formation should happen in dialogue with both the faith tradition that underlies the form tradition and with its actual pluralistic fields of congenial and compatible faith implementation, presence, and action.

Evidently formational symbols are crucial for the process of transmission and maintenance of form traditions. In contrast, informational signs are not symbols. They have not sufficient affective-cognitive formation power to keep a tradition alive. This insight compels me to look deeper into the meaning and function of symbols as distinguished from informational signs. I will do so from the viewpoint of my formation anthropology.

Informational Signs and Formational Symbols

In my formation anthropology, I make a distinction between an informational sign and a formational symbol. When we view the wondrous performance of dolphins, we are amazed at how well they pay attention to the signs given to them. They see the movement of the hand or the showing of a hoop through which they have to jump; they hear a word or the sound of a bell, and they obey perfectly. All of these function as informational signs, informing the mammals of what feat to perform. The word, the hoops, the bell, the moving hand have their own meaning and value. In themselves they are more than mere signals for functioning in certain external ways; the particular worth, meaning, and dignity of what they are in and by themselves remains concealed from the dolphins. Their informational use is not preceded, accompanied, or complemented by a truly formational knowledge of the particular nature or inner form of that which is commanding them to exercise a special movement.

Formational understanding is different. This knowledge of inner form is observed only in human life. Beyond informational knowledge, it discloses to us something of the particular inner form of that about which we receive information. The disclosure of the basic particular inherent form, in and by itself, in its own essence, can be mediated by what I call the formational symbol. Why formational? It discloses to us something of the original and originating inherent form and meaning of what is disclosed to us. In this sense it is unconcealing, revealing, epiphanic of what is hidden, concealed in, and under the information we receive. Simultaneously this disclosure by the formational symbol has a potentially formative influence on our own life form and its formation.

Living Words as Primordial Formational Symbols

The affective-cognitive, formational words we speak or write are a primordial form of the formational symbol we are considering here. The life-word as formationally symbolic and epiphanic gives form to our distinctively human apprehension and appraisal of the basic inherent forms of people, animals, events, and things, and of the multiple manifestations of this inherent originality. The painter, sculptor, or musician capture such manifestations in design, color, or melody. A formational word gives us not only functional information about what we should execute functionally in a certain situation, like a user's guide for cooking on an oatmeal package. It lauds the goodness, the gift of the grain itself. It refers us to the nature and unique form of each person, to the individual form of each planet, animal, thing, or event. These can become for us more than a mere point of departure for effective functioning. Formational symbols light up for us people, events, and things in their own uniqueness and/or individuality.

The beauty of human awakening to the epiphanic power of formational symbols is strikingly described by Annie Sullivan, the teacher of Helen Keller. With gentle patience she enabled Helen, who was deaf, mute, and blind, to enter the human world of formational-symbolic thought and expression. She had taught the girl a few words. Still these words were merely informational to her. As such they could only point to things without disclosing their individual form, worth, and meaning. Helen confused the words *mug* and *water*. For her they were mere informational signs about the function of drinking. They did not reveal anything about the inner form or generic, special, and individual essence of the mug or the water itself nor about their forming power for our life of thought, feeling, imagination, memory, anticipation, and action.

At one point Annie let Helen keep her mug under a stream of pump water. When the cold water gushed down and filled the mug, she spelled "W-a-t-e-r" in Helen's free hand. That the word so immediately followed the sensation of cold water streaming over her hand seemed to surprise her. She let the mug fall and stood rooted to the ground. A new light came over her face. She spelled time and time again "Water." Then she let herself fall on the ground and asked the name of that movement. She gestured toward the pump and the grill, asking their name. Suddenly turning around she asked the name of her teacher. In a few hours she added several more words to her vocabulary.

Helen herself recalled the experience. She told how she suddenly stood still, her whole attention riveted on the movement of her fingers. Suddenly she experienced a misty consciousness as if of something that she had forgotten, a thought returned. She said that in one or the other way the mystery of language was revealed to her. She knew at that moment what "w-a-t-e-r" meant: the delightful coolness streaming over her hand. She told how that living word awakened her spirit, how it gave her light, hope, and joy, and set her free.

The story of Helen Keller shows us that the formational symbol is more than an informational sign. It is disclosure, epiphany, revelation. Distinctively human formational words are the primordial matter of form traditional symbols. In fact, however, everything in our field of presence and action can become a formational symbol. This happens when an appearance in our field discloses a uniquely human or an individual prehuman form in itself. It appears to us as a source of a wonderful plurality of meanings, all springing from that unique or individual ground form. As forming symbol it means infinitely more to us than a mere informational stimulus to one or other type of practical functioning.

Endless Range of Form Symbols

The range of possible form symbolic meanings is endless. Certain symbols refer for many people only to one meaning, for example, the written word "two" refers for most people only to the number "two." Other formational symbols carry more than one meaning. Some symbols express the essential form of bodily sensations, such as the symbols cold, warm, tired. Others refer to affective experiences, such as anger, spite, love, resentment, disappointment. Others refer again to the unique form of a person or the individual form of an animal or thing. The symbols in these examples usually refer to forms that are immediately clear. But we also have symbols that refer to formational meanings and directives that are initially unfamiliar, obscure, or mysterious. Examples are dream symbols, the symbols in certain myths, legends, fairy tales, and mystical writings, and other veiled expressions of faith and formation traditions.

Therefore, I make a distinction between the formation of direct and indirect symbols. The formation of direct symbols prevails in our civilization since the emergence of a predominantly functional-scientific approach to reality. The formation of mythical form symbols, mediating indirectly less obvious forms of reality, is typical of form traditions that preceded the prevalence of functional-scientific thought. In that period of formation-history, *formational imagination* prevailed over *functional imagination*.

Human Life Form as "Animal Symbolicum"

Only the basically spiritual or human life form can receive and express forms in its field of presence and action by means of formational symbols. We can call the human being as *animal symbolicum* the "formational-symbolic animal."

Only humans receive new knowledge by means of symbolic words and concepts. This enables them to know forms in their uniqueness or individuality. These symbols are more than merely informational signs for functioning. In other words, the human person is form receptive, essentially open to all inherent essential or basic forms. In this sense Thomas Aquinas could say: "Homo quodammodo omnia," in some way the human being is all things, or all forms he or she knows.

The human life form is not only form receptive; it is also form expressive. Because of its basic form symbolic potency, the human life form is practically without limit in its power of symbolic form expression. We can connect all kinds of symbolic references with anything that appears in our field and its horizons. For example, a tower may be a symbol of pointing to the gods in heaven, of the phallus, of the pride of a fortress city, of a warning against invaders, of the power of a king living in a palace with a tower, of a place pointing Muslims to prayer, and so on.

This formational symbolic potency sets us free in our formation field. Animal life does not have the power of managing its life and world by an endlessly diversified understanding through ever new symbols of formation. The animal is not an *animal symbolicum*, for it fits in its given environment as a hand in a glove. It has an instinctual consonance with its surroundings. The animal does not have to change its given environment into a compatible formation field as humans have to do by means of symbolic apprehension and appreciation. An animal is bound instinctually and inflexibly to the given vital significance of things for its survival. If their fitting field of life disappears or is destroyed, animals die out.

In that sense, animal life, unlike human life, is one-dimensional. Its basic form is identified with its vital-instinctual dimension. Human life formation is not the result of its vital dimension only. Human life can transcend all vital-formational signs of the appearances in its field of form reception and expression. For unlike animal life it is pluridimensional, plurispheric, pluritraditional, and form symbolic. Its functional-transcendent, transcendent, and transcendent-functional dimensionality give it the potency to open up to all forms in their essences and multiple symbolic connotations. The human life form can use anything as an image of something else. This is not to deny that the vital dimension keeps sounding through and reverberating in all human formation. This dimension must keep humans alert for the vital meaning of all things, but they are not bound to these meanings exclusively. Transcendence enables people to distance themselves from what is merely vitally significant. They can subordinate vital form directives to the functional and transcendent vital directives. The power of symbol formation lifts people beyond direct vital domination by the environment. Formational symbolizing makes possible the constitution of a compatible formation field that is either typically or distinctively human.

Symbol-Introduced Distance
between Form Reception and Expression

Within the human life form itself, the creation and use of formational symbols breaks through the inflexible connection that we observe between form receptive and form expressive potencies in animal life. The animal is receptive only of sense impressions that are instinctually relevant. This instinctual form reception evokes automatically a corresponding vital instinctual expression of form in its biological environment.

In humans the formational symbol creates a distance between form reception and donation. This distance makes it possible for us not to react immediately on the basis of the information and first insight we receive. We can reflect on what is possible and desirable in our life. Reflection and appraisal of this kind are also sources of our experience of problems, crises, and conflicts. Our necessary reliance on mainly our formational-symbolic potency makes us uncertain, vitally impoverished, and instinct deficient. Because we often feel uncertain and insecure, we may be tempted to flee into an obsessive attachment to a stilted form tradition. We may try anxiously to pin it down in a rigorous set of unchangeable formulae. We deny the dynamic essence of formation tradition, demanding us to retrieve its treasures critically and to renew its movement continuously.

A frozen form tradition has lost is dynamism of flexible responsible compatibility. This leads to a diminishment of human freedom. For example, the anxious clinging of aging Soviet leaders to all facets of the Stalinistic form tradition destroyed their freedom to respond compatibly to economic-political crises in their collapsing empire.

Formational Symbolic Power
and Retrieval of Classical Formation Wisdom

Formational symbolic power enables the human life form to keep, retrieve, and update the classical formation wisdom created by the human race over the millennia of its formation history. In this sense, symbolic power conquers time consciously as no animal or plant can do. By means of words and other symbols, the human life form can accumulate its experience of formation over thousands of years and pass it on to coming generations. Birds and bees did not learn anything basically new over the millennia of their existence. Humans do. At any time people can change the form tradition they critically retrieve. What becomes known to people about changes in their formation fields can lead to new appraisals and, therewith, to alterations in their form traditions. For the same reason differences in form traditions will always emerge between different communities of people, even when they adhere to the foundationals of the same faith tradition. Each community faces a different formation field. Therefore, their appraisal of how the form tradition should be made compatible without compromise will be necessarily different. The same Islamic faith tradition, for example, is implemented in numerous different form traditions in different ages and countries.

Form Traditional Appraisal Systems and Formation Symbols

To appraise is to disclose what is appreciable and depreciable in the people, things, and events we deal with in daily life. In doing so, we assign to them a certain symbolic meaning. This symbolic designation of a particular kind of appreciability or depreciability can give form in turn to our life.

For example, when a mother leaves a note for her children that the milk has turned sour, they will avoid drinking it. When the TV weather reporter shows on his map how beautiful it will be tomorrow, this symbol may give rise to a directive to plan for a hike in the woods. This illustrates again the power of formational symbolism in our everyday lives. The same applies also to form traditions. Their ethos contains formational symbols about the appreciability or depreciability of certain ways of life.

Symbols have a forming influence on the life directions of the participants in their tradition. For instance, the architectural symbol of the mosque in the Islamic formation tradition points to the faith and form directive that one should never portray Allah in an anthropomorphic image. Only the Koran, whose Arabic texts may be ornamentally engraved on the bare white walls, can point to the divine.

Appraisal can thus be expressed in specific formation symbols. In that light, we can look at formation traditions as systems of shared appreciations and depreciations and their expressions in formation symbols. Such appraisals will generate common form traditional directives. These again can be expressed in particular formation symbols. For example, the dissonant form tradition of the Ku Klux Klan uses the symbol of cross burning to express its inhuman directive of racial and religious hatred and discrimination.

Studying formation traditions from the viewpoint of the appraisal systems which they contain deepened my understanding of them. I want to share these insights in the next chapter. There I will consider formation traditions insofar as they are appraisal systems. I shall further reflect on the implications of this important observation.

CHAPTER 13

Form Traditions, Human Needs, and Aspirations

I n volume 1 of this series, I discussed human life insofar as it manifests itself in its sociohistorical, vital, functional, and transcendent dimensions. I showed there how vital desires and functional ambitions or performance strivings give rise, respectively, to directives of gratification or satisfaction. Not only functional satisfaction but also vital gratification is in part served by the functional dimension. For example, the vital need for food is quelled by the gratification of our hunger and the pleasures of the palate. But this gratification is made possible only by the practical functions of, for one thing, baking bread, slicing, serving, and eating it. At the same time, this functioning in service of gratification, if it is done well, satisfies the functional performance ambition of this dimension.

Another set of directives, beyond those that are vital-functional, is transcendent. These are rooted in the aspirations, and inspirations of the transcendent dimension of life. When Gandhi went on a hunger strike for the sake of freedom and justice, he bypassed his need for food in favor of his aspirations and inspirations. Sakharov chose exile in Siberia above a comfortable life in Moscow. He, too, put aspiration and inspiration above gratification and satisfaction.

Both need-gratification and functional satisfaction can be consonant with the fulfillment of aspirations and inspirations. Take a family Thanksgiving meal with all the prayers and trimmings, or a high-priced dinner organized to assist AIDS patients or aging people with Alzheimer's disease. Often, however, tensions evolve between gratification or satisfaction directives and aspiration and inspiration directives.

What applies to our lives as such applies also to the traditions that teach us the art of living. This chapter deals with the answers traditions give to our needs, aspirations, and inspirations, and to our struggle for their wise integration. A powerful means used by form traditions to direct and facilitate integration are the symbols tradition attaches to what gratifies the vital needs or satisfies the functional ambitions of our life form.

Symbols Free Us from Vital Bondage

Transcendent traditions teach us that we should not be the slaves of our needs, though, of course, we should take them into account. Therefore, consonant traditions help us to see how we can be people with high aspirations and inspirations, who, at the same time, care for the fulfillment of our needs. If we do not heed these needs, we lose the vital energy to carry out our aspirations and inspirations. An undernourished teacher has not enough strength left to give form to her aspiration to inspire students with enthusiasm for the spiritual literature they may be reading for her class.

What sets us free from control by our needs is our power of symbolizing. We can give all kinds of meanings to our needs and to what arouses them. An animal fits into its field of life completely. It cannot take a stand over against the arousal of its instincts by its environment. Animals cannot add higher symbolic meanings to these stimuli — meanings that evoke aspirations and inspirations. When a female animal is in heat, the only meaning the male animal can give to it is that of an occasion for sexual pairing. The human male may be sexually aroused, but he is able symbolically to give a deeper meaning to the woman he encounters. He may see her as a unique person with freedom and dignity, who would be humiliated if she were seen or used only as a sex object. His aspiration to be distinctively human in respecting her humanity is coformed by symbols pointing to her dignity; many such elevating symbols are given to us by our form traditions.

No matter how powerful need directives keep sounding through our enfleshed life, we can transcend them. The human person can take distance from everything. Through our use of symbols we cut the tie between the final form we give to our thoughts, feelings, images, acts, and the physio-chemical stimuli that initially arouse us vitally and organismically.

This explains the distinction between form reception and form expression. Our mind can take in any form that appears in our field, but we are not forced to keep it within ourselves as it has been given to us immediately and initially. Inwardly we can give all kinds of symbolic meanings to the forms we have inwardly received. Subsequently we can recreate or express ourselves outwardly in the forms we have expressed creatively and symbolically within. A striking example is the life of an artist. A painter sees the same house, tree, or sunset we see. Like us he gives his own inner form to it by his own unique-communal power of symbolizing. But unlike us he has the added power to make others experience the symbolic form he has given inwardly to what he experienced uniquely in his field of life.

Form Traditions, Symbols, and Freedom

Formation traditions form us through symbols. They expand the store of symbols available to us. They provide us with transcendent symbolic forms for what we experience in life. They give us visible, audible, touchable symbols, such as rites, directives, books, poems, paintings, sculptures, music, architecture, parables, and other narrations. They help us through and with a traditional community to give symbolic form to our aspirations and inspirations and to their relation to our needs and everyday experiences. We can keep a tradition alive only by keeping its symbols alive or by expanding or renewing these symbols, if necessary. Transcendent form traditions serve the freedom of humanity to go beyond its being ruled by needs alone.

To remain alive a tradition requires steady renewal of the deeper sources of spiritual freedom through renewal of its symbols. Many people hesitate to take the risks that freedom of renewal entails. Paradoxically, their fear of living traditions creatively will lead to enslavement to past forms and their meanings, even if they no longer have a significant meaning in the present. Such people may turn tradition into a straitjacket. To break out of it will cost them dearly. Fearful of the original openness of their tradition, they do not enrich it with new symbols that represent the transcendent meanings of new directives that come to them from their present field of observation and action.

New directives call for new symbols. What is given to us as hard facts can always be appraised and symbolized in new ways. Differences in formation traditions are the outcome of the different ways in which groups of believers in varying fields appraise and symbolize the same event, thing, person, or position. We have only to look at how different traditions attach dissimilar symbolic meanings to the same appearances of the sun, the stars, the heavens, the mountains, the colors white, red, or black, the king, priest, preacher, or guru, fatherhood, motherhood, childhood, birth, sex appeal, sickness, death, burial, femininity, masculinity.

Form Traditions as Symbolic Systems

Traditions help us to appraise what we meet in life. Appraisal is served by our power to give symbolic meanings to what we are appraising. Appraisal entails a special use of our symbolic power. This is also true of the appraisal dispositions that mark form traditions. Each form tradition is a system of formative symbols linked with the appraisal dispositions fostered by the tradition.

Within this overall traditional system of symbols, I distinguish three subdivisions that somewhat overlap. I see first a subsystem of symbols that is for the most part cognitive. They inform us about the tradition. Examples are the theological or ideological statements of religious or ideological faith traditions insofar as they sound through in our form traditions or have become formationally meaningful in a more proximate way. They make us know how to do things even before we have a full appreciation of them. For example, in the Buddhist form tradition beginners are taught how to sit in meditation. I call such an informational-formational set of directives the informational-formational system of a tradition.

Second, I distinguish from this more cognitive-informational system the system of symbols that serves mainly our appraisal of things. It is linked with a system of appraisal dispositions. These symbols serve as a model for the appraisal systems that the followers of the tradition are encouraged to develop in their life. For example, the Christian form tradition disposes Christians by many of its symbols to appreciate profoundly the Bible and hence to appreciate devout attention to its words. I call this the symbolic appraisal or appreciation system of a tradition.

Third, I find in each tradition a symbol system that is mostly concerned with concrete formation directives. Each tradition gives directives to its followers. For example, the Islamic form tradition directs people to pray five times a day. This directive, given in written word symbols, is reinforced by the audible symbol of the sound from the minaret calling people to this prayer. I call this the symbolic form directive system of a tradition.

The form tradition gives each of these three respectively informational, appraisal, and directive symbols systems its own due. It maintains also the intimate relationship between these subsystems. The same symbol can have informational, appraisal, and directive meaning. For example, the symbol of the covenant in Judaism as informational-formational tells Jews what Yahweh did for them in history; as an appraisal symbol, it disposes them to appreciate their dignity as the chosen people; as a directive symbol, it exhorts them how to direct their life in consonance with Yahweh's deeds in their history and with their election as the chosen ones.

Dispositions and Attitudes

Each disposition symbolized by a tradition gives form to a variety of attitudes. Attitudes adapt the symbolized basic dispositions to various situations in which the disposition has to be implemented. The basic Islamic appreciation of a prayer custom will give rise to a different attitude — in regard to its public implementation — in an Eastern Islamic community and in a pluralistic Western city. It would be incompatible with the Western situation were the follower of Islam to kneel and bow down on his prayer mat in a bank, on the metro, or in a restaurant. Changing their attitude toward the posture of implementation does not mean changing the basic appreciation disposition of these Islamites. For disposition and attitude are not the same. A Muslim in a modern Western metropolis can be as much rooted in his commitment to this prayer disposition as when he publicly engages in the ritual. As a faithful follower of the Koran, he is filled with the directive disposition to engage in this prayer as well as possible in any given situation. How he gives form symbolically to this disposition in new ways is a question of implementing new attitudes of form donation required by the shared formation field in which he finds himself.

Gratification Directives, Aspiration and Inspiration Directives

What is the difference between gratification directives and aspiration and inspiration directives? When marriage partners make love, they gratify their physical sexual needs. These needs direct to some degree what they enjoy sexually. They also aspire to humanize their sexual encounter by tenderness, loving mutuality, attractive surroundings, and respect for each other's form tradition. They complement mere vital need directives with aspiration and inspiration directives.

Need directives are primarily about gratification. They tell us symbolically how we should gratify or satisfy our needs. Form traditions in turn dispose us by their symbols to gratify or satisfy our needs in certain ways. For example, our style of eating is guided by a Western form tradition. We are told to eat with a knife and fork instead of with our fingers. This traditional directive has become a custom. This custom then initiates a need in us, the need to eat in that manner. On top of this, our custom of eating evokes new needs. The use of forks, knives, plates, and a table leads to needs for a nice table cover, for forks made of a fine metal, for clean trays and glasses. These give rise to new traditional forms. Often it is difficult to say where gratification directives end and aspiration as well as inspiration directives begin. Our concern for a beautiful table setting serves often an aesthetic aspiration.

What is the basic mark of a gratification directive and of an aspiration or inspiration directive? The main mark of a directive to gratify is that it directs us to do or to use something mainly for the satisfaction of a need. What we do or use is only valued insofar as it can gratify our needs. There is no appreciation for what the person, thing, or deed gratifying us are in themselves, or what they look like in the light of our higher aspirations and inspirations. The gratification directive is absorbed by its sole function to direct us toward fulfillment of a need. That which gratifies our need is not appreciated as a reality which has value in itself, whether or not it fulfills our need. We pay attention to it only insofar as it indulges the need we have.

Aspiration and inspiration directives transcend directives for gratification. They direct us to rise above mere need fulfillment; they enable us to appreciate the need-transcendent preciousness of persons, things, and events in themselves. Even if they can no longer fulfill our needs, we keep appreciating them for what they *are*. Transcendent preciousness goes beyond vital or functional form directives. We aspire after what is transcendently appreciable long after our needs have been fulfilled. We appreciate and admire a beautiful crystal fruit bowl, even if we do not use it to serve fruit. Our dog cannot admire its feeding plate when not filled with food.

Transcendent aspirations can be falsified. We do not always recognize our needs as needs; we may mistake them for aspirations or inspirations. Formation science tells us about the confusion between needs and aspirations or inspirations. We can do something because of an aspiration or inspiration or because of a merely sociohistorical, vital, or functional need. It is not always easy to tell which is which.

This formational approach runs counter to that of the Freudian view of culture. Freudians are bound by their prescientific traditional presuppositions to search for organismic drives or needs as the exclusive ultimate sources of culture and tradition. Some anthropologists, such as Malinowski, use the Freudian premise in their own probes of cultures and traditions. I tried to complement and correct this onesided approach, not by denying its limited usefulness. Appreciating the insights we gained from it, I stress also the role of aspirations and inspirations. I highlight, moreover, symbolizing form traditions. For me traditions carry more weight in the story of human formation than their weak reflections in pluralistic cultures. I maintain that we can enjoy some relative freedom in the process of giving form to and receiving form from our formation traditions. I realize, of course, that my theory is at odds with any thought about the driving force of organismic needs or strivings as the *exclusive* source of human life and tradition. Briefly I do not believe that *all* of culture and tradition is but a sublimation of libidinal needs.

Human life is distinctively human insofar as it is marked also by aspirations and inspirations and not only by needs. The same is true of distinctively human formation traditions. If we hold that needs are the sole source of human formation, we have to think up ever new needs to explain why we do things. We cannot trace all human formation to needs alone. Is the sacrifice of comfort, safety, and fame by Sakharov only to be understood as need gratification? Or was there some higher aspiration or inspiration at work? Did he not strive for freedom, appreciated as a good in itself, even if this striving did not fulfill his organismic needs.

In a well-ordered formation tradition, the gratification of needs is not denied as good and desirable; it is seen as ultimately to be guided by aspirations and inspirations. As Dorothy Lee puts it, " . . . culture is not, I think, a response to the total needs of society, but rather a system which stems from and expresses . . . the basic values of society, or as I would prefer to say, of traditions" (see Lee 1959, 76).

My formation theory of personality takes needs into account. I am aware that every formation tradition spells out ways of its acceptable gratification and satisfaction. But both my theory and transcendent traditions hold that aspirations and inspirations are more fundamental than needs. The former should direct the latter and not the other way around. The balance between needs, aspirations, and inspirations is as different in each form tradition as in each life form. Persons as well as traditions can grow from a life of being ruled by needs to one of needs being ruled by aspirations and inspirations.

Auxiliary sciences of formation science such as psychoanalysis and other schools of psychotherapy point only vaguely to the mazes, knots, and tangles between the initial power of needs and the birth of aspirations and inspirations. They usually do not go beyond the pretranscendent plane of what they call ego and superego or what I call the pretranscendent subordinated "I" with its conditioned pretranscendent lower conscience. I take critically into account the remarkable theories about the complex dynamics of pretranscendent character formation by psychoanalytic and other disciplines. I try to purify, however, their findings and theories from deterministic, rationalistic, or mystifying anthropologies. Then the empirical insights and data they disclose can be assimilated in my formation theory of personality and related to distinctively human transcendent aspirations and inspirations.

Mixture of Form Traditions

The form tradition of people who live in a pluralistic culture is not only an embodiment of their faith tradition. A form tradition is the outcome of ongoing conversation between the faith tradition, everyday life, and the form traditions that have already put their symbolic stamp on the culture they share with others as well as the form traditions and symbols they come directly in contact with without mediation of the general culture.

Each of us, as we have suggested in an earlier chapter, is a pyramid of symbolized form traditions. At the base of the pyramid is the form tradition we believe to be a more or less faithful embodiment of our faith tradition. Beyond this basis, we take in traditions that other groups unfolded in their conversations with everyday life and with other form traditions in our shared field of presence and action. The thin top of the pyramid stands for the current outcome of all these traditions in the way we give form to our life here and now and for the penetration of our pyramid into our shared formation field.

People who live in the same society tend to appropriate in their tradition pyramid elements of other traditions that have been absorbed into the general culture of their society. In a society like ours bent on consumption, individualistic self-actualization, and economic achievement, the free-floating traditions of vital gratification, functional satisfaction, and economism have marked its general culture. Those who belong to an orthodox Jewish, Islamic, or Christian form tradition must somehow give form to their life of needs, aspirations, and inspirations in ways that take into account the buying-and-selling form traditions instilled in our general culture by consumerism and economism. Their struggle is not to betray their faith tradition and yet not to be totally out of touch with the achievement and selling-buying patterns in their culture. Whether they like it or not, such free-floating traditions play some role in their "form tradition pyramid." To bring the former in line with their basic form tradition as believers is seldom without flaws.

A Christian family, for instance, may say a table prayer or do a Bible reading before the meal. Yet, during the meal, the talk may be about how to afford excessive luxuries or how to gain wealth and professional advancement at any price. Many consumer needs are instilled in us by free-floating form traditions that have exalted consumption, status, and income as an aim, as a cultural ideal or idol in themselves. In other cultures, such as those formed by a Hindu or Buddhist tradition, the other side of the coin prevails insofar as people are taught not to live by desire but by detachment from desire.

In my view of balanced formation we should make room for reasonable timely fulfillment of consonant pretranscendent desires as well as for timely detachment if any desire tends to become ultimate, thereby fostering deformational coercive dispositions. Similarly we should advance the optimal formation of a pretranscendent I that is as firm, effective, keen, and assertive as possible. This managing I of practical field incarnation can never be strong enough. The more astute and tough, however, our pretranscendent instrumental I becomes the more we should make sure that it remains the flexible servant of our higher transcendent I with its unique call and rootedness in the radical and cosmic mystery of formation.

Human Needs and Transcendent Form Traditions

I hold in my formation anthropology that the formation ideal should be neither need negation only, nor need fulfillment only, but need transcendence. Need transcendence means the wise gratification or satisfaction of needs in light of an appraisal that is transcendent, in other words, one that puts form traditional aspirations and inspirations first. An example would be our need for tasty meals in an atmosphere of pleasant togetherness. We cannot let this need rule our lives to such a degree that we cease to be content with less rich meals should our health be harmed by them or should we have to follow a form traditional aspiration for fasting at certain times.

No form tradition can allow itself to negate needs. No matter how lofty our form traditional aspirations and inspirations may be, we must find a way to remain in consonance with our basic needs. Otherwise our aspirations as such will become skewed. Neglect of basic needs will backfire. Having refused to acknowledge focally and prefocally their reality in our life, we will seek their gratification or satisfaction nonfocally by dressing them up as aspirations or inspirations. For example, a preacher who can never give vent to his need to talk out anger in daily life may angrily preach only "hell and damnation" to the faithful in the illusion that he expresses aspirations and inspirations to save their souls.

In some cult-like subformation traditions, aspirations and inspirations are raised to such height that needs are spurned or forgotten. This can harm the health, peace, and joy of uptight followers. Psychoanalytic and Marxist faith and form traditions have pointed out that we should be suspicious of the bent of form traditions to turn group needs of ruthless acquisition, exploitation, and possession into aspirations. What is good for a particular free-floating tradition such as economism is good for all and that after which all should aspire. The insights of particular disciplines into the masking of selfish needs could be helpful in this regard. Their onesided stress should be complemented and corrected by the integrative approach of a formation science that specializes in a comprehensive attention to all spheres and dimensions of the human formation field, integrating the rich insights and data generated by the specialized attentiveness of other arts and sciences to particular aspects of that field.

Erich Fromm (1967) reports on an inquiry among whites in the U.S.A. They were asked two questions: Are all men created equal? and are blacks equal to whites? In the South at that time 61 percent answered the first question with *yes*, but the second received only 4 percent positive answers. From the standpoint of formation science, this statistic exemplifies the clash between faith and formation traditions. The first answer was the answer of their Christian faith tradition, the second of their form tradition, which had been coformed by their search for like-mindedness with other political Southern traditions. In this case, the need for compatibility with the Southern form tradition overtook the aspirations expressed in answer to the first question.

Needs play a powerful role in shaping a form tradition. They are often linked with aspirations and inspirations. A search for the basic directives of a form tradition calls for skill and patience. It is made more difficult by the fact that form directives are often nonfocal. In formation science, the nonfocal region of consciousness takes in all awareness that is not at our beck and call in the focal (and vocal) regions of consciousness. Such directives are unspoken or hidden in the ways in which we give form to everyday living. Therefore, they can be a source of bafflement for followers of other traditions, who may perceive a marked discrepancy between our faith and form traditions.

Compatibility and Form Traditions

In this chapter I looked at needs and aspirations gratification or satisfaction directives, and appreciation directives as well as their underlying need and aspiration dispositions. Then I took up the role form traditions play in the ways in which we gratify or satisfy our needs and fulfill our aspirations and inspirations. I asked also what part the growth of a form tradition takes in the field of life. Other sciences have asked the question — not about form traditions per se since this is a new idea rooted in my theory of human formation — but about culture. Many of them came to an answer different from mine. They prefer the terms *adaptation* or *adjustment*, concepts derived from biology where it makes sense when speaking about the forms plants and animals take on in reaction to their surroundings. There is some likeness between people and animals or plants insofar as people, too, have a genetic heritage whose form can be altered over time in response to events such as the changing climate, the quality of nourishment, the habits of work. But this is not the whole story.

Formation science looks at human life as distinctively human, as transcending the merely genetical, as more than a biological organism. Transcendent formation traditions are not concerned primarily with purely biological needs, but with typically human needs and distinctively human aspirations and inspirations and their interformation. Without overlooking biological needs, the focus of formation science is on human needs, aspirations, inspirations, and the answers to them in form traditions. It stresses that neither human culture nor formation traditions are like biological organisms of adaptation or adjustment. Because of their formation traditions, people can, beyond adaptation, also creatively change the form they give to their field of life.

In the course of formation history, they have done so to an extent that we cannot observe in the adaptation of other organisms. A form tradition is not as overbearing as the process of biological adaptation. Not only is there some freedom to change a form tradition — in the light of free and creative human insights — but also the same people can live in different form traditions at the same time. People can change their adherence to a form tradition and choose another one. Plants and animals cannot in the same way choose another biological-genetical adaptation tradition once nature has imposed one on them.

I find the concepts of adaptation and adjustment, as applied to animal and plant formation, too broad to make sense of all facets of typical and distinctively human changes in formation traditions as well as in people's personal lives. Adjustment to one's surroundings does not by itself alone make clear why so many forms of a tradition of an earlier time and place remain intact and do not represent an adaptation or adjustment to the field of tradition we know today. Neither adjustment nor adaptation are sufficiently wide and concrete concepts to make clear how people and their form traditions allow themselves to be changed or not changed by their surroundings.

I found it necessary to offer a new approach to this problem, one for which I use the terms *compatibility* and *compatibility striving*. I do not deny that we in some ways adapt or adjust like plants and animals do. I say only that this does not fully explain all facets of our typically human and distinctively human changes. Compatibility means that we, as free and thinking people, strive for consonance with our field of life insofar as it does not harm our congeniality with what we, as humans and as followers of a tradition, are basically called to be. Our transcendent formation traditions, with their underlying faith traditions, help us — insofar as they are consonant — to be compatible with our field here and now without losing congeniality with our human nature as transcendent. They teach us how to give form to our aspirations and inspirations in ways that enlighten the gratification or satisfaction of our needs in reasonable compatibility with our field of presence and action.

The common formation tradition that my science proposes hypothetically can never take the place of any particular, especially any classical, form tradition. The necessarily sparse and general elements of the hypothetical common tradition should always be complemented and corrected by the richness of the faith, doctrines, rituals, symbols, literature, and immense spiritual power of a classical faith and form tradition to which one is committed. An eventually agreed upon common formation tradition of humanity would by itself alone be too anemic to inspire and nourish the transformation in depth of any human life. Besides being an instrument of rational structuring, one of its main purposes should be to foster some elementary mutual understanding and cooperation between the various form traditions. Another one of its aims is to offer not only formation scientists and their colleagues in other human and social sciences but also representatives of specific faith and formation traditions an instrument to structure and formulate their critical-creative observations and reflections, enriching and clarifying the formational wisdom and practice of their own traditions and enhancing their effectiveness.

CHAPTER 14

Traditional Form or Field Directives

In my formation theory of personality I use the term *form directives* to answer the question: What are the basic bearings that give form to the life of form traditions or of persons within them? How do they see the field in which they find themselves? Because of this second question, I call these bearings sometimes "field directives."

In the field view of formation, directives have not only cognitive but also affective coformants. As the term *directive* shows, they are basic guides as to how we ought to give form to our life. For example, the directive of the Islamic form tradition in some Muslim countries is for women to veil themselves. Devout Muslim women in such a field of Islamic formation not only know the dress directive (the cognitive coformant); they also appreciate it as a sacred and attractive directive (the affective coformant). Thus both cognition and affection strengthen the directive power of guiding their way of dressing.

This aspect of my personality theory, like many others, is so different from theories of others that it raises questions such as, How did I come to the concept of the term *form directives?* Why and how do I contrast it with the present-day popularized connotations of the terms *values* and *value clarification* as introduced by Abraham Maslow, Carl Rogers and William Coulson? I formulated my terms seminally during the World War II phase or the first phase of the development of my theory. During the Dutch Hunger Winter of 1944–45 I observed that some people around me were more apt than others to fall apart under the threat to their lives, their families, their possessions. Among them were those who had not wisely assimilated basic traditional life directives. They had been subjected to what in Holland was called *vrije opvoeding*, literally translated *free education*. Central in the program of free education was the imagined or pretended freedom from direction by any formation tradition. Instead the children in such families or programs were trained to find in themselves alone their own values. How they really individually felt was supposed to guide their life. They were encouraged to be the soloists of their own existence. Often what they hailed as their individual values appeared to me as an idealization of pretranscendent needs and desires, which they were not taught to check out against the age-old wisdom of any classic formation tradition.

118

These exclusively self-disclosed values had no binding character to them. Because they were self-invented they could be self-rejected or changed at any time. As a result their life lacked stable direction rooted in a traditional wisdom shared by numerous others over generations. Their vacillating condition exposed them more than others to the ups and downs of their feelings. They were also more vulnerable to the unpredictable changes in events and rumors assaulting all of us in that dreadful winter.

To help them in their search for a direction that would enable them to face courageously the reality of the field in which they had to live here and now, I introduced my concept of traditional form or field directives. I explained the art of appraisal of such traditional treasures and its difference from values clarification. I did not deny that clarification of values could be explained in a sense that would be compatible with my emergent anthropology. Sometimes I myself would do so. My lingual concern was that, formatively speaking, it would be difficult, if not impossible, to remove effectively the nondirective connotations this expression had gained in free education.

Dialogue with Maslowian and Rogerian Theories

Working later in the United States to refine my theory and especially the concept of form and field directives, I realized the basic divergence between what I saw and the Freudian, Adlerian, and Jungian formation traditions and also the positions of my colleagues Abraham Maslow and Carl Rogers in America. I had intense personal dialogues with both of them about the differences between our three personality theories. Unlike in mine they did not base life's formation on a personal or unique yet consonant assimilation of form traditional life directives within a uniquely modulated form traditional pyramid. To me they seemed to underestimate the central role of form traditions in all personal and social life. Maslow's concept of self-actualization means in effect the actualization of the pretranscendent individualistic *I*, expanded by him to include only what I identify in my theory as the functional-transcendent gnostic dimension of the self. Neither would the intraformational dialogue of this self-actualizing person include the unique transcendent life call as appraised in the light of explicitly acknowledged formation traditions. It did not take into account all facets of the formation field construct I had developed in the Netherlands. I missed also the social justice concern of the sphere of interformation and the ecological concern of the outerspheres, not to mention the transcendent sphere of the mystery at the heart of the field. There was little mention of the objective directives coming from those spheres, independent of desires for self-actualization.

Carl Rogers, with whom I also worked and whom I admired in many ways, as I did Abraham Maslow, was even more outspoken. He put at the center of the person's world the principle of nondirectedness by outside traditions and forces. He was a gentle master in accompanying the idiosyncratic life melodies of his clients without ever referring to any objective form traditional directives they might be able to disclose in their field of life and, within their intraform of life, in their own prefocal pyramid of traditions. His radical nondirective approach culminated later in California in his well-intentioned initiation of nondirective education in a large school system of a religious order. With his intimate cooperator there, Professor Coulson, the whole teaching system was recentered around the concepts of individualistic self-esteem, individualistic values clarification, and individualistic absolutized decision making outside the parameters of formation traditions. This approach reminded me of the "free education" approach of some psychologists and educators in the Netherlands. The Maslowian, Rogerian, and Coulson approaches, however, were far more systematized and radicalized than what my personality theory had to reckon with in my home country.

I thought it only fair, as the initiator of a quite different theory, to become as familiar as possible with their opposite views without any premature appraisal. I decided to immerse myself under their personal tutelage in their theory and practice, putting temporarily my own theory in parentheses, as it were. This would enable me to disclose the implicit form traditions at the root of their approach. I hoped to be able to spot and integrate any empirical-experiential findings of these colleagues in the body of my formation science if they would be compatible with it. Accordingly, after finishing my graduate studies in psychology I spent one year with Carl Rogers at the University of Chicago doing counseling in his nondirective style under the supervision of himself and his staff. After discussions with Carl during this period, he invited me graciously to private meetings at his home with his closest cooperators. A year later I spent a long summer with Abraham Maslow at Brandeis University. His integrity as a scientist and his openness to any critique was amazing to me. He invited me for a year to take his place as a visiting professor of psychology at Brandeis and to teach his courses to his own students while he would take a sabbatical. He allowed me to teach them my own formation theory of personality.

During my first American phase in psychology I had already to name my formation theory differently in order to be acceptable in American psychology departments. For the time being I called it *existential psychology*. One reason to select that temporarily convenient name was to express my opposition to existentialistic psychologies that put existence before the directive essence of the mystery and the founding life form. Another reason was that I wanted to emphasize that my formation theory was based on the ex-sisting, the standing outside or beyond one's individualistic *I* or pretranscendent group-*we* toward the formation mystery and its directive epiphanies in the consonant traditions, spheres, and dimensions of a distinctively human formation field.

The Maslowian theory was more developed than the Rogerian. It offered me more points for comparison and critique. Always open and searching, Maslow, or "Abe" as I soon came to call him, was always eager to discuss the basic differences between what he preferred to name in his sometimes somewhat solemn fashion the divergencies between the Maslowian and van Kaamian theories of personality. After finishing my teaching at Brandeis as his substitute, he invited me back at various times to address the student body and to engage in prolonged private dialogues in his office or at his home. He visited me also at Duquesne University to continue the interaction while he used one of the rooms of our Trinity Hall community. I invited him to address our students, to which he graciously assented.

Consonant Direction, Dissonant Under- and Overdirection

The contacts with Carl, Abe, and their followers seemed to confirm for me my own theory of formational direction. It had struck me already during my counseling of people in the Hunger Winter that the enthusiasm of some for nondirectiveness was often an understandable kind of reaction formation against what I defined then as the deformative impact of overdirection. Earlier in my theory I had made a distinction between consonant and dissonant direction. In dissonant direction I distinguished between over- and underdirection. Both interfere with consonant human life formation. Consonant formation, on the contrary, is congenial with the here-and-now disclosures of the probable life call of the person in accordance with her or his age. It is also compatible with the inter- and outerspheres of the actual formation field, including form traditions.

A number of those who were hiding had been subjected to unnecessarily coercive direction during their own youth. Ideally they should have moved from such overdirection to consonant direction. This reasonable moderate direction should have made them more congenial with their unique life call, more in tune with their formation traditions, and more compatible with the inter- and outer meanings of their formation field as apprehended and appraised in the light of these traditions as well as their own life call.

Children should not be the victims of either over- or underdirection by representatives of their formation traditions, especially their parents. Neither should they, because of underdirection or nondirection, be compelled to invent their own life direction by independent values clarification. Children are too young, too underdeveloped in life experience, and unlike animals too instinct-deficient to live wisely without the light of form traditions that crystalize the life experiences of generations. They should not be forced prematurely to make their own decisions in regard to basic distinctively human life orientations. The opposite extreme is overdirection. Within the parameters of the basic tradition-directives, reasonable room should be created gradually for decision making on small subdirectives in congeniality with the emergence of the first tiny indicators of their own possible unique life call to be realized within the overall direction of their formation traditions. Overdirection would beget the opposite results of respectful reasonable direction. It would generate deformative guilt about the impossibility to integrate consonantly within one's uniquely unfolding personality the fundamental directives of one's form traditions. It might instill infrafocal resentment, a secret resistance that later could explode in a focal striving for nondirective education as I observed in some of the proponents of this theory of personality development.

Underdirection would create similar problems. Underdirected children do not learn the wisdom of form traditions. Lacking the instinctive endowment of animal existence, they would also miss out on its superior replacement by form traditions. They would have no compass by which to steer their life wisely, reasonably, and effectively. They would not know to give order formatively to inner and outer chaos. As a result they, too, may come to believe in the myth of nondirective education and absolutized self-actualization. They are not initiated and do not initiate their own children in the art and discipline of disclosing personal life directives in the light of age-old apprehensions and appraisals of humanity-in-formation. They create the illusion that children should become the inventors of their own nondirective values, free to be changed at any time, more or less arbitrarily, by new values clarifications.

Maslow's Theory Correction

I told my friend Abe Maslow of my theory of form traditional direction developed during the Dutch phases of the initiation of this new theory and science of formation. We argued back and forth. Initially disagreeing, he still listened carefully. Then he seemed to relent a little. Later I heard that his concern for a beloved granddaughter made him aware of the dangers of absolute self-actualization, independent values clarification, and decision making, as well as nondirective education.

The moment of crisis came for Maslow in the aftermath of the dramatic failure of the well-intentioned attempts by Carl Rogers and his colleagues to introduce traditionless nondirective education, premature independent decision making, and self-actualization in the sixty schools offered to them for experimentation by a religious congregation of school sisters in California. The deformational consequences, the resulting complaints by parents and children, and the scientific appraisals by experts of the outcomes of this experiment were devastating. To the horror of Maslow and Coulson other schools, educational institutes, and programs began blindly to imitate the experiment. They did not consult the outcomes of the scientific evaluations. Honestly admitting that they had unleashed a monster in American education, Coulson and Maslow tried to control the damage that began to spread through the whole nation and even in other countries. Coulson traveled all over the country to warn educators and parents that he himself, Maslow, and Rogers had been wrong in their expectations of nondirective education.

As one of his colleagues later revealed, Maslow — a heart patient — driven now by his sense of responsibility worked himself literally to death the last twenty months of his life. He expanded and edited two volumes of journals to undo the harm that he had done unwittingly. They were published posthumously, no longer supported by the grants that had widely spread his former contributions and largely ignored by most of his followers, not even mentioned or given equal time in posthumous reviews of his works. Not many people have the courage and candor to admit that they have been wrong in their life long investment in ideas, some of which ultimately proved to be ineffective.

Initially Abe was not too sure of his shift. He probably was also afraid that others, finding his journals in case of his death, would not allow their publication. He knew where I stood in my theory of personality and of reasonable wise life direction. The last time I visited with him he begged me to take under my wing manuscripts he was writing. He gave me the key to a box filled with these writings, which he would send to me with a student of his who had now become on his advice a student in the graduate program in psychology that I had organized at Duquesne University. He asked me not to open the box before his death. In case he survived long enough he would ask me to send the box back and to begin work at their publication. I found a safe hiding place for the box in the basement of our priests' residence on campus where I was living. It was a most unlikely residence for the writings of this noble agnostic, who honestly tried to do the best he could for his numerous students and followers.

A few years later Abe called me and asked me to return the box with the same graduate student, who had told him that he would visit him. He was now ready to make these notes public with many others he had collected. That was probably the beginning of the twenty last months of his life spent in feverish preparation of his journals for publication. This publication, as reported in detail by Coulson, confirmed me, at least indirectly, in my own theory of formative life direction in the light of consonant formation traditions.

Form Directives for All Formation Traditions

Formation science as foundational helps us not only to disclose the form directives of any particular tradition. It also shows what are the ideal directives at the root of consonant formation in any form tradition. I have concluded that ideal form directives are marked by the following traits:

1. They are in principle common to all consonant human formation.

2. They are ordered hierarchically in consonance with the higher and lower dimensions of the human life form. (For instance, gratification and satisfaction directives should not rule out transcendent appreciation directives.)

3. They are effective in the consonant receiving and giving of form in one's life.

4. They help people to tell the difference between directives that are consonant or dissonant with their field of formation.

5. The basic life and field direction endows people and their respective form traditions with the power to apprehend more clearly what appears in their field, how to appraise it more wisely, and how to direct or bring about more effectively the outcome of their apprehension and appraisal.

Any formation tradition, insofar as it articulates these basic conditions, helps people to comprehend the events that show up in their fields of life.

Common Questions for All Form Traditions

Are there common questions about human formation that can be posed to any form tradition? I believe there are. So far I have found the following, indicated here in the form of questions.

1. How do form traditions take into account the human life form's preformation or given nature in ways that foster consonant formation?

2. How do form traditions help people to apprehend, appraise, and deal with the interformation between people in ways that foster consonant formation?

3. How do form traditions help people to apprehend, appraise, and deal with the structures of their human life form and its field in ways that foster consonant formation?

4. How do form traditions help people to apprehend, appraise, and deal with local situations, and with cosmic and world happenings in their field of life, in ways that foster consonant formation?

5. How do form traditions help people to apprehend, appraise, and deal with crises, conflicts, sickness, suffering, and death in ways that foster consonant formation?

6. How do form traditions help people to apprehend, appraise, and deal with the field extensions of time — of present, past, and future — in ways that foster consonant formation?

7. How do form traditions help people to apprehend, appraise, and deal with the focal, prefocal, infrafocal, and transfocal regions of their consciousness and the interformation of these regions in ways that foster consonant formation?

8. How do form traditions help people to apprehend, appraise, and deal with other form traditions (and with the marks they put on one's shared culture) in ways that foster people's consonant formation?

9. How do form traditions help people to apprehend, appraise, and deal with the uncanny and the mysterious or the mystery in their field of life in ways that foster consonant formation?

Different Answers of
Different Form Traditions to Universal Questions

Not all form traditions try to answer all of these basic questions. For example, the ideological form tradition of Stalinist Marxism will have no explicit answer to the ninth question about the mystery. The underlying Marxist faith tradition would not even give rise to a search for the answer. By the same token, the form traditions of one and the same faith traditions do not necessarily answer all of these questions. For example, the everyday form tradition of some groups of Slavic Christians did not try to answer the eighth question about dealing consonantly with other traditions insofar as it would be concerned about the apprehension and appraisal of the Jewish form tradition. Neither do all formation traditions give the *same* answer to these questions. For example, the answer to the first question about formatively dealing with human nature differs in traditions that see our nature as good, as a mixture of good or bad, or as bad.

Likewise the fourth question about the human life form as related to cosmic and world happenings is answered differently by Hispanic American form traditions that view the human life form as controlled by nature; Chinese and Japanese form traditions that view our nature as in harmony with the cosmos; European and American form traditions that see human nature as master over cosmic forces. Looking at time, as in the sixth question, old Chinese form traditions emphasized the past; Hispanic American traditions the present; North American and European ones the future.

Different form traditions will respond differently to the second question of the interformation between people. Some, like ancestral form traditions, stress linear interformation between the followers of the tradition today and those of the past and future. Others are concerned with here-and-now interformation between people near to one another, for instance, in traditions that foster a joint family life. Others again dwell on individual self-sufficiency, lessening the width and depth of interformation and instead fostering individualism.

Another example of the same concerns the ways in which form traditions deal with illness, the fifth question. Some traditions treat sickness as restricted to only physiological causes; for others sickness is a symbol of the dangers that threaten the group from nature or their own members. Some traditions look upon illness as an unfortunate accident, while others raise it to the divine heights of a providential life direction.

Formation scientists can distinguish and rate form traditions on the basis of their answers to these key questions as potentially raised by people at all times everywhere in the world.

Flaws and Changes in Form Traditions

Transcendent form traditions help people to bring together their needs, aspirations, and inspirations, but they are not without flaws. No form tradition is fully coherent. Any one of them has its dissonances, its unevenness, its whimsical irregularities. Why did followers of the Christian form tradition hold slaves without sensing a dissonance between that form directive and the opposite directives of Christianity as a religion of love and freedom for all in Christ? Form traditions are the outcome of a ongoing conversation between one's faith tradition and the historical field of life in which one has to carry out its lofty goals and rules. Each form tradition is the outcome of a historical formation process. It is a silent settlement between many forces. Failing to look at a tradition from the viewpoint of formation history, as a whole, it may seem a patchwork.

Consonant form traditions are marked by openness. The development of a form tradition is unforeseeable because of the, as yet, unknown events that will change its course. Some forms of a tradition come and go because a tradition-as-forming is challenged time and again by new formation fields. Changes in form tradition seem to follow certain rules:

1. What stays on is often of a lower level than the ideals of the faith tradition. Basic human needs that followers cannot yet fully tie in with the aspirations and inspirations of their faith tradition may linger, often prefocally, in changing fields of accommodation.

2. Many forms of a tradition endure while their meanings change. The same forms may be filled with added or different meanings. For example, the forms of the feast of Christmas may stay the same while pointing to added meanings, such as gift giving, the setting up of the creche with its figures, the tree, the lights. Briefly, the forms

of a tradition are often more stable than the initial meanings they point to.

3. Form traditional patterns can become empty and without meaning. They then have to be changed. They begin to bore people because they do not know any longer what these forms signify. This factor sheds light on the changes in the traditional forms of ritual, music, literature, painting, architecture, dress, movies, and plays.

4. Another ground for change in the forms of a tradition is the emergence of new needs and aspirations. These have their beginnings in changes in the field. Take, for instance, forms of courting. They change many times in answer to new social situations in which people have to find ways to come to know each other more intimately and to express their love in forms that make sense and are still acceptable within their faith and form traditions.

Apprehension and Appraisal of Form Traditions

Before the establishment of formation science, one could have concluded (wrongly) that all formation traditions would have to go through the same line of unfolding. Persons were tempted to make the line of unfolding of their own tradition the rule of appraisal for the growth of any other tradition. Formation science has shown that form traditions are more or less consonant. They are more or less adequate, unique-communal, historical answers to the basic formation questions of humanity. These answers are unique insofar as they are affected by the limited challenges a form tradition has to go through in its succession of particular formation fields. Insofar as the discoveries of each tradition are basic and consonant, they have an important part to play in the unfolding of the fundamental human knowledge of consonant formation as a whole. Insofar as these discoveries are meaningful only for the particularity of a tradition, or even dissonant with it, they do not expand or deepen the fundamental overall formation tradition of all humanity. Because of growing interformation between many different traditions, we are now aware of a basic likeness between them. We are more willing to enrich our own tradition by the discoveries of others as long as they can be formulated in ways congenial with the tradition to which we adhere.

In appraising the influence of secular form traditions on those that are transcendent, formation scientists seek the help of such auxiliary sciences as political science or economy. Take, for example, the difference in influence of the democratic-liberal form tradition, as in the Netherlands, Scandinavia, or England, and that of the democratic-capitalistic form traditions, for instance, in the United States and in Germany after 1945. In some way, such secular form traditions affect the transcendent form traditions of those living in these countries, enhancing or diminishing their consonance and consistency, depending on their style and success of assimilation.

Knowing Other Form Traditions in Service of Interformation

To appraise our own form tradition, we should be aware of how deeply it is touched by other traditions. The primary concern of formation science and its articulations in specific form traditions is not with the underlying faith traditions and their theologies or ideologies as such but with the faith tradition only insofar as it is practically and concretely implemented in everyday formation traditions. We should not take for granted that we grasp what other traditions tell us about themselves. Often we are too caught up in our own tradition to have an open mind for what they are trying to say to us. A few fundamental starting points about interformation instead of interdeformation between traditions would be:

1. Form traditional interformation always takes place in a shared experiential formation field, not in a field of theological or philosophical abstractions from the field. Not only words but also silence, deeds, art, symbols, movements, and repetition can be interformational on the level of formational experience.

2. Each message of a form tradition not only gives some information about the tradition; it can also be formative insofar as it gives, at least implicitly or potentially, form directives to our thoughts, feelings, imaginations, anticipations, memories, and actions.

3. Next to the focal (and often vocal) message, there is also a nonfocal (nonvocal) message whose influence is difficult to escape in view of the situation in which the interformation happens. For example, a Christian tells a Jewish person, "Some of my best friends are Jews," but at the same time her tone is somewhat defensive and condescending. In response the Jewish person is somewhat withholding, for the message as a whole is, "I like you people but don't come too near to me." The Christian in turn may mistake the message of the subsequent slight bodily symbolic withholding of her Jewish partner because she is unaware that she herself also sent out a hidden ambiguous message. She brings the conversation to an end and may leave with the mistaken notion, "No matter what you say nicely to these people, they always hold back." Both leave with a false view of each other's form tradition.

4. Interformation is always many-sided. It is a maze of open and hidden messages and directives, of symbols and changing contexts. The verbal interformation between the followers of different form traditions always goes together with facial expressions and often with at least minimal gestures. Each interforming communication, moreover, is tied to earlier and later interforming communications. One cannot take a message out of this context without falsifying the message of one's own or the other's tradition.

5. The language of a (for us) strange form tradition can make sense only

when it is heard in the everyday lifestyle of that tradition. Its language will be understood insofar as we enter into that tradition itself *as* experientially formational. We cannot coexperience the concrete formational everyday experience of the adherents of a formation tradition through the theological or philosophical abstractions from that experience. Coexperience helps us to appraise not only what binds us together as human forms of life but also where in our own form tradition we are fundamentally unlike other form traditions. We need to acknowledge this difference in order to remain faithful to our own core self insofar as it is form traditionally committed to our own basic form tradition.

6. Looking at the interformation between different form traditions, we should first and foremost look at what we can see directly. We must not begin with what we have heard or read about each other's form traditions, or what is said theologically or philosophically about their underlying faith traditions. Form tradition is an ongoing happening. Slight or considerable changes can take place at any time. To begin to know what the experiential form tradition is like here and now, how it is at present both alike and unalike our own form tradition, we must first of all look again and again on all direct and indirect formational-experiential messages, words, deeds, gestures, and postures, the usual as well as the unusual. Only then can we appraise and integrate it as a whole without twisting it to suit our preapprehension and preappraisal. In terms of the general conceptual framework of formation science, form traditions themselves *as form* traditions here and now do not usually give us a frame of reference that shows clearly how everything comes together into some kind of formational-experiential system. On that score, form traditions are unlike faith traditions, especially the classic ones. Classical faith traditions themselves, unlike many of their numerous form traditions, give us some overall ideological or theological outline of the whole of the faith.

In regard to supplying the missing outline of a form tradition, a main help may be the general conceptual framework of human formation traditions developed by formation science on the basis of formation theory and anthropology. This theory of traditions in turn learns much from open, objective observation of any form tradition as such.

Transexperiential Coformants of My Methodology in Light of My Basic Concern with Form Traditional Articulation

This insight in the central role of form traditions in human experience *as formational* may deepen one's understanding of the research methodology that I developed for formation science and its final articulation in formation traditions. This new understanding will teach us that in the execution of these methods this final articulation should be kept in mind from the beginning. The methodology remains the same but the selection of authors, other form traditions, and scientific theorists during the consultation stage should be in part directed by the final articulation of the specific formation tradition one has in mind.

For example, one may have chosen, as I did, a Christian formation tradition as one's final articulation object. This final implicit purpose of one's research should be somewhat prepared for in the choice of, for instance, the works one wants to discuss in the consultation phase of one's scientific research. This will not change the scientific methodology itself in any significant fashion. For I designed the methodology as generally and inherently oriented for any final articulation of any formation tradition. My methods are not meant to produce a mere qualitative, experientialistic, or existentialistic description and elucidation of human experiences as such, if this is at all possible. Our object is human *form traditional* experiences. I mean by this our human experiences, first in their general characteristics, but then in the way in which they are always already affected by form traditions. Hence I outlined in volume 4 as one research task the consideration and consultation of other form traditions and theorists. Such traditions and theories should be appraised also from the viewpoint of their form traditional origin as well as their impact on the experience under study, its formulation and explanation. Students of the science may select a Christian formation tradition as their final articulation object. In that case they will already from the beginning prefer for consultation those contributions of other form traditions and scientific theories and findings that seem to affect positively or negatively the formation experience under study in regard to the Christian form traditional meaning of the experience.

What all of this amounts to is that my methodology should not be misunderstood as merely qualitative, experiential, phenomenological, or hermeneutical. While these and similar methods can be useful and sufficient for excellent qualitative research, they can never be sufficient for the form traditional appraisal of the fidelity or infidelity of the formational meaning of an experience to the ethos of a form tradition and its subsequent directives. For this comparative apprehension and appraisal I needed to develop the insights of my formation anthropology, of my formation theory of personality, and of the developing body of knowledge of my formation science. I devised my methodology with the ultimate or crowning phase of this research in mind, which is the consonant articulation of the formational articulation of one's traditional object of choice. This inherent orientation is general and implicit in the methodology of formation science, specific and explicit in its final articulation phase. Without this understanding one could be caught in the trap of an experientialism that could deform one's apprehension and appraisal of the formation tradition under study.

Sometimes I compare this analogically with the pretheological integrative philosophies of Christian thinkers such as, among others, Søren Kierkegaard, Blaise Pascal, and Thomas Aquinas. They tried to develop a critical integrational, speculative, or literary prerevelational philosophy that could be acceptable in the light of human reason and intuition to their contemporaries even if they were not or were no longer believers in the Christian faith tradition. Yet above all they wanted their philosophies to serve the theological articulation — in the light of reason and intuition enlightened by revelation — of their Christian faith tradition. From the outset their minds were also oriented toward the final task of Christian theological articulation. In their intentionality philosophy was meant to be the handmaid of theology. Analogically in my own research methodology I aimed at the initiation and development of an empirical-experiential formation science useful for non-Christians as well as Christian formation traditions. At the same time I aimed personally at making my science serviceable to the empirical-experiential articulation of Christian formation traditions while encouraging different articulations by other religious and ideological faith and form traditions. Such articulation is meant to be done in the light of my, in part, transphenomenological and transexperiential anthropology and formation theory of personality.

CHAPTER 15

Formation Traditions as Systems of Appraisal

W e can look at formation traditions as systems of appraisal. Traditions help us to appraise what happens to us. If I get ill, and I am a Muslim or Christian, the illness has another meaning for me than it would have for those who are formed by an atheistic tradition. The Islamic or Christian tradition disposes me to appraise my illness as allowed by God. Form traditions instill in us dispositions to appraise things in light of their ethos. A Marxist tradition disposes its followers to appreciate what people can do in common, to depreciate private gain and unique personal life formation. Underlying this tradition and its style of appraisal is an ideological faith tradition. In this example it is an ideological belief in the prescientific assumptions of Karl Marx.

Dispositions and Attitudes
People may share as a disposition of appraisal that of depreciating private ownership of property and unique personal unfolding. This basic disposition may give rise to different attitudes in accordance with the situation in which people implement it. I call these *implemental attitudes*. I distinguish them from the basic, comprehensive dispositions in which they are rooted and which they attempt to implement in daily life.

Implemental attitudes vary, for instance, between socialists who live in Russia, Cuba, China, Great Britain, Italy, or the Netherlands. From the beginning of formation science, I saw that a formation disposition is more basic than its subsequent attitudes. As the example shows, one and the same appraisal disposition can be translated into various attitudes, depending on the situation. A disposition must be in consonance with one's life call, with one's form tradition, with one's other dispositions, and with one's attitudes subordinated to such dispositions. We can appraise the correspondence of these attitudes with the disposition and, through it, with the tradition the disposition stands for.

A traditional disposition changes when the formation tradition itself changes in regard to the deeper appraisal at the root of that disposition. An attitude can be changed without a change in one's traditional disposition. The reformation of an attitude can be meaningful. Still even then it does not necessarily imply a change of one's disposition. It may mean only a change of attitudinal, implemental direction of the implementation of one's disposition. For instance, a salesperson may change the attitude of manifest arrogance, for it hinders the marketing of his wares. But that change does not necessarily mean that he has changed his disposition of feeling superior inwardly. This disposition in turn may be a form traditional disposition. For instance, the seller belongs to a Muslim form tradition that may dispose its members to feel inwardly superior to clients who are "infidels."

Changes are radical if they give another form to our dispositions. For example, the radical disposition of racial discrimination, not simply its implemental attitudes, must change into racial appreciation if racism is to be eradicated.

Inconsistencies in Systems of Appraisal

Traditional attitudes of formation are rooted in a system of appraisal dispositions. This intraspheric system works usually in ways we are not aware of. If one is a true Marxist, one feels unconsciously uneasy when giving in to the need to make something one's own domain or to listen to one's own unique life call. A convinced Marxist may not be aware of why he or she feels this way. This appraisal system has become so much his or her own that it guides one prefocally.

No system of appraisal is perfectly cohesive. Inconsistencies between some of its dispositions are to be expected. They are especially to be watched for if we live in a pluralistic formation field. A pluriform culture is filled with backlashes of many traditions. They filter through our appraisal systems, fostering dispositions that are at odds with the appraisal dispositions of our own basic tradition. When not sufficiently appraised, they may become a source of dissonance. For example, a disposition of sexual promiscuity in a pluritraditional culture may filter into an appraisal of sexuality by people who have been formed basically in a Jewish, Islamic, or Christian tradition. A clash between dispositions and conflicts of their form traditional conscience may be the result of such an invasion of secularistic traditions.

Foundational Form and Core Form of a Formation Tradition

In volume 1 of this series, I distinguished between the foundational form, dynamically speaking, our unique-communal life call, and that to which it gives rise, namely, our core form of life. I can now apply the same distinction to formation traditions. Any form tradition has two aspects: the form tradition itself and the faith tradition that inspires it. We can look at the faith tradition as the founding form or the inmost dynamic faith call of the form tradition that implements it.

We have seen earlier that the founding form of our human life is the hidden ultimate criterion of the consonance of our empirical life formation with itself as giving rise to our unique-communal life call. Applying my concept to a faith tradition as a whole, I may say that this faith as made catechetically or ideologically explicit is the ultimate criterion of the consonance of any specific empirical form tradition with a unique-communal faith tradition.

In the same way we can compare not only the founding form but also the core of our empirical form tradition with the core form of human life. I have shown that the core of our empirical life is a set of basic dispositions. These guide the disclosure and implementation of our unique-communal life call. Analogously I can now say that also the core or heart of any form tradition is a system of basic appraisal dispositions. These guide the empirical-experiential implementation of our unique-communal faith in our inner life and in our daily fields of presence and action.

For example, the foundational form of the faith tradition of Christianity implies as a dynamic call that we should love our neighbor as ourselves. How we implement this tradition empirically depends on the situation. Jesus himself gave an example of such implementation in his story of how a robbed and beaten traveler was empirically helped by the good Samaritan. Over the centuries Christians lived in a wide variety of fields of needs of neighbors. Many of these were different from that of the robbery victim, both in regard to the nature of the needs and the means to alleviate them. Different fields give rise to different traditions of how to give form concretely to the faith tradition of loving one's neighbor. Out of such empirical experiences grew different systems of appraisal dispositions for different formation traditions. This system is the guiding core of the life of an empirical form tradition's giving form to its faith tradition. This core takes in both the appraisal dispositions and the basic form directives as well as the implemental attitudes and directives that flow from these dispositions.

We can more fully understand a form tradition if we disclose its core of dispositions and directives. We should also clarify the relation of this core to the grounding faith tradition as well as to the field in which an implementation of that faith had or has to take place. To describe a form tradition without a disclosure of its core of hierarchical appraisal dispositions and their relation to faith and field, would offer us nothing more than a laundry list of disparate items.

Ideal and Actual Directives of Formation Traditions

I observed during the war that there is a difference between the ideal and actual directives of the tradition of the people I helped to hide. I concluded then that the essence of a tradition-as-formative is known to us through the core of appraisal dispositions. These can tell us ideally what should direct the form its followers should give to their daily life. In actual life, the followers of a tradition often drift away from such ideal directives. This happens under the pull and push of their respective neuroform or conditioned nervous system, temperform or temperament, core form or character. Added to these are field changes and especially the subtle seductions of other traditions, their backlash in a pluritraditional culture and its language. The study of such actual directives, unlike that of only the ideal ones, gives us a more realistic view of the actual influence of traditions on people.

For example, we can look at the ideal directives of the Dutch Reformed Church as given by its early founders in the Netherlands. We can then study the actual directive of apartheid as lived for a long time by the Dutch Reformed Church in South Africa. This was a response to the threat of wholesale slaughter of the first pioneers by marauding tribes. Once this disposition of apartheid became part of the core of their form tradition, it was initially difficult for them to overcome it when the field had changed.

The same can be said of the appraisal system of the Catholic form tradition of landlords in South America who felt they had a divine right to their holdings and the power it gave them. Neither was the appraisal system of the poor *campesinos* in tune with the ideal directives of their form tradition, for they were not disposed to protest the exploitation of their families and did not develop in time attitudes for various ways of effective implementation of a Christian resistance to social injustice. The attempts to raise their actual formation consciousness in this regard can be seen as a move to restore a lost ideal directive of the Christian form tradition.

Social Symbolism

In the previous chapter, I dealt with symbolism; in this one with appraisal systems. Is there some connection between them? Their interforming relationship becomes clear if we keep in mind that traditional systems of appraisal can endure only if they are kept alive in the hearts and minds of those who carry them out. This can be done by the use of symbols. The minds of the faithful are filled daily with profane customs, rituals, things, and events that are common among the people in their secular field of daily interaction. To rekindle in their minds the tradition-related meanings of such things, the tradition may add a symbolic meaning to their common everyday sense. I call this process *symbolic attunement* of common sense to the sense of one's tradition.

To give some examples of a few symbolic attunements, only in the area of words and greetings: the "in God we trust" on the American dollar; "Grüss Gott," as an everyday greeting in Bavaria; "Heil Hitler" during the short-lived National Socialist tradition; "Comrade" during the period of a Stalinist-Marxist form tradition; "Citizen," in the early French revolutionary tradition.

Form traditional symbolic attunement of ways of greeting, of tasks, of things, events, and everyday words can strengthen traditional directives already alive in the mind and heart of believers. More often than not, symbolic attunements can come alive only in the inward appreciations of the participants in a tradition. For instance, a Christian nurse may see her service in a state-run hospital as an expression of her faith in Christ-in-the-patient without being allowed to verbalize this faith publicly. This Christ symbol would not move a nurse less inspired by the Christian form tradition. Attunement symbols can wear out in the course of time. They can become so functional that they lose their inspiration. Then other symbols have to be found to replace them.

Symbolic attunements take in informational as well as formational meanings. The informational message tells us something about the symbolically attuned person or group. The martially uniformed bands of National Socialist marchers pass on as information a new faith and form tradition that is unyielding and powerful, that will take care of any foe. The singing of the Horst Wessel hymn gave a formational message to many listeners by its appeal to a people crushed by Allied punishment after the loss of World War I. It reformed in many the disposition of defeat and hopelessness to one of fight and hope. They were inclined to omit serious, critical reflection on the dissonant ideological belief system underlying the National Socialist form tradition.

Symbols and the Nonfocal Region of Consciousness

Form traditional symbols can set forth the ethos of a tradition directly or by means of attunement. An example of the first is the symbol of the cross in Christianity or that of the crescent moon in Islam. An instance of symbolic attunement is the painting of the dove of peace on a flag that is already symbolic of a country or movement.

Form traditional symbols are beamed not only to the focal region of our consciousness. Often more influential is their bearing on our nonfocal consciousness. Its hidden power may be difficult to escape. We cannot wholly avoid its impact. Take as an example of both focal and prefocal symbolic influences a white Christian speaker asked to address a black audience about the problem of racial intolerance. There may be an inconsistency in his own inner appraisal system. As a Christian, he is for tolerance; as a prosperous participant in a white middle-class form tradition he has developed a hidden disposition of superiority toward blacks. Focally he thinks and says the right words. The black public is with him. At the same time the listeners, in their region of nonfocal consciousness, may sense uneasily some inconsistency of symbolism. The words of the speaker do not fully match his body language. Some postures, gestures, and a tone of voice seem to tell something else. The answer of the listeners is hesitant because the message seems double: I am for the humble service of all people as preached in our Christian form tradition. Therefore, work with me for kindness, gentleness, humility, and justice for black people. Nonfocally, however, another message is given symbolically by his body language. Do not expect that I personally will give up fully my feeling that I am somewhat superior to black people. After all I am a successful white middle-class business person, highly regarded in our community as you are not. Possibly, the basic form tradition of Christianity of the speaker is overshadowed by the rivalry, one-upmanship, achievement, and career-at-any-price disposition of the free-floating tradition of secular individualistic functionalism.

Interformative Patterns of Traditions

A pluralistic culture reflects different traditions. To take part in such a culture is to expose oneself to the remnants of the traditions that have put their stamp on that culture as formative. We are immersed in complex traditional patterns that interform with each other. Their messages and channels of influence, their responses to changing field situations, their focal and nonfocal symbolic interactions, keep us moving in an ever-expanding web of interforming dynamics.

On top of this, each traditional response is interwoven with preceding and following responses. This context of time, of a past and future of traditions, adds a symbolic sociohistorical meaning to each present utterance of these traditions. It is impossible, for instance, to fully appraise the form traditional meaning of a ritual expression of another tradition without knowing its emergence in history. One must be enough aware of the symbolic historical reference to related rituals in the past. They are still implicitly in the form they give to ritual here and now. Each ritual act of a classical tradition is laden with unspoken historical symbols.

Implications for Research

For these reasons I keep insisting that formation scientists in their research of traditions should focus first of all on what they observe directly. They should not start out from constructs, inferences, and language uses they may borrow from psychological, anthropological, sociological, political, or economic theories. Otherwise they are in danger from the beginning of putting upon a traditional symbol, alien to them, a theory built on observations of basically different form traditions, usually those with which they themselves are familiar in their own formation field.

Once attention is focused on the observation of a form tradition in its uniqueness, the researcher should try to find out what is truly different in this tradition. Only after such examination is the researcher ready to relate this difference to the overall theory of formation science. This may result in a deeper, more critical understanding of the form tradition under study.

Such a critical scientific appraisal in the light of formation science can be helpful to the participants in the tradition as well as to sympathetic outsiders and malinformed opponents. In addition, the new knowledge of the particular form tradition may enrich, complement, and correct the theory of formation science.

CHAPTER 16

Alignment of Vital Dimension
and Form Tradition

I n my formation theory of personality I distinguish as indicated previously six dimensions of human life: the sociohistorical, vital, functional, functional-transcendent, transcendent, and transcendent-functional. Each of them gives form to life by its own particular power. This is one of the theoretical principles on which I built my science. One of the other principles is this: the four dimensions that are pretranscendent should be transformed by the ones that are transcendent in such a way that the latent deepest striving of these lower dimensions finds its fulfillment. Their transformation happens through an alignment of their particular strivings with the strivings of human life as a whole for the peace and joy of universal love and consonance. A disposition for alignment is inherent in each of these dimensions. In turn transcendent transformation does not violate but fosters the potencies, directives, and strivings that are typical of each dimension.

In this chapter we shall apply my principles of alignment to the vital life as well as to the operations of our form traditional pyramids.

Founding Life Form and Vital Dimension

How is our vital life related to our founding life form? I see the latter as our unique transcendent form of life *in* its pristine embodiment. Its immediate enfleshment has two aspects: primarily, an incorporation of our transcendent form in our genetic make-up and, secondarily, our embodiment in a parental ambience starting in the womb of our mother. To summarize: Our transcendent founding form is enfleshed by two coformants, the genetic and the parental as starting in the maternal.

Our founding form as embodied is a gift of the mystery of formation. It contains the seeds of a unique life call to be disclosed over a lifetime in dialogue with our fields of presence and action. The leading *transcendent* uniqueness of our founding form is the gift of the radical mystery directly to us. It roots us in the cosmic mystery as well as in the radical mystery itself. The radical mystery keeps us in being and enables us to be receptive to its gracious inspiration. Those who do not espouse a theistic faith tradition may believe in the cosmic mystery as their ultimate ground.

The lasting *genetic* embodiment of the founding form is the indirect gift of the mystery. This gift is mediated by the cosmic epiphany of the radical mystery for those who believe in the latter. Our genetics are formed through the cosmic interplay of genetic formations, reformations, and interformations over generations, culminating in the genetic code we inherit from our parents. This embodiment roots us genetically both in our parents and in the generations preceding them.

The secondary initial embodiment of our founding form is the *maternal* and by extension, the paternal and familial. This, too, is an indirect gift of the radical mystery. It is mediated not only by the cosmically formed maternal-paternal organic ambience, but also by the society-formed parental traditional ambience. Therefore our initial maternal embodiment roots us both in the maternal organismic influence as well as in the parental tradition pyramid. The latter is a point of departure for the formation of our own tradition pyramid later in life. This parental pyramid provides our first encounter with the sociohistorical dimension of our life form and field.

Prevalence of the Maternal Ambience

At the beginning of our life, the leading transcendent center of our founding form is hidden. So is our genetic embodiment except insofar as its genetic form potency is activated by the maternal ambience, starting in the womb of the mother. What directs our initial formation more immediately is the maternal ambience in which we are immersed as fetus and as infant.

The vital formational influence of the maternal ambience (and its extension in the familial ambience or its substitute) marks us for life. It never leaves us totally. Unwittingly we seek to return to its warmth and safety, to restore it in some way or to find it later in other people if we missed it in our childhood. Even our resistance to it is formed indirectly by what we resent or oppose in the parental pyramid of form traditions. Much wisdom and effort is needed to grow beyond the gentle or firm dominance of the initial maternal ambience. We have to restore the maternal coformant to its appropriate position in our life. We must realign it with our leading unique transcendent coformant and with the reasonable and realistic compatibility demands of the inter- and outerspheres of our successive formation fields. Often a long and arduous process of detachment is necessary. For in some way we have to unfasten our life from the nostalgia for the lost maternal-parental ambience and its later substitutes in our life.

Crucial in this process is our appraisal of our own tradition pyramid. The right appreciation turns our pyramid into a path to joyful consonance. The wrong appreciation will keep us in an unhappy state of dissonance;

transcendent love and joy will elude us. Most of us alternate between these two worlds of appreciation.

Functional-Vital Compromise

The maternal coformant of our founding form prevails in early infancy. Our vital life receives its first traditional form from the maternal, parental, and familial tradition pyramids. Parental demands impose this tradition. The original license allowed to our infantile vital life begins to be disciplined when our functional dimension emerges. The awakening of the functional life invites a greater influence by the paternal tradition pyramid. In many traditions today the paternal pyramid is still more functionally oriented than its maternal counterpart.

The functional dimension is activated when the infant becomes able to learn and perform simple functions as in toilet training. Infants are trained — in accordance with the form traditions of their families — in certain ways of functionally regulating the vital tendency merely to let go of waste products at any time or in any place.

By itself alone the functional regulation of the vital life cannot align our vital striving for pleasure and sensation with the striving of life as a whole for transcendent love and joy. What we observe in infants is not an alignment but a compromise between the functional and the vital. At this early stage traditional directives have only a functional meaning for the infant. In spite of the fact that vital directives are experienced as more pleasurable, they have to be restrained because of traditional functional directives imposed by the parents.

Such compromise solutions in childhood set the tone for further attempts to come to an integration between vital desires and functional obligations.

Insufficiency of the Compromise Solution

The compromise solution cannot be ultimately effective. The functional in and by itself is unable to align vital life with the human spirit. It can impose, control, or compel from the outside. It cannot effect a change that inwardly aligns the striving of vital life with the transcendent striving for ultimate happiness and consonance. For such inmost alignment something more is needed than the functional dimension, something that transcends mere functional skills of external control. This something more is the transcendent dimension.

An infant does not yet have the receptivity for the alignment of its vital life by the life of the spirit. He or she is only receptive to functional ordering by parents or their substitutes. Parents find directives for such ordering in their own tradition pyramids. The infant lives mostly in the tension of a vital-functional compromise. Compromised formation may mark a long period of our life, for many, perhaps the remainder of life. As long as the inmost transformation of both the vital and functional dimension is not granted to us, transcendent joy and peace will elude us. We will seek anxiously for ever new vital-functional compromises, feeling compelled to persevere in that search because of our innate striving for transcendent joy and consonance. Transcendent traditions point to the path of true inner alignment.

Sublimation as a Sophisticated Compromise

Our compromises become more sophisticated when we grow older. Some theorists designate what happens then as "sublimation." While this may sound more "sublime," it is not effective in an ultimate sense. I hold that the construct of sublimation is based on a faulty theory of personality as well as on the assumptions of an insufficient pretranscendent formation tradition and anthropology. Sublimation as an ultimate explanation category in other theories is an attempt to gratify the needs of the vital life in a socially acceptable way not by transcendent integration but by disguising them as some higher functional or functional-transcendent aspiration. Such a cover-up is acceptable to our functionalistic society. It is a kind of external exchange. Instead of integrating, we exchange. For instance, a vital sexual gratification is exchanged for a socially acceptable satisfaction or expression that is functional or functional-transcendent, such as the dance.

Our functionalistic society tries to bend the meaning of our tradition pyramids in the functional or functional-transcendent direction. This robs them of their deepest transcendent integrational meaning and power. Traditions are then made subservient to the functional-vital compromises of society. Functional or functional-transcendent sublimation takes the place of the inmost alignment of the vital life that in my personality theory only our transformative spirit can effect. The term *sublimation* may suggest to us that we have found the final solution for dissonance. Yet, even if we apply it successfully we are still far away from the joy and freedom that is our birthright. We give up our journey to the land of consonance long before we have reached its shore. We refuse the helping hand of consonant and classical form traditions with their original transcendent symbols and meanings.

Candid Appraisal

We may experience conflicts in our life as well as in the pyramid that guides it. These dissonances should be appraised candidly. Refusal to face them leads to a split between our focal and infrafocal regions of consciousness. I term *focal conscious* that of which we are clearly aware, such as people, events, things, feelings, and images on which we can focus our attention at will. Infrafocal are those that are so far below (infra) our power of attention that we cannot focus on them at all.

Traditions in our pyramids can be focal or infrafocal. We may refuse to admit to ourselves that some free-floating traditions in our society, such as the hedonistic or functionalistic ones, have also gained a foothold in our own pyramids. We may keep them out of focal awareness, yet beneath (infra) that awareness, they shape and strengthen our vitalistic strivings. The reason we bar them from focal awareness is that they are in conflict with our more basic transcendent traditions. Unable to live with such a discrepancy, we push the conflicting tradition out of the *awareness* of our tradition pyramid as a whole.

Infrafocally we may strive for a merely vitalistic life of self-indulgence as portrayed in novels, movies, or commercials that reflect the free-floating hedonistic formation traditions in our society. At the same time, our focal consciousness is disposed to give form to our apparent life in accordance with the acknowledged transcendent traditions in our pyramid. Every time this happens, the tension deepens between our infrafocal and focal life as well as between the corresponding infrafocal and focal traditions in our pyramids.

As long as the infrafocal source of tension is not made focal by formation therapy, counseling or direction, or by a healing friendship, we cannot grasp from whence the tension or depression is coming. We cannot deal with it in a healing fashion. Our tradition pyramid may not be available in its totality to our appraisal because we have not allowed ourselves to be focally aware of the conflicting tradition directives it secretly contains.

The refusal itself of candid focal appraisal is infrafocal and, therefore, hidden from our focal and prefocal attention. Infrafocal refusal works powerfully within us and within our pyramid of traditions. As long as it succeeds in keeping vitalistic life directives out of the light and power of our focal and subsequent prefocal appraisal, these emotion-ladened directives will grow unchecked and become stronger and stronger. As a result, our acts of giving and receiving form become increasingly ambiguous. They are anxious compromises. Some of them, while self-centered, are sustained by high-sounding motivations. We borrow them from our transcendent traditions. But they are really directed by vitalistic impulses. Fake transcendent motives are like ships loaded with contraband sailing under false flags.

Genetic and Maternal Coformants as Hiding Our Founding Form

Transcendent traditions point to paths that may disclose our founding form or unique-communal life call. This form as transcendent is rooted in the formation mystery itself and is continuously illumined and nourished by that mystery. Its direction was at first hidden from us. For infants the maternal ambience stood out as powerfully embracing their entire field of life. Later our reflections on life experiences and our assimilation of the symbols of transcendent traditions let the light of our founding form shine through as ultimately leading our journey. This light prepares us for the pilgrimage back to the sacred sources of our being.

A hindrance to this homecoming in our transcendent founding form can be posed by two other coformants. They determine our life as embodied spirit by its individualizing genetic and maternal enfleshment. We can choose to focus on either one or both of these two subordinate coformants at the expense of paying attention to the transcendent base of our life direction. This wrong choice can be confirmed by scientific-ideological form traditions in our tradition pyramid. Some of these traditions reduce the ground of all formation to genetics and/or parental determinants.

Flight from Functionalism

Resentment of the harshness of a functionalistic world may drive us back to our maternal beginnings. This reaction can obstruct our path to the deeper, always present transcendent origin of our emergence in time. Transcendent traditions teach us how to find easement in this blessed origin from the severity of a functionalism that hardens the human heart, misled by our quasi-foundational pride form. Without enlightenment by tradition, we may misread the longing of our heart. We may read into it a reaching out, not for our transcendent home, but for the lost maternal ambience with its vital consolations. We may reduce even the transcendent mystery itself to a vitalistic supermaternal ambience. The symbol system of some subformation traditions can be affected by the needy search of adherents for a shelter of vitalistic maternal soothing by the Most High. Any form tradition can be infected by directives that are stuck in vitalistic strivings for felt gratifications that have not been inwardly transformed and aligned by the transcendent dimension under the guidance of transcendent traditions. A master of transformation as John of the Cross candidly unmasks such attachments hidden in piety, devotion, and spectacular enlightenment.

A transcendent tradition itself can deteriorate. It can be infiltrated by elements of pretranscendent traditions that interform with each other and with elements of transcendent traditions in the same tradition pyramid. A transcendent tradition can end up as a compromise; it can be experienced as a symbol of vital gratification. Adherents intend focally the transcendent meanings of the symbolic system, but intrafocally they seek vital gratifications as ultimate. These can be camouflaged as transcendent ecstasies. For example, followers of an excessively emotional cultic tradition may focally intend union with the transcendent while sweeping themselves into an ecstatic frenzy. Infrafocally they may be in pursuit of outlets for vitalistic erotic desires that are not yet respectfully penetrated, transformed, and given their ultimate fulfillment in the light of consonant transcendent formation traditions.

Obstacles to Living in the Light of Transcendent Traditions

Transcendent traditions point us to paths that may lead back to our original form of life as hidden in the mystery of formation. This pristine form in its transcendent leading core was at first hidden from our awareness. What stood out in infancy as embracing the whole of reality was the maternal ambience. Later, we grow up and experience life outside this motherly universe; we reflect on these new experiences as rooted in our own inner resources. At the same time we begin to assimilate personally the symbols of our traditions. All of this allows the light of the mystery to shine through as leading us. The star in the firmament of our life brightens a little. We suspect that there has to be more to our life's destiny than sheer genetics and a maternal ambience. We become ready for a pilgrimage back to the lasting sources of our being.

A hindrance to this homecoming is again posed by the two other co-formants of the ground of our life as embodied spirit: the genetic and the maternal. We can choose to focus onesidedly on either one or both of them, usually under the influence of reductionist form traditions. We can reduce all of human formation to genetics alone or to parental determinants alone.

Resentment or fear of the harshness of a functionalistic society can drive us back to our maternal beginnings, but this is not a necessary or predetermined course. Transcendent traditions teach us how to find easement from the severity of functionalism by abiding in the mystery at the root of our founding form in its transcendency. Without the light of tradition, we may misunderstand the call of the transcendent as the call of the lost or never enjoyed maternal paradise with its real or imagined consolations. We are tempted to reduce the mystery itself to a supermaternal ambience of tranquilizing comfort. The symbols of some traditions accommodate this anxious pursuit of a sublime shelter of cosmic soothing.

Any tradition is vulnerable to infection by directives that are stuck in vitalism. These directives have not been inwardly transformed and aligned by our transcendent dimension. They turn alignment into mere compromise or sublimation. The warped tradition becomes a sophisticated symbol of vital gratification. Such adherents intend focally the transcendent meaning of the symbol. Infrafocally they are in search of vital gratifications, at times camouflaged as sublime experiences. In other words, people may strive focally for absorption in a cosmic transcendent realm while infrafocally they aim for vitalistic fulfillment as ultimate.

Transcendent Formation, Conditioning, and Form Traditions

Let me clarify my distinction between transcendent formation and conditioning. Both have a place in the story of our unfolding. Transcendent formation is guided by spiritual choice and insight. Conditioning should be secondary and subordinated to transcendent formation. A conditioning or programming of our neuroform should be directed by the spirit, but this is not always the case. At times conditioning takes place directly. It bypasses, so to speak, the spirit and hence eclipses transcendent control. In infancy this is unavoidable. Later in life it happens too. A shocking event, such as the fall of a German missile that malfunctioned near my neighborhood in World War II, conditioned my neuroform for some time to uncontrollable anxiety reactions any moment I heard an explosive sound. My lower vital-functional brain triggered the sense of mortal danger I felt before. My spirit can only give new human form to this reaction by making me slowly aware of its irrationality, of the difference in situation, of the possibility of integrating it in some transcendent view of life and death. Then my forming spirit reconditions my brain, its hormonal output, its impact on my autonomic nervous and organic systems. Briefly it relieves and modulates the neuroform of my life. A consonant life is marked, therefore, by a certain ease in regaining the balance between transcendent formation and subordinated conditioning every time this harmony is lost.

I apply this same insight to the inner alignment of our vital dimension. Remnants of its early infantile conditioning stay with us even when we attain adulthood. Such residues will sound through in our transcendent form traditions without necessarily deforming them in a significant fashion. People who for some reason reject a transcendent tradition will point to such vestiges of immaturity to suggest that the tradition as a whole is nothing but a regression to infancy. Careful observation will disclose that such people tend to generalize prematurely such remnants of immaturity in adherents of a tradition itself.

We should strive for a balanced formation of our own tradition pyramid. As its base we should want a transcendent tradition. Beyond this base other traditions need to be aligned with the fundamental tradition to which we are committed. We want all of them to become increasingly congenial with our given unique-communal life call. What may hinder us in this call to unique-communal formation is the reemergence of certain facets of the pyramid of our parents we thought we had grown beyond completely. What is the story behind this reemergence of past parental forms?

Reemergence of Parental Pyramid

We receive our original tradition pyramid from our parents. After this reception in childhood we entered a formation phase that I call *the period of confrontational appraisal*. We no longer accept without any personal appraisal all forms of parental and familial tradition. Some of them we dislike and reject. Not having worked through this rejection, unable to live with our resentful refusal in daily relations with our family, we may push them out of our focal and prefocal consciousness. They sink into its infrafocal region. Because this happens impulsively and is maintained compulsively, it is not a transcendently formed refusal but a vitally conditioned rejection, the price of which will be paid later in life. We may discover to our surprise that much of our tradition pyramid looks strikingly like that of our parents, even the facets we rejected long ago with such vehemence. They may have gone underground for a period of latent formation, but they have come back with a vengeance, with an even more intense formational power than they had before. Our original vital-affective identification with the parental tradition pyramid proved stronger than our emotional refusal in adolescence and young adulthood. This process of the reemergence of what is rejected can happen for better or worse. It all depends on the consonant or dissonant quality of what is now powerfully reemerging in our tradition pyramid.

No superficial sublimation can save us from the power of early traditional conditioning of the vital life. Only its inner transformation through alignment with the life of the spirit in the light of transcendent traditions will recondition the vital dimension.

Eros, Transcendent Love, and Formation Tradition

Human life is a dynamic aspiration for transcendent, universal love and consonance. Consonance with all that is and with its creative source is the wellspring of transcendent peace, happiness, and joy, at times reverberating in our pretranscendent life. Potentially corresponding with transcendent aspiration is eros on the vital level. If vital eros becomes aligned inwardly with transcendent love, it will be a source of consonance. It will grow into what I term *transeros*. Eros points already in its very makeup to a transcendent consonance. It is more than mere vital desire. A penchant for deeper consonance, for a deeper pleasure called joy, be it ever so faint, covibrates in the human eros. Therefore, we cannot speak about eros in animal existence. This covibration of a hidden longing for transcendent love and joy explains why some form traditions over the centuries have confused eros and love as totally identical.

Earlier I introduced my notion of an autarkic self-centered form of life, the pride form. This form is a powerful interloper. It pretends to be our true founding form, but there is an abyss between the two. Our original form is basically open to the not-self, the other, the cosmos, the radical mystery; it is always in search of connection, of the joy of loving consonance. Our quasi-founding form is closed in upon itself. It keeps the eros of our vital life self-absorbed, seeking relationships for its own gratification alone. It is averse to an expansion of selfless love. The autarkic pride form paralyzes the inner tendency of eros toward alignment with transcendent love, toward becoming transeros.

Tradition pyramids are susceptible to distortions by the autarkic form of life. Our aspiration for true love and consonance is drained by a blocked pretranscendent eros that has become exclusively self-indulgent. The vibrant energy of transformation is sidetracked in erotic attachments to exclusively preferred persons, events, things, and situations in isolation from the whole of the formation field, its wider horizons, and its cosmic and radical mystery. These ties carry the delusive promise of ultimate love and consonance. They stir in us the fear of losing what we desire so ardently. Inordinate, isolating attachments create in us the "never enough" syndrome. For the pretranscendent limited erotic forms in which we invest our hope for happiness will never be enough to give us the security, joy, and peace, the fulfillment of dreams for which we are yearning in the depth of our being. We become obsessed with a need for more and more under the misappraised longing for we know not what. We shall never be satisfied.

Our inordinate attachments grow, stretching themselves out further and further. Our hearts become encumbered by an increasing variety of safety and security directives to protect these attachments. We are filled with desires for exciting conviviality with others, for pleasure and sensation, for satisfaction of our pretranscendent will for power and control. We find ourselves caught in a network of isolating, frustrating attachments. We identify with this strangling web as if it were all of our life, our real self. Any threat to it evokes anxiety. To cope with this anxiety people tend to develop what I call *self-shielding traditions* that protect and hide the false delusional form of life. They justify one's attachment system by sharing it with like-minded others within these traditions. They create directives of personal and social life that are driven by anxiety and proliferating security strivings instead of by love and reason. The subtradition of many Christian landlords and military rulers with their death squads in South America or the apartheid tradition of leading groups of white South African Christians or of anti-Semites are examples of such absolutized self-shielding form traditions. They may turn basic Christian form traditions into exclusively self-shielding subtraditions.

Other subtraditions invent seemingly magical directives. They misinterpret symbols, sacraments, devotions, blessed objects as magic protections of one's piously colored selfish interests. We can say that such self-shielding traditions are shared *contraformations*. We give them their defensive, aggressive, or magical form over against (contra) the threats to our self-centered dreams, false ideas, warped affections, possessions, things, or privileges to which we are desperately strapped. We believe them to be indispensable sources of an imagined ultimate happiness. These powerful bindings are indirectly energized by unacknowledged longings in our transfocal consciousness for the joy of universal self-forgetful love and consonance, liberating us from our isolation. Some of this transfocal dynamism infiltrates our nonfocal consciousness. Deformed by its delusional elements this region of consciousness deepens our attachment strivings. It intensifies our inclination to make some of these ties absolute.

A self-shielding form tradition becomes a finely developed safety mechanism. It is the sum total of efforts made by adherents to devise a security system that neutralizes their anxiety. This anxiety is evoked by threats to their shared isolating attachments to certain goods, customs, and privileges as ultimate.

All traditions of one's pyramid can be perverted into self-shielding systems. At the height of Nazi power in Germany, groups of people interpreted every form tradition in their pyramid in the light of self-shielding of the Aryan superrace. Examples are the German philosophical tradition as in the case of the Nazi-appointed university president Martin Heidegger; the religious tradition, as in the groups of Christians for Hitler and the fatherland; the art tradition, such as the entourage around the Wagner festivals; and the medical tradition, such as the eugenetic physicians.

A society as a whole can be deformed by a significant number of people with such flawed tradition pyramids. Within such a society, as long as the self-shielding tradition holds absolute political power, everyone who shares this tradition pyramid is rewarded with better chances for social acceptance and promotion. Society itself, however, becomes a parody of what human life should be like.

In the Synoptic Gospels, Christ speaks about the perversion of traditions: "You have made a fine art of setting aside God's commandment in the interest of keeping your traditions! For example, Moses said, 'Honor your father and your Mother'; and in another place, 'whoever curses father or mother shall be put to death.' Yet you declare, 'If a person says to his father or mother, any support you might have had from me is *korban*' (that is, dedicated to God), you allow him to do nothing more for his father or mother. That is the way you nullify God's word in favor of the traditions you have handed on. And you have many other such practices besides" (Mark 7:9–13). In this way tradition pyramids can become sources of malformation.

Usually our tradition pyramids are partly consonant, partly dissonant. To the degree that unsolved anxiety dominates our life, we are tempted to distort our traditions. To cope with anxiety we look out for anything that can turn tradition directives into protectionist walls against our feelings of insecurity and insufficiency. We may clutch at any meaning that can be used against real or imagined powers that intimidate us.

For many these intimidating powers are symbolized by the paternal tradition pyramid. In early childhood they were confronted with the father figure as a first threat to their awakening to vital-functional freedom. As a consequence, later in life they may be anxiously seeking in their own pyramids how they can find contraforms against anything that reminds them of paternalistic power. This search turns symbols and sayings of any of their traditions into the weapons I call contraformations.

To summarize what I have said so far, a self-shielding and self-serving tradition pyramid is:

1. riddled with prefocal and infrafocal anxiety-evoking protectionistic contraformations;

2. strives at times to return to our real or imagined or hoped for maternal ambience of infancy in the form of substitutes;

3. is a source of inner dissonance, tension, and crisis;

4. thwarts the formation of trust, love, and consonance in everyday life and society;

5. leads to judgmentalism, discrimination, prejudice, and social injustice.

Form Traditions and Interformation

Formation traditions are interformational systems. As such they cannot be fully understood from an imagined isolated inner formation of the intraform of our life. Our intraform assimilates first of all the interformational facets of our tradition. For example, children born into the Quaker tradition assimilate its form of life by spontaneous interformation with their family and other members of the Quaker community. Interformation is first. The inner formation of children accompanies or follows it.

In accordance with this principle of interformation, the ways of formation are not only the source of new form traditions; they are also the product of interformation with elements of former traditions. For example, the Marxist tradition of the former Soviet Union is in great measure the result of Bolshevik ways of giving form to society; yet it is also in part a product of certain autocratic facets of the Czarist formation tradition. Elements of this tradition survived in the form given to the tradition pyramid of Stalinist communism. The Czarist tradition in turn was formed over centuries of giving form to the revered notion of an absolute monarchy.

Contra- and Counterformations

Form traditions are sources of pluriform cultures in which they play a significant role. We can trace such cultures back to elements of these traditions, no matter how deformed by syncretism or compromises as well as by contra- and counterformations they may be. My distinction between contra- and counterformation is important here. *Contraformations* evolve over against something inside or outside of us that we fear, reject, or oppose as such, for instance, some people absolutely reject all authority. *Counterformations* are expressions we use to counterbalance, check, or complement something we accept and respect. For instance, in a constitutional kingdom we counterbalance monarchical authority and privilege by laws and by a democratic representation of the people.

From these examples it may be clear that both contra- and counterformations, evolved by various traditions, play an important role in a culture. In our American culture, for instance, we see the many counterformations, the systems of checks and balances in the government. Many of them emerged from the traditions of people who fled governmental persecution in European countries of that period. Contraformations are expressed in the numerous allowed and protected protest movements against practices that are rejected by various traditions in our pluritraditional culture.

Relative Autonomy of Form Traditions

Form traditions are not subject to the arbitrary whims of their followers. These traditions are in part autonomous. They have a power of their own. As such they determine in some measure the formation of our vital-functional strivings. It is true that our vital make-up modulates to some degree a personal living out of our form tradition, but this does not mean that it takes away the primacy of these traditions.

For example, a particular Scotch Calvinist gentleman may be vitally more temperamental and emotional than a Catholic southern Italian. He may change his style of self-expression slightly as compared with the common style of Scotch Calvinist traditions. He may be somewhat more outgoing, more warmly affectionate than other adherents of his faith. Yet he will not be as exuberant in word flow and gesticulation as the southern Italian, who may share the vital emotionality of the Scot. Conversely a southern Italian lady of Sicily, with less emotional vitality than her Scottish counterpart, will still express her limited emotionality in a more exuberant fashion than she would if she were born and raised as a lady in Edinburgh.

This principle of my personality theory applies to all vital drives. It is opposed to the prescientific assumptions of some representatives of the social sciences who are less focused on the formation field as a whole than I am. They observe in therapy that patients have lost their freedom of form expression because of a domination by vital aggressive or sexual drives. This affects the way in which these patients see the meaning of the symbols of their traditions. Obsessed by libidinal problems, they may see, for example, church towers only as phallic symbols. The theoreticians of the school, impressed by the repetition of such cases, under the influence of certain local and temporal traditions, created a whole system of meanings of such symbols for all people, no matter their particular form traditions or personal life formation. What they were in fact creating was a new ideological form tradition that, by means of the media, may be popularized and may affect then the formative symbol systems of large groups of people. A highly cultivated system of libidinal meanings of symbols is made available to people, many of whom would not have seen before the same symbols in the light of this interpretation. By now some of these symbols may have become part of their own tradition pyramid.

CHAPTER 17

Transcendent Form Traditions and the Vital Erotic Facet of Human Love

I n previous chapters I introduced the issue of vital erotic formation and its relationship to tradition. This facet is crucial for human unfolding. All kinds of derailments and conflicts are possible here. Therefore, the topic merits more consideration in this chapter. Let me first summarize what we have reflected upon thus far and make it more explicit.

Tradition and Formation

Our founding life form or call is initially preempirical. This means it is not yet known by the infant him- or herself in an empirical-experiential way. Nevertheless the child begins already to give form to the core of his or her emergent empirical-experiential life. The form that this core will gradually assume is one of relatively enduring basic dispositions that in turn give rise to manifold attitudes and acts that congenially and compatibly implement these fundamental dispositional directives in one's formation field. Dispositions are symbolized for the child by formational-directive symbols in its formation field.

This field is coformed by the initial maternal ambience and its gradual extension in the paternal and wider familial sphere with its particular form traditional structure. Another more internal but still veiled aspect of the forming field of childhood is the child's genetic predispositions as well as vague hints of his or her founding life form or the call to which it gives rise.

The formational influence of the early vital erotic facet of human life is considerable. It is at the center of our initial core or character formation. Remnants of the initial vital erotic core formation tend to reemerge later in life. Important in this stage of formation are the infantile erotic reactions that easily become vitally aggressive when vital erotic needs are not fulfilled. These resistances are reactions to attempts by formationally significant others to force the vital erotic life of the infant prematurely into the personally or idiosyncratically modulated form traditional pyramid of the family.

The forms these reactions take, their effectiveness or ineffectiveness, their interformation with the genetic predispositions of the child, their observed influence on the responses of others, will mark the emergent character formation of children for a lifetime. They will implicitly give form to the child's prefocal dispositions toward the form traditions in which they are raised insofar as these traditions with their familial modulations are transmitted by the parents to their children.

Core Formation and Interformation in Infancy and Childhood

Infants cannot yet develop a focally appraising, personally interforming relationship with the traditions offered them in infancy. They cannot yet use the transcendent appraisal power of their human spirit. The form potency of transcendent appraisal is still latent. They do not yet sense the call of their own uniqueness. Each infantile striving is rooted in the child's genetic, vital, biochemical make-up. This rootedness is not yet complemented by the child's own appraisal of its genetic predispositions. This appraisal later will be enlightened by one's own pyramidic structure of transcendent traditions. There is thus a separation between the infant and the form traditions embodied in the maternal ambience.

If deformed traditions are anxiously imposed by modes of coercion in fearful families, they have mainly a repressive function. They do not initiate real inner growth and openness to future self-disclosure and change. Consonant transcendent form traditions should be communicated not by *modes of coercion* but by *modes of appeal*. Appeal has an animating, confirming, and creative function. Modes of appeal in infancy and childhood are implicit. They are embedded in the relaxed loving care, patience, and discipline of the parents. As such they are merely sensed, not explicitly known, by the child, yet their impact may last a lifetime.

Both the parentally lived transcendent tradition structure as well as its lived deformations give form in the child to a vital incorporation of a form traditional set of core dispositions. These constitute the base of the traditional coformant of the core form. The traditional coformant of the core form embodies dispositionally the traditions to which people adhere. Once the awareness of the founding life form emerges, a process of interformation with this basic ground begins to unfold. It is a dialectical interaction between emergent inner manifestations of the call to uniqueness and the basic expressions of the form traditions initially received on the vital level in infancy and early childhood.

The observable reality of this unfolding interformation leads me to deny the assertion of some theories of social sciences that the directives of childhood are all powerful, that they definitely determine all later formation of life. The interformation between the core form of people, received in childhood, and their own unfolding and changing tradition pyramids is dynamic. This dynamism is enhanced to the degree that traditions are understood and lived in their transcendent meaning and power. This implies that through this relatively free and insightful interformation, new needs, ideas, images, symbols, ideals, and corresponding directives can emerge. Through them people can change the core form, heart, or character that they acquired in childhood by vital symbiosis. For example, I integrated critically, after much appraisal, some elements of the form traditions of the social sciences into my own tradition pyramid. I gained new ideas and form directives. After a period of incubation, they changed and enriched some of my traditional core dispositions adopted in childhood.

Deformed traditions, transcendent as well as pretranscendent ones, may be fearfully and coercively imposed. We submit to them merely as shields against anxiety. Used in a protectionistic way they can encase our whole existence in infantile contraformations.

Vital Eros and Transcendent Form Traditions

Transcendent form traditions are rooted in underlying transcendent faith traditions. They are not merely the result of infantile vital eros. Formation traditions emerge from the historically ongoing interformation between two sources of insight and option. A first source is the foundations of the faith tradition, including their authoritatively agreed upon theological or ideological developments. The form this authority takes depends on the faith traditions concerned. In some, for instance, it may be the majority consensus that functions as authority, in others a hierarchical authority. The other source of insight and option is the historically and personally changing traditional coformant of the core form, heart, or character of the adherents of traditions. This traditional coformant of the core form changes through another type of interformation, namely, our core interforms with the successive formation fields in which the faith tradition has to be lived compatibly and effectively. We can observe in the history of formation an ongoing interformation between the foundationals of the faith tradition and this ongoing change in their traditional implementation. This change results from the disclosure of the unique-communal life call by adherents of a tradition and their dialogue with successive changes in their formation field. At times of great change in the field, this process is accelerated. Such change may result in a temporal vacillation in the traditional coformant of the core form of the parents. Children born and raised in such a period may assimilate this vacillation in some way in their own emergent core form. This will make their initial core form different from that of children in more stable periods of the history of formation.

Traditions as Camouflaged Expressions of the Vital Eros

Dealing with the interformation between vital eros and tradition, we are faced with the orthodox psychoanalytic theory that all cultures, religions, and, by implication, all religious traditions are camouflaged expressions of, or protections against, our libidinal erotic drives. We have to ask ourselves what grain of truth may be pointed to in this assertion and what in it may be incompatible with our observations in formation science.

First of all, we should not too glibly charge such theorists with a merely biological outlook. This is too simplistic an interpretation of their formulations. My comprehensive field approach has taught me how strong the interformational drift is between all dimensions of human life, whether they are biological-vital or transcendent-spiritual. This interformation influences even the formulations and observations of theoreticians who may seem to claim they are exclusively biological in their approach to human life. Because of this always ongoing interformation, I can say, as a comprehensive field theorist, that our biological nature is always already in some measure affected by some typical human life directives.

When I study Freud in this light, I am struck by his emphasis on *meaning*, which is not a biological notion. When he introduces the notion of meaning, he opens the door to all kinds of meanings, including transcendent ones. Appraising the case studies of psychoanalysis, I realize that patients tell as fact what often proves to exist only in their imagination. Psychoanalysis is indeed about the imaginary form that people give to their field of life by means of the formative power of imagination. We have the form potency and corresponding inclination to give form to images and symbols. These in turn have a formationally directive influence on our life. Psychoanalytic thought is about the existence and dynamics of images and symbols, their meanings and dynamics, as they emerge in our unconscious. In my theory and terminology the Freudian unconsciousness can be somewhat likened to my notion of the infrafocal region of consciousness. These images and symbols are linked by the psychoanalyst to the repressed libidinal-erotic and aggressive drives in the unconscious. Freud himself would explain culture, religion, and by implication all religious traditions as camouflaged expressions of these unconscious symbols and images and their underlying drives. The authority and genius of Freud makes me cautious. Is there something in our transcendent form traditions, especially when they are deformed, that made him observe these libidinal influences in the way in which his patients talked to him about their religious traditions?

Vital Erotic Symbols, Meanings, and Form Traditions

From psychoanalytic case studies, it becomes obvious that what is decisive for human formation and its traditions is not what happens objectively. What forms people is how they experience what happens. We are not allowed to reify, that is, to make merely an objectified measurable thing or fact out of an event that is reported to us by people as having a forming influence on their life. In my science I would ask what is the formational meaning for this person or this tradition? How does it give formative or deformative direction to his or her life? The same could be said for adherents of a form tradition. What does an event, symbol, or image mean to them? How does it direct them to give form to feeling, thought, and action? Can camouflaged erotic meanings play a role in a form tradition? How can I faithfully describe these formational meanings in both individuals and traditions?

The emergence, selection, option for, and elaboration of images, symbols, and their meanings is dependent on individual persons or groups of adherents. One cannot predict them with absolute certainty. One cannot claim a priori that the meaning of these symbols is always and everywhere identical in all details. This ties in with my principle of formation science that there is no exhaustive list of all possible symbols and images nor of their possible meanings and directives. We cannot exactly predict the future meanings and directives of a human formation field. The reason is that this field of presence and action, including its ubiquitous coforming traditions, is not merely a collection of objective facts. Each so-called fact or event receives its formational meaning and direction from people who experience and live these events in the light of their formed and/or deformed pyramid of form traditions.

Unfortunately the real intention of many outstanding theorists of the social sciences is often obscured by their own creation and use of a system of mechanistic constructs they apply uncritically to all the meanings of the symbols, myths, and images they disclose in patients or in the formation traditions of these patients. Certain patients may use the symbols and myths of their transcendent tradition to express exclusively their own repressed dreams and desires. This is an instance of personal deformation of the classical meaning of their tradition. But such incidents of therapy, even if multiplied, do not prove that the classical meanings necessarily correspond in all adherents of all periods of the tradition with the personal added meaning given by these patients.

Formation Traditions, Collective Unconscious, and Analogical Formation Power

Against my conception of numerous potential meanings of symbols, the following argument may be raised. Many social scientists have pointed out that the same meaning of a symbolic object is expressed in many cultures or in their underlying traditions. And this happens in widely divergent periods and places, often independent of each other. There must thus be an unchangeable meaning of symbols to be found in a "collective unconscious" of humanity, to use a popular Jungian phrase.

I do not find this argument cogent. As a formation theorist, I make a distinction between the *actual* meaning given to symbols by individual persons or specific populations as well as by faith and form traditions, and the *potential* meaning. Potential meanings *can* be disclosed by the imaginative form potency, which is shared by all people of all times because of their shared basic human form of life. I call this the *analogical form potency* of humanity. A person, animal, plant, thing, or event may have characteristics that make them potentially analogous, that is, partly alike. This similarity between their appearances evokes our universal human imaginative form potency to follow its laws of analogical thought and imagination. These are laws of similarity and of formational relevance. In accordance with these laws, the analogical power in any human being, group, or tradition of any time can give a similar meaning to a similar object relevant to a same formational concern.

For example, people can be obsessed with coercive sexual fantasies and desires due perhaps to sexual problems that emerged under the influence of their deformed traditions or their resistance to them. Their analogous imagination can make them disclose in every pointed object, be it a regal scepter, the staff of a shepherd, or a broomstick, an erected male genital and in every hollowed receptacle, such as a bowl, a vagina. They disclose this analogical form because there is a resemblance between the two. All humans of all times, places, and traditions are endowed with the same creative analogical form potency. All of them are subjected to the same laws of analogy and formational relevance. Therefore, all are liable to see under the same circumstances the same resemblances and to give analogical symbolic form accordingly. By the same token, under other circumstances, their analogical formation power will disclose other resemblances relevant to their different experiences as modulated by different form traditional structures.

In summary, when exposed to other conditions in their field of life, the analogical formation power of people will disclose other resemblances in the same symbols. For example, the adherent of a particular religious form tradition can see a pointed church tower as pointing to heaven, an empty bowl as an image of our self-emptied receptivity for grace and forgiveness. It is also possible that one and the same object is endowed with different imaginary symbolic meanings in accordance with the different form traditions in our pyramid that come into the foreground selectively in the varying situations we meet in our field of presence and action.

I conclude that nothing demands the construct of a mysterious collective unconscious of humanity. I submit that my concept of an analogical formation potency can explain sufficiently why similar symbolic forms may emerge when people anywhere are faced with similar objects of analogical resemblance within a somewhat similar field situation.

It can take a long time and considerable skill for the formation therapist to disclose the individual meanings and dynamics of image and symbol in a person and how these are related to the symbols and meanings of the individual's tradition pyramid. The same applies to the traditions themselves and their nonfocal symbols and meanings. For the same reason it is not always possible for our auxiliary social sciences to disclose the nonfocal meanings and symbols that play in our form traditions.

Eroticized Traditions

Traditions as such are not derivatives of the infantile eros. They have their own creative power and function. Core dispositions in children are coformed by parentally transmitted traditions. They are not innate and unchangeable instincts. They vary with the variations of tradition pyramids and their interaction with one's unique life call and field. For example, the Oedipal disposition is not a given of nature but a form traditional given. This explains why we cannot find this disposition in the adherents of all form traditions in all cultures, continents, and countries. In other words, a formation tradition cannot be adequately explained out of the history of one's individual vital-erotic formation in childhood. On the contrary, beside our genetic preformation our form traditions with their individual parental modulations are also an important source of the diversity of the initial formation story of people.

There is thus a basic difference between traditions and the vital erotic life. Their dynamics can fuse with one another, but each has a different origin. Vital erotic drives can embed themselves in the rivers of traditions, but they do not create these rivers.

The same applies to the myths, rites, and symbols of a tradition. Their original, classic meaning can be understood adequately only out of the traditional system itself and its history, not out of the childhood problems of those who adhere to these traditions. It is something else again that these classic givens of the tradition can be used by people to image their vital erotic problems and relationships in their search for a solution.

Formation science, therefore, does not say that the sexual-erotic becomes desexualized by a transcendent tradition and so becomes acceptable in the tradition and in society. I would put it the other way around: a tradition sometimes becomes eroticized in a pretranscendent fashion by a number of its adherents. All traditional symbols and relationships can be colored by the erotic strivings of individual adherents or groups of them. Religious tradition and eros can penetrate each other. Religious form traditions should guide and facilitate the alignment of erotic and transcendent strivings. But that does not prove that a religious tradition as such finds its origin in pretranscendent erotic desires alone. It would only mean that a religious form tradition can either be degraded to a mere tool of expression of an autarkic, self-centered, isolating vital eroticism or present a guiding warm enlightenment for integration and alignment of eros and transcendence, so that transeros may emerge. For example, the interpenetration of religious experience and erotic arousal can sometimes be observed in affective sensual religious ecstasy. The emotional ecstasy may radiate from one brain center to another. This radiation can also touch the center for vital erotic sensuality.

An example of a mixture of religious transcendence and not yet wholly transformed eros is given by Reverend Oskar Pfister, one of the earliest students and friends of Freud. He brought to light the refused eroticism of Count Ludwig von Zinzendorf as manifested in its return in camouflaged forms in his ecumenical pietist spiritual life. The count was a cofounder of the Hernhutters (1700–1760). (See Pfister 1925).

If the symbols of tradition and their meanings do not necessarily arise out of camouflaged vital erotic strivings, from whence do they come? They have grown out of the need of any tradition-community to assert and communicate its form identity and direction. We are faced here with a set of dynamics essentially different from those of the vital eros. Therefore, it generates different symbols. For example, one such symbol is that of the meaning of marriage within a tradition. Marriage binds people together, not only two individuals but whole groups. It has implications for the community as a whole. Therefore, a transcendent form tradition will express this union in a rite that symbolizes the sacred ties that keep the new community together and fills marital eros with a deeper meaning.

I conclude that transcendent traditional myths and symbols as such are originally not the expression of a repression of the dynamics of the vital eros. They belong to a totally different realm of reality. They express the sacred relations, aspirations, and inspirations characteristic of a transcendent tradition, yet the same traditions should facilitate the alignment and integration of erotic and transcendent love.

Encounters and Collisions of Form Traditions

If different form traditions encounter each other, something happens to them. Often there is a collision. Some anthropologists have tried to explain this collision in terms of anxieties evoked by a return of the repressed vital eros with its unsolved relationship problems within the family. As a result, the adherents of a tradition would feel threatened by the other traditions. Their infantile repressed eros seems embattled again in its competition for eros fulfillment in the family. Hence a collision and deeply emotional feuds occur between traditions. The repressed infantile dispositions, rebellions, and guilts are then projected onto the other form traditions entering the arena to fight for loving adherents.

From the viewpoint of my formation science, I do not deny the possibility of such dynamics. I only want to point out that they are not necessarily operative or primary in all collisions of form traditions. For the formation scientist things are more complicated. When one tradition encounters another within a pluritraditional culture, a complex process of selective interformation begins to develop accompanied by fear of loss of identity and territorial power. The process in most adherents is either pre- or infrafocal. It is quite possible that in a number of them it becomes an occasion for a simultaneous return of repressed aspects of unsolved problems of competition for eros fulfillment in infancy. This complicates the collision for them, but the return of the repressed eros competition is not necessarily the main origin of all collisions between formation traditions.

Processes of Reinterpretation and Selective Reformation

The processes of encounter, mutual appraisal, and unavoidable social and professional interaction as participants in the same formation field put one's initial rejection and misinterpretation of the alien tradition into question. The disclosure of consonant aspects in the adherents of this other tradition makes one ask if they can enrich one's own tradition. All of this can take place in the prefocal region of consciousness. In the long run, this process leads to a reinterpretation of our basic form tradition as well as of elements of other traditions already represented in some way in our form traditional pyramid. Initially the need for reinterpretation and reformation of our familiar tradition structure, in which we invested so much, is resented, feared, and rebelled against. But the necessity to live and work compatibly with adherents of the other tradition, to answer together effectively the same demands imposed on all by the ongoing changes in the shared field of presence and action, renews the resented quest for corresponding reformation of one's own tradition. After prolonged periods of collision, we may come to a reinterpretation of denied consonant facets of the other tradition and in that light reinterpret our own structure of traditions.

This reinterpretation is followed by a long and arduous process of critical selective reformation of one's pyramid. This often prefocal selection is guided by commitment to one's basic faith and form tradition and by the appraisal of one's unique-communal life call in a corresponding formation field. This guidance leads to the modulated adoption of some elements of the alien form tradition in one's tradition pyramid while other elements can be dismissed as uncongenial. The selected elements often receive a new meaning, one that is congenial with the core dispositions of one's tradition as well as with the dispositions evoked by one's unique-communal life call and genetic individuality. Also taken into account is the compatibility of the adopted elements with the inter- and outerspheres of one's field of presence and action.

For example, adherents of the Islamic form tradition in secularized Turkey took over such secular tradition elements as discarding the veil for women and not propagating holy war as a means of spreading the message of the Koran. Other secular elements, such as the neglect of prayer five times a day, were not taken over by committed adherents. The holy war ideal was not totally dropped either but received a new meaning, that of spiritual warfare.

Notice well, I do not deny that the dynamism of our vital eros, its problems, plots, and history, can play a powerful prefocal part in the encounter between formation traditions. My contention is only that they are not necessarily the exclusive or prime explanation of what happens in the collision of traditions. Not everything is vital erotic. A fusion of the erotic with the dynamics of the transcendent form tradition in such a collision is often to be expected. In that case it adds to the intensity and violence of the clashes between traditions that have to share the same field of presence and action and to appeal to the allegiance of the same population.

Similar processes of encounter and collision can take place between different form traditions of adherents of the same faith tradition. Examples can be found in the collision in early America between German and Irish Catholic form traditions, at present between certain Catholic white and certain Catholic Afro-American and Hispanic form traditions. We see the same between different Christian form traditions as well as between different Islamic form traditions in Lebanon. One cause of these violent clashes within the households of the same faiths is that the formation tradition is far more directly intertwined with the personal everyday life concerns and interests of people than are the theological faith traditions. Many of their adherents may not be emotionally evoked by a theological debate on the faith tradition, but they are aroused to passionate involvement the moment one touches upon their everyday familiar form tradition. If such involvement becomes complicated by a return of repressed eros conflicts in childhood, the inflamed passions may know no bound and the ensuing violence may be unconscionable.

CHAPTER 18

Transcendent Traditions and Transformation of Eros

Eros and Libido

My concept of eros differs from Freud's concept of libido. The distinction is rooted in our divergent theories. Freud put the libido at the heart of formation. I ascribe this central position to the "transcendence dynamic." Freud, seeing the libido as merely biopsychological, believes it to stay the same essentially, while accidentally changing itself in terms of objects, forms, and strategies. One common way in which this happens is through what he calls sublimation. In his thinking sublimation does not transform and enrich the libido itself inwardly and transcendently.

My theory integrates the biopsychological libido in the potentially or actually biotranscendent eros or what I call the transeros. This eros is at the core of our vital dimension, albeit latently initially. In the beginning it is overshadowed, temporarily at least, by the biochemical coformant of this dimension, which includes the physical aspect of the sex striving. Where Freud's and my theory differ is that I see the human eros as inherently and potentially receptive of an inner transformation that completes and fulfills its deepest latent orientation. This transformation turns eros into an infrastructure of transcendent or agapic love and appreciation. I do not mean a mere sublimation of only the objects, forms, and strategies of an unchanged eros. Eros with its powerful sexual and psychological coformants finds the fulfillment of its own deepest form-receptive potency when it becomes an infrastructure of distinctively human love and appreciation, also in its consonant sexual expression.

The human potency for expressions of transcendent love is neither isolated from nor identical with the human potency for pretranscendent expressions of libidinal and erotic love. Expressions of transcendent love strive to suffuse expressions of pretranscendent love inwardly, transforming them in the process. Eros, as initially pretranscendent, is inherently preformed and predisposed to this possibility of transcendent transformation, which will enhance and deepen its bioerotic beauty, power, and passion.

The call to distinctively human love dwells in us from the very beginning. It is latent in the depths of the human form of life. Slumbering in our hearts, vitalized by our passion, it is not the fruit of sublimation but a source of transformation of our pretranscendent bioerotic passion that dimly longs for infinite fulfillment.

As children we are not yet fully awakened to our inmost gift. Mostly we live by our vital eros. We feel animated by this potency for vital love, felt appreciation, lust for life and nature, vivid sympathy, not only in our relations with ourselves and people but also with nature, exciting events, familiar surroundings at home and neighborhood, flowers, trees, plants, stuffed and real pets. Eros vitalizes all human-cosmic interconnections.

In early childhood we are not yet open to the epiphanic meanings and form directives of what we like or love. We are bound sooner or later to be disappointed by the limits of what we enjoy vivaciously. Our boundless passion for life and bliss runs blindly into unyielding walls. Through the disillusions of eros in its pretranscendent phase we awaken to the possibility of a transcendent fulfillment of the deeper hunger hidden in its tempestuous craving. We experience disappointment and subsequent depreciation of what we thought would fulfill our erotic dreams and wishes. This may lead to a certain detachment from singular people, events, and things as ultimate sources of the ultimate, deepest meaning for our life. Detachment may be followed by incidental experiences of the reception and expression of gifts of transcendent appreciation and love in the depth of our being, renewing and purifying the fire of blunted erotic desires. Our eros, if still self-centered in the pretranscendent way, may abuse this gift. We can prevent or heal such perversion through the assimilation of the wisdom of classic transcendent traditions.

Eros and Transcendent Traditions

Transcendent traditions can be described as systems of symbolic structures that guide us on the way to transcendent love. This is a love that discloses the epiphanic depth of any form in our field. Transcendent love is dynamic. It expands and deepens continually if not interfered with. In the end it embraces cosmos and humanity as epiphanically appearing in our field and its horizons.

One recipient of transformation by this love is our vital eros. Transcendence and transformation in formation science do not mean a simple leaving behind, an indifferent passing by, or a rejection of what is transcended. On the contrary, in its very going beyond, transcendence discloses, affirms, elevates, and celebrates the authentic ground form of that which is surpassed. Transcendence liberates us from what we mistakenly and coercively appraise to be final and exclusive in and by itself alone.

Eros remains eros even if it fully shares in our graced transcendence. Transformed, it stands revealed in its inmost and richest possibilities. When I say "graced" transcendence, I am not using the term here in its technical, philosophical, or theological meaning as in a particular faith tradition. In pretheological formation science I use it as an indicator of the universal sense that the ascendance of eros is a gift granted by the mystery beyond us yet dwelling within us. It masters us instead of us mastering it. I distinguish this from what I call either "functional" or "vital" or "gnostic" transcendence. They refer to attempts to master side benefits of preliminary transcendence that can be manipulated. Gnostic Jungian, much New Age, Maslowian, Rogerian, transpersonal-psychological, and related techniques of "value clarification," of individualistic self-esteem, and of personality development partly represent such attempts. By their effectiveness in self-actualization or individuation, they may paradoxically and unintentionally block access to the higher path of graced transcendence. The good can become the enemy of the best.

Transcendence as aimed at in classic transcendent traditions brings us in touch with our finest aspirations and inspirations. Everything else in these traditions serves in some way this graced dynamism at the heart of our humanness. A classic transcendent formation tradition is a consistent structure of symbols, directives, and practices that point the way to transformation. They serve the formation of transcendence-oriented dispositions. These facilitate the joyous affirmation as well as the gradual transformation of our eros by distinctively human love and aspiration.

I believe that this description can make sense to a significant number of transcendent traditions in our pluriform world. The description distinguishes (not separates) my generic concept of a transcendent form tradition from more specified related concepts of any theological, ideological, or special spiritual tradition.

Key to Transcendent Affirmation of Vital Eros

What is the key to transcendence of the vital eros? I believe that it can be found in a double polarity. The first polarity is that of "appreciation and depreciation," resulting from the appraisal process. The way in which we appreciate and/or depreciate what we experience as gratifying our vital eros will have an influence on the degree to which we open or close ourselves to the transcendent dimension of life. Spiritually abused children whose bioeros was not helped to open up to warm vital interformation with parents, others, and nature are not spontaneously disposed to open up later in life to the transcendent fulfillment of an eros-in-transformation.

Intimately interwoven with this first polarity is the one that exists between pretranscendent appreciations/depreciations and transcendent appreciations/depreciations. We must experience the relativity and contingency of our pretranscendent appreciations and depreciations in the light of those that are more fully transcendent. Then we can give up our absolutized or inordinate attachments to what gratifies merely pretranscendent libidinal-erotic longings. Our vital passions may have become tyrannically coercive via our neuroform. We can liberate them not by denouncing them but by changing them in the light of traditional wisdom into *relative* appreciations that no longer dominate our strivings absolutely. Transcendent traditions of transformation are thus guiding lights on this path of eros elevation.

Depreciative experiences can collapse the pretranscendent hopes and dreams of our frustrated vital eros in its pretranscendent phase. They can stimulate us to open up to the power of transcendent appreciations. These are the cornerstones of transcendent love. Depreciation of the gratifications of an absolutized pretranscendent eros can be the result of many mutually related experiences. Among them are disappointment, low-grade depression, dejection, despondency, discouragement, frustration, let down, failure, boredom, disillusion, despair. All can lead to a depreciation of what the gratification of vital eros alone, before its graced transformation, can offer us.

Appreciation is at the heart of love. I can love only what I appreciate, cherish, long for, strive after. Transcendently I can love only what I appreciate and embrace as an epiphanous revelation of transcendent goodness, truth, and beauty. In our pretranscendent life, love usually means a vitally, erotically tinted appreciation of people and nature, of cosmic and aesthetic forms in exclusiveness and isolation. Such pretranscendent experiences have little or no reference to the epiphanic ground forms of what we appreciate. Missing also in them is an experience of covibration with all other forms and their mysterious source. This limiting and isolating type of appreciative love carries the seed of depreciation. For the finitude, contingency, and inherent transience of the objects of our lust for life may at any moment announce themselves. We fall into disappointment, grief, mourning, or enraged frustration.

The disappointment of mere pretranscendent erotic gratification may potentially disclose the gift of transcendent love. At the borderline of the frustrated pretranscendent eros, the gift of disclosure points implicitly to the joy and peace of ultimate transcendent love. Our readiness for this awareness is fostered by lingual and other symbols of transcendent faith and form traditions. These point to the basic dimension of everyday life and experience rightly called transcendent. Already the erotic infrastructure of this love, before it fully functions as such, contains hidden clues to the horizon to which it is oriented implicitly.

The transcendent epiphanic love dimension of human life can best be viewed by reflection upon the disappointment experienced in merely pretranscendent erotic love. Repeated disappointment in anticipated gratifications fills us with a passing or lasting depreciation of its promises. Disillusionment raises questions to which a response that we can properly call transcendent becomes meaningful. The preceding experience of depreciation of a mere pretranscendent erotic gratification is a key for understanding the distinction between pretranscendent and transcendent love. It is not as much a question of separation between erotic and transcendent love as it is a search for similarities and differences between these two kinds of love in service of their mutual integration. Without the warm, affective, at times passionate, animation of its erotic infrastructure, transcendent love grows cold and distant; it is easily perverted into an affair of the mind, not of the heart. On the other hand, vital erotic love cannot sustain its fire without completion by a loving appreciation of the epiphanic mystery in the beloved. Without this experience, erotic love is like a fast-burning match that ends in the ashes of disappointment and depreciation. The tediousness of everyday confrontation with the imperfections of one another and of nature deadens the song of mere pretranscendent erotic excitement.

Transforming Transcendence
Instead of Denial or Fulfillment of the Pretranscendent Life

Central to transcendent formation traditions is a concern for the transcendence of our pretranscendent life and its transformation. Many humanist formation traditions, to mention a few, the gnostic Jungian, Maslowian, Rogerian, some New Age spiritualities, and transpersonal psychologies, make functional-transcendent individuation, self-actualization, pretranscendent self-esteem, or self-fulfillment their basic concern. They foster an often sublime erotic love of self or of a group, of humanity or of aspects of the cosmos. They may propose sophisticated techniques to nurture mainly the lower, initial manifestations and side benefits of our transcendent life dimension.

These traditions do not demand an unconditional abandonment to a sovereign forming mystery, even at the cost of our own pretranscendent self-esteem, self-actualization, and individuation, were this its plan for our life. In this sense their central concern is for autonomous higher self-fulfillment, not a full transcendence of a mere pretranscendent love for self, individuals, cosmos, or humanity. Functional, manipulative transcendence is not real, full transcendence; it is handcuffed still to the functional autarky of the pretranscendent self-actualizing *I*. In the end it does not make a difference whether we are bound by a heavy cable or only a slight functional-transcendent thread to self-actualization as ultimate. Bound is bound. We cannot fly before we are redeemed from any binding.

According to classical traditions, one lives in true transcendence to the degree that one goes beyond an exclusively pretranscendent life. One can be aided in this ascent by the directives of formation science as articulated further in one's own basic form tradition and its transcendent directives.

Basic Transcendence Directives of Formation Science

The basic transcendence directives of formation science, as also related to transcendence of our bioeros, can be formulated dynamically as follows:

1. Awakening to the transcendent call to a unique-communal life of joyous love and service, animated by transformed eros.

2. Growing in the courage of candor to disclose the present demands of this call as well as our denials, resistances, and distortions in this regard. Disclosing candidly the guises a merely pretranscendent bioeros assumes, to give the appearance of transcendence to what is only a quasi transcendence.

3. Appraising and appreciating in all things the epiphanies of the mystery of formation. Appreciating the playfulness of the cosmic mystery in the gift of eros to humanity.

4. Being attentive to congeniality with one's call insofar as it manifests itself in daily life. Paying attention to the directedness and the intensity of eros. Being attentive to the degree of faithfulness to one's call to transform and enrich eros wisely and patiently.

5. Being compatible — without a compromise of congeniality — with the challenges and opportunities in the inter- and outerspheres of the formation field one shares with others. Being compatible not only in a cool rationalistic fashion but also in a warm vital way.

6. Growing in the courage of commitment to concrete flexible implementations of one's call in everyday life in docility to what is disclosed to one inwardly and outwardly. Growing in the courage to let vital-spiritual love tell its own heart-warming tale in the implementations of one's life call.

7. Growing daily in a transcendent joyous love and appreciation that affirms, celebrates, integrates, and wisely modulates the ardor of eros or lust for life in accordance with one's life call, tradition, and situation.

I believe that my seven transcendent form directives are among the basic conditions for the possibility of a distinctively human life formation and transformation, including the elevation and celebration of eros as transeros. In one way or another we find some of all of them in any transcendent form tradition insofar as it is consonant with the truth of the mystery of formation. We must come to understand and live these conditions as paths of transcendence. This requires regular exercise of the basic disciplines of formation as taught in classical traditions. Continuing spiritual transcendence, also of eros as merely pretranscendent, demands a detachment that often falters, inviting new efforts on our part.

Appreciation-Depreciation Questions

In our search for transcendent love, classical traditions inspire us to ask what I call appreciation-depreciation questions. Why does love and desire for oneself, for people, humanity, nature, animals, plants, and things meet with disappointment? How can we make sense out of our longing for endless love? Why are we unable to find any hope of fulfilling this desire when we look at our life experiences so far? Does anyone ever have an experience of appreciation and love without a secret fear of loss, disappointment, and the subsequent let-down of a period of depreciation? Can we, in the light of the teachings of transcendent traditions, go beyond or deeper into what we ardently love and desire? Do we then disclose in ourselves and others a ground so deep and embracing that it cannot disappoint us? Why and how does disappointment of pretranscendent love throw us at times into the abyss of depreciative existence?

Such questions, inspired by classic traditions, disclose to us both the borderlines of a merely pretranscendent erotic love and the unboundedness of transcendent love. Spiritual love penetrates, elevates and transforms our eros, our lust for life, enhancing, not killing, its amazing animation.

Transcendent love and appreciation present us with a final or grounding horizon for our love experience — not what some novels or movies may claim as the summit of love nor what the media and talk shows may propose as standards of appreciation. The truth of distinctively human love is not unveiled for us in the everyday babble of the crowd. The transcendent standard of love and appreciation lies within the horizon of our own distinctive humanness. To make our home in that horizon, we need to immerse ourselves, directly or indirectly, in the treasure of transcendent traditions. There we will find intelligent, reasonable, and responsible grounds for our loving appreciations. These classics will help us also in courageously implementing their wisdom in responsible action. Our use of the gift of reason, as illumined by classical traditions, will serve as a bulwark against the infiltration of a merely pretranscendent erotic self-centeredness into the ecstasies of spiritual elation. We are taught not only how to appreciate and love transcendently, but also how to experience that each of us is infinitely and uniquely loved and appreciated by an all-embracing mystery. A divine eros lingers at the heart of our existence. This graced experience grants us a fundamental affirmation of the unique dignity, worthwhileness, and warmth of our life, its meaningfulness, and its intelligibility.

The presentation thus far points to the depreciation that follows the disappointment of a merely pretranscendent eros. I see depreciation paradoxically as a gateway to transcendent love and appreciation. This insight is confirmed by classical transcendent traditions as well as by an analytical appraisal of disappointment and depreciation in everyday life. Formation science benefits from the unmasking of the deformations of classical traditions as concretely lived by people. We find such exposures of deformations in thinkers like Feuerbach, Marx, Freud, and Nietzsche, as well as in the scriptures and writings of many spiritual masters of various traditions. Their disclosures support our attempts to reform possible distortions and deformations in our tradition pyramid that hamper our ascendance to transcendent appreciation, love, and joy.

Disappointment-Depreciation
in Our Everyday Field of Formation

Depreciation situations evoke feelings of disappointment. Despondency may veil our liveliness when our eros can no longer vitalize our loving appreciations of the people with whom we are involved or of the tasks and pastimes in which we are engaged. Such disappointments and various states of depreciation emerge especially at occasions of failure, guilt, embarrassment, homelessness, loss of employment, rejection, fear, powerlessness, vulnerability, illness, heightened awareness of personal contingency in the face of one's own death or that of others, historical upheavals and social injustice. All such occasions remind us of the precariousness of life within an always changing society and wider world, which can betray our well-being at any moment.

Other awakening experiences imply the opposite. They are not depressing but uplifting, even exhilarating. These are experiences of heightened appreciation about what is good in life. They may emerge in the pretranscendent realm of life and rise to their fullness in life's transcendent dimension. We suddenly experience this higher dimension as a possible source of profound joy in our daily doings. These are experiences of aesthetic rapture, of inspiration and creativity, of deep delight about the goodness of life, of intimacy with God, with others, with art and nature. Some highly gifted people in the realm of self-expression, such as artists, actors, composers, and poets, can bring such experiential moments to life for us. Their own everyday existence may be lived in the shadows of pretranscendence. At the privileged moment of inspired acting, speaking, writing, or composing, they may dip into their transcendent life dimension and touch us by the genuine expression of what they truly sense spiritually, be it perhaps passingly. We may wonder about the abyss between those heights and the sometimes sordid quality of their public and private lives. These exceptional cases notwithstanding, many of us have had experiences that made us aware of passing the borderline of merely pretranscendent eros gratification. We found ourselves touching upon the transcendent dimension of love and joy. This experience can offer yet another clue to the life and love of the spirit.

Epiphanic Experiences

Let us return to the first point I mentioned, that of grave disappointment and the depreciation of life to which it leads. These "down" times can cause us to reflect on the boundaries of our pretranscendent erotic vivacity and lust for life. For example, when an intimate but merely pretranscendent love relationship is shattered, we may question the meaningfulness of a life that does not sufficiently go beyond pretranscendent erotic appreciation. This questioning may be enough to awaken us to the possibility of a life animated by eros yet transformed by transcendent love.

I call experiences of profound appreciation that slide over into the realm of transcendent appreciation *epiphanic experiences*. These are appearances or epiphanies of our call to transcendent joy and love. At moments of enhanced appreciation, we sense that we are called graciously to rise above absorption in appreciations stirred by our vital eros as merely pretranscendent. We implicitly experience the pointing of eros to an erotic-transcendent appreciation. Transcending appreciations cannot be adequately captured in terms of the rousing of pretranscendent eros alone. They put us in touch with a mystery indwelling cosmos, earth, and above all our human hearts. We cannot arouse ourselves to transcendent-erotic love by our own power of merely pretranscendent erotic love. We find ourselves in the power of a higher love that surpasses us while suffusing our hearts. We are spontaneously affirming our epiphanic appreciation of the transcendent meaning of that with whom or which we are in love. The gift of epiphanic appreciation enables us to transform and ground in a deeper way pretranscendent appreciations. Participating in transcendence, they, too, begin to disclose their deeper meaning.

Recall that I am speaking here generically from the perspective of formation tradition, not from that of a particular religious faith tradition. When we speak from the viewpoint of generic human formation about transcendent experiences as such we do not necessarily express them in the terms typical of any particular religious faith tradition.

Fundamental Option of a Basic Tradition

Our potential receptivity for the transcendent is sustained profoundly in its actualization by the transcendent tradition we have chosen as the basis of our tradition pyramid. In early childhood this can only be a borrowed option, implicit and prepersonal. As children we absorb by symbiosis the tradition pyramid of our family. Gradually we gain some freedom for a more personal option. Initially this will be a semifree cooption with our family. In that formation phase we begin to introduce hesitantly our first personal modulations. We may also seek some enlightenment from the sources themselves of the tradition transmitted to us. Such resourcing can grant us some distance from the familial or group modulations imposed on the original traditions during their transmission. Later in life we may enjoy the freedom of a personal option. We may freely commit ourselves to either our own personally chosen or personally ratified basic tradition. Insofar as it is a formation tradition, this option may entail personal modulations.

When a chosen tradition is ardently loved and appreciated, it will direct the unfolding of eros itself as well as that of the objects eros leads people to adhere to fervently as their focus of involvement. I think here not only of eros's animation of love for special persons but also of its enlivening of involvement in other things, such as nature, art, an enterprise, a system of thought, a community, a country, or political cause. Here, too, the basic tradition for which the artist, the entrepreneur, the thinker has opted codirects the unfolding of the consuming concern the impassioned appreciation of eros may have released.

A philosopher, for instance, can become fervently engaged in structuring a brilliant system around experiences of a tradition he or she intensely appreciates. The initial option in animated appreciation of this tradition will somehow color the unfolding of philosophical thought and imagination. The fiercely preferred tradition will guide his or her engagement in consonant or dissonant directions.

For example, people raised in one or more of the many formation traditions of Islam may believe passionately that the delights of paradise will instantly be theirs if they are blessed with death in holy war. True believers go into battle filled with inflamed animation, dying there without a trace of regret.

These examples illustrate how eros, both pretranscendent and transcendent, is not only itself given direction by traditions. Eros in turn influences the poignant choices of adherents who have fallen in love with their tradition. This applies not only to traditions but to all things and enterprises passionately appreciated in the light of one's tradition pyramid.

CHAPTER 19

Wounded Eros
and Transcendent Tradition

W hile eros rules the vital relations of infants within their surroundings, this is an eros not yet on the path of transformation. Infants
are not yet capable of the transcendent love that complements and transfigures vital eros. While young children are immersed in the traditions of
the family, they cannot yet personally grasp the deeper message of the transcendent customs communicated to them. Their erotic sympathy revolves
around their own vulnerable incipient selfhood. Like all human forms of
life, infants, too, live and grow in interaction with a limited field of presence and action, of care and play. They are receivers, not yet givers, of
care. They do not plan their life but live it from moment to moment. This
absence of rational concern enhances the influence of the vital eros with
its emotional swayings between sympathy and antipathy, feeling accepted
and rejected, desire and gratification.

Formational Meaning of Self-Centered Eros Phase in Infancy

Infants cannot develop a lively faith in the presence of the mystery at
the heart of their field of life. This mystery of grace and love cannot yet be
the transfiguring center of their existence. Instead eros makes them sense
themselves as the point of convergence of all facets of their small, still incoherent field of sensual presence. We should not see this as a calamity.
In the great scheme of life's gradual formation, reformation and transformation, this short period of self-convergence, unillumined by the inmost
meaning of the pointings of transcendent traditions to the mystery, has
a formational function. It is a remote preparation for the road to transformation later in life. It lays the groundwork for the experience to come
of "I am uniquely important and lovable" as well as for the experience
that "Nobody and nothing around me can fulfill my insatiable desires for
appreciation, love, and confirmation."

Children experience gradually the limits of the fulfillment of their self-
convergent eros fantasies. Their view of their field is challenged by reality.
They become aware that people, things, events are not turning around
them alone. They begin to experience that others cannot fulfill their bound-

less desires for eros gratification. During this crisis of eros, parents imbued with the wisdom of their transcendent traditions can help children to cope with the disappointing discovery that their surroundings are not there for the mere gratification of themselves alone. This disclosure marks the ambivalent beginning of a hesitant reaching out of eros beyond the self-centered fantasies it engendered. It sets the stage for a lifelong contest between self-love and love of others. Parents enlightened by tradition prepare the way for the later opening up of the infantile eros to the transcendent epiphanic meanings of things.

None of us can bypass this brief phase of eros formation necessarily initiated by a primitive eros that centers our field of life around an infantile vulnerable existence, crying out for protection and survival in a strange powerful world on which early life is totally dependent. Without inner direction and certitude, infants are moved by an unenlightened eros that they cannot control. They need for a short while this centering of their field around "his or her majesty, the baby."

Wounded Eros Later in Life

When parental confirmation is withheld, children may find it difficult to grow in the inner independent affirmation of the dignity of their unique-communal life call. Their eros may stay wounded; it may develop an insatiable hunger for external confirmation. For a lifetime such children may be in search of the confirmation they missed in childhood. Confirmation has to substitute for their lack of confident, inner self-affirmation in the light of transcendent traditions communicating to them their absolute worth in the eyes of an eternal mystery. Everything they imagine, think, anticipate, remember, and do is then appraised mainly from the prefocal perspective of "how can it gain me external confirmation that shores up my own unstable and weak inner affirmation?" The eros orientation toward others is infected by an overwhelming eros for self. One becomes oversensitive to any sign of absence or presence of confirmation by others. Others are mainly appraised as possible or actual sources of confirmation. The joy and peace of life is lost in this idle pursuit of a wounded eros for perfect confirmation that will converge every facet of the field of life on a constantly disappointed self.

All of us want some confirmation. Within the bounds of reality and reason, this is a healthy and normal desire. The question is how deep and comprehensive is this striving for confirmation, how much does it dominate our life, how seriously does it prevent the transformation of eros?

Our eros may be vulnerable because of our own lack of affirmation of our life call. This may give rise to an insatiable hunger for confirmation. This hunger can turn into a famine because of disappointment in others, who do not or cannot grant us the confirmation we want. Because of prolonged disappointment, we may sink into a low-grade chronic despondency.

Confirmation Highs and Confirmation Depletion

People who suffer from the syndrome of the I-convergence-need of childhood may always be in search of situations that will substitute, by means of endless confirmations, for their own missing transcendent self-affirmation. At times they may find abundant confirmation. Their eros is revitalized. They are lively and elated as long as it lasts. If circumstances end their supply of confirmation, their eros sags; they suffer confirmation depletion. When others attack them or expose their vulnerability, they suffer excruciating feelings of confirmation-disappointment. They are most vulnerable to this kind of disappointment. Its pain is deepened by the focal and nonfocal remembrance of untimely and inappropriate eros deprivation in childhood. This experience keeps pervading their infraconsciousness.

At times honor, status, success, power, and position may grant them passing "confirmation highs." Many people are inclined to pretend confirmation to those who are powerful, rich, or famous. They may pour streams of exuberant praise on those whose name, influence, and favors they want to share. I once asked a friend of mine who became a bishop what, if any, difference he experienced before and after his elevation. He smiled and said: "You know I am a rather dry person, not blessed with wit. Before being a bishop nobody laughed at my feeble attempts to joke; now they roar."

When fame, success, and power wane so does the flow of lavish confirmation, of bounteous applause, of servile admiration. The vulnerable wounded eros shrivels again when the wells of confirmation dry up unexpectedly by changes in the fluctuating history of success in one's life. The crisis is profound. Emptiness pervades one's heart. The animated vivacity eros brings to life seems frozen. Despondency begins to clog vital spontaneity. As long as the victims have no recourse through transcendent traditions to the inner affirmation of their unique-communal life call, they may have difficulty in resurrecting the spontaneous animation of a depressed eros. In the glorious past, now eroded by vacillating history, they clung to their confirmation highs as a source of the pseudo-meaningfulness of life. But these confirmations are no longer available to them. Without them, they cannot maintain a sense of self-appreciation, no matter how precarious it may seem. They attributed to power, possession, and popularity excessive importance. These assets of a triumphant pretranscendent life pale and stand demythologized in the cold light of their present everyday reality. They realize that respect can be replaced at any time by scorn and derision.

New Lesions and Impairments of Eros

The immense disappointment amounts to a new lesion of the eros. This leads to what I call *eros impairment* or a loss of the effervescent, childlike lust for life. In volume 1 of this series, I described and diagrammed the human formation field. Among the many determinants of our field consciousness, I spoke not only about spheres, dimensions, and regions but also about ranges, such as the personal, familial, and communal. Each range specifies our outlook on this field. We ourselves choose the influence we allow each of these ranges to have on our field vision. Problems develop when a particular range colors our experience of field facets to such a degree that it renders us out of touch with the autonomous reality or ground form of that facet.

For example, a family tradition of depreciation of people belonging to minorities may distort our vision so much that we can no longer see the real contributions of such persons to our shared field of life. Something similar can happen in the case of personal prejudices. Overwhelmed by the need for confirmation, we incorporate, as it were, autonomous facets of our field into our personal range alone. We see them no longer as also independent from us but merely as parts of our personality. At any time, however, they can reassert their independence and no longer give us the confirmation we hunger for so desperately. We make that field aspect an exclusive part of our personal range. It becomes for us an interiorized source of dependable confirmation. If we lose it, it feels like the amputation of a limb without which we cannot walk. Hence the new eros lesion leads to eros impairment.

We should listen to the message that every pain conceals. It cries out to us: face, appraise, and relinquish the anxious search for the convergence of your whole field of presence and action on your self-confirmation alone. No external changes can heal the lesion and impairment of eros. The cure has to come from the inside, from the intrasphere of life. We must have the courage of candor to realize that rage and anger come from a much deeper disappointment than the upset we normally experience when people let us down. It goes back to our basic eros lesion and impairment. The ground for it was laid perhaps in the parental neglect of the need for temporary field convergence on our vulnerable infant selves.

Healing of Eros Lesion and Impairment
Usually the parents who withhold their confirmation of what I call the *eros-convergence phase* in childhood have experienced the same in their own childhood. They passed their own eros deprivation on to their children. They may have been vaguely convinced by a deformed family tradition that this withholding would be best for their offspring.

The solution for a recurrent excessive confirmation need is not to keep trying to draw one's field of life exclusively into one's individualistic range of concern for confirmation. No inter- or outer aspect of the field should be made an integral and exclusive part of one's personality, of one's personal confirmation rights and sources. The only answer that works is to assess patiently for as long as it takes the eros lesion and impairment that is reawakened by present-day disappointments.

Immersing oneself in the wisdom of one's transcendent tradition can be of immense help in this labor of disclosure. So can formation direction, counseling, or transcendence therapy. One must begin to pay attention to moments of early emergence of the hunger for confirmation, to appraise it in the light of one's formation tradition, to link it to similar moments during one's life, a chain that goes back to infancy. One must allow oneself, to feel the emptiness, the useless and deformative suffering with its adverse bodily consequences that result from this tension. Then it is necessary to opt for another train of thought, imagination, desire, and action, enlightened and supported by one's transcendent tradition with its transformative wisdom.

There are many symptoms of the need for convergence of the whole field of life on a confirmation of oneself. Among them are fixation of one's eros on confirmation by others, even in such intimate relationships as those of marriage and family life. Other instances include: unrealistic self-exaltation; envy of those who are confirmed by persons one would like to be confirmed by; a secret striving for confirmation control; a hidden demand for signs and symbols of respect and deference; an anxious perfectionism in order to prove to God, oneself and others how well one deserves constant confirmation; the reduction of religion to a fullproof ethic system of behavior that guarantees divine and human confirmation; frustration, anger, and envy when some higher-placed person in an organization, who coordinated, inspired, and guided the use of the aptitudes of co-workers and subordinates, receives confirmation because of the overall success of the enterprise.

Wounded Eros and Wise Use of Aptitudes

Confirmation can come to us from many sources. Examples are a job well done, a work or organization wisely administered and developed, a company made prosperous and efficient, scientific research effectively performed, social justice strategies well planned and executed. None of them can be done in our contemporary complex society without the aid of other people. Nor can other people succeed in many of their enterprises without a wise use of our own aptitudes in one or the other aspect of their work.

Such necessary aid can involve a variety of aptitudes for organizing, making deals, and strategizing, for public relations, typing, filing, computing, editing, drafting proposals, cleaning, teaching, and so on. The great art and duty of creative leaders is to use wisely the aptitudes of those who work with or under them in service of a cause that is greater than all of them. Conversely such creative leaders must be willing to let their own aptitudes be used well with those whom they serve in the enterprises to which they are freely committed.

Notice that I speak about using aptitudes — not persons. We should never use other persons in violation of their own unique-communal personhood or founding form of life. Nor are we allowed to let ourselves, as persons of conscience formed by our own transcendent tradition, be used by others against our conscience and its underlying tradition. The crime of Hitler was not that he used the aptitudes of well-trained soldiers to defend the country if attacked, but that he violated their personal conscience by using them to attack other countries, to inflict death and torture on Jewish people and others, against the faith and formation traditions in which many of these soldiers were formed originally.

What we cannot avoid, if we are to be effective in the present interdependent world, is to make use of the aptitudes of other people and to allow others to make use of ours once we have committed ourselves to their enterprises. Nothing of consequence would otherwise get done. We should be careful not to make the increase of confirmation of ourselves the ultimate aim of the use of these aptitudes. Transcendent classical traditions teach us that they should be directed to a cause, work, project, or inspiration that surpasses all of us and that in some way serves humanity.

Unavoidable Confirmation of Effective Leaders

We cannot avoid confirmation of our work when we succeed with the aid of others. We should let them share in this confirmation. Whether we want it or not, often the visible leader of a project receives a greater share of confirmation than those whose aptitudes he or she enlisted in the project.

A bishop who uses the aptitudes of his clergy to the benefit of his diocese will be confirmed by most people who enjoy the better services and the growing reputation of their diocese. A hard-working administrator of a university department who uses the aptitudes of her faculty and staff cannot escape being confirmed by outsiders who see the growth of this department. A writer who makes use of the typing and computer skills of his collaborators will find confirmation when the published contribution to science or humanities is highly lauded.

Some of those who aid us may be suffering from eros impairment and confirmation hunger. Seeing the confirmation we cannot avoid as leader of a diocese, country, city, school, department, or industry, they may feel inundated by waves of envy. It reevokes the pain of wounded eros in their childhood. Their dream of the whole field of life converging on confirmation of them seems to become true for the praised leader only. She or he seems to get what their wounded eros longs for so desperately. Infraconscious anger, frustration, and rage may explode in gossip and accusation.

By contrast, people not plagued that way since infancy can rejoice that their limited aptitudes were wisely used in service of a higher aim, product, or project that benefits humanity in some fashion. But those who suffer hunger for personal confirmation will gripe: "I as a person was used; I was only used for a gain in the confirmation of gifted leaders, a confirmation I myself am so desperately longing for; what they have done is not at all serving a higher aim surpassing each of us, such as the good of my church, the country, the company, the diocese, the university." The overwhelming personal need for confirmation, the lack of joyous faith in one's own unique-communal life call, no matter how simple, the need for praise and applause is projected onto the envied persons of public achievement. They, like all others, had to put to good use the aptitudes of people engaged with or under them for the advance of a cause that is larger than any one of them. Transcendent traditions can teach us the wisdom and courage to graciously rise above this vulnerability.

Dealing with the Attacks of Eros-Deprived People

Many effective, inspired leaders of humanity had to cope with assaults of people, some of whom were effectively famined by the absence of confirmation in their infancy and by a lack of their own affirmation of their transcendent life call. Even saintly spiritual leaders suffered from this explosive rage of those under or around them. They, too, had to enlist the aptitudes of those who could not fathom the unique-communal life call and mission in those they were asked to follow. Abbot Benedict of Nursia, the founder of the Benedictine order, narrowly escaped poisoning by some of his enraged and envious monks. Teresa of Avila had to run out of a church when the faithful tried to attack her under the influence of the gossip spread by clergy and religious. John of the Cross was imprisoned and daily beaten by his own Carmelite confreres; later he was expelled from any leading function in the Carmel monasteries he himself had helped to establish and reform. Francis Libermann, the second founder of the Spiritans, was called by some of his confreres a schemer, a plotter, a fake, and a fraud, who manipulated the amalgamation of their new community with the old one of the Spiritans.

The exemplary strength of such great women and men persevering joyously despite such accusations was rooted in the inner affirmation of their unique-communal mission in life and world. Their immersion in their own transcendent faith and formation tradition deepened this commitment to their life call. Their belief in the message of their faith and formation tradition healed any remnants that could still have been lingering on as a result of a thwarted childhood hunger for confirmation.

The deeper our tradition-supported affirmation of our own unique-communal and mysterious life call is, the less vulnerable we are to any denial of the gift of confirmation by others. Instead of weakening us, attack and gossip will entrench us in our call. We shall go our way steadily as Teresa of Avila says with "determined determination." We will be enabled to heal any remnants of a wounded eros and to transform this impairment in the light of our transcendent formation traditions. Along the lines of the examples mentioned, we will keep alive the spontaneity, strength, and youthfulness that comes to us from the "fountain of youth," which is eros transformed by transcendent love and joy and to which the title transeros rightly applies.

CHAPTER 20

Reaffirmation and Transcendence of Eros in the Light of Transcendent Traditions

I n my formation anthropology I affirm eros as a coformant of the vital dimension. At the same time I believe that its integration with the
transcendent coformant of our life brings eros to its full richness within the
disposition of distinctively human love for people, cosmos, earth, events,
and things as epiphanies of a loving "mystery." To situate our transcendence as well as our affirmation of eros in the framework of my formation
anthropology, I must look again at the project of formation science and
its anthropology as a whole. What may be helpful in this consideration
is a comparison between our situation today and that in which the philosopher and theologian Thomas Aquinas found himself in the thirteenth
century. It was a time of confusion in many minds due to the clash between
popular philosophies of the day. To stem the tide of confusion, Aquinas
found it necessary to locate the contributions of these philosophical disciplines in the overall framework of a philosophy that was universal and
integrational. For this purpose he used a language that was quite different
from the biblical and theological languages of his religious faith tradition.
He demonstrated how his universal philosophy, based on human reason-
as-speculative, could be articulated in the particular theologies of faith
traditions as well as making sense for people outside of these traditions.

Similarly, in preparation for the year 2000, formation science aspires to
give form not so much to an integrative philosophical, but to an integrative
empirical-experiential science. It tries to do for the popularized as well as
academic formational outlook of the empirical-experiential and therapeutic sciences what Aquinas did for the philosophical outlook of his time. I
want to propose in formation science and anthropology some principles
for a basic frame of reference that could integrate systematically those insights of formation traditions and experiential sciences that are relevant
to transcendent formation.

Like Aquinas's philosophy, formation science too creates a metalanguage of its own to set this discipline apart from specific faith and

formation traditions as well as from particular sciences or any of their schools. It shows how a generic and integrational understanding of formation and of form traditions, as formulated in a generic language of its own, can later or simultaneously be articulated in the languages of specific formation traditions. This is analogous to the way in which certain aspects of Aquinas's philosophy could be theologically articulated in faith traditions as well as philosophically in other philosophical frames of reference.

In the two preceding chapters, I considered the Freudian formation tradition. I analyzed some of its main constructs critically from the viewpoint of formation science and its anthropology. This discussion necessitated the use of such terms as *libido* and *eros*, which are not typical of formation science and its underlying formation anthropology. There are disadvantages to using terms that originate outside of one's own science and its specific language. They may carry connotations that are somewhat at odds with the model of consonant transcendent formation we draw upon.

Because the question of love and its relationship to eros is central in my formation anthropology, I find it necessary to consider this problem at length. After so doing, I will return to the critical consideration of other traditions. I will discuss in the following chapters theories based, among others, on the neo-Freudian, Marxist, and capitalistic form traditions. First, however, after my critical appraisal of the Freudian libido construct in the preceding chapter I must reformulate in my own terminology the role of eros in the anthropology of formation science, especially in relation to my concept of the transcendence dynamic.

Timeliness of Reformulation of the Formational Rule of Eros

This reformulation seems especially significant in view of our changing times. Humanity seems to be at the beginning of a dramatic transition in the way it apprehends and appraises itself. One area where the emergence of this shift is apparent is in the critical reconsideration of Western individualism and its impact both on the eros and on the love life of humanity. Individualism deforms human life into an arrogant, isolating, sometimes bellicose enterprise. It separates us from one another, from the cosmos, and from the formation mystery. Individualistic self-esteem paralyzes love and eros. It generates isolation, loneliness, depression, persistent addictions, and violence. Individualism gives rise to therapeutic traditions that often neglect to complement pretranscendent healing by a therapy that radically transcends individualistic concerns.

One source of the newly emerging, postindividualistic worldview of formation science was the terror I witnessed during World War II, the destruction caused by its battles, bombings, and concentration camps. Another source of this outlook was the failure of fascist and communist collectivistic systems. But I saw also the backlash of an unmitigated individualistic capitalistic tradition. These were the reflections I shared with the intellectuals whom I helped to hide from death and deportation threats in the Dutch cities and countryside. Our discussions confirmed my growing conviction that I should initiate a new formation anthropology that would help us to transcend individualism. I dreamt of a new vision of loving interformation of each of us with cosmos and humanity and their all-pervasive mysterious ground.

Still another source were my discussions with university students in hiding during the long winter evenings, discussions about the implications of the new quantum physics. We felt that this new view, too, could help Western humanity to rise above its individualistic bent. It would be one of the means to regain a vital relationship with the cosmos in ecological care and concern. We realized that the universe was no longer apprehended and appraised by quantum physicists as a machine liable to random failure, a collection of separate entities arranged like building blocks. Rather it was seen as a magnificent network of interforming connections in which each object and person was called to play a responsible and essential role in the unfolding of cosmos and humanity. It was my dream that this new scientific insight would make it possible for pretranscendent formation traditions to transcend their individualistic and isolating presuppositions. This dream deepened my aspiration to disclose the dynamic of transcendent love hidden deeply in all of us.

The transcendence dynamic inspires us to see cosmos, earth, evolution, history, humanity, and their forming mystery as called to unfold as a universe of vitally loving relationships. My considerations during the war gave rise to a wholistic anthropology of distinctively human formation. Basic in this approach is the awareness that everyone and everything should be appreciated for its interformational human and cosmic significance. Individualistic autarky paralyzes eros and love, awe and wonder. People and things begin to exist only insofar as they can be measured, quantified in statistics, or put into laboratory test tubes.

The New Paradigm of Formation Science

In the new paradigm of formation science, everyone and everything is considered to be interforming with everyone and everything else. Each person or thing that exists is appraised in terms of its interforming relationships with others and with the forming mystery. In the light of our epiphanic consciousness, our formation field as a whole becomes a dynamic web of interforming events. Within each transcendent tradition adherents are in some way reminded that they are a unique expression of an always forming mystery.

When we learn to recognize the mysterious interformation of cosmic and human appearances, we begin to appreciate and love in a new way the inherent dignity of the founding epiphanous form of everyone and everything. Our thoughts, feelings, and actions are directed by the appreciative apprehension that everything is interforming, that all we do is affected by and affects everything else. This elevation of our vital eros makes us love earth and universe as sacred, not as mere sources for exploitation. Our interforming love reaches out to the underprivileged, the discriminated against, the sick and the poor, the homeless, the aging, the handicapped, and those suffering from starvation and any form of human deprivation. All of these people are we. We are at one with them in the transindividualistic history of love and compassion whose spark is in all of us.

Without a resurrection of the forgotten transcendence dynamic, we cannot survive as a species in a world that daily grows smaller and more interdependent than ever before in history. It is no longer a question of the survival of one or the other transcendent formation tradition to which we adhere, but of the survival of humanity as a whole. One of the necessary means for preservation of us as a people is that each formation tradition rekindle in its adherents the transindividualistic dynamic of transforming love for all that is.

Without this transcendent love, life itself becomes in the end as hollow as a desert crater. We search frantically for answers to what to do with ourselves. The dynamic of transcendent love goes beyond and yet is coformed by vital-erotic love. Only this love can help us to begin to hear the basic message of our life's calling. Drugs, alcohol, promiscuity, or consumerism cannot substitute for this deeper message or meaning of universal love.

Pretranscendent overwhelming needs interfere with this emergence of transcendent love. Proliferating unchecked, these needs will rob our joy and erode our peace of mind and heart. Such tugs and pulls of the pretranscendent are warning signs, little red flags. They tell us that we are out of touch with our transcendence dynamic, that we are no longer animated by our vital eros as permeated by the mystery of transcendent love. At such moments we cannot even love ourselves. For we have lost our intimate consonance with the mystery of love within us. This mystery grants to us our ultimate identity, our founding life form and unique calling.

Often pretranscendent therapies help us to find workable compromises. They can provide us with considerable relief from our tensions. While this partial solution is helpful, it is in itself insufficient to endow us with ultimate lasting peace and joy. What is missing is the light of a vision of life as ultimately meaningful and benevolent. This vision can only be glimpsed in the light of the transcendent love our transcendence dynamic is longing and striving for continuously. One condition for this love to manifest itself is the subjection of our pretranscendent "I" to the transcendent "I" of our founding life call and its mysterious source. In this regard transcendent therapy can complement pretranscendent therapy.

Another condition is the assimilation of the wisdom of transcendent formation traditions. These sources of insight plant seeds in our transfocal and prefocal regions of consciousness. There they keep germinating until they are brought to fruition by the indwelling mystery. Then these seeds begin to blossom in focal awareness, filling us with dispositions of appreciation and transcendent love that transform our everyday prefocal region of consciousness. Ultimately, our transcendence dynamic of awakening love is rooted in the unique call to be loving of the mystery in the depths of our being.

Transcendent Purification of Our Love Life

Longing love may draw us into a "dark night." We find ourselves on the borderline of transcendent love. We long for it, we sense its dawning but we are not yet there. Our love needs purification for it is still too vitalistically erotic, too functionalistically prone to self-actualization, too eager to conform to sociohistorical crowds and collectivities.

Purification happens in the "dark nights" that masters of transcendent traditions speak about. We lean still too much on lower levels of love as crutches. One by one they will fail to support us ultimately. Until our love focuses on the radical mystery of formation as central, we will not know the joys of true consonance.

At times of disappointment and desperation, it may seem as if we do not even have the mystery to lean on. It feels as if the Presence is absent. What we are really losing is not the mystery and its soundless love but our too willful, too controlling lower-I bound love. This blessed loss is accompanied by a new awareness of the mystery that wants to transform us by its purifying presence. Once we are lifted up by the mystery, we begin to live in transcendent love in a peace and joy that at times may seem indescribable in its beauty and intensity. Before the cleansing process occurs by means of the mystery itself, we remain inclined to filter everything through our lower self-actualizing *I* whose processes are so well described in pretranscendent psychologies and personality theories. Being released by the mystery of transformation, transcendent love begins to transform our love life. No longer are we dominated by the two different functions of our lower "I" and our lower "super-I." The Freudian concepts of "ego" and "superego" seem to point analogously to some facets of this lower *I* and lower super-*I*. Yet their overall meaning is different from my concepts because of their embeddedness in a philosophical anthropology that differs essentially from my formation anthropology.

In the light of what is happening to us, we begin to realize that we are called to be not merely *good* women and men but *transcendent* beings. This does not mean that we diminish our effective presence in our field of life. As a matter of fact, we will live, love, and labor in the world even more affectively and effectively than before. The difference is that we are no longer overly immersed in the worldliness of the world. We have in effect a wider vision of all that is, ourselves included. There will still be moments or periods of brief or long duration in which we lose this gift of consonance. This may be due to the fact that we are either too onesidedly pretranscendent or transcendent.

Onesided pretranscendence means that we give in temporarily to the exclusive dominance of our individualistic self. The other extreme is a willful attempt to be transcendent only. This exclusively transworldly attitude may be fostered by deformations that may have emerged in some transcendent formation traditions. Their mistaken directives may have tempted adherents willfully to insulate transcendent love from its necessary continual embodiment in our pretranscendent life. This means in effect that we lose transcendent love in its fullness.

Transcendence can be real only when it participates in the human spirit as an openness to all that is, meaning among other things the loving permeation and elevation of our pretranscendent life. We must, in other words, go beyond or go deeper into our pretranscendent life without eradicating any essential part of it. The mystery enables us to regain time and again the balance of loving consonance while we walk the high wire of incarnated and incarnating living. If we fall momentarily and lose our balance, the mystery, so to speak, catches us in the safety net of its all-sustaining love. It inspires us to keep pursuing in a balanced, consonant way the adventure of life and love for which we have been created. It uses transcendent faith and formation traditions as channels of this inspiration.

Tradition, Eros, and the Life of Transcendent Love

The Freudian libidinal concept of eros points to an important aspect of distinctively human love. It is related to one of the six coformants of transcendent love, which I shall consider in the following chapter. This specific coformant is designated in my formation anthropology as the "vital coformant." The libidinal eros, as presented by Freud, is in itself only one aspect of this more encompassing vital coformant. Moreover, like other pretranscendent coformants and their facets, this facet, too, will be transformed together with the vital coformant in such a way that it goes far beyond its limited role and meaning in individualistic formation traditions.

To understand this subordinated function of the vital coformant with its libidinal eros aspect, it will be necessary for me to expound on the life of transcendent love as pointed to in many transcendent traditions.

Our life of higher love is nourished by the growing awareness that our latent founding life form is always already in implicit interformation with cosmos, humanity, history, and their all-pervading mystery. Once we allow this interforming founding form to be reflected in our hearts, it enables us to begin to appreciate all appearances as epiphanic of the expressive presence of the mystery of formation everywhere manifested. In our core form we grow in an awareness of an all-pervasive love that begins to transform our unique, individual, and communal life profoundly. This transformation also impinges upon the vital-erotic component and its libidinal erotic facet that coform our human life continuously.

The transformed life can assume many forms. What form it takes in each of us depends in great measure on our particular form traditional pyramid, which happens to be ours in a certain place and time of history. Any traditional style of living that allows for the unfolding of our transcendence dynamic will serve the increase and expression of our life of higher love. It will make this love expressive in our own historical time and space; it will reflect our genuine contemporary care. No matter how timebound and limited each consonant form traditional style of loving may be, it will let shine forth a deep and primal rhythm of love that begins to permeate our whole being. This epiphanic love is a gift in time of the transtemporal and translocal source of all distinctively human love.

The transcendence dynamic of love sets us on an inward journey that gradually spirals outward into all spheres of our formation field. First this dynamic inspires us to a deepening of self-knowledge, disclosing to us the limitations of the sociohistorical, vital, and functional coformants of our life of love. Through this disclosure it readies us for the discovery of the transcendent dimension of love. The other coformants of love should be coordinated with this dimension in increasing consonance. The transcendent coformant of love thus opens for us the epiphanic perspective. The person in transformation begins to experience in love the epiphanic depth of all appearances in the inner, inter-, and outerspheres of the formation field.

A full life of love is possible only to the degree that it is appraised wisely and disciplined gently by the transcendent coformant of human love. The transcendence dynamic strives toward the total transformation of a person. It enables us to apprehend and appreciate the various dimensional coformants of love as they concretely affect our unfolding in time and space. The particular transcendent formation tradition to which we adhere enlightens us. It points to ways in which we may foster consonance between these coformants of transcendent love.

Transcendent love involves love for ourselves as unique expressions or images of the mystery. This love of the hidden formation the mystery gives to our life differs essentially from the esteem we feel for our lower individuality. Transcendent love discloses our transindividualistic deepest *I*. This transcendent *I* is unique insofar as it is a unique image and call of the mystery. At the same time it is basically communal insofar as it shares lovingly in the universal image of the mystery as expressed in its universal human and cosmic manifestation. Therefore, on this level of love, we are paradoxically most alone and most at one.

Sociohistorical Form Traditions
and the Expression of the Transcendence Dynamic

One main principle of formation science is that we cannot escape the sociohistorical dimension of human life. I developed this dimension in order to point to the social and historical form traditions by which we receive and give form to our lives. It follows that the form in which the transcendence dynamic of love manifests itself is profoundly coformed by our traditions. We formatively receive these by means of the specific language and the other symbols that express the style of each particular form tradition. Traditions in turn coform the corresponding dispositions of our heart during its process of unique traditional transformation by the transcendence dynamic.

I always feel the need to emphasize the essential interforming relationship between daily experience and language formation. These two agents of human and traditional formation coform each other continuously. Neither formative language nor experience can be considered as prior to the other. I contend that there is no tradition-free or language-free formation experience. Neither can there be a tradition- or language-free unfolding of the transcendent dynamic of love. Our transformation always happens in a sociohistorical, hence experiential and language-bound context.

The inner form of our life and its transcendent dynamism has thus been coformed by the presuppositions of our pyramid of form traditions. Among all the traditions we formationally receive in and through language, those that are transcendent should prevail. The intraform of our life is influenced by the particular traditions that are alive in the sociohistorical inter- and outerspheres of our formation field. Our intraform unfolds in continual interformation with these spheres. The formational receptivity of our intraform is undeniably experiential. It is not primarily a critical act of our functional-analytical or speculative intelligence. Formational receptivity of traditions affects the experiences and subsequent dispositions of our core form, heart, or character. The disclosure of our unique transcendent life call and its transcendence dynamic occurs simultaneously with the disclosure of the living truth of the presuppositions of our faith tradition as sociohistorically and experientially implemented in our formation tradition.

Three Essential Facets of Our Founding Life Form

Each consonant form tradition presents us with an ideal form or model of how to unfold a life of transcendent love. This ideal form strives to be consonant with three essential facets of our founding life form. These are, first of all, the generic facet of the human life form we all share; second, the specific sociohistorical traditional facet we have been discussing; and, third, the unique facet of our life call. These three facets of our founding life form as unfolding and implementing itself in daily existence interform with one another continuously. It is their interaction that gives concrete form to the experiences and dispositions of our core form or character. One cannot function without the other. None of those preformed potencies of our founding life formation can be known initially and directly in their concrete actualization. Before actualization and implementation of these latent potencies, we cannot know them in themselves empirically-experientially. In that sense and in that sense only the unactualized founding life form is preempirical. During a lifetime of actualization and implementation we will know them empirically-experientially only insofar as they are realized in and through our formation field.

Most historical traditions of transcendent transformation and transcendent love point, usually implicitly, to the threefold generic, specific traditional (sociohistorical), and unique facets. This point of departure for human formation differs essentially from the points of departure characteristic of pretranscendent human developmental theories. The latter are rooted in the traditions and sciences of the pretranscendent life. These tend to start out from a pretranscendent solitary or group individualism. They are prone to absolutize individualistic development of a person or a group at the expense of the distinctively human communal formation typical of generic humanness. Such an approach is inclined to underestimate not only this generic facet but also the power of the traditional facet of human formation. Likewise it tends to bypass the unique facet of our founding life form. It replaces the transcendent mystery of the unique life call by the self-development, self-actualization, and self-esteem of the pretranscendent life in its individualistic personal, family, or group isolation.

Presuppositions and Directives
of Transcendent Formation Traditions

Each transcendent formation tradition has its own set of presuppositions and formation directives. These give form to the manner, style, and process of unfolding of the transcendent dynamic of love. Each offers a profile of an ideal traditional form of the transcendent life. Each tradition also gives form to its own formational language, writings, images, and symbols. In this way each of them articulates in its own particular fashion our general human formation anthropology as well as the foundationals of its own sustaining faith tradition and its implementary form traditions. It is primarily through the language and ideal form of a formation tradition that its adherents have access to the life of transcendent love. Against this background of one's form tradition one's life of transcendent love plays itself out in its particular self-expression.

Formation traditions that are focally and explicitly transcendent point by way of many different symbols to the aim of the transcendence dynamic. I envisage this aim as an interforming life of love between humanity and the transforming mystery, including its myriad epiphanies in human fields of formation.

This interforming love engages the human life form and its field of presence and action as a whole, but it has its birth as well as its initial and ongoing unfolding in our intraform of life. As I explained in volume 1 of this series, the intra-, inter-, and outer forms of human existence are not conceived by me as divorced from one another. Following most classical traditions, I assign to what I call the *intraform* in my personality theory — especially to the core form or heart within that intraform — the priority. The heart is for me and many others symbolic of the luminous bridge of love between humanity and the mystery, including its countless epiphanies in our field of life. The transcendence dynamic, starting out from this core form, moves the human life form as a whole in all its spheres and dimensions to an increasingly closer intimacy of love. Transcendent love becomes an entire way of life.

Tension between Pretranscendent and Transcendent Realms in Transcendent Form Traditions

Most transcendent formation traditions point, as I do in my own way in my formation anthropology, to a tension between the pretranscendent and transcendent realms of human life. This tension plays itself out between the appeal of the transcendent love coformant and the attractions of the lower socio-vital-functional and functional-transcendent love coformants. Our mind and will as formational participate in this tension. Our lower will and mind as executive, as managing, functional, and vital, dominate the pretranscendent area of our life. Their operations should ideally be consonant with or coordinate with our mind and will as transcendently inspiring and aspiring. But our lower mind and will, as merely directing our vital-sensual-functional and functional-transcendent self-expression, is tempted to absolutize itself, to become independently self-actualizing, to lose itself in individualistic functionalistic self-esteem and in desperate concerns for confirmation by others.

The transcendence dynamic moves us to appraise what the directives coming from the mystery may beckon us toward. It moves us also to appraise how we may align our pretranscendent mind and will and their directives with those that are transcendent.

In practice, people are formed in the means to engage in the dynamic of transcendent love by the formation tradition to which they adhere. There is no other way. People are traditional through and through. To be human is to be traditional, to be always formed by traditions. Each consonant transcendent form tradition is rooted in the foundational scriptures, doctrines, or ideologies of its sustaining faith tradition. Through the various subsequent implementations of form traditions, the foundations of the faith tradition itself may be developed and nuanced over the centuries in dialogue with the formation fields in which such basic scriptures and doctrines have to be given form to concretely.

Universal formation science and anthropology can never replace or substitute for the richness, the symbolic power and wisdom, of the specific classical traditions of concrete implementation. The science provides a means of clarifying, systematizing, and appraising these traditions by relating them to the general, distinctively human structure of life and experience as called to transcendence. It also makes possible an enlightened dialogue between many different formation traditions. Its theoretical-integrational methods enable adherents to be more aware of and faithful to their own identity and difference while dialoguing with each other critically and creatively in areas they may have partially in common.

This limited yet basic commonality is rooted in the distinctively or transcendently human make-up of life shared necessarily by all adherents of formation traditions insofar as they belong to the same species. Thomas Aquinas aided his faith tradition and its theologies by developing a general philosophy and philosophical anthropology meant to apply to all humans and their world. He sought to make manifest the links between a faith tradition and the basic constitution of human life and world as examined by the philosophical sciences. The same has been attempted by thinkers like Pascal, Hegel, Kierkegaard, Ricoeur, Marcel, be it in different styles and ways in conformity with their own background and situation. Something similar had to be done today for the then not yet existing social and human sciences in their formational relevance. Hence I tried to outline possible principles for a general empirical-experiential formation science with an underlying formation anthropology. One of these suggested principles is that there exists a basic structure of human life formation. Another is that this structure is explored, among others, by the empirical-experiential arts, sciences, formation traditions, and anthropologies thus far available to us.

The image of the mystery of formation — while it is uniquely expressed by each person and each formation tradition — is not the sole possession of any of them. It is unique but not individualistic. It has a generic coformant shared by all humans, albeit more fully by those who allow their transcendence dynamic its free unfolding. In the process of implementing this dynamic in their own personality, they develop this generic image in their own unique way. I call this the unique aspect or coformant of our image of the mystery. People give always and unavoidably form to their life in the light of some formation tradition, the one that happens to be theirs as sociohistorically situated people. Hence they take into account the form traditional coformant of their unique image of the mystery. Again, this course of formation is inevitable because the transcendent dynamic of love demands expression in a sociohistorical way of life. The transcendence dynamic as such transfigures human forms of life into expressions of the transforming mystery of love, recreating life in the image of that mystery.

CHAPTER 21

Autism, Eros, and
the Six Coformants of Love

Transcendent love is rooted in the image of the transforming mystery latent in the generic founding life form of humanity. It generates love for the epiphanies of that mystery in cosmos, humanity, and history. It is already secretly operative in the longing and outreach of the vital-erotic coformant of love in childhood and infancy. It makes the child reach out in wonder, excitement, and affinity to people and things, to parents and siblings, to toys and shining objects, to cuddly pets, to stuffed animals like teddy bears. Infants and toddlers tend to explore these things by putting them in their mouths or gripping them with their fingers. If the nervous system or neuroform of the child, by some inborn deficiency, prevents the unfolding of the vital-erotic coformant of love, the child suffers from the debilitating handicap of innate autism. This condition should be distinguished from that of acquired autism later in life. Then people may become so isolated and deficient in loving intimacy with others that they tend to live exclusively by individualistic, isolating formation traditions.

Life becomes distinctively human through a cultivation of love in all of its coformants in the light of the transcendent coformant. Love, as the saying goes, is a many-splendored thing. It is not a one-dimensional disposition. Love is richly textured. In my theory love is coformed by six major coformants, rooted in the six dimensions of the human life form. These are:

1. the all-pervading sociohistorical form traditional coformant, said to be so because our expressions of love are always and unavoidably coformed by our form traditions.

2. the vital coformant that gives rise to the sexual and the vital-erotic expression of love.

3. the functional coformant that enables us to make love concrete by its expression in loving service and by its embodiment in practical functional tasks for the people we love, the ideas or causes we espouse, the country to which we belong, tasks done with dedication alone or in cooperative teams.

191

4. the functional-vital transcendent coformant of love. Here it is important to note that the functional-vital and transcendent coformants of love imply a first disclosure of the transcendent love coformant. It is functional-vital-transcendent insofar as the transcendent coformant is still dominated by vital and/or functional modes of love.

5. the transcendent love coformant that overcomes the socio-vital-functional dominance of facets of transcendent love. This coformant enables us to experience the original love power of the transcendence dynamic. It strengthens and deepens our loving will, even if vital love pleasure and functional love satisfaction are at times absent or diminished by unforeseeable circumstances.

6. the transcendent, socio-vital-functional love coformant. This coformant represents the transforming permeation of the pretranscendent love coformants by the transcendent coformant. This transformation does not destroy but complements and deepens their own unique role in the richly textured disposition of distinctively human love.

These coformants are rooted in the six form dimensions of human life as human. They do not represent discrete loves but six interforming coformants of one distinctively human love. The phrase "distinctively human love" refers in my formation anthropology to a central and many-layered concept. In various classical transcendent formation traditions, this basic anthropology of human love may be alluded to by different symbols and words. In the measure of their transcendence and distinctive humanness, they will grant to the transcendent dynamic of love a central position. They will also point to the mystery as essentially loving, compassionate, and benign. This pointing is symbolized in their particular use of language and in their choice of image and metaphor.

Human Love and the Love of the Mystery

These traditions may portray human love also in its sociohistorical, vital, and functional aspects. But they will somehow relate these aspects to the love or compassion of the mystery, no matter by what name that mystery is called. The more consonant and mature these traditions become, the less inclined they are to isolate any coformant of human love from the love of and by the mystery. On the contrary, they begin to see the love of the mystery as shining forth or expressing itself epiphanically through the transcendent dimension in all love coformants of human life. By loving the mystery in itself and in its epiphanies, the adherents of these traditions are drawn back to the mysterious source of their founding life form. They also point in their own language and symbols to the opposite of this inspiration by the mystery of love. Formation anthropology identifies this factor as the quasi-foundational autarkic, individualistic, or illusionary pride form.

When the counterfeit pride form of life takes over, the benefits of vital and functional love may be sought as ends in themselves. They do not function as coforming parts of a basically transcendent love. This betrayal of love as a many-faceted gift of the mystery leads to a life of illusion. Transcending self-centered love is a transcendence of illusions. Many form traditions confirm this transcendence in a wide variety of narratives and symbols. They also point to the fact that the human life form by its own individualistic power alone cannot be saved or redeemed from these illusions. A higher redeeming power is necessary. They differ in what or whom they identify as that higher power. How they conceptualize and image the process of redemption from the illusions of love depends again on their different assumptions, revelations, or intuitions as well as on the basic doctrines of their sustaining faith traditions.

The awakening and implementation of the transcendent love coformant as primary points to the highest pinnacle human love can reach. Without it love's other coformants may become less than human due to their isolation from this supreme coformant. Love robbed of its latent transcendent power, love that does not go beyond individualistic self-centeredness, is no longer love in a distinctively human sense. Love ceases to acknowledge its dependence on the transcendence dynamic. It becomes incapable of recreating the image of the transforming mystery in one's actual form of life and throughout one's whole formation field. This being the case, the core form or heart can no longer represent fully our inmost founding form. Its transcendence dynamic becomes paralyzed. The core form may sooner or later be dominated onesidedly by the pretranscendent I and its dissonant lower sub-I's along with the individualistic life forms to which they give rise.

Reformation and transformation of the heart through a reawakening of the transcendence dynamic of love are necessary if we are to be redeemed from the illusion that lesser loves can ever satisfy this longing. Only in the light of the transcendent is the homecoming of the heart in the mystery of love made possible. Only then can the other coformants of love become conduits through which we meet the mystery in its fullness along the road of life in its epiphanic appearances in cosmos, humanity, and history, in people, events, and things. Fired by love's longings, we can express this all-embracing mystery in social service, in ways of caring that are vitally affective and functionally effective. The pursuit of love in its multitextured richness is thus seen as uniquely and individually as well as socially and ecologically responsive.

The transcendence dynamic of love implies a dialectical tension between all of its coformants. This tension is implicit in the paradox of our being both pretranscendent and transcendent, a truth transcendent traditions continually remind us of. To pursue a life of distinctively human love is to assent to one of the main directives of a transcendent tradition — namely, that we will never be able to resolve the tension that is at the heart of our pretranscendent-transcendent "amphibious" life of love. Only when we accept this tension and live within it can we begin to approximate the kind of consonant love that keeps in balance the dynamic coformants that together constitute transcendent human love.

Love of oneself, of other human beings, of cosmos and nature grants us a foretaste of the fullness of love by and for the mystery of formation. The mystery discloses itself, if only epiphanically and through a glass darkly, in self and others. Such glimpses of what is "really real" unconceal while at the same time concealing the nature and meaning of the transcendence dynamic at work within us. Through this dynamic, humanity participates in the transformation offered by the mystery itself. Transforming love gives rise to the affective imagery of the heart in its most exquisite acts and dispositions. Likewise it enables us to transcend the anxiety of separation from and longing for the person or thing we most love. It is also the source of the transcendent love imagery we find in the art and literature of many traditions. Transformation of the pretranscendent coformants of human love by the transcendent thus readies us for a taste of consonance between our love for the mystery and our love for its countless human and cosmic epiphanies.

Power of the Vital Coformant

We might wonder what is the originating lasting power that keeps alive the transcendence dynamic that awakens the other coformants of love? Sheer observation reveals that it can be nothing less than the power of the vital coformant itself. Already in early childhood, this basic coformant of love is the first manifestation of the latent transcendence dynamic. Later it initiates, accompanies, and keeps love alive in its other coformants. The transcendence dynamic moves the child vitally to go beyond enclosure within its pretranscendent self. It enables her or him to be in touch affectively with people and things in the surroundings of home and family. By contrast, in an innately autistic child, the transcendence dynamic is inhibited by factors not fully known to science. If the inhibition of the vital-affective reaching out beyond the isolated self is not overcome, the transcendence dynamic will be unable to "vitalize" the affective outreach that is typical of the other coformants. The dynamic interforming quality of the human love disposition remains absent or severely deficient. The love directives of transcendent traditions cannot reverberate vitally in the hearts of the victims of innate autism. The vital longing for consonance and intimacy with other persons, with nature, cosmos, and humanity, with epiphanic appearances and with their pervasive mystery of ongoing formation is sadly silenced.

Purification of the Vital Coformant

Transcendence traditions teach their adherents how to purify and enhance the raw vital or vitality coformant of their love. Such enhancement does not suppress the vital coformant. On the contrary it elevates and transfigures it inwardly, disclosing its own deepest direction. We could say in effect that the vital love coformant is thereby redeemed from the unenlightened raw drive that only strives to gratify the pretranscendent individual *I* as dominated by its vitalistic sub-*I* as if it were an end in itself.

The transcendence dynamic, in dialogue with our life experience and the directives of our transcendent traditions, enables us gradually to appraise the unique power and limitations of each love coformant. This appraisal then directs us to place all the coformants of love in the light of the transcendent.

This being the case, I still maintain that the access to love is and remains the transcendence dynamic in its initial embodiment in vital affective longing and reaching out to what is beyond the self-enclosed pretranscendent *I*. This vitally embodied transcendence dynamic passionately strives for ever fuller transcendence. It turns the vital affective coformant into the servant of transcendent love, granting our transcendent outreach warmth and vivacity. As love comes from the mystery that is transforming humanity in its own image, so love returns humanity into that originating mystery.

The language of the transcendence dynamic of love finds different variations and symbols in the great variety of transcendent formation traditions that emerge within each specific faith tradition as ways of its implementation. Their task is to facilitate for adherents the embodiment of their underlying faith tradition in the matrix of everyday life and experience. When they are matured to consonance, transcendent formation traditions present to their followers ways of interforming with their pretranscendent individuality and with their field of ongoing formation. They present alternatives to the way of individualism. People learn to listen to a different drummer, to a tradition that in its transcendent directives is at variance with pretranscendent pulls to care only for oneself. Committed followers of a transcendent tradition come to know that this kind of selfism comes to a dead end. They begin to depreciate the dissonance and disparities of a merely pretranscendent existence. They grow in appreciation of the increasing consonance that is the first fruit of a life of transcendent love.

Ideal Form of the Transcendent Life

The transformation of our pretranscendent life is guided by the ideas, language, and symbols of transcendent traditions. We must remember that human formation is sociohistorically and essentially a communal as well as a unique personal story. It is the communal formation tradition that offers to its adherents a central ideal form of the transcendent life as situated sociohistorically. This ideal form of how life ought to be in faithfulness to the transcendence dynamic gives adherents of the tradition access to the mystery of love and its embodiment in their shared sociohistorical world.

The dynamic of transcendent love leads to a progressive dying to the individualistic directives of an exclusively pretranscendent way of life. Simultaneously it raises adherents through the power of the mystery of transforming love to a life of love that is increasingly transcendent yet fully embodied in the pretranscendent dimensions of life. Any transcendent tradition insofar as it is consonant with reality will admit that such a transfiguration is granted usually only over a lifetime. The path to transformation, as we know, is replete with trial and error. We fall down and rise up, behold with clarity love's call and watch it sink back into obscurity. We experience along the way of transforming love ambivalence and clarity of direction, confusion, and elucidation.

The language of a transcendent formation tradition assists its followers to nuance, clarify, and direct the often stormy journey from pretranscendent pointers to the transcendent goal. Within the shared framework of a faith and formation tradition, each adherent has to find his or her unique expression of the tradition. Each one has to give form to a way of living and loving that is congenial with one's life call yet compatible with the basics of one's tradition. Each of us has to learn how to be compassionate with unavoidable setbacks and failings in self and others. Each person has to grow in the art and discipline of competently proceeding along the path ordained by the mystery.

Traditional Languages of Transformation

Each formation tradition has its own metalanguage. This language has a decisive bearing on one's experience of implementing the basics of the sustaining faith tradition as well as on the subsequent style of transformation. Language becomes the channel through which adherents of a tradition can give meaning and expression to their own corresponding experiences of formative implementation and transformation. By languaging these experiences, transformation itself is realized in the core form of one's inner life. Through the language of one's transcendent formation tradition, one comes to appreciate more and more the richness and beauty of the manifold coformants of love as enlightened and harmonized by the transcendent coformant. In short, the language of one's tradition gives form to the direction of our life as an embodiment of transcendent love. It provides the parameters for all other interforming relationships within one's field of life.

Appreciation of Pretranscendent Coformants of Love

Pretranscendent love coformants should not be depreciated. They should be incorporated into a fullness of love that becomes basically but not exclusively transcendent. Growth in the lived primacy of the transcendent basic love coformant implies a necessary mitigation of the dominance of pretranscendent coformants in our life. It further calls for a relinquishing of our idolizing of their objects as sources of ultimate fulfillment and happiness. However, this mitigation does not negate the necessity of respecting each love coformant and the relatively valuable quality of the love facet and object it discloses to us.

The transcendent coformant of love acknowledges each subordinated coformant as significant. The qualities of beloved persons, events, and things disclosed by the pretranscendent coformants of our love life should not be used for our own social enhancements, vital pleasures, or functional satisfactions as ultimate. We should appreciate their limited contributions but our appreciation should not degenerate into dispositions of lust, greed, and possessiveness. It should be elevated to an appreciation of the epiphanic quality of what or whom we love. We must always place our love within the context of love for and by the mystery. This gives to our love a kind of cosmic and human expansiveness. Our growth in the primacy of transcendent love within the parameters of our life call also has to take place in dialogue with the wisdom of classical transcendent traditions. This dialogue demands that we listen to and learn to respect the strictures placed on the ways in which we are to receive and give form to the pretranscendent expressions of our love. Paradoxically, these restrictions may become the surest avenue to our being able both to release the power of transcendent love and to enhance the potencies of all pretranscendent coformants of our love.

The transcendence dynamic as understood in my formation anthropology is a power inherent in our founding life call. This dynamic propels its own reflection in the unfolding consonant dispositions of our core form and through them to the spheres and dimensions of our formation field. It draws us in love to the mystery as epiphanous in our unique founding form of life as well as in the inter- and outerspheres of our formation field. All love coformants, when directed by the transcendence dynamic, point in the same direction. Mature, wise, and time-tested classical transcendent formation traditions show us this same basic dynamic of love in a wide variety of symbols, practices, and metalanguages. Rooted as they are in sustaining faith traditions, these expressions enrich and make concrete this formational structure in a way formation science of itself could not.

The transcendence dynamic of love reaches its apex when it discloses and implements the primacy of the transcendent coformant. This summit of love implies a fully consonant and transfigured vision of cosmos, humanity, formative evolution, and history as pervaded by an infinitely loving mystery. The greatest gift of the mystery to the human form of life is the dynamic of transcendent love.

Fullness of Transcendent Love

Transcendent love is the source of real growth in distinctive humanness. Disclosing and implementing one's unique life call is not something one does alone. It happens in transindividualistic relationships with others. The transcendence dynamic, as celebrated in classic formation traditions, fosters personal relationships of intimate love. It helps us to appreciate the rich vital pleasures and functional satisfactions that may accompany the wonder of intimacy. We should gratefully cherish, while also going beyond, these pretranscendent gratifications. They should not dominate our lives exclusively. Each private relationship of intimacy is meant to bind us also to the larger world around us.

The transcendence dynamic cannot be kept encapsulated in relationships of one-on-one intimacy. Without losing its dynamism, the embodiment of this dynamic in friendship, in marriage, or in small community life has a profoundly social aspect. These relationships are channels of love toward others and the wider world. Consonant love moderates individualism; it fertilizes the transcendent love dispositions of the heart. True love tames our eagerness to enrich our turf by trampling on others, to make a name for ourselves at the expense of another's good or by any means of advancement available to us.

The call to transcendent love is ideally experienced in private settings, in community, family, and close friendships. These relationships are havens in a sometimes heartless world of cut-throat competition, one-upmanship, and endless struggles for individual promotion in career, status, achievement, and survival. The world in its worldliness is dominated by form traditions bent on promoting independence, not interdependence. Self-reliance, not reliance on the formation mystery as fostered by transcendent traditions, becomes the goal.

Intimate community, friendship, and family relationships offer the solidarity, mutual acceptance, openness, and interdependence in which the latent transcendence dynamic of love can awaken and begin to blossom forth before it is frozen by the cold winds of a functionalistic society bent on its own aggrandizement, often at the expense of the poor and underprivileged.

Transcendent love, as upheld by its corresponding traditions, is not a passing whim; it is a way of life, a style of being, an expanding presence at odds with self-bolstering individualism. This love longs to contribute to the common good, to heal the ecological wounds inflicted on cosmos, earth, and nature, to relieve the plight of the spiritually, aesthetically, and educationally poor as well as those who are poor physically and discriminated against because of their race, sex, color, appearance, accent, or place of origin. Above all, transcendent love hungers for intimacy with the mystery that nurtures all that is.

The Consonant Heart

Any community or communion of transcendent love gives primacy to a heart steadily enlightened but not paralyzed by analytical reason. The enlightened heart listens also to higher reason; it can be calculating when necessary but is guided above all by gentle wisdom. The consonant heart in many transcendent traditions symbolizes the wellspring of a life that is distinctively human. While being solid, committed, and persevering, it is not harsh or willful. The transcendent heart's intimacy with some people is not insulated from the encompassing context of family and of the wider community, of humanity, cosmos, and its always sustaining mystery.

This heart is not a closed enclave but a spring of love, generating a network of interforming relationships as wide as the world itself. It shows preferences but not callous judgments. It builds walls not against others but against insidious individualism and the vicissitudes of subjectivism. The state of being in love marks this heart's flow with all that is while growing in deep respect for one's unique call within the limits of time and of the music of eternity vibrating in an unfolding universe.

Transcendent love embodies one's deeper transcendent *I* in the sacred context of that which interforms us and all things mysteriously. One feels grounded yet free, interdependent yet liberated, at home in one's rightful place in universe and history yet at one with all that is. Only the transcendence dynamic, when we allow it full reign, can grant us that easy certainty of universal love for which all of us are secretly longing.

Transcendent love is a beautiful blending of spontaneity and solidarity, of effusiveness and sobriety, of receiving and giving, of sharing and wisely withholding, of self-formation and interformation, of solitude and togetherness. It is feeling at home in the universe and with other people, being comfortable with who one is with one's defenses shut down. It is not melding but merging.

Vital Love Coformant and the Vicissitudes of Feeling

The art of love, as taught by transcendent traditions, points in the same direction as formation science. I emphasize the hierarchical unfolding of the six coformants of love under the aegis of the transcendent love coformant. The primacy of the latter entails that when one or the other coformant cannot be activated under certain circumstances, love will be saved and sustained by the transcendence dynamic. For example, the vital animating coformant will always be present as long as love is alive, but the spontaneous emotionality that may accompany vital animation may at times be absent. Paradoxically, this diminishment of vital emotionality, not vitality itself, may purify love as a disposition of being with and for another for his or her own sake.

Emotional sensations are often linked with self-centered and self-seeking pleasure. Beneficial when not inordinate, such effusiveness when made ultimate can become harmful to the outgoing self-transcending essence of love. An excessive search for romance only can be a sign of pretranscendent selfishness, of looking at relationships for merely pretranscendent vitalistic thrills.

The momentary loss of emotionality can be purifying for another reason. It can free our transcendence dynamic of love in such a way that it transforms our love from within. It makes it less individualistically self-serving. It activates our transcendent will to love people, events, and things not for the pleasure or advantage they can give us but for what they are in themselves potentially or actually as loving gifts of the mystery.

We cannot command the ups and downs of our emotions or affections directly or immediately. Our transcendent mind and will can give form to a loving commitment to disclose what must be appreciated as more than the individualistic I that at times dominates our concerns. Through the action of transcendent mind and will, we can be committed also to the implementation of the inspirations and aspirations that flow from our love experiences. Transcendent love, while animated by our vital-erotic life, is ratified by our transcendent mind and will. Through love's commitment, they activate and transform pretranscendent coformants independently of the subjectivistic fluctuations of our emotionality or the ebb and flow of our feelings.

Our transcendent will is formed and directed by the transcendence dynamic. This transcendent will in turn transforms our pretranscendent managing will and its subordinate coformants. In this process our emotional life too is transformed and activated. In contrast with hedonistic and individualistic form traditions, transcendent traditions do not believe that transindividualistic love can depend on subjectivistic pleasant feelings. They come and go unpredictably, they can rise and fall as rapidly as mood swings.

The endurance of transcendent love cannot be guaranteed by the fast changing, vulnerable forms our emotional life assumes. It is based on our commitment to and disinterested service of whom and what we love. The vital animation of love's commitment and service can be even more profound when our feelings of subjective pleasure are low or absent. The feelings of pleasure that may or may not accompany our vital animation of transcendent love are by themselves alone too unstable a base for a life of transcendent love to last. This love entails a lifelong commitment to loving coformation with the forming mystery of cosmos, earth, humanity, and history, especially with the mystery of people with whom we are called to be more intimate.

The vital coformant of love will prevail when we are still dwelling in the pretranscendent realm of human existence. Often the "chemistry factor" of the vital dimension moves people at moments of vital affinity. They feel wonderful, vitally attractive and attracting. Pretranscendent free-floating hedonistic and individualistic formation traditions in our formation field exalt this vitalistic love. It is the stuff out of which soap operas are made. No one would doubt its initial impact. The trouble is that such traditions doom our love life to unhappiness by raising the empty promise that such feelings will be lasting, that they are an essential sign that this is the "real thing." We are doomed to lives of failed love if transcendent traditions do not come to our rescue and redemption.

The excited feelings that accompany love cannot be guaranteed to remain perfect and continuous. They can, however, be sustained on a deeper level. This happens when we grow in transcendent commitment and loving service. The stability of our transcendent love life can be guaranteed only by this recurrent option to see problems, crises, and dissonances in the everyday field of life as opportunities to grow more loving. Reality, for better or worse, may blot out pleasant feelings but transcendent love can always survive this emotional ebb and flow. Felt affections will return after such nights of emotional blandness. Now our affections may be more purified, more transcendent and refined. No longer do feelings define love but transcendent love defines feelings. This is the aim of the transcendence dynamic when it lets us temporarily dwell in deserts of emotional deprivation.

Personal Intimacy and Universal Love

The classic masters of the great transcendent traditions speak in many symbols and in various languages about the purification of a love that is still too vitalistic in a pretranscendent emotional way. The faith traditions that are the wellspring of transcendent religious or ideological formation traditions can tide us over when our changeable feelings of excitement die down or become eroded away by the tediousness of the tasks to which we are committed by our life of transcendent love.

The love of personal intimacy, as in marriage or friendship, is not meant to close us off from the universal transcendent love to which our transcendence dynamic calls us. On the contrary, relationships of loving intimacy should join us to the all-encompassing transcendent love that can grant us moments or periods of peace and joy no matter what. Personal relationships of loving intimacy are preferred entrances to the mystery and poignancy of transcendent universal love. Personal private love relationships are condensed manifestations of the universal love that reveals the maturity and fullness of our distinctive humanness. The more we experience personal intimacies of love as privileged entrances to universal love, the more freeing this intimacy will be. Such gifted relationships are grounded, secure, deep, and lasting. Only through the love of commitment to something that transcends our pretranscendent individualistic preferences or needs for fulfillment can we glimpse the lost paradise of universal love, peace, and joy.

Within the primacy of this transcendent love coformant, all other pre-transcendent coformants can be gradually transformed and come to fruition in their own unique way. Such transformed coformants will take into account gratefully and graciously the insights and contributions of pre-transcendent traditions, arts, and sciences after wise and critical appraisal in the light of the transcendent coformant. To live in transcendent love is to enjoy the best of both worlds in beautiful consonance.

CHAPTER 22

Sociohistorical Freudian
and Transcendent Traditions

The previous chapters dealt with our vital-functional dimension. How could its vitality, its eros, be transformed inwardly? How do transcendent traditions help us to make such transformations? In this chapter I want to consider the transformation of the sociohistorical dimension, asking again about the influence of transcendent traditions.

I shall look at the general drift of the psychoanalytic tradition to see what it can teach us about our sociohistorical formation. I shall deal mainly with the general orthodox Freudian tradition. Here I shall show that this perspective taught us much about our vital-functional formation but little about our sociohistorical formation. In the following chapter we shall see how the neo-Freudian tradition was a reaction to this onesidedness. The neo-Freudian tradition is mainly concerned with the forming power of sociohistorical events and structures. Conversely it may not give sufficient attention to vital-functional formation.

Orthodox Freudian Tradition

One objective of my methodology is to compare critically from the viewpoint of transcendent transformation the relevant contributions of other auxiliary sources to this ultimate process of human life formation. This essential aspect of the theoretical-critical approach of my methodology, in the light of my formation anthropology and personality theory, goes far beyond a merely experiential, qualitative, or phenomenological description of human experiences or their heuristic analysis.

One of the sources of such to be corrected contributions is the psychoanalytic faith and form tradition. I examined the possible input of psychoanalytic thought to the sociohistorical dimension of my formation theory of personality. I discovered a basic difference of opinion between orthodox and neo-Freudian traditions. The older tradition holds at least implicitly that the sociohistorical dimension as such does not basically change the fundamental life direction of people. This belief ties in with their assumption that the core form of our life, established in infancy, rooted in early libidinal development, is basically unchangeable.

This perspective differs from my own. In my personality theory, only the transcendent founding form of human life, as embedded in genetics and the initial maternal ambience, is relatively unchangeable. This founding form generates, among other aspects, the enduring side of our temperament or temperform, which is different from our core or character form. The latter should be congenial with our founding form. To that degree some element of lasting stability of character enters into our core form. But in other ways less basic core dispositions can be altered in the course of life by the forming influence of sociohistorical traditions and institutions.

My personality theory holds also that a once-established core disposition usually remains in us *radically*. "Radical" refers to the Latin *radix*, which means root. The root, even of a now replaced disposition, can usually not be eradicated. To give an example, a rehabilitated alcoholic has replaced the disposition of alcoholism with that of sobriety. Yet the root of the former disposition remains as a radical predisposition, leaving him or her more vulnerable to a reawakening of the replaced core disposition. The rare exception is, as I shall argue later in my forthcoming volume on transcendent articulation, the person who is purified and elevated by the formation mystery itself to the summit of transcendent union. In that supreme process the mystery itself may eradicate some of these stubborn predispositions during the night of the spirit, at least in their functional if not physiological ground.

In terms of my science, I would say that the early disciples of Freud explained the formation of our basic character as well as of sociohistorical traditions and institutions on the basis of the history of the formation of the vital-erotic dimension of individuals. This would mean that the sociohistorical dimension would be a by-product of the vital-functional dimension.

Laforgue, for instance, claims that one should understand the sociohistorical institution of the police force as an expression of the need of people to be punished. This need is envisaged as a remnant of the conflictual infantile formation history of one's eros (see Reich 1969, 7).

In my theory only certain neurotic individuals, coping with an imaginatively magnified threat of the police force in their life, may relate it infrafocally to their repressed need for punishment. One of my assumptions is that any of our dimensions, including the vital-functional ones, *co*form our dispositions and attitudes toward sociohistorical institutions. My concept, however, of potential or actual coformation by all dimensions excludes that our vital dimension, as modulated by its early individual formation history, is the only explanation of institutions such as the police force. I would call this an a priori "monoformational" explanation. It overlooks the possibility that a "pluriformational," "coformational," or "multidimensional" explanation may be required.

View of Formation Science

To return to my example, certain people may have a pre- or infrafocal need for punishment. This need can be expressed in many ways, such as in coercive dispositions that may lead to scrupulosity, self-torturing behavior, or psychosomatic symptoms of excessive guilt and self-condemnation. It is difficult to see, however, why this need would be the exclusive necessary and sufficient explanation of the establishment of police forces in human history.

One cannot deduce a sociohistorical phenomenon from the vital-functional dispositions of individuals alone. I would go so far as to say only that the formation story of the vital eros could have a coformational role to play in the establishment of police forces as appraised by certain individuals.

A basic assumption of my personality theory is that people can and do learn from their form traditions in ways that surpass the dispositional formation of their vital eros in early childhood. In infancy such traditions are vitally assimilated from the family. Later people learn more directly from the sociohistorical institutions and structures themselves in which traditions are embedded. Exposed to them, they learn how they can receive and give new form to their life. Especially when people interform with other traditions in their pluriformational society, their core dispositions may change significantly.

Subordination of Eros
to the Sociohistorical Dimension of Life

The eros at the heart of our vital dimension energizes our loves and hates, our likes and dislikes, our labor and leisure; it animates, ideally in a subservient way, our scientific, artistic, and idealistic pursuits without being reduced to any of them. The vital eros is extremely plastic as shown in the myriad adaptations of its energizing formation power. This endless adaptation opens the vital eros to numerous new impressions. A great number of these come from our sociohistorical situations. The vital-functional structure of life is to a high degree affected by the prevalent sociohistorical, political, and economic form traditions embedded in the systems in which we find ourselves. These give rise to everyday pulsations in society that touch our daily lives.

For example, Afro-American slaves were vitally-functionally dependent on their white owners, white governments, police forces, and preachers. This sociohistorical situation made them Christians but it made them initially also unable to savor the Christian message of liberation of the oppressed and of the dignity of their unique-communal life call in Christ. It did not empower them to cultivate an inner disposition of resistance to degradation by white families, especially those that kindly yet condescendingly took good care of them. Many black women were entrusted with the motherly care of white babies and children. Their vital eros would be expressed in this care; it would also dampen their inner power of critique of their sociohistorical situation. Sociohistorical phenomena like these cannot be explained totally outside of the vital formation of people. Neither can the biological structure of the vital eros fully explain the dispositions of black women. Without taking into account a sociohistorical form tradition of the master-slave relationship, we cannot fully understand the relationship between Christian white slave owners and their black Christian slaves.

Similarly the revolt of blacks against the government of South Africa cannot be unmasked as merely a disguised and delayed vital rebellion against the father they resented in their childhood. In dialogue with the psychoanalytic tradition, my science can examine how far unsolved vital-erotic conflicts with the father may also play some role in the motivations of individuals who participate in the insurrection against white suppressors. However, the basic anthropological assumptions of my science do not allow to turn this father-son conflict into the only or main explanation of this historical event as a whole.

Need for Dialogue with Other Social Disciplines

Not all sociohistorical expressions in people are always and exclusively the result of their vital-erotic history. The protest of Midwestern farmers when their lands were threatened by mortgage foreclosures ought not to be explained by means of vital-erotic motivations or by a phrase like "rebellion against the father." The sociofunctional structure of the life of most people is mainly formed by the form traditional sociohistorical structures to which they are exposed daily in their society. Vital conflictual motivations *may* be involved in sociofunctional processes but only when such postulated motives are really operative should we acknowledge the role they play.

Therefore, I made an essential part of my methodology the dialogue with auxiliary disciplines other than the discipline of psychoanalysis, for instance, disciplines such as cultural anthropology, sociology, political science, economy, and socio-linguistics. In this case aspects of their data and theories that are more directly relevant to the formation of the sociohistorical dimension of life should be critically examined in the light of formation theory. What is their relevance to distinctively human formation? How is transcendent transformation facilitated or hampered by sociohistorical traditions and their impact on the formation of the sociofunctional structures of people's lives? For example, certain traditions of capitalism or socialism may hamper the transcendent transformation of people, others may not.

Social and Individual Relationships

Relationships between classes of people, each with their own particular social traditions, are different from those between individuals. Affective relationships between individuals, each with their own personality, are modulated by their tradition pyramids and by their history of conflicts and clashes with parents and others. As such they are more open to childhood motivations. The conflicts between social classes, as, for instance, in a strike of workers, is due more to a difference in their sociohistorical traditions than to the search for a solution of childhood conflicts. It is not impossible that a strike has something to do also with inner conflicts that stem from the childhood experiences of employees. Perhaps all had conflicts with their fathers, but the principle of multidimensional coformation should prevent us from explaining the strike as only a revolt against the father. What is the impact of formation traditions? It is possible, for instance, that both conflicts between fathers and sons as well as conflicts between employers and employees may stem from the same sociohistorical tradition, for example, one that is patriarchal. This tradition in some situations can give the specific explanation of both types of conflict.

As I have shown, the family relationship itself is directed by its tradition pyramid. This pyramid contains also traditions of contemporary society as a whole. That the labor class let itself be exploited for so long and adapted itself to its degradation is the result of sociohistorical traditions. To reduce their revolt against this condition to merely an infantile-irrational rebellion against the father is to cover-up its deepest cause: the sociohistorical tradition of oppression imposed on society by the leading classes. Such a cover-up can delay or paralyze the battle against a socially unjust tradition by the oppressed.

Summary of Implications for Formation

The implications for formation of what we have seen so far can be summarized in the following points:

1. Form traditions influence the formation of our character or core dispositions, especially the traditional coformant of our character.

2. The initial formation of core dispositions does not depend exclusively on the biogenetic structure of our vital dimension but far more on patterns of childhood formation as directed by the sociohistorical traditions assimilated, modulated, and transmitted by the parents.

3. Childhood formation is a process of interformation between the tradition patterns of the parents and the emergent patterns of vital erotic life in their children.

4. This initial interformation explains why young adherents of a specific tradition share similar dispositions. As children of adherents of that tradition, they have been subjected to its patterns of childhood formation and deformation.

5. This initially similar core with its typical structure of dispositions does not necessarily determine the core form and the whole life of the child in the future.

6. In the course of life each adherent of traditions gives form to her or his tradition pyramid and subsequent core form through interformation with successive sociohistorical life situations and with other traditions as well as through personal modulations of the initial parental and later freely chosen or affirmed formation traditions.

7. A pluritraditional society offers more room for expansion and modulation of one's tradition pyramid than a monotraditional society. During humanity's history of formation many populations were conceived, born and raised, not only in a monotraditional family but also in a monotraditional society, for example, in an American Indian tribe before the appearance of white men and women on this continent. The striking similarity of the core dispositions of the members of such a society are the result of monotraditional patterns of childhood formation and lack of exposure to different traditions and related sociohistorical situations later in life.

8. The deeper one is transformed by a transcendent formation tradition the less one is at the mercy of parentally modulated tradition pyramids assimilated in infancy and of popular sociohistorical pretranscendent traditions pulsating in one's formation field.

CHAPTER 23

Sociohistorical, Transcendent, Marxist, and Neo-Freudian Traditions

In the previous chapter I discussed mainly the general reductionistic drift of the orthodox Freudian tradition. I especially considered the role of this reductionism in the Freudian explanation of the formation of the sociohistorical dimension of our life. I did so because my science focuses in part on sociohistorical form traditions. In this chapter I shall consider the general drift of Marxist and neo-Freudian traditions. I will give special attention to the areas where these two types of traditions seem to have something in common.

Human life is sociohistorically coformed by the socioeconomic and political traditions that prevail in our field. Among other things they coform such social support and maintenance systems in our society as those of nutrition, business, means of production, employment, administration, health care, housing, retirement, foreign relations, travel, transport, and recreation. Tradition pyramids as well as cultural elements that reflect some facets of some of these traditions coform such systems. Formation traditions and these cultural reflections strive to maintain themselves by means of these and other sociofunctional structures.

Limited but Real Formation Power
of Sociohistorical Traditions

We should neither under- nor overestimate the forming power of such sociohistorical support and maintenance traditions. An example of overestimation can be found in the Marxist tradition rooted in the belief system of historical materialism. This tradition holds that the ethical, intellectual, and artistic core dispositions of people are determined by the particular socioeconomic forms that prevail in a specific society, be it a capitalist, socialist, democratic, or totalitarian state. I would agree that sociohistorical and political traditions, expressed in social maintenance systems, do exercise a forming effect on those who have to live their daily life within such systems. I would not elevate them, however, to the status of the ultimate or only formational factor to which all agents of formation could be reduced. A particular tradition whose leaders are power hungry may take over society and try to form citizens by the introduction of socioeconomic, political, and administrative form traditions that reflect their own traditional presuppositions and political interests. In order to survive, persons traditionally opposed to these systems may have to adapt to them in their public apparent form of life. Meanwhile their own silenced traditions may keep exuding a forming power inwardly.

In other words, traditions that manage to prevail sociohistorically are not all-powerful, even if they are in control of socioeconomic and political maintenance systems on which the survival of people depends. No matter the oppression to which they are exposed, different groups of people and different individuals respond inwardly in their own way to the same imposed socioeconomic and political traditions. Their deeper response is coformed by their own personally modulated traditions.

This is equally true in a democratic society like India. A Mother Teresa of Calcutta, a poet or scientist, a Muslim or Hindu, an Indian socialist or capitalist, a Sikh or Buddhist, will respond differently to the same socioeconomic conditions facing them in their country. The difference in their response is rooted in differences in their personalized traditions.

More particularly, transcendent traditions inspire their adherents to hold on to directives that go beyond those of pretranscendent traditions and their socioeconomic and political expressions. They enable people not to succumb to them. Examples would be the Christian, Jewish, and Islamic traditions that survived in the Soviet Union after decennia of persecution and the forced exposure of adherents to the forming power of the Marxist socioeconomic and political maintenance and support traditions.

Indirect Formation Power of Imposed Traditions

I have observed here and abroad that imposed traditions have some effect on people. Many Christians, Jews, and Muslims, exposed for many years to a Marxist tradition, may see things in a somewhat different light than those who did not go through this experience. Some facets of the tradition in question may have entered their own pyramid. They may, for instance, look more critically on the limitations of a capitalistic or neocapitalistic socioeconomic tradition.

At times the impact of the formational and deformational politico-socioeconomic form traditions of a society can be profound. An example would be a society that for centuries was structured by a onesided patriarchal form tradition. Many people may accept the superiority of patriarchal males as if this were a given of nature rather than the effect of a sociohistorical formation process of a particular form tradition. Such an absolutized onesided tradition is rightly criticized by its opponents. At times the critique may deteriorate into an excessively resentful reaction formation that can no longer distinguish between faith and formation tradition. Such confusion may be due to the fact that a onesided patriarchal tradition can be mixed with other traditions in our complex pyramids and contaminate them.

For example, we may confuse absolutized patriarchalism with the classic religious faith traditions of those who happen to support or impose this way of life via a form tradition. We overlook the possibility that their own temporal and local understanding of their faith tradition may have been deformed in the process of adaptation and compatibility under the influence of a dominant patriarchal form tradition. That being the case, the underlying faith tradition as a whole, its very essence, can be mistakenly thought of as identical with, in this example, an absolutized patriarchal form tradition. The Marxist tradition, to cite another case of a tradition unaware of my distinction between faith and form tradition, looks at religious faith traditions as merely the outgrowth of a patriarchal (bourgeois) socioeconomic tradition. The mistaken Marxist conclusion is that religions should automatically disappear when the form tradition here in question loosens its hold on society.

Infrafocal Base of the Marxist and Freudian Views of Tradition

Both the Marxist and the Freudian formation traditions see focal consciousness as a reflection of infrafocal form potencies, dispositions, traditions, directives, and dynamics.

In Marxist thinking, the politico-socio-economic traditional infrastructure of a society determines the way in which one gives form to rational, spiritual, religious, and political thoughts, memories, imaginations, and anticipations. In their view these infrafocal socioeconomic and political traditions shape "quasi" transcendent superstructures of art, religion, culture, ideology, and education, including the politico-socio-economic traditional forms we give to our society.

As I have argued earlier, the Freudian faith and form tradition makes infrafocal libidinal erotic form potencies and drives the real source of our "sublimated" quasi-transcendent superstructures. By contrast, the Marxist faith and form tradition makes infrafocal politico-socio-economic traditions of a society the source of its focal traditional superstructures. The really transcendent forms that classic traditions foster are reduced by them to camouflaged expressions of either the politico-socio-economic or the libidinal infraformation of human life.

Neo-Freudian Use of Both Reductionistic Formation Views

The Freudian and Marxist traditional reductionistic views of life are reconciled by neo-Freudian theorists such as Erich Fromm. He stresses that the infrafocal (and I would add "pretranscendent") vital-erotic directedness of our life is itself formed by the socioeconomic structure of society. The family is envisaged by him as the agent of a particular socioeconomic and political tradition of society. In his view quasi-transcendent form traditions — as reflected in social structures — use families as their agents to give form to affective relationships, worship styles, and ideals, and to the dispositional structure of vital drives, especially the vital-erotic.

In some populations powerful quasi-transcendent traditions manage to give form to the sociohistorical structures of their society. Such a society transplants in the hearts and heads of people through their families directives of overly compliant submission. These directives may be camouflaged as religious virtues. Power directives are piously dressed up in the guise of spiritual life directives. They are used, often prefocally, to gain or maintain power and dominance for a politico-socio-economically established form tradition. Even those who use them for gaining power may believe in their own apparent pious intentions. They may repress any awareness of their equally powerful nonfocal control, possession, and position ploys.

Fromm would envision the task of psychoanalysis as an exploration of the various sociohistorical reformations of the dispositions of our vital form potency, especially the libidinal. His guiding question would be in my terminology: How are these reformations of our core or character structure the consequence of a particular socioeconomic political tradition?

More Comprehensive View of Formation Science

My view is different. It is the task of my formation science to explore not only the reformations but also the inner transformations of the vital form potencies, especially in their central erotic power. For me this exploration implies the study of any formation or preformation in any sphere and dimension of one's formation field, not only the intrasphere or the vital erotic or sociohistorical dimension. This approach includes but does not restrict itself to formations and reformations in socioeconomic political traditional structures. I believe that all such field changes should be appraised in the light of the question: How do people really appreciate and depreciate the meanings of any vital erotic or sociohistorical event that happens in their field of personal or shared presence and action? We should ask what changes *mean* to people. How do they perceive and respond to them under the influences of their own tradition pyramids? This research should also include an examination of the transcendent traditions that enable people to give a higher or deeper meaning to the traditional structures in their field.

Use of Neo-Freudian Views to Explain Deformed Traditions

Having defined the parameters of my investigation, I can now critically use, complement, and correct certain insights of social psychoanalytical thinkers. Some of these can help us to explain the possible deformations found even in classical transcendent traditions. These may be due to well-meaning attempts to be compatible with other sociohistorical traditions such as, in this case, the neo-Freudian faith and formation traditions. Why, for instance, do patriarchal or Chinese communist societies remain stable and powerful for such long periods of time? In my personality theory such stability is based not only on coercion by means of a police and a military machine in conspiration with cunning authorities. Beyond that their domination is made possible by the deformation of the dispositional core structure itself of many victims of such regimes. The core deformation is preceded or accompanied by a deformation of their own tradition pyramid. As I have shown, our tradition pyramid, with its personal modulations and deformations, directs our core or character formation.

The vital eros, for example, of many South American *campesinos* or of Afro-Americans in the United States was directed by the Christian form tradition. They themselves under the pressure of the oppressors deformed these form traditions prefocally and unwittingly. This deformation occurred in order for them to survive by adaptation. To live in quasi congeniality with their suppressed unique life call many of them learned to experience their coformation with the oppressors as virtuous, humble, reverential submission to the political and economic powers of landowners or American slave owners. The oppressors in turn had deformed their own Christian form tradition to justify their exploitation of the dispossessed. A similar dynamic explains the past submission of abused women and children to men. The strength of the deformed elements of such traditions makes it difficult for courageous women and men who set out to revitalize classical traditions in their original purity. They try to rally the victims of deformation behind them, to awaken them to resistance to their meekly revered male oppressors, to restore the tradition to its original purity, or to expand it in compatibility with newly emergent insights.

Oppression Facilitated
by Deformative Disposition Formation

Distorted family traditions can become the vehicles, the Trojan horses so to speak, that sneak into our hearts and mediate to us such overly submissive or abusive core dispositions. For example, the deformed tradition of absolute patriarchism initiates people in core dispositions of blind submission. They are reared in unquestionable respect for the father of the family, no matter his disrespectful dispositions toward them. They are trained to overrate his rights and powers. Such core dispositions instilled by deformed elements of traditions, mediated by the family, dispose children to the overdependency and the blind obedience they may later live out in relation to all father substitutes. They are worst off when a despotic tradition gains overwhelming power in a society, such as happened with the National Socialist tradition in Germany. Such a regime musters the power to reshape bureaucracy, government, security services, the military, and especially state education and criminal law in accordance with its onesided tradition of absolute dominance. The form that the triumphalist adherents give to these institutions is meant to maintain and deepen in their hapless victims the misdirected vital-erotic core dispositions of enthusiastic submissiveness. The submission to the father is now transferred to submission to idealized leaders. The traditional core form of the vital eros of the adoring victims of such regimes is one of the main means used to keep people docile and submissive to their oppressors.

Perils of Sudden Reformation of Social Structures

A society may undergo basic reformation. In its wake people may experience a conflict between the shared traditional core form to which they are accustomed and their suddenly changing field situations. The traditional facet of their core form comes into question. Suddenly, bereft of their familiar ways, people become uncertain, anxious, and frustrated. They seek wildly for new ways of life or fall into the trap of a deformative defensive traditionalism. They are vulnerable to all kinds of self-styled social prophets and gurus propagating new, often exotic, untested traditions. Society may break apart like melting ice, leading to catastrophic consequences. Balanced adherents of consonant classic traditions may find themselves crushed between the onslaught of wildly proliferating new traditions and the bunker mentality of an irrationally closed traditionalism.

The disturbed reactions of many people in the Soviet Union to the *glasnost* and *perestroika* reformation of Gorbachev are an example of what can happen when the traditional core form of a population is unexpectedly put into doubt. Reformation and transformation should try, if possible, to prevent sudden changes in familiar ways. Ideally, the replacement of deformed traditions by classic, more consonant traditions, should be gradual. Alas, this is rarely possible when a revolutionary reformation of a dictatorial society into a democratic one is taking place. Examples of attempts to foster a basic transformation of some facets of the traditional core form of people, without falling into traditionalism, are the work of Gandhi in India and later of Mother Teresa in Calcutta, of Bishop Tutu and of Nelson Mandela in South Africa, of Martin Luther King and Cesar Chavez in North America.

Helpful in this process of an inner liberation of an encapsulated core form can be my concepts of the founding life form and of the unique-communal life call. This call transcends and should direct the formation of our core form. Congeniality with this life call — in the light of classical transcendent traditions — will protect us against overcompatibility with unjust or unwise sociohistorical traditions as well as with traditionalism, no matter how fervently they are propagated as "the" ultimate solution for all that ails us.

Transcendent Transformation and Sociohistorical Structures

The process of transformation is a never-ending progression of situated free appraisals and options. Each of us is confronted with sociohistorical challenges at every point throughout our life. We must choose between the safe pleasures and satisfactions of overcompatibility or the transcendent joy of growing beyond oppressive structures without betraying our basic traditional identity. We must decide between overdependence on coercive powers and fidelity to our own unique life call with its risks and challenges. We must opt for the path of regression or progression, of immaturity or maturity, of dynamic open tradition or closed traditionalism, of transformation or deformation. When one can think only, "I am the helpless victim of unjust traditional sociohistorical structures," one is on the path of irresponsibility and regression. But when one admits, "It is not the unjust traditional structures alone that make me feel that way, but it is me who makes myself feel like a victim," one is already taking responsibility for one's reformation.

What destroys us is the disposition to put the responsibility for our life in sociohistorical events, people, and situations. One may say, "My family, friends, or employers make me feel overly guilty whenever I think for myself or when I begin to behave a little less as a conforming, colorless, family- or company-person." This is self-defeating talk. It is an example of the irrational process by which we give up fidelity to our unique-communal life call. We make our life the responsibility of traditionally oppressive elements that are embedded in our sociohistorical institutions. We let them manipulate our guilt feelings. We make them the sources of our emotional self-appraisals. We become dependent on the sporadic moments of leniency and benevolence when our oppressors are condescendingly kind to us because they happen to need us for their comforts and projects. Looking for cheap rewards from the powermongers among us, we lose our soul. We must reclaim our own responsibility for the unique-communal aspect of our life. Yet at the same time we must strive for compatibility with reasonable elements of sociohistorical traditions, structures, and events with which we are confronted in our formation field.

The Transcendent I and the Subordinated I

We live in sociohistorical contexts, which may not be conducive to our transcendent transformation. Involved in such situations, we must do our part; we must function as well as we can. The pretranscendent central "I" of my theory that directs our functioning in socially acceptable ways is *not* our deepest I. This lower central *I* aims to integrate the relevant messages of its pretranscendent sub-I's, such as the sociohistorical, the vital, the functional, the functional-transcendent I's and their respective articulations. To keep on the path of transcendence, we must disclose in ourselves the deeper "I" that my theory also poses. This is the *I* that goes beyond, that "transcends" sociohistorical conditions as well as our lower *I* with its sub-I's. We must take these into account, but we are no longer their slave. Sometimes I designate this deepest I in my personality theory as the *beyond-I*. Our *beyond-I* is the *I* of our unique-communal life call. This "I" is responsible for inspiring and guiding our lower executive or central "I." The *I* of the life call directs this subordinated *I* to implement our unique-communal calling in life not only congenially but also compatibly. For the implementations of our life call should be reasonably compatible with the right demands of the sociohistorical institutions in which we have to implement our faith traditions. We must do so in the belief that the mystery of transformation speaks not only in us but also in our formation field.

Sociohistorical events and situations may often seem alien, unfamiliar, isolated, and "out there." The transcendent *I* enables us to find in them what is consonant with our calling in life as it slowly discloses itself over a lifetime in continual dialogue with people, events, and things. It empowers us to maintain our feeling of personal meaningfulness within day-to-day social structures in which we have to operate as well as we can. Our *beyond-I* is the power in us to appreciate and love ourselves as significant participants in the compatible processes of sociohistorical enterprises and happenings, not as moveable pieces on a chess board.

The true art of transcendence or *beyond-ness*, as inspired by transcendent traditions and theoretically clarified by formation science, entails learning how to be beyond things in the midst of everydayness. It means being a part of social structures insofar as they are consonant with the allowing will of the mystery of both tradition formation and of world and history formation. We are to disclose and maintain a sense of our own meaningful calling within the awesome formation story exploding in space and time. To experience this kind of maturity, we must make sure that our life call remains somehow effective within, and in spite of, leveling social institutions. I deem this aspect *call efficacy*, which is intimately linked with the consonant "C" of formation competence, which I introduced in volume 1 of my series.

Call efficacy is a key to transformation of self and world. How we choose to appraise what is happening to us in social systems and their traditions actually affects what happens to us personally within these systems and what we can do about it. Our body chemistry, too, forms itself in continual reaction to our appreciation of how competent we are in handling wisely and firmly the infringements of socioeconomic and political form traditions on our life call. If we are able to strengthen our own appreciation of our overall call efficacy, our fear responses and accompanying chemical secretions will be diminished. We must tell ourselves, "I am not made fearful by powerful social form traditions and their structures; it is I myself who allow myself to be overly impressed by them. I may have the feeling of fear of social oppressors, but I am not that fear. I can do something about these feelings and about what traditional social form structures do to me."

A reader may say, "I understand the hold that sociohistorical form traditional structures can have on my life, but I cannot really believe that I can rise above them." This amounts to a confession of having *become* these structures and of having little appreciation of one's own call efficacy. Call efficacy begins to manifest itself the moment we take responsibility for our own freedom from oppression and for the meaningfulness and effectiveness of our own tradition pyramid. My chapters may make readers aware of elements of oppression in their life, but this should not imply that anyone *is* her or his oppression.

Call efficacy is a coformant of the transformation response. It implies an appreciation of our own form potency, a sense that the mystery of formation through us can and shall be effective in its own time and way. Fidelity to our call can only be effective when our functional I — with its sociohistorically conditioned response — is subordinated to our higher I rather than the pretranscendent I taking precedence over the transcendent I.

Life Call Affirmation

Another coformant of the transformation response is our affirmation of our own life call with its nourishing transcendent traditions. This is to be distinguished from confirmation by others. The strength and the prominence of our higher I as an epiphany of the mystery deepens at any time we affirm our unique-communal call in faith, hope, and love. Life call affirmations should be part of our daily self-talk. They can then facilitate the transformation of our entire bodily and mental form of life.

We must not give in to discouragement. We must never talk to ourselves or others as if our life were meaningless because of oppressive social traditions embedded in social structures that hamper our ascent. Such talk tempts us to bypass an opportunity for transformation. It demonstrates that we are out of touch with the best of our own transcendent traditions. Often we ought to ask ourselves: "How am I talking to myself?" We need to watch our language, for language is the software directing our body's computer system. When we learn to say to ourselves, "I *myself* upset myself about adverse social traditions," or "I am 'catastrophizing' my social situation," we will notice a restoration of our sense of control, of our power to give effective form to our life in spite of a depressing past or of present or anticipated sociohistorical calamities. This will affect not only our emotions but also our physical well-being.

Suggestions for Life Call Affirmations

Let me offer a few suggestions for life call affirmations. By reflecting on them, readers may make their own affirmations in their own language.

1. Transformation is a never-ending process. The way in which we *personally implement* our formation tradition always changes because our sociohistorical conditions are always changing.

2. We are transformation-in-process. Our transcendent *I* — enlightened by transcendent traditions and inspired and empowered by the formation mystery — makes transformation happen in the midst of and in spite of adverse sociohistorical traditions, events, and structures.

3. Our vital life may get upset, irritated, angry, and aggressive when we feel oppressed by social situations and the traditions they express and foster. But our higher *I* is not reducible to any of these feelings. If we refuse to become any of them, they will diminish and even vanish in time.

4. The reformations we want in social situations and traditions are all temporary and passing. Our higher *I* is lasting and, therefore, transcends them all. We are not identical with past, present, or future sociohistorical form traditions, changes, and conditions.

5. Our impatient need for social reform is not the longing of the transcendent *I*. Our vital-functional *I* has needs, but our higher *I* is needless; it lives by inspirations and aspirations nourished and symbolized by transcendent traditions.

6. Our pretranscendent *I* experiences vital pleasures and displeasures, functional satisfactions and dissatisfactions, about what happens in our sociohistorical scene, but our transcendent *I* is not fully identical with any of these emotions. It enables us to appraise these lower feelings from an inner distance, as it were, and to change them if we want to in the light of transcendent traditions and symbols.

7. Our lower subordinated *I* has exciting or depressing thoughts about our sociohistorical predicaments and the traditions they represent, but these thoughts are not the whole of who we are. Our higher *I* should appraise and gently yet firmly control our thoughts and our *attentiveness dispositions* in the light of consonant transcendent traditions.

8. To feel helpless under the overwhelming power of dominant sociohistorical traditions and structures is an invitation to let the mystery empower our higher *I* so that it may shore up our defeated vital-functional *I*.

9. Our transcendent *I*, as empowered by the mystery, is in control of our transformation in the light of the disclosures of that mystery in transcendent traditions.

10. Sociohistorical oppressors in the family or in any social institution may affect our vital-functional life, but they cannot affect directly our transcendent life. Our transcendent *I*, enlightened and strengthened by transcendent traditions, determines the ultimate effect people will have on our life and its ongoing transformation.

CHAPTER 24

Transcendent and Capitalist Traditions

E lements of the capitalist or neocapitalist tradition influence the character or core form of most people in Western societies. I call this a *free-floating tradition* because capitalism, not as a mere economic system, but insofar as it affects the formation of the core dispositions of human life, is not institutionalized like Jewish, Christian, or humanistic formation patterns are. What is institutionalized are not its hidden powers of shaping all of human life but only capitalistic economies, enterprises, lobbies, laws, pragmatic trainings in economic techniques and principles. All of these can affect the formation climate of a society. They can modulate the overall outlook on life of people who participate in such undertakings or are educated for them. I call this in my personality theory the form traditional aspect of capitalism. As a form tradition, capitalism is not institutionalized and formulated as some others are. Within our pyramids of tradition, the free-floating implicit patterns of a capitalistic life formation interform with those of other traditions. Similarly, dispositions initiated or stimulated by the capitalist tradition interform with those fostered by other sources of formation.

Of special interest to my formation theory are the interactions between early childhood dispositions and later acquired elements of capitalist dispositions. Certain problematic dispositions in childhood can influence the later selection and excessive cultivation of similar dispositions in one's form traditional pyramid. Some of these dispositions are formed under the influence of a capitalistic outlook on the meaning of life as a whole. Psychoanalysis, one of our many and varied auxiliary disciplines, has much to say about this issue. Within the context of this book, I cannot give a detailed critique of the capitalistic tradition in all its formational ramifications. I shall restrict myself to a concise consideration of the general drift of this tradition. My main question will be: How can I relate this tradition to transcendent traditions?

Obviously I am not dealing here with capitalism as an economic system, developed in Europe since the fifteenth century, based on the principles of private enterprise and of the private ownership of means of production. This system takes on different forms in different countries, cultures, and periods of economic history. As such, economic capitalism is the object of study of disciplines like economics, political science, business administration, history, and geography.

Capitalism, if made by people into a basic faith or belief system, holds that our inherent striving for happiness can find the best conditions for fulfillment by owning and expanding money, valuable possessions, economic status, and power. The moment we turn it into the foundational belief system at the base of our pyramid it becomes relevant to our life formation as a whole. Under this aspect alone it falls under the formal object of formation science.

Psychoanalysis and the Capitalist Tradition

What is the general drift of psychoanalytic thought about the correspondence between certain traits of infancy and analogous elements in the capitalist tradition? I shall channel my observations in this regard along the lines of the comprehensive theory of formation science. As usual this translation will help me to go beyond the restrictions of particular auxiliary disciplines dealing with other aspects of the same topic.

Infants find themselves in a confined field of life. They are not yet able to open up to their environment as adults do. They do not have at their disposal the power of well-trained accurate sense observation enriched by lifelong experience. They have not yet developed the possibility of empathy. Mature empathy would allow them to open up affectively to people, events, and things in their uniqueness and individuality. Neither is there fully available to them the power of affective, imaginative, rational appraisal, and of accurate sense observation. These are our bridges to the realities that surround us. In summary, their channels of contact with their environment are still severely restricted. Infants cannot yet sufficiently actualize their basic form potencies for form reception and expression. Actualization of these potencies requires mental and sensual openings to the forms of reality as they appear in our environment. Only then can we exercise our human powers of receiving and modulating them.

Yet infants' inherent form potencies with their still latent dynamics compel them to open up to their small world in any way available to them, no matter how primitive and limited in their scope. Because of the lack of development of their higher channels of contact, they fall back on other organismic body openings. Initially the oral opening with its original sensitivity is most immediately available to them for interaction with aspects of their field of presence and action. They experienced this channel of contact with reality in the process of feeding by the mother. This still highly sensitized oral opening is utilized by their form potency to receive and give form in their field. Their mouth sensitivity makes it possible for them to take in and probe various forms of nourishment. In a similar fashion, they tend to receive and explore other forms in their environment. That is one of the reasons why we have to watch carefully what infants put into their mouth, which is their main form receptive channel for almost everything.

Infants are endowed not only with a form receiving dynamic but also with a form-giving or form-modulating dynamic. Biting and chewing, molding with the oral muscles, spitting out, sucking in, are ways of working upon received forms, to make them somewhat their own while slightly modulating their form in the process. These are primitive modes of minimal form donation.

Experiences of Consonance and Dissonance

What I call basic experiences of consonance and dissonance with one's world may, for certain individuals, go back to these first experiences of oral form reception and expression. For them the experiences of consonance and dissonance later in life may still be determined by remnants of their experiences as infants. Their initial flowing with or excessive resistance to people, events, and things in their infantile attempts to realize their oral receptivity and oral form-giving may still be with them. As adults they may still be seeking for satisfaction of frustrated oral sucking, tasting, and biting in infancy, be it now in a symbolic fashion. This may play a role in certain sexual erotic desires and patterns of sexual behavior or in their aggressive moments when they clench, for instance, their teeth.

If infants experienced sufficient consonance with their environment and the people within it, these pleasant experiences can be the root of later dispositions of appreciation and hope that things will work out well in the end. In other words, elementary favorable vital-oral experiences may foster primitive appreciation and hope dispositions. Like the vital eros experience of infancy, this embryonic hope has a latent transcendence capacity. It can be transformed by transcendent hope at the appropriate time in one's formation history. This hope suggests that somehow a benign mystery of formation will make all things well for us in the end.

In some cases infantile experiences of consonance may contain the seeds of a naive trust in all individuals just as they appear to us in their apparent form. It may take a long time, much pain, and disappointment to learn the lesson that no person, event, or thing appearing in our pretranscendent field of life can be trusted unconditionally. Innate imperfections, neurotic conditions, the fancies of the autarkic pride form, unpredictable or unrecognized life experiences make it impossible for any of us to be perfectly and consistently trustworthy at all times under every circumstance. Only the transcendent mystery is fully trustworthy. We can hope for the best in every person. We can love, if not always like, people and appreciate what is actually or potentially good in them. We should love them as loved and called uniquely by the same mystery who is calling and loving each of us uniquely. It would be a mistake, however, to base our life formation on absolute trust in people just as they appear to us in their apparent form. We then set ourselves up for a life of disappointment. While not judging them ultimately we must daily grow in appraising them practically to facilitate the competent implementation of our unique life call.

In place of consonance infants may primarily experience dissonance in their attempts to receive and modulate forms in their surroundings through their sensitive oral channel of communication. This may be the unknown root of such core dispositions as the expectation to be disappointed, which can lead to dispositions of depreciation, withdrawal, low-grade depression, despondency, and despair later in life.

Anal Formation Phase

This next phase is of special interest for our exploration of possible connections between infantile experience and the possessiveness that may be fostered in certain individuals by the way they tend personally to interpret and live the capitalist tradition.

In this phase children experience a fundamental change in their field of daily formation. Parents or their substitutes begin to restrict a thus far uncontrolled area of form reception and expression through their imposition of toilet training. This involves another sensitive body opening in the initial primitive actualization of the form receptive and form expressive potencies of the child. Children discover that one way of giving form to their faeces and also to their relations with others (interformation) is made possible by control of their holding up or letting go what presses to pass through the openings of their own bodies. They dimly realize that their performance is of concern to their parents. This enables them to experience the power of giving form to their relations with them by holding in, keeping to oneself, conserving, sparing. For some individuals this can be the beginning of a basic disposition of their character or core form. This disposition may engender attitudes of stubbornness, obstinacy, autarky, avarice, excessive self-assertion, being thrifty and overly regulated.

As with the vital eros and the oral hope disposition, so the vital anal disposition — when not excessively thwarted by the parents — is inwardly receptive to later transformation by the transcendent preservation disposition. In the light of transcendent traditions, this disposition asserts and conserves fidelity to one's transcendent life call and to all that proves to pertain to its congenial and compatible realization.

Some psychoanalytic thinkers relate this anal formation phase to the capitalist tradition. Freud was the first to write about *character and anal erotik*, or in my own terminology, the influence of the vital-erotic anal formation phase on the disposition formation of our core form or character. Freud claims that patients whose character disposition is strongly influenced by withholding attitudes of the anal formation period are marked by a compelling sense for order, neatness, and thrift. He added that this concern with filth can be pursued further in compelling money concerns, hence, perhaps, explaining the expression "filthy lucre."

Ferenczi interprets the further formation of children, their pleasure in playing with mud and clay and later their inclination to collect things as a replacement, respectively, a sublimation, of their interest in their own faeces. I see this interest as also an expression of their latent need for form expression, especially by toying with pliable forms of faeces that are most near at hand. Ferenczi sees the roots of capitalism in the subsequent pleasure of the child in collecting. From the viewpoint of my own personality theory, I cannot go along with this observation of Ferenczi in its universality.

Capitalism and Anal Formation

My first question is: What is meant by the term *capitalism?* I also ask how far one can reduce a universal economic system called capitalism to the anal formation problems of individuals? The individual ways and motivations of striving for property formation are different from those fostered by capitalism as a merely socioeconomic tradition. As a formation tradition, capitalism goes beyond individuals and their private histories. It is an economic tradition concerned first of all with the efficacy of functional-economic processes. Of course, I do not contend that the compelling drive to pile up and save more and more money, gold, and valuables is necessarily propelled by functional-economic directives alone. In a number of individual people who suffer from the coercive form disposition of hoarding possessions, the therapist may detect its irrational and erotic roots in unsolved childhood dispositions.

Even so, I am not convinced that all forms of avarice in later life can be explained as merely aftereffects of an infantile conservation of faeces. Neither can I deny that some connection may be possible between holding up faeces and the collecting and coercive holding on to monies and other valuables or, by analogous extension, an irrational holding on to individualistic opinions that fill one's mind and heart. My question is: What is it in people that makes it possible for a number of them to link in their nonfocal memorial consciousness the past experiences of their infantile holding in of faeces and their later coercive holding on to possessions and opinions? Are both of them rooted in some basic need of human life?

Fulfillment Aspiration

In formation science and theory, I have pointed out that at the base of human life are certain fundamental aspirations rooted in the founding human life form and latent in our transcendent or "trans" consciousness. One of them is the aspiration for *fulfillment* in a deep, distinctively human sense. One is not at once awakened to this aspiration in its fullness. Yet its hidden dynamic can indirectly stir fulfillment strivings on the pretranscendent level of life. Also, analogous symbolic metaphors of this latent aspiration can express themselves in some people's lower striving for material fulfillment. A basic pretranscendent need for material fulfillment, for keeping filled up, for finding pleasure in feeling filled in one way or the other can take the place in some of an as yet undisclosed transcendent fulfillment aspiration.

One possible concretization of this pretranscendent analogous need can be the craving to collect more and more money or other valuables. In some cases it can become the coercive disposition to stuff one's consciousness with images, opinions, ideas, and information to which one stubbornly clings as a filling of the mind. One seems somehow driven to maintain such fillings at all costs. It is as if the very meaning and solidity of one's life were at stake.

The source of the urgent demand for unlimited increase in possessions is thus not exclusively the holding up of, the keeping filled with, faeces in infancy. This can be a secondary source in some individuals. But this urge itself to keep filled up in childhood can be another analogous substitute for the transcendent fulfillment aspiration deep within every human being. Both the craving to fill up with money or information and the primitive infantile urge to keep filled up with faeces could express in some cases also a general need for material fulfillment. This need in turn is one of numerous possible ways to express pretranscendently an ignored or not yet awakened basic transcendent aspiration. As with all transconscious aspirations, this, too, can radiate in camouflaged forms into the prefocal and focal consciousness of people.

I realize, of course, that certain spiritual traditions stress the aspiration of "emptiness" or the "void," "nada" or "nothingness." Examples are the Christian subtradition of John of the Cross or Meister Eckhardt or the Buddhist tradition of "emptiness." A closer look at what they mean points us still in the direction of the transcendent fulfillment aspiration. They may speak, for example, of an emptying of the heart of all attachments so that it might be filled more fully by what can alone satisfy this aspiration: the abyss of divine love, mystical union with all that is, or, in some traditions, becoming at one with the fullness of the mystery of being.

Inexact Generalizations of Individual Experiences

As may be evident by now, my awareness of the role of traditions in formation makes me cautious in my appraisal of the generalizations of childhood experiences of individuals no matter how much similarity there seems to be between them. I do not want to generalize uncritically. I do not think that the possible reactions of a number of infants to a specific tradition of toilet training — modulated by individual parental idiosyncrasies — should be too easily transferred to a universal reaction of all infants exposed to different traditions of toilet training. One of our auxiliary sciences, anthropology, shows that the practices of toilet training in different traditions differ considerably. This data makes me wary of linking too generally the formation of the core form of people to their toilet training in infancy.

This caution should not go so far as to overlook the possibility of certain relationships between eating and drinking and thrift. Some ancient traditions believed that by the eating of someone's flesh and blood, one shared in the substance of that person. To eat and to drink is, after all, the most primitive example of receiving, assimilating, and "having" some form.

The immense plasticity of our imaginative, metaphoric, and symbolic formation powers also makes possible a connection between money and faeces and between the craving for collecting money and anal eroticism. Some of Freud's patients associated constipation with money. In dreams, myths, and folklore, the relationship between money and filth returns again and again, for instance, in the First Letter of the Apostle Peter: *turpe lucrum.*

Again it would be unwise to explain on the basis of such individual symbolic meanings and cravings for money the character of the capitalist tradition as a whole, which primarily developed as a mainly economic tradition. The question with which the comprehensive formation scientist is faced time and again is: How far can one explain a general socio-historical tradition out of individual formation dispositions, dynamics, and directives?

Economy in Ancient Traditions

Consulting anthropology as an auxiliary science, we see that it is the consensus of anthropologists that in ancient traditions money had a sacred meaning and that an earlier primitive economy, related to these traditions, did not know about exchange of goods for the pursuit of gain. Archaic patterns of exchange were intimately interwoven with the all-pervading faith and form traditions of the tribes involved. Not material profit but the mysterious order of the world as known to them gave form to the patterns in question. Adherents of these traditions did not work for profit. Neither did they develop a distinct tradition of barter and exchange based on merely economic motives and separated from their faith and form tradition. Individual collecting of material goods merely for private profit was unknown. The economy of barter and exchange was submerged in social relationships that guided the patterns of interformation. What was crucial in their traditions was not the amassing of individual possessions but social standing, social claims, and assets. Material possessions were appreciated only insofar as they helped safeguard one's standing in society.

Capitalist Tradition

We can compare the meaning of material possessions in ancient economic traditions with our own capitalist or neocapitalist tradition. The basic features of the capitalist tradition in regard to material possessions can be summarized as follows.

1. The capitalist tradition in and by itself does not give a transcendent, sacred, or epiphanic meaning to what we collect or possess or to the ways in which we collect, preserve, or use such possessions.

2. The capitalist tradition inclines us to give form to every exchange in such a way that we make a profit.

3. The capitalist tradition further inclines us to put a monetary value on all things, events, actions, jobs, and careers. This can influence our rating of the worth of people. We may be tempted to esteem highly those who gain the most or who can help us to acquire more material resources. Conversely we may underestimate those who gained the least or less than we ourselves did or whose lack of resources makes them less potentially material supporters of our own projects.

4. The capitalist tradition suggests that we should always and everywhere labor for remuneration. It may already give a capitalistic form to the normal everyday services children perform in the family by rewarding them with small allowances for the chores they do.

5. The capitalist tradition fosters a concern with the "marketable" apparent form we ought to develop in order to gain the position, status, and power that improve our possibilities for economic gain.

6. This tradition directs our appraisal process by the criteria of economic success. How much people make becomes a main measure of their worth and achievement.

7. The capitalist tradition fosters the art and discipline of accomplishing as many economically advantageous tasks and projects as possible with the least loss of energy and within the shortest time, because time is money, and with the least possible distraction by noneconomic concerns.

8. This tradition can lead to an underformation of motivations that are transeconomic or that do not foster side-effects favorable to our economic possibilities, such as the cultivation of one's marketable apparent form.

9. Spontaneous human love and sympathy, trust and warmth, celebration, festiveness and playfulness, contemplation and worship, art and beauty can become subordinated to traditional capitalist styles of togetherness. Companionship may be increasingly restricted to a progressive specialization and rationalization of individuals collaborating within productive teams. This formation may spill over into aspects of relationships in marriage, family, friendship, and other associations.

10. Capitalist formation tends to reinforce behavior that strengthens profit production by smoothly functioning teamwork. Reinforced are also behaviors that enhance the marketable skills and appearances of all par-

ticipants in money-making enterprises. This smooth, somewhat flat yet charming style may spill over into other relationships, diminishing the intimacy and spontaneity of human encounter. It may influence the formation of children of adherents of the capitalist formation tradition.

11. The capitalist tradition gives form to an open market, characterized by free competition and the pursuit of material gain. To stay competitive in such a market presupposes that one develops a core form or character disposed to compute, manipulate, strategize, and to use politically one's gift of charm. This tradition in and of itself neither instills nor forbids a transcendent appreciation of the unique worth and dignity of the human persons involved in such interactions. Practically speaking, however, if no transcendent tradition fosters such appreciation-in-depth, a participant in a mainly capitalist tradition may not maintain or develop this deeper appreciation.

12. Because the capitalist tradition may direct people to enhance their marketable apparent form, they may dispose themselves to merely imitate some external "winning" ways and demeanors that may give the impression of transcendent appreciation. This leads to a virtuosity that may prevent the formation of the real virtues of transcendent presence. Such deformation may gain some foothold in a capitalistic society at large.

13. As with every form tradition, so too the capitalistic tradition can be partly motivated in certain individuals by irrational needs. These can co-form one's life as a whole. They can be explored in the auxiliary discipline of psychoanalysis, which in some instances might disclose their roots in unsolved erotic infantile conflicts. Individual irrational motivations, however, cannot sufficiently explain the general, powerful, and rational tradition of economic capitalism as a whole. Not all adherents of this tradition share these erotic infantile conflicts and needs. Historical studies demonstrate the presence of other influences in the development of the capitalist tradition since the fifteenth century in Europe.

14. The capitalist tradition, as other traditions, has its own general system of rational or rationalized objective functional directives. While these cannot prevent the intervention of irrational motivations of individual participants in the tradition, they do surpass them. Therefore, the capitalist tradition as a whole cannot be reduced to a mere effect of unsolved problems of childhood.

15. Individuals participating in the capitalist tradition do not necessarily make it the basic tradition of their own tradition pyramid. If their transcendent tradition is the matrix of their life formation, they will not be dominated by their added capitalist form tradition. They will subordinate it to their basic transcendent tradition. They will adopt mainly those practical forms of the capitalist tradition that are compatible with their own faith and form tradition. They will not accept all tenets of the faith tradition that animates an absolutized capitalistic form tradition.

16. Conversely, one's transcendent tradition can be contaminated by

one's secondary capitalist tradition. For example, people may make contributions to churches and works of charity or they may participate in public religious ceremonies and activities mainly in service of their own economic interests. They may do so focally or nonfocally to enhance their marketable apparent form within a community of believers whom they appreciate as potential cooperators or customers or as coformers of a favorable local climate for their enterprises.

Interformation of Capitalist and Transcendent Traditions

My introduction of the notion of a tradition pyramid raises many questions. One of them is that of the interformation between the different traditions that are operative within the same personal or group pyramid. The possibilities of such interformations are legion. One example of the interformation of traditions has been worked out by Max Weber in regard to the interformation of the Protestant and the capitalist formation traditions (see Weber 1963).

His study extends itself in fact only to one Protestant form tradition, that of the Anglo-Saxon Puritans and probably that of the Pennsylvania Quakers. The predestination doctrine of their Calvinist faith tradition led to rigid life directives in their form tradition. The puritanical form tradition flowered in precise workmanship, dedicated skillful labor, honesty, reliability, thriftiness, and sobriety of lifestyle. To understand their form tradition requires that we look more closely at some of its salient directives.

Formation Directives of the Puritanical Formation Tradition

The Puritans frowned upon a spontaneous and carefree appreciation of the joys of life. For example, they resisted the *Book of Sports* promoted by law by the English kings James I and Charles I. Both monarchs wanted to foster and defend the enjoyment of sport against the emerging more rigorous form tradition of the English middle class in that period.

The puritanical form tradition distrusted the vital-erotic as well as the vital-functional dimensions of life insofar as they could be sources of time- and energy-wasting pleasures. Such times and energies should be used instead for worship or for profit-producing labor. Soon this distrust extended itself to all social and functional enjoyments that could not be justified in terms of their predestinational formation system. For example, the sober and conscientious study of science could be appreciated in the light of their tradition. Therefore, they honored and promoted it. But time spent in literary pursuits — the reading of plays and novels, poems and short stories — was lost time, exposing oneself to frivolity and occasions of sin and temptation. Condemned were dance, theater, other arts and lighthearted amusements. People favored by the Lord are on the earth not to amuse themselves but to labor and to prosper economically as a sign of their predestination for eternal salvation.

The puritanical form tradition rejected also ventures or endeavors to which one could ascribe a magic power, such as liturgy or folk festivals ranging from popular Christmas celebrations to Maypole festivities. Theatrical performances were especially suspect. The puritanical city government of Stratford on Avon closed the theater of the town while Shakespeare was still alive (1564–1616). The puritanical form tradition instilled a disposition of fear for anything that could lead to an idolizing of creatures. Its adherents fulminated against idle talk, superfluities, and the vain ostentation promoted by fashion. One should honor God alone and protect oneself against idle thought and fantasy by an ethos of sober functioning, matter-of-factness, and daily industriousness. One should not spend money idly but save it and labor ceaselessly to increase it. To be ostentatious or to strive for riches in and by themselves was sinful. However, to acquire goods as a result of an irreproachable life of dedicated functioning, thrift, and sobriety could be seen as evidence of divine approval and predestination for salvation.

Interformation of Puritanical and Capitalist Traditions

Obviously there are points of interformation between this stern, thrifty form tradition at the base of the puritanical pyramid and the emergent American capitalist tradition. The directives of the puritanical tradition but also those of the Quakers in Pennsylvania could not but benefit the development of an economy dominated by the steady formation and effective use of capital. The amassing of great capitals for the industrialization of America has been made possible by the implementation of the traditional puritanical form of life. The success of capitalism on this continent was in great measure the triumph of the functional-economic virtues of the Puritans. It was sanctioned by their belief that prosperity was a sign of being chosen by the Divine.

Flaws in Max Weber's Work

Weber tends to magnify unduly the formational impact of the Puritans on the capitalist tradition. He makes it sound as if the capitalist tradition itself is a mere outgrowth of the Protestant tradition. Unfortunately, Weber could not be aware of my distinction between faith and form tradition or of my notion of a form tradition pyramid with the subtle interactions between its multileveled traditions. These constructs could have protected his great work from the flaws of confusion and of the exaggeration of his hypothesis.

As with all faith traditions, so too the Calvinist *faith* tradition should not be made identical with any Calvinistic *form* tradition. There is a basic Calvinist faith tradition; there are numerous diverse Calvinistic form traditions. Not all of them translate in the same fashion the predestination doctrine of their underlying faith tradition into a practical everyday form tradition. The Puritans turned this doctrine of their faith into a set of everyday directives that gave form rigidly to every facet of their life and thought. Many other Calvinist and generally Protestant form traditions are not as exclusively guided by these form directives. Their directives allow for a reasonable enjoyment of food and drink and the simple pleasures of art, life, beauty, sport, and entertainment. Therefore, the title of his work, *The Protestant Ethic and the Spirit of Capitalism*, is a misnomer that exemplifies what could happen before there was a systematic understanding of the crucial distinction between faith and form tradition. It was not the Protestant faith tradition Weber was talking about, but only one of the numerous Protestant form traditions and one of its particular implementations in everyday life formation. Moreover, as I said earlier, the rise of capitalism also has sociohistorical roots other than the Puritan form tradition. These are, at least in part, older than the Puritan tradition itself.

In spite of these flaws the work of Max Weber is an outstanding contribution to our understanding of the dynamics of interformation between transcendent and capitalist traditions when found in the same tradition pyramid of a group or of an individual.

Applying my notion of the tradition pyramid, we can see that within the Puritan pyramid a basic form tradition interforms with the emergent tradition of capitalism without becoming identical with it. Therefore, the inherent dynamics of the capitalist tradition itself would lead to an increasing distancing from the transcendent elements that the Puritans had injected into it during the process of interformation. Interformation is a circular process. Interforming traditions are at the same time a cause and a consequence of each other's form directives.

Capitalistic Deformation and Transcendent Transformation

I am not qualified to evaluate the economic system of capitalism with its many different faces in a wide variety of cultures, countries, and cultural periods. My concern is how capitalism as a formation tradition can influence our distinctively human formation. The word *capitalistic* with the ending "istic," as I use it here, is meant to point to incidences of individual and group formation in which a capitalistic mentality has taken over, has become the basis of one's tradition pyramid, taking the place of transcendent traditions, and hence fostering the deformation instead of the transformation of life.

It is all right to foster a subordinated position of the capitalist form tradition somewhere in one's tradition pyramid. This does not exclude transcendence. Transcendent transformation, as I see it, is "a going beyond while going into." It is a transcendent movement that is at the same time an immanent one. For example, in the light of transcendent traditions, I go beyond pretranscendent anxious possessiveness. I relativize the false life directive that having and collecting things is "the" path to ultimate happiness, but I do not reject a reasonable concern for my possessions or those of others. I care for them without being overly attached to them or not caring as a good steward for the needs of others. I appreciate them as useful and agreeable means to attain a balanced and effective life, serving my family and society. Such relaxed detachment and appreciation is a fruit of the transformation that becomes possible only when I rise above my obsession with possessions, which can be a side-effect of the capitalistic mentality.

Possessiveness

The capitalistic tradition becomes deformative if it leads to possessiveness. Concern for possessions is constructive; possessiveness is destructive. Care for possessions is compatible with transcendence; anxious possessiveness blocks the road to joyous ascendence. To grow in peace, joy, and love, I must awaken to the perils of sheer economism. These always threaten me in a capitalistic culture. The ways of detachment from material holdings have been tried and tested for thousands of years by the classical transcendent traditions of humanity.

When we try to live by capitalist traditions alone, we install in our lives a mechanism of instant overreaction the moment we feel that our possessions are threatened. This automatic emotional reaction is a symptom of possessiveness. It affects not only our mind and feelings but our vital make-up as well, especially in its constitution of what I have identified as our neuroform. Adrenalin flows into our bloodstream. We feel ourselves tightening up. Our whole attention is absorbed by the imagined or real economic threat. No room is left for attention to anything other than safeguarding and expanding our threatened possessions or opinions. Others are seen only as competitors. We fight with them for a bigger piece of the economic pie.

When we suffer for a long time from coercive possessiveness, we may become paranoid in the world of money, promotion, and commerce. We are swallowed up by the urge to dominate the market or our shaky job environment. We imagine that survival and happiness depend on economic success, on outdoing others in the realm of career, profit, and the market place. We lose the ability to tune in to the overall situation in which we are involved. We do not see ourselves or the people around us as they fully and truly are, nor do we appreciate all facets of our field here and now. We are perceptive only of the economic dimension of reality.

At times of threat such economic fixation leads to automatic anger, fear, and aggressiveness. We do not flow with the world; we are at the world. Rapid heartbeat and a fast release of adrenalin and other hormones into the bloodstream may be the consequences, harming our health, lowering our immunity system, stealing our energy and *joie de vivre*, aging us before our time.

Rising above the Capitalist Game

In our economic interactions, possessiveness magnifies molehills into mountains. If we do not rise above the capitalist game that we have to play in our society, our autonomic nervous system becomes geared to instant fear, anger, paranoia, and dissonance from competitive others. The paradox is that a transformation of this dissonance into basic consonance, love, and compassion would serve our economic efficacy much better in the long run. For in return we would receive cooperation, confirmation, and trust from dependable people in society. Sooner or later they would seek us out. They would feel safe and at ease doing business with us or promote us in our jobs. Of course, that should not be the main motivation for our transcendent life formation; however, it can help us to overcome the conviction of some people that to be honest and loving is bad for business.

Possessive Life, a Life of Dissonance

Possessive, paranoid people live in painful dissonance with their own better selves and with others. They cannot warmly love themselves and others. Their main intimacy is with money and money games. Feelings of inner lostness and tension accumulate. They tend to get high blood pressure, ulcers, dermatitis, heart trouble, indigestion, and other diseases. Classic transcendent traditions show us how to rise above our economic obsessions without forfeiting reasonable monetary concerns. They teach us how to override our economic "jungle mentality" so that we can enjoy all of our life, not only its economic facets.

The endless struggle for more and more profit yields lives of constant suspicion, dissonance, incompatibility, lack of compassion, aggression, frustration, fear, and resentment. Everything possessive people tell themselves they must have to be happy ends up yielding more disappointment than satisfaction. The more successful a person is in making money, turning a profit, getting ahead of the game, collecting possessions, the less consonant, congenial, compatible, and peaceful one may find himself or herself in the long run. Even if one wins there is always the fear that one may lose what has been amassed with so much diligence and cunning.

Internal Coercive Attachment, Source of Anxious Existence

It is not financial success in and of itself that creates a tense and anxious life. It is the inner coercive attachment disposition or compelling urge for material acquisition and maintenance that keeps one from enjoying the transcendent beauty and meaning of human existence. Possessiveness is a misinterpretation of our aspiration for fulfillment; it is a faulty way of looking for it. Some may already have been conditioned this way in their anal-erotic formation phase. When fulfillment is sought for in *having* and controlling instead of *being*, we become vulnerable. Having more and more things cannot fulfill us. We will never have enough to make us content.

There is always the fear of nonfulfillment. We are constantly afraid that someone will take a source of income, of promotion or customers away from us. We are anxiously scanning our business or job environment: Is somebody invading our profitable relationships or tricking us otherwise? We feel bored if we do not experience an increase in our good fortunes. We are eaten up by worry if our income goes down, over-elated when it rises, then asking again if we could not have done even better than that. Briefly, as long as we are possessive we have no chance of living joyful, consonant, peace-filled, wise, and effective lives.

Changing Absolutized Attachments to Relaxed Appreciations

Transformation of this unhappy state occurs when we realize the utter futility of trying to live a joyful life by economic efforts alone. To grow in transcendent happiness, we have to transform our possessive dispositions and attitudes in the light of classical transcendent formation traditions. This presupposes that we become aware of these unsavory dispositions, especially of their routinization in the programmed reactions of our autonomic nervous system. Our neuroform will react coercively the moment issues of money, profit, economic loss or gain enter the horizon of our life. It is the foolish patterns of "happiness-through-money" in our head, our economic hang-ups, that perturb life. By changing these absolutized attachments to relaxed appreciations, we will be able to become economically effective, peaceful, wise, and loving. We will be free of a constant barrage of excessive concerns about profit. Because transcendence is "going beyond while going into," it does not require that we change our flexible relaxed appreciation and wise management of economic matters. We can be "going beyond" most effectively if we stay appreciatively with our present business, with our reasonable attempts to make a profit, and continue our relaxed concern with job advancement in service of the needs of our family and of society.

Once we have grown with the aid of spiritual formation traditions to a more transcendent awareness, we can become more fully perceptive of our life situation as a whole and the place of our economic concerns within it. Only then will we be granted the wisdom to make suitable changes in our economic position in case a deeper insight into our unique-communal life call would direct us that way. Our aspiration to become free from possessiveness will be our best teacher. It will disclose to us how we can appreciate every economic situation as also an opportunity for human growth. It will make us aware of the inner work of transformation in which we should be involved daily. Each step of liberation from possessiveness will immediately add to our experience of relief and give us more enjoyment of life. Transformation is not a distant goal; it is an ongoing project, an indelible part of our here-and-now situation.

Since almost everyone around us in a capitalistic or neocapitalistic society seems to be dominated by the coercive formation disposition to appreciate money as the main road to a meaningful and happy life, we may have given up looking for any other way to peace and contentment. We may even have decided that peace of mind and joy of heart is an impossible dream. Our transcendent traditions teach us differently. They show us the true pathways to peace and joy to which we have been blinded by anxious obsessiveness with possessions.

CHAPTER 25

Formation Tradition
and Formation Mystery

Throughout this book I have attempted to make clear that each formation tradition is a special way of implementing a faith tradition.
One cannot implement what one does not know. Hence a first require-
ment is to seek sufficient understanding of the foundationals of the faith
tradition that a form tradition is meant to implement. Obviously each adherent of each formation tradition cannot be an accomplished theologian
or ideological philosopher. For the majority of believers it is information-
ally desirable that they have a basic grasp of the fundamental authoritative
doctrines of their belief system.

While this is enough for their cognition, it is not enough for the effective
formation and transformation of their life. They must grow in a faith that is
not only cognitive but also formative, not only an affair of the mind but also
of the heart, not merely open to the speculative but also to the implementing intellect. The disposition of believing must become so easy, constant,
and attractive that it is comparable to a second nature, a disposition we activate instantly and continually if the situation calls for it. This disposition
is the fruit of repeated transcendent formative acts and experiences that
flow from a faith to which we are freely committed. Briefly, we need not
only faith, but formative faith.

Four Coformants of Formative Faith

Any formative transcendent disposition contains four coformants: a
functional cognitive, a vital affective, a transcendent loving, and an effective formational coformant. These four are related respectively to the
functional, the vital, the transcendent, and the sociohistorical dimensions
of human life. The four coformants of the disposition of formative faith
complement each other. They can be more or less consonant or integrated
with one another.

In religious formation traditions, for example, adherents prevalently
disposed to transcendent contemplation tend to be less disposed to
functional-cognitive analysis of the processes and contents of their faith.
On the basis of this preference, some of them may develop particular con-

templative formation traditions like the Sufi in Islam, Zen in Buddhism, or the Carthusian in Christianity.

Others again may be predisposed to give form to their faith tradition through the formation and reformation of the sociohistorical dimension of their field of life. They may be less contemplative, less affective transcendent as well as less intellectually analytically disposed. Their way of expressing transcendent love and presence manifests itself preferentially in formational strategy and action. A number of them may develop particular form traditions of social service and care.

Others tend to lean mainly toward the functional-rational-speculative dimension of their faith tradition. Some may become professional theologians and ideological philosophers of their various belief systems. In relation to formation traditions they may choose to become formation theorists and scientists. In some cases a corresponding underdevelopment of the vital affective and contemplative transcendent life of love may become so prevalent that one's passionate love for God or of felt concern for the sociohistorical dimension may seem almost absent.

Another type of believer is inclined to develop mainly the vital affective facet of the faith tradition. If this affective component would exclude the other coformants of the faith disposition solid faith could be replaced by emotional devotionalism.

Consonant formation of the faith disposition in well-developed transcendent traditions respects people's preferential inclination toward one or the other of its four components. Such preferences, however, even if dominant should always be lived out in a balanced, healthy, or consonant relationship to the other coformants.

Because of the complexity of the formational faith disposition, formation practitioners, scholars, and students are often faced with the problem of dissonance between the functional cognitive and the transcendent affective facets in adherents of a faith and formation tradition.

Functional Cognitive and Transcendent Affective Faith Formation

In my formation theory of personality, I stress the impact of initial traditional formation as modulated by the parents. Because of the particular modulation of the parental pyramid of traditions, early interformation with one's original family influences considerably the further unfolding of one's form tradition.

Transcendent transformation is rooted in the increasing disclosure of one's unfolding unique-communal life call and founding life form. The appraisal of this call must take into account the following aspects:

1. The basic and the additional coformants of one's tradition pyramid; their mutual consonance and dissonance; their consonance and dissonance with one's unique-communal life call; their consonance

and dissonance with the spheres and dimensions of one's formation field.

2. One's vital temperament and one's core, heart, or character formation. The vital dimension comprehends not only one's temperament or temper form but also and more basically one's neuroform. This congenitally given and acquired form of one's nervous system must be taken into account.

3. The vital sensual, vital sexual, and vital affective dispositions engendered by initial interformation with the parentally modulated form traditions and with one's neuroform and temper form.

4. One's individual basic talents, deficiencies, aptitudes, and limitations, ultimately rooted in one's genetic neuroform, later activated in one's acquired neuroform.

5. How one's personally modulated pyramid of formation traditions tends to take up the vital affective dispositions of initial interformation and the propensities of one's genetic and acquired neuroform.

6. How one is inclined to give form inwardly to a cohesive field image that can optimally serve as an increasing source of consonance between the coformants of one's formation field.

Formation Crises

The disclosure as well as the implementation of one's founding life form or life call within the parameters of one's tradition pyramid is usually accompanied by formation crises. These are evoked by conflicts between new and past apprehensions and appraisals of one's unique-communal call. The tentative implementations of new appraisals can lead to new conflicts, now between the differences in congeniality and compatibility of a variety of experimental applications.

For example, many experience a crisis when the assertion of their life call and its corresponding modulation in and by a form tradition demands liberation from the paternal modulation of a form traditional pyramid. If, for instance, the paternalistic living out of a religious tradition implied severity, excessive control, and constant threat of punishment, the dispositions of anxiety, resistance, and ambivalence are formed in the child and easily transposed to the formation tradition itself and the God image to which it points. I have tried to describe this process in my biography of Francis Libermann, the son of a devout and strict Orthodox rabbi, in relation to his original paternalistic religious tradition (see my *Light to the Gentiles*).

People in crisis may transcend the dissonance they are experiencing in many ways. One of them is by means of the utilization of dispositions evoked in their relationship with a caring, loving mother figure. Unfortunately the mother of Francis Libermann died when he was quite young. The Catholic tradition he later embraced provided him with the corrective coformative dispositions needed for consonance, but only gradually.

Francis at first began to experience a basic dissonance between himself and a loving mystery of ongoing formation that can never be sufficiently mirrored in any parent. It can only be pointed to. The deepest message of classical transcendent faith and formation traditions is such a pointing. Francis Libermann was graced with a basic appreciative abandonment in faith to the divine forming mystery as announced in his Judeo-Christian tradition. He gained the transcendent wisdom that no feat of pretranscendent mastery, feeling or control could engender; he tasted the consonance the human heart aches to attain.

Francis's history of transformation is comparable to our own. It unfolds along the lines of consonance and dissonance, appreciative and depreciative abandonment, refreshing solitude and depressing loneliness, awe and indifference, attentive abiding and exhausting distraction and dispersion. These and other elements, which I have described in previous volumes, are highlighted in transcendent faith and formation traditions.

Transcendent Maturity and Critical Reason

The great traditions of formation point the way to transcendent maturity. This does not exclude that we mature also in our pretranscendent individualizing life. On the contrary, a mature transcendent tradition presupposes and fosters pretranscendent unfolding. Transcendent traditions teach us not to neglect but to subordinate our pretranscendent maturation to the transcendent disclosure and implementation of our life call.

Crucial in the unfolding of our pretranscendent life is the right formation of critical reason. This analytical aspect of human reason is at the center of the functional-rational dimension of our life. We need to develop a critical sense. We must learn to resist the uncritical acceptance of unrealistic fantasy and mystification. Critical, analytical knowing has a necessary function in human life. It fosters our growth in insight, wisdom, and maturity. It enables us to resist irrational impulses and compulsions. It protects us against premature religious or ideological excitements. Such rational resistance to either religious hysteria or compulsion is necessary. Yet we must be able to benefit also from the wisdom of transcendent intuitive reason. Our resistance to the threat of irrationality can become excessive and unreasonable. Then we may lose our reasonable receptivity for a higher way of knowing, the way of transcendent faith. Faith as truly formative does not make superfluous our critical, analytical, functional reason. It welcomes, complements, and elevates it.

Initially our faith is inspired by the transcendent roots of human life. The potency for faith is latently present in the graced depth of our being. Formation traditions bring us in touch with this hidden ground in its practical implications for our life. But, as I have argued, the parental transmission of sustaining traditions can be both enriched and marred by the parents' particular idiosyncrasies and modulations. Dissonant pretranscendent modulations can appeal to our childish fantasies. Our parents' basic tradition may have also been distorted by insufficiently appraised additions of elements of other traditions in the familial tradition pyramid.

Formative Faith and the Advent of Critical Formative Reason

Children experience an implicit formation in the faith. Central in this experience is a spontaneous abandonment to a mysterious higher power. This higher power is reflected for the child in parental, situational, and cosmic powers it cannot understand or control. It is a first uncritical, and hence unfree, abandonment. It is primitive, without a realistic nuancing of the epiphanic signs of the mystery. Later the formation of the functional powers of critical reason and perception begin to push the adolescent out of the paradise of primitive abandonment in faith. This can lead temporarily, sometimes lastingly, to a rejection of a faith life as such. What may be rejected is not necessarily confined to the mistaken signs and images of a childish formation tradition. The temptation is also to ignore or deny the profound and mysterious symbols of the depths of one's transcendent tradition. Such denial leads to inner isolation from one's inherent aspiration for transcendent presence, from one's transcendence dynamic.

What is needed is a reintegration of new critical rational apprehensions and appraisals with the primordial aspiration for the transcendent. We should be newly inspired by the deepest symbols of our faith and formation tradition, but now actively appraised by us in the light of our new rational insights. Then we may be graced with a secondary core disposition of *appreciative* abandonment. This secondary phase is not simply the *"naive" abandonment* of childhood. It is a new type of abandonment, an appreciative abandonment, supported now by critical appraisal. We integrate within this more mature form of abandonment the successive appraisals of both the transcendent faith dimension and the pretranscendent dimension of our maturing critical reason. For most people this process mainly happens prefocally.

I would characterize transcendent maturity as a creative, fluid consonance between transcendent formative faith and pretranscendent rational knowledge and unfolding vital affectivity. Transcendent formative faith itself is now coformed by the deepest symbols of one's faith and form tradition. At the heart of this maturing faith is the *secondary appreciative abandonment disposition*. I refer to it as secondary because it transcends the first childhood disposition of naive abandonment, unenlightened by personal appraisal and appreciation. This deepened faith abandonment is formational insofar as it empowers maturing persons to give faith-filled form to their life and world in the light of personally appraised and assimilated faith and formation traditions. Both faith and form traditions are about the experience of lived faith. However, formation traditions consider the faith experience primordially insofar as it directs the multivaried concrete implementation of the faith. This implementation implies the congenial and compatible reception and expression of forms of faith in one's life and in one's pluritraditional formation field. In contrast, faith traditions, particularly their theologies or ideologies, deal primordially (not exclusively) with what one should believe about the doctrine and about the more general basic rules of moral implementation of one's faith.

All faith is always inherently formative. Formation tradition and formation science are marked by their focus on the formational facet of any transcendent faith tradition.

Creative Fluid Consonance
between Formative Faith and Formative Reason

I see the consonance between formative faith and formative rational knowledge as creative and fluid. Consonance is not a fixed state once and for all frozen in solid immutability. Formation, reformation, and transformation of the depth and outreach of living faith as well as of the deepening and expanding of human reason leads to change. Any change in one or both areas demands a creative search for a corresponding updating of the consonance between these facets, hence my term *creative fluid consonance*. Every new situation we face and any facet of that situation may imply a momentary adaptation of our consonance-striving to that situation. Such adaptation should be creative and fluid yet guided by the parameters of our form tradition.

For example, when formation scientists are invited to address an audience less familiar with this field of study, they will look for facets of their own experiential consonance that can be communicated attractively and understandably to an audience. After the talk they may meet with a few people in the audience who are aware of formation science, its terminology and scholarly critiques. Now the principle of *fluid consonance* enables the formation scientists to flow immediately with this new situation. They call upon their scientific disposition and its trained patterns, again within the parameters of their own and others' form tradition pyramid.

The road toward transcendent maturity usually entails many detours. Dissonances can block the way to the prudent exercise of creative and fluid consonance. It is obvious that critical, creative, rational appraisal is necessary to purify and order our transcendent attentions, apprehensions, and appreciations. This appraisal can be consonant, balanced, realistic, and reasonable, or it can be the opposite. It all depends on the disposition from which critical appraisal emerges in the first place. It may be deformed by an anxiety disposition or by a disposition of paranoid maintenance of an absolutized pretranscendent *I*. In that case, like for instance in that of compulsive religiosity, our critical appraisal power is likely to be abused by our pretranscendent *I*. It deteriorates into an instrument aimed at closing us off from any relaxed receptivity to transcendent inspiration and aspiration, from any form of appreciative abandonment, any openness to the depths of our traditions.

This refusal of traditional formation-in-depth does not necessarily lead to a rejection of all facets of our form tradition. For instance, we may restrict our interest to a mere rational theological or philosophical-ideological concern. We may then write, teach, speak, and analyze, perhaps brilliantly, but we may seldom be sparked by transcendent inspiration. Neither may we be profoundly moved by an abandonment to the mystery that is awesomely affective and appreciative.

Vagaries of Formative Attentiveness

Our attentiveness should not be exclusively directed to only the functional-rational dimension of transcendent traditions. For such one-sidedness can lead to an exclusively intellectual theological, philosophical, or scientific interest in one's own and other faith and formation traditions. One of the consequences could be an underformation of the vital affective and the transcendent affective dimension of the "traditional coformant" of one's core form.

By contrast, adherents of some cults and of many forms of New Age spirituality manifest an opposite onesidedness. They pay minimal attention to the functional-rational and the informational dimension of spiritual traditions. Their main emphasis is on affective dedication, excessive compatibility, or even homogeneity. They tend to underestimate reasonable congeniality with one's own unique-communal life call. Neither do they sufficiently appreciate the rational cognitive substructures of classical faith and form traditions.

Formation in the *effective* life of transcendent faith presupposes not only the unfolding of the functional-rational dimension of one's tradition. One should also be formed in a transcendent, higher, or supreme disposition of attention.

Our pretranscendent *I* engenders necessarily a critical-functional attention to our formation field. This enables this lower *I* to protect, maintain, and competently implement the inspirations and aspirations of the higher *I*. By contrast the transcendent or higher *I* opens itself to optimal consonance with all horizons, spheres, dimensions, regions, and ranges of the formation field. This supreme *I* abides in attentiveness to the mystery of formation as embracing and permeating all of one's field of life, shining forth in its manifold epiphanies. The mystery itself generates dispositions of transcendent awe, abiding, attention, apprehension, praise, and appraisal. Transcendent attention aims also at a disclosure of and consonance with one's own life call and its particular unfolding through one's own form tradition pyramid and its modulations by self and others.

Transcendent attention and appraisal in faith results in the acceptance of what the mystery of formation has allowed to be here and now. This here and now includes all our present possibilities and limitations, consonances and dissonances. Abandonment in faith fills the trusting heart with hope. One finds the courage of patience. In this abandonment we escape the traps of functionalistic willfulness. We rise above our impatient, compulsive, and impulsive strivings that coerce us unwisely to change instantly ourselves and our form traditional core dispositions.

Transcendent traditions point to the beauty and the mysterious epiphany of our life and world. They teach us to overcome the isolating anxiety of our individualistic *I*. They keep our transcendent participant *I* and its history of transformation operative. To learn to see with transcendent eyes through the mediation of classic transcendent traditions, assimilated through interformation with others, is a sure path to consonance.

Briefly transformation demands that our functional-rational and our informational attention be elevated and nourished by the faith attention to the transrational (not irrational) formation mystery as pointed to by transcendent traditions.

Presentation of the Formation Mystery

The formation practitioner is called to bring to light the transforming mystery in the traditions of those entrusted to his or her care. Outside of this awakening to the mystery much can be learned cognitively about one's tradition, but no real transformation can take place.

Formation practitioners, mentors, counselors, or teachers must learn how to be at home with a joyous faith, in their own life call, faith and form tradition. They must be at ease with their own always spotty formation story with its failures and contradictions. Practitioners should grow in the disposition of a continual search for consonance between their analytical grasp of the faith and form tradition and their disposition of abandonment in faith to the mystery to which the tradition points.

This pointing by traditions to the mystery happens through symbols of transcendence. Transcendent attention and appreciation are evoked and kept alive by traditional symbols. Symbol receptivity and sensitivity is necessary for effective interformation with one's tradition. Symbols of transcendence point to what cannot be expressed in merely informational language and functional rational concepts. The making present of the mystery by traditions demands symbols.

Transformation presupposes an abiding with the mystery of transformation. Formation science implies necessarily a formation anthropology, a formation theory of personality, and a scientific experiential-empirical methodology. These scientifically necessary operations could become an obstacle, were they not complemented by a transscientific openness to religious symbols. They could obscure the essential operation of transcendent formation praxis, which is to awaken people to the mystery of transformation as announced in symbols of transcendence.

What we do in formation science, and especially in the articulation of this science in specific form traditions, is a rational critical appraisal of the mystery as formative. This implies an intellectual clarification and purification of irrational and unreasonable vital affective disfigurations of the mystery and its operations. It means preparing the mind for transcendent goodness, truth, and beauty. Intellectual apprehending is one of the many possible articulations to be executed by the functional dimension of our life. We may not have been able yet to subordinate this dimension to the transcendent dimension. Then our analytical mind may be anxiously driven by prefocal needs for power, control, and manipulation. But when we try to control the mystery, conceptually or otherwise, the mystery as mystery eludes us. It may also elude those whom we try to assist in their journey of transformation by this mystery.

Mystery of Formation and Scientific Blueprint of Formation

Formation science as science tries to order the empirical-experiential phenomena of formation and of formation traditions in a surveyable and systematic fashion. This is necessary to gain a critical orderly view of the relative position of the various coformants, the formation phases, the role of formation dynamics, the facilitating and hindering conditions of formation. The science highlights, moreover, the varied importance of the great variety of form traditional directives for the overall process of formation. The danger is that the blueprint of the formation process will be mistaken for the mystery of lived formation itself. Conceptualization cannot replace inspiration and aspiration. An intellectual inventory of distinctions cannot substitute for the inspiration and wisdom of a living form tradition.

Formation science and its articulation should be only a preceding purification, a means, a servant, a preparation for the evocation of the awed attention for the mystery by means of the ever-expanding transcendent symbols of one's tradition pyramid. The effective practitioner is both a formation scientist and a poet of the symbols of the tradition. One of the tasks of transcendent formation is to awaken symbol receptivity and sensitivity. This sense for the mystery as well as for transcendent traditions belongs to the integrity of the distinctively human form of life. To be at home with the symbols of our tradition demands that we are in touch with the power of our transcendent or epiphanic imagination. Functionalism and rationalism have paralyzed the epiphanic imagination in many. This has separated them from both their vital and transcendent affectivity, from their creative imagination, and therewith from the transcendent symbols of their traditions.

Symbol, Tradition, and Consonance

The consonance of human life as a whole depends in part on receptivity to symbols of transcendence, kept alive by transcendent traditions. It is our awakening to the mystery announcing itself in symbols that opens us to consonance with this mystery and its epiphanies in our life and world. We lose our distinctive humanness when this mystery is banned from our attention, when we are no longer in touch with the symbols of our traditions. This paralysis of the most distinctive dimension of our humanity diminishes the peace, health, and effectiveness of our personality as a whole. Receptivity to the transcendent symbols of traditions is a condition for the fullness of human existence. We are on the path to this fullness when we allow the transcendent symbols of traditions to interform with the concrete realities of our everyday living.

Functionalism and rationalism tempt us to reduce symbols to the categories of rational systems of explanation. We do not allow the traditional symbol to remain a symbol. Symbols of traditions are transcendent precisely because they have a transfunctional, transrational meaning. This meaning exceeds our systems of functional conceptualization. By attempting to explain or interpret the symbol, one talks it away, castrates its pointing power.

For example, the mandala, a symbol of Eastern formation traditions, evokes awe for the integrating mystery of all that is. It may do so immediately for adherents who have grown in receptivity to the symbols of their tradition. One can compare this with the affective symbolic meaning of the American flag or the national anthem for those who adhere to a patriotic tradition in America. We would diminish its impact and kill its appeal were we to reduce it only to an explanation like: "This is a piece of cloth with stripes and stars. The stars stand for the states that form the federation."

In formation science, and especially in its varied articulations in numerous formation traditions, the concept "symbol" is central. Each formation tradition is filled with symbols: the symbols of its history, of its transcendent events, of its stories and parables, of its description of nature, cosmos, humanity, of its epiphanic events. Transcendent symbols are necessary to express what cannot be put fully into words. Formation traditions that are transcendent are about the unspeakable mystery that penetrates us and all reality, that forms and transforms us continually. Therefore, it is the central function of any transcendent form tradition to evoke our sense of mystery by its symbols.

Renewal and expansion of the symbols of a form tradition are often necessary. Symbols can lose their plausibility for people when the sociohistorical dimension of their life estranges them from existing symbols. For instance, the symbol of the Red Cross coming from a Christian form tradition was foreign to adherents of Muslim traditions. They had to replace it with the symbol of the crescent moon.

Loss of Formative Symbol Receptivity

We find in every tradition adherents who have lost or who have never enjoyed formative symbol receptivity. Let me suggest a few causes of this lack of receptivity for the formative symbols of traditions:

1. One cause is the general functionalization of our world and the rationalization of our mind. Hearts and imaginations are easily impoverished in such a climate.

2. Another cause, related to the first one, is the often onesidedly rationalistic approach to a theological, philosophical, or ideological explanation of the underlying faith tradition or belief system.

3. This onesidedness can be compounded by excessive demythologizing. When extreme or exclusive, this approach can kill the power of myth, story, and symbol.

4. Particular formation traditions are modulated or even modified, for better or worse, by families or wider formation communities. They are the sociohistorical carriers of traditions. Negative accretions or overwhelmingly pretranscendent dispositions may obscure the deeper symbols of a tradition. As a result, transformative, transcendent symbol receptivity may be paralyzed or never awakened. Transcendent appreciation is replaced by a pretranscendent rationalistic or vitalistic depreciation of traditional symbols. They are no longer experienced as pointers to the mystery of formation, the cosmic as well as the radical mystery.

5. Traditional symbols are rooted in affective experiences of personal and sociohistorical life. Many of them express also lively experiences of the cosmos announcing itself in universe, earth, and the vital dimension of human existence. Many people are alienated from cosmos and humanity, from life and love. They are more robot than poet, more computer than meditator. Traditional symbols of transcendence have grown out of the lively age-old conversation of human life with earth and cosmos, nature, humanity and history, art and literature, suffering and death. Without immersion in this nourishing ground, one cannot affectively appreciate the symbolic pointing beyond oneself of these experiences as they are taken up and transformed by form traditions.

6. Sociohistorical conditions of human life, of its environmental scene, of its understanding of cosmos, earth, and nature are always changing. The transcendent symbol system of any form tradition should take change into account. It should always ask the question: How can we enrich existing symbols or add others that enable adherents to see the transcendent meaning in new personal and common experiences, evoked by facets of present-day formation fields?

7. For some the search for new symbols, when exclusive, may paradoxically lead to impoverishment instead of enrichment. This search should always be inspired and accompanied by a formation in classical symbol systems. These are nourished and deepened by the use of generations.

They are profoundly interwoven with the original faith tradition that early followers sought to implement in their art of living competently, yet epiphanically in their own here-and-now situation. As early heirs of this faith tradition in its pristine nobility, truth, beauty, and inspiration, they were most sensitive to the faithful consonance of formation symbols with faith symbols. Without our abiding with the *faithfulness* of their symbols, our additional symbols when insufficiently appraised may detract from the consonance between our faith and form tradition.

Formation scientists and practitioners, in order to become affective and effective servants of a form tradition, must reflect on the traditional formation story of their own life. Is there any facet of the problem areas I have summarized in these seven points that has affected their own form traditional or their own formation-symbol-receptivity in some fashion? The discovery of such deformational elements should not be discouraging. It should be welcomed as a precious formation opportunity, an undeserved gift and grace. Any improvement in their form traditional dispositions will benefit those they are called to assist in their own formation in a particular transcendent tradition. Such newly gained wisdom and inspiration may help others to give form to their own unique-communal life call in a way that is consonant with the basic directives and symbols of their shared tradition. We may hand over this purified form tradition, kindly protecting our own offspring or disciples against premature modulations or modifications under the influence of insufficiently appraised alien traditions in their form tradition pyramid. Good formators may thus feel themselves responsible for generations of people. They influence future parents and grandparents of coming generations. As humble channels of the formation mystery formators are called to enlighten those in their care by the symbols and the rational substructures of the transcendent faith and formation traditions.

CHAPTER 26

Dealing Formatively with Failure in One's Life Call and Tradition

During my war experiences in Holland I conceived the idea of a unique-communal founding life form. This seminal concept became one of the central ideas of my formation science and formation theory of personality. This transcendent, eternal ground form, this deepest *I*, is at the root of our existence. I expressed in the term *life call* the dynamic directive power of this ground form. Our actual unfolding empirical life form is called to be faithful to this direction. Our life must strive increasingly to be congenial with this deepest invitation by the mystery of formation. This life call is symbolized in various formation traditions in different ways.

When I began to work with my new concepts in the counseling of people hiding with me in occupied Holland, I realized at once that my creation of the concept of a "transcendent *I*" would make things more complex than many representatives of the social and human sciences could have imagined. It did not diminish my respect for their theories about the "pretranscendent" personality. On the contrary, I became more grateful for these theories for they granted to all concerned a simpler, more elegant, and more insightful view of the complex dynamics of the pretranscendent life. Compared with what was known before, the elaboration of these theories of pretranscendent existence and education gave us a more sophisticated view, even if I, from the viewpoint of formation science, could not agree with all their assumptions. In some way I regretted that I had to complicate these useful systems of thought by an additional dimension that would force me to reconceive, complement, and sometimes correct the formulations of insights into pretranscendent existence that were excellent in many, if not all, of their facets. I felt that the already established social, human, and educational sciences would probably have to stick to the historical path they had chosen: the disclosure in many ways and by many methods of the developmental dynamics of pretranscendent existence. There is always more to know about the pretranscendent life, its development, crises, and conflicts, its ways of education, therapy, and counseling. We owe a lasting debt of gratitude to pioneering thinkers and researchers in these fields and to their present and future successors. Their contributions notwithstanding, I became deeply aware that the added dimension I envisaged would demand a new experiential-empirical science, not one about primarily pretranscendent human development, education, or self-actualization but a science of transcendent formation, always attentive to the forming mystery that sustains and embraces all that is.

Life Call: Congenial and Compatible Implementation

The unfolding of the mystery of the life call, as I envisioned it, not only encompassed its announcement in the intraform of our life but also in the inter- and outerspheres of our successive formation fields. Foremost of influence in the interformational sphere of life are the formation traditions or tradition pyramids that profoundly coform the shape we give to the concrete implementations of our life call and our faith. Traditions are the most significant channels the mystery uses to communicate to us what we are called to be. The outerspheres of our formation field, namely, our changing immediate situations and our mediated cosmic and mondial situations, as well as our changing grasp of them, tell us in the light of our unfolding traditions, how we should competently implement our life direction here and now.

I was asked during my war period of hiding and resistance to assist the people around me to respond anew to their faith and form traditions, often forgotten and neglected, but now emerging again in a time of fear, pain, and loneliness. I was asked to help them to grow in wise compatibility with their new life situation as war fugitives. This crisis inspired me to develop the concepts of compatibility and compassion as a complement to that of congeniality with one's unique inner call. Their plight made me aware that a wise and effective implementation of the life call rests upon the consonance of congeniality with the inner as well as compatibility with the outer messages of life in its situatedness. I also realized that I alone or any other counselor would never have enough wisdom and experience to bypass the treasures of insights stored by generations in the transcendent formation traditions that some of these people began to rediscover under the duress of deprivation and the threat of extinction. The famed diaries of Anne Frank and Etty Hillesum, and the writings of Corrie ten Boom are striking testimonials to the rediscoveries I saw happening around me and in which I was privileged to play a modest role.

Failing Life Call and Tradition

I soon discovered that a new awareness of the forgotten call of life and its sustaining traditions could lead to debilitating feelings of failure in many of the depression-prone people who came to me. They did not realize that nobody is perfectly faithful to life call and tradition. This is no reason for discouragement or despondency. As long as we do not willfully give in to harshness of heart and obduracy of mind in relation to the directives of our traditions, we are on the right road. In abandonment to the mystery and trust in our transcendent tradition, we must serenely flow with the deficiencies we cannot yet fully overcome.

My war experiences confronted me with the formation question: How responsible are people for failing their life call? Later I met many more people who lived in considerable fear of a life failure in regard to tradition. Many refused to deal candidly with these kinds of failure. Yet they manifested in their personality make-up acknowledged or unacknowledged traces of excessive guilt and shame about real or imagined failures of this sort. Often I met parents who were tortured by the anxiety that they had failed the parental facet of their call because their children had left the form tradition they had tried to instill in them. There is much deformative, pretranscendent suffering in people. It often clusters around real or imagined failures to listen to one's life call and to live in fidelity to one's tradition.

This suffering can be especially poignant in relation to failures in the form traditional facet of our life direction. One reason may be that representatives of each particular form tradition tend to imprint in focal and prefocal regions of consciousness the pretranscendent implementary, educational aspects of the do's and don'ts of their traditions. This is all to the good provided they do not neglect the communication of also the consoling and inspiring transcendent experiences at the root of traditions. In other words, they may be tempted to express failure mainly in terms of individual failed self-actualization not in terms of the transcendent invitations by an always loving, gracing, healing, and forgiving mystery. Unwittingly they live by pretranscendent simplifications of transcendent form traditions and by the self-actualization "fixation" of some representatives of the social and educational sciences.

I want to appraise the failure of the life call, especially in its traditional coformant, from the viewpoint of formation science.

Faulty Individualistic Appraisal of Failure

The experience of failing the life call — especially in its form traditional facet — depends on how we appraise what failure is. Perhaps our appraisal is pretranscendent only. It may be based on a onesided emphasis on merely our individual self-actualizing potency. Appraisal, by contrast, ought to be rooted in a transcendent appreciation-in-faith of our unique communal life call by a loving, healing mystery. Do we respect and accept, in the light of this loving call, the actual possibilities and the realistic limits of our own and of others' individuality? Failure in individual implementation should not be confused with failure of our transcendent life call as a whole. Our life call implies that we bear with passing or lasting individual limitations, including the boundaries of our temperform and neuroform. They are part of what it means to grow in transcendence. Growth in transcendence is not the same as the successful evolvement and education of pretranscendent skills, aptitudes, acclaim, and achievement.

The forms the implementation of our life call assumes must be disclosed by us in dialogue with successive life situations. These tentative, current, or lasting forms change with our phases of formation, reformation, and transformation. The younger we are, the more provisional, tentative, and ambiguous will be the forms in which we seek to express who and what we think we are called to be. We look at prototypes or *protoforms* of life within the form traditions with which we feel most at home. As children we are not yet able to apprehend and appraise fully the meaning of these protoforms. Their availability for us as protoforms for our own life and their congeniality or uncongeniality with our own unique-communal call cannot yet be clear to us at that early stage. That we fail these provisional protoforms is not a final failure of our life call itself. On the contrary, such so-called failures can make us more open to our true calling.

Transcendent maturation means maturing in our appraisal capacity. The more we grow in transcendent maturity, the better we can appraise what may be consonant with our mysteriously founding life formation. We also begin to realize that the concrete forms of implementation of our call are partly free and partly conditioned by our field of life.

Formation freedom is field-conditioned freedom. What may appear to be a failure of the life call is often the result of field limitations. These can hinder certain idealized implementations of the life call but not the life call itself. Our life invitation can be implemented in countless possible ways. Foremost among our field limitations are the traditions to which we have been exposed.

Courage of Candor, Courage of Implementation

To appraise the provisional or enduring implementations of our life call within the limits and possibilities of our field and its traditions, we must grow both in the courage of candor and the courage of implementation. We must dare to face candidly where, how, and why we fail our life call. We must also have the courage to implement the insights gained by this candor in new forms of expression of our founding form, if other expressions have failed.

Failures in our tentative implementations of the life call are normal and to be expected. They only threaten our final fidelity if we refuse lastingly to reappraise courageously our consonances and dissonances with the life call. This call will more clearly disclose itself to us over a lifetime of trial and error, of purification and clarification of our tradition pyramid.

When we try to appraise if we perhaps failed our life's direction, we must ask ourselves first of all what is that direction. What is disclosed to us here and now about what we are meant to be? How does our tradition fit into the understanding and implementation of this mysterious project? Only then can we see where and how we failed this veiled light at the center of our existence.

Excessive fear, shame, and guilt on the level of pretranscendent self-actualization can block candid appraisal of our unique-traditional call as it is currently disclosed to us. We may try to escape candid self-appraisal. We may blindly follow the automatic life directives offered to us by co-ercive dispositions, exclusively controlled by the vital life dimension's articulation of our neuroform. Such coercive dispositions are a signifi-cant aspect of the particular neuroform that is ours. Our free dispositions, too, have their coformants in our neuroform, but they do not compel our life direction irresistibly. We can resist and change them. By contrast coercive dispositions are no longer at the immediate disposal of human spirit and reason. They can replace the wisdom and freedom of tran-scendent appraisal, the candor and clarity of correcting and informing functional reason, and the enlightenment of our always unfolding tradition pyramid.

Necessity of a Basic Transcendent Tradition to Cope with Failure

Excessive fear, shame, and guilt linked with the awareness of failure in self-actualization or pretranscendent perfectionism can lead to the de-nial of the necessity of a transcendent tradition. We all need a tradition that is personalized in a way that is unique, yet still consonant with its basic wisdom. This tradition must be alive and unfolding. For the wis-dom of tradition is the guardian of our consonant appraisals. Often the higher beneficial fear, shame, and guilt evoked yet mellowed by the wis-dom of transcendent traditions are not recognized as such. Instead they are confused with their deforming counterparts in our insulated pre-transcendent life. There an immense burden of lonely responsibility for our self-actualization rests upon our own shoulders alone. To escape the tortures of excessive self-actualizations, we may try to live without a basic formation tradition. For, misunderstood by us, it reminds us too cruelly of our failures and detours along the way.

In that case, instead of gaining an imaginary freedom from all tradi-tions, we become the defenseless toy of floating diverse form traditions and the chance elements uncontrollably pulsating in our formation field. When we don't dare to face and appraise possible or imagined failures in self-actualization, our fear of failure increases. Fear becomes a nonfocal anxiety or dread. It can lead to devastating vital and functional defor-mational symptoms, affecting our neuroform and through it our spiritual, mental, and organismic health. Relief may be sought in excessive consump-tion sprees, promiscuity, drugs, wild partying, manipulation and abuse of others, and sometimes even crime or suicide.

Night the Mystery Allows

Transcendent appraisal of a failure of the life call or its implementation should be marked by awe-filled praise and appreciation of the forming mystery. The forming will of the mystery allows at different formation phases only limited disclosures of our failures. Similarly it grants us only gradually deeper insights into our formation field and into the wisdom of our traditions. We should not force either a premature disclosure or rash implementation of the life call. We must live in reverence of form traditional wisdom that has to coform our commitment continuously. Awe-filled appreciation of the night the mystery allows in our life lets us flow humbly with the pace of grace.

Much fear of failure finds its ground in a premature sense of responsibility for dissonant dispositions and directives we anxiously suspect but cannot yet disclose and clarify. It is part of our life call that we have to live with only partial disclosures of its directives in our successive here-and-now situations. The same applies to certain facets of our tradition pyramid. This flowing with the pace of disclosure is not a failure. It is obedience to the limits of the disclosure and implementation of our life direction in each situation.

Certain popularized versions of psychology, psychiatry, psychotherapy, and pretranscendent education and theories of self-help and self-improvement may unwittingly have increased in many a debilitating fear of failure. In some people the sciences that were supposed to help them have served only to awaken unrealistic expectations and therewith anxious feelings of responsibility in regard to instant self-exploration in depth and the subsequent burden of successful self-actualization or pretranscendent perfectionism.

Wise and candid appraisal of failure enhances the effectiveness of our disclosures and implementations and enables the wholeness of our existence at the present moment. We must patiently accept and affirm our gradual growth in perceptiveness and candor of sense and mind, in clarity of functional reason, and in the wisdom of higher reason or spirit.

Fear of Failure and Form Tradition

From what I have said so far, it may be clear that one crucial factor in regard to the fear and uncertainty we feel about consonance and dissonance, about failure and success of life, is the absence of a basic classic form tradition to which one can be fully committed. A transcendent form tradition entails directives that can help us to distinguish between what is basically consonant or dissonant. It can facilitate openness to possible options at crisis moments in our life. Moments of conflict are necessary. They mobilize our form receptivity and creativity. They inspire us to seek the deeper sense of our traditions; they enlighten our choices.

Any one of us can fail our call if we refuse to grow in candid self-appraisal. If our appraisal remains encapsulated only in a pretranscendent search for social security in the sociohistorical dimension, for pleasure, excitement (even devotional excitement), and sensation in the vital-emotional dimension, and for satisfaction and control in the functional dimension of life, we may never sense the greatness of the consonant life to which we are called. If our potency for transcendent appreciation does not unfold, no transformation in consonance with our deepest *I* can take place. If we adhere only to an appreciation of our achievements, of what is pleasant in our life, if we refuse to appraise candidly and courageously, yet gently and firmly, also what is dissonant, our faults and failures, we may remain blind to our call for transformation. If we never grow in the wisdom of our basic faith and form tradition, it will become difficult for us to see where the mystery is leading us.

The transcendent call of human life, pointed to by transcendent traditions, should become transparent for us personally. The gift of formation crisis shocks us out of our enslavement to pretranscendent strivings and certainties as "the" way to ultimate happiness. Received with integrity, it makes us form receptive again for the always healing, forgiving, and transforming disclosures of the mystery of formation.

We fail our transcendent life call if we try to find ultimate happiness only in absolutized pretranscendent security, pleasure, satisfaction, and control. If we invest our inherent longing for happiness mainly in pretranscendent coercive dispositions, we are bound to be disappointed. Then we may by-pass perhaps not the apparent but certainly the inmost wisdom of the great transcendent traditions that in the end make life worth living.

CHAPTER 27

Traditional Formation as Central in Formation Science

I n this chapter I want to expand and integrate some of the main points of traditional formation touched upon in the course of my work thus far. Let me reiterate first of all the centrality of my idea of a "form tradition pyramid." Each of us is formed by a plurality of traditions. We also have common traditions. French, German, Dutch, Italian, Mexican, English, American — each of these populations share certain life directives. Yet each person and group within each of these common cultural traditions his or her own life call and usually has chosen his or her own basic faith and form tradition, which is complemented by a sprinkling of directives of other traditions in that society.

One's commitment to a form tradition means that one gives priority to its fundamental directives. Such directives tell believers how their faith tradition can be embodied compatibly in their everyday field of life.

Intermingling of Traditions in Our Tradition Pyramids

My concept of tradition pyramids clarifies the intermingling of directives of traditions that coexist within a pluritraditional society. Examples of such coexisting traditions are legion. Think only about such traditions as the Protestant, Catholic, Episcopalian, and Jewish; the capitalist, agnostic, atheistic, individualistic, esthetic, hedonistic, or functionalistic; the upper-, middle-, and lower-class traditions; the Hispanic, Afro-American, Caucasian, Asian, and Native American. Add to these such categories as the academic, the military, the clerical, the corporate, and one sees immediately the possible effects of a pluriformity of traditions on everyday formation.

My pyramid suggests further that many of us are standing on the solid base that we have chosen or ratified as the fundament of our own particular pyramid of traditions. That base is the tradition to which we are committed as the ground of our life. The increasingly smaller lines in the pyramid above this base suggest that other traditions in our society also have a definite, albeit a lesser, influence on us than our basic tradition does. People committed to their own tradition of necessity limit their acceptance of other traditions. They submit them to creative and critical scrutiny by themselves or by others. They welcome alien directives only insofar as they are compatible with the foundations of their own base traditions.

For example, people committed to a Marxist form tradition will affirm only those religious or capitalist directives that are compatible with the fundamentals of the Marxist belief system.

The wise appraisal of the compatibility of directives of other traditions with those of our own is a complex process. Even more demanding is the implementation of the results of such appraisal in our everyday life. Initially, in spite of our best efforts, the diverse traditions we spontaneously live by are not yet well integrated with our basic tradition. At first our pyramid is more like a syncretic collection than a harmonious quilt.

For example, under the past Stalinistic regime, Russian traditions of peasant adherents to Orthodox religious form traditions were a syncretic mixture of Orthodox, collectivistic, patriotic, and rural traditional directives. In true believers, the Orthodox form tradition prevailed insofar as it still could be maintained inwardly and limitedly expressed outwardly in a collectivistic state professing atheism.

To appreciate the essential role of tradition in the history of the human species, we must understand the predicament of humanity in cosmos and world. Why and how is the emergence of traditions rooted in the evolutional and historical emergence of humanity? The insight thus gained will facilitate the integration of my theory of traditional formation into my general theory of human formation. When appropriate, I will also discuss the implications of such integration for our everyday way of life.

Cosmos, Chaos, Formation Fields, and Formation Traditions

The human life form is not endowed with sufficient instinctual directives. Hence it cannot instantly and automatically order the cosmos into predictable fields of human formation. Prehuman sentient life forms are instinctually able to translate formationally relevant aspects of their cosmic surroundings into instinctually predictable fields of life. To human life, however, the cosmos appears initially as chaos.

The first striving of humans is to turn the chaos into rationally predictable fields that can serve their survival and unfolding. I distinguish a proximate and an ultimate mode of transformation of the experienced chaos into a humanly livable environment. The proximate mode is a vital-functional-rational ordering of our inhospitable surroundings. The ultimate way of creating order is a transcendent one that goes beyond mere vital-functional organization. It orders and gives meaning to chaos, also transcendently, by means of the disclosure of a higher meaning. This disclosure renders the cosmos, both in and beyond each immediate life situation, also ultimately meaningful. This meaningfulness is sought in terms of the relationship of cosmos and situation to the mystery that shines forth in them while transcending them.

Proximate Formation of
Predictable Formation Fields and Form Tradition

The quest for a proximate ordering of predictable formation fields out of the experience of chaos gives rise to the five following questions:

1. How can I order my immediate life situation in a way that is congenial with my personality, life call, skills, and aptitudes, yet compatible with the reality of the situation? The question of *congeniality*.

2. What kind of reactions and responses can I anticipate in people, animals, things, and events, when I try to order my life situations congenially and compatibly? The question of rational *predictability*.

3. What must I do to be effective in my life together with others who share my life situations? How can we help each other? The question of *interformation*.

4. How can I maintain a sense of self-appreciation, of form potency and effectiveness? The question of *form potency appreciation*.

5. How can I with my unique life call and individual neuroform attain maximum consonance with my immediate formation field? The question of *functional consonance*.

These five functional questions can be answered in dialogue with the functional dimension of the form traditions to which I am exposed during my lifetime. Let me now turn to the five transcendent questions.

Transcendent Formation of
Predictable Formation Fields and Transcendent Traditions

Our *spiritual* quest gives rise to five transcendent questions. These are:

1. What is my unique transcendent life call? What does it mean in the context of the meaning of my life situation? The question of *transcendent call and meaning*.

2. What response of the forming mystery can I anticipate in faith, hope, and love when I respond to the epiphanic meaning that is disclosed in my life situation? The question of *predictability rooted in faith, hope, and love*.

3. What kind of traditional transcendent acts and exercises do I have to engage in with others to be or remain spiritually effective in my

life here and now? The question of *spiritual interformation through sharing in transcendent traditions*.

4. How can I, as spiritual, direct my transcendent engagement within a life situation with others in a way that deepens and expands my hope-filled faith and loving appreciation of the gift of my unique life call, form potency, and effectiveness? The question of *transcendent life call appreciation*.

5. How can I in my life situation attain maximum obedience to and subsequent consonance with the forming mystery and its messages in my life? The question of *transcendent consonance*.

These five questions should be answered in dialogue with the transcendent dimension of the form traditions to which I am exposed during my life.

The five earlier vital-functional questions are concerned with signals of my environment that can tell me something about the effects that can be anticipated when I move within this field practically. Things become formatively meaningful for us in the measure that we can anticipate their effects on us and our world. Our functional form traditions help us to disclose such meanings.

To prepare for effective functioning I must disclose predictable possibilities of effective action. This disclosure is made possible by the development of my potencies to apprehend, appraise, and anticipate the consequences of my performance. This is not always easy, for all of my life situations are surrounded by the threatening unknown, the awareness of which I may have refused to acknowledge. Formation traditions help me to overcome this refusal through faith, hope and love in regard to a benevolent mystery in and behind the unknown.

Concern of Transcendent Formation

The second set of transcendent questions is concerned with transcendent meanings. They make a transcendent appraisal possible. This appraisal is influenced by the memory of transcendent form traditions to which I have been exposed. Such traditions present me with networks of transcendent meanings and their symbols.

The life situations in which I daily move should have for me not only functional but also transcendent meanings that deepen my loving faith in the mystery. Such meaningfulness has beneficial implications for my consonant life formation. Chief among these are:

1. The transcendent meaningfulness of my everyday life allows me moments of miniretreat from the pressures of its vital-functional meanings and directives.

2. Such miniretreats may restore my transcendent potency for loving appraisals and appreciations when I have lost my joyous flow with the stream of the creative and liberating mystery in which my life, each of its situations, and all present manifestations of the universe are like fast-passing waves.

3. Miniretreats from everyday tensions may allow the flow of my formation energy to restore and replenish itself in contemplative presence to the mystery as manifesting itself in my tradition as well as in my pains and pleasures, limits and duties, labors and leisures.

4. Presence to the transcendent meanings of my life that are essentially open meanings (human spirit is the potency for universal, multidimensional openness) enables me to relativize my present situations. This relativizing may help me to regain my freedom of spirit.

5. Openness to transcendent meanings enables me to infuse the vital-functional directives of my working life with a transcendent depth of power and meaning.

6. It creates space for resourcing myself in my transcendent traditions. It enables me to disclose their relevance for my situation here and now.

Such disclosure is made possible for me by a potency for transcendent aspiration that is inherent in human life itself. To activate this potency I must grow in intuition, appreciation, and symbolization of signs of presence of the mystery in my everyday life. The wisdom of traditions teaches me how to grow, both by practical directives and inspiring symbols. I must keep a wise balance between these inspiring symbols and a practical commitment that is reasonable, realistic, and relaxed.

In extreme cases of deformation a person's whole life may become merely symbolic, imaginary, idealistic, mythological, or mystified. In the formation history of most people, moments or periods can be found in which the right balance between symbolic and practical formation becomes distorted. The effects of such distortions should not be underestimated.

A coercive concentration on one's "spirituality" is liable to the danger of imaginary, symbolic deformation and mystification. The danger increases in the measure that we lose touch with the practical life directives of formative traditions and communities. Even then dialogue with these directives should be complemented continuously with personal reality testing. We must try directives out in everyday life situations.

Origin of Form Traditions

I trace the initiation of form traditions to our original human condition. The cosmic epiphany of the formation mystery enables all forms in the cosmos to emerge, expand, and maintain themselves until they are submerged again in the cosmic energy field or emerge as other forms. This primary epiphany of the formation mystery as creating a cosmic energy field infuses all forms with their own foundational form potency. Their given form potency implies a form direction. This form direction enables them to develop form directives that are congenial with this foundational form direction as well as compatible with their own formation situation.

Presentient cosmic forms, such as minerals or atomic and subatomic particles, form themselves congruently in automatic consonance with their inherent form direction. The cosmic epiphany of the formation mystery provides them with a built-in formation-readiness.

Sentient cosmic forms are organisms equipped with instinctual form directives. These innate form directives correspond with those pregiven form appearances of the surrounding world that are relevant to the survival and expansion of these specific organisms. Their concrete basic formation field is predetermined. They form themselves congenitally and congruently in automatic consonance with their instinctual life direction.

Human life emerges in the cosmos with almost no instinctual directives. Devoid of sufficient preformed directives, human life has to disclose its own directives. We do so in interactions with other human beings over the generations. The cosmos does not automatically manifest itself as a ready-made, well-articulated formation field for the human life form as it does for the instinctual forms of life. Accordingly, human life has to bring into relief those appearances of the cosmos that would seem to provide opportunities for its unfolding. It has to make them stand out in their relevance, to enhance them as such in its ever-expanding fields of life. For example, human life as intellectually-emotionally auditive and musical selects, enhances, transforms, and creates sounds in the cosmos in such a way that they form a significant aspect of human existence.

Role of Formation Symbols in Personal and Traditional Formation

Formation symbols radiate a form directive power into human life and society. Not all human symbols exercise this influence equally on all people. For example, mathematical symbols do not have the same impact on all persons. While they may be known as symbols, they are not experienced by most people as formation symbols.

Human life discloses receptive and expressive form directives. It relates them to corresponding stimulating aspects of the world. Together people enhance, elaborate, expand, and reform these selected aspects. In this way they give form to traditions and to the inter- and outerspheres of shared fields of life and action. In this process human communities develop rich sets of symbols. Such symbols signify and keep alive fields and traditions that are handed over from generation to generation.

Formation symbols are basic tools that human life has available to disclose, maintain, and elaborate, in mutual collaboration, transinstinctual form directives. Only by means of symbols can people set fields of human meaning and purpose apart from the overwhelming unknown cosmos. For humanly significant environments are not articulated as such in nature.

Symbols are necessary to point to humanly preferred aspects of nature. Certain micro- and macrocosmic appearances are symbolically highlighted, staged as it were, and put into relief as relevant to human existence in the world. Such symbols are internalized in both common and unique ways. When assimilated uniquely they articulate inwardly one's personal path of life. The internalized sets of symbols and their implied directives begin a life of their own in the realms of human intraformation. People can inwardly draw countless experiences from these symbols, play with them imaginatively, reflect on them thoughtfully, structure and restructure them in their mutual relationships in numerous ways. One can do so with focused attention, but mostly it happens prereflectively. The internalized symbols have their origin in interconscious symbols that are externalized in the many expressions of the form traditions of humanity. The intraconscious play with symbols should maintain a dialogical relationship with the symbolically externalized interconsciousness of humanity, and society. At times we may be tempted to flee from interconsciousness into our intraconsciousness with its inner symbols alone. This inclination tugs on our heart when life seems to let us down or threatens to overwhelm or destroy our sense of form potency. This threat may be real or imaginary. When real, a momentary strategic withdrawal may prove beneficial. It may enable us to restore our energy and to resource ourselves in our traditions.

Human life has disclosed a rich and nuanced tapestry of symbols of formation. Disclosures by numerous generations have overlaid cosmos, humanity and its history with a net of symbols that reflect the meanings of our societies and their sustaining traditions. No individual alone, nor a few passing generations, could in isolation from other generations amass sufficient experience and insight to propose optimally helpful life directives. Only traditions that take into account the wisdom of past generations can function as effective guides for present and coming generations. For the wisdom of living cannot be based only on the fleeting situations to which a few evanescent generations would have been exposed.

A continuous purification of form traditions by many generations is necessary if they are to retain plausibility. Each new generation must separate accidental accretions, due to particular situations, from the disclosure of foundational truths of the perennial art and discipline of meaningful human existence. Universal, transcultural form directives are usually hidden within the particular form directives handed over by former generations.

Foundational and Sociohistorical Facets of Form Traditions

As we have seen, the word *tradition* comes from the Latin *tradere*, which means "to hand over." I coined the term *form tradition* to refer to the form directives that go beyond the mere general faith directives. They have been handed over in a coherent fashion from generation to generation in specific communities of memory; they give direction to the concrete receptive and creative formation of life within societies. Form traditions are intimately related to the corresponding faith traditions in which they are rooted. They should, however, not be confused with such faith traditions.

I call a form tradition *foundational* to refer to that aspect of the tradition that has a universal validity at least for past, present, and future adherents of that specific tradition and community. Beyond this, certain directives of a specific tradition may even have a universal validity for all humanity.

Any form tradition is a mixture of foundational lasting directives and particular sociohistorical accretions. Such accretions may remain effective for the society or community concerned as long as the sociohistorical situation, which is in need of that particular response, continues to exist.

I am particularly interested in fundamental form directives disclosed by classic form traditions, for some of them may point to directives that are relevant to all human life. I translate them in the language of my science, integrating them in the body of knowledge about foundational human formation. In this way they may serve the ongoing development of a science of universal transcendent human formation on which many people of good will and clear reason may be able to agree in principle. This science of transcendent formation is essentially different from the disciplines of education and of human development.

Faith Traditions and Form Traditions

The power of transcendent form traditions lies in their presuppositions regarding the formation mystery and its epiphanies. The deepest formation question is about the mystery of formation. We cannot reasonably deny that the ultimate nature and meaning of the formation processes in universe and humanity are a mystery. Daily formation of life and world can proceed effectively only if we somehow abandon ourselves to this mystery, at least in some implicit elementary fashion. The faith presuppositions of a transcendent form tradition facilitate this abandonment.

A religious faith tradition offers basic beliefs in regard to the formation mystery and its epiphanies. The faith tradition provides meaningful revelations, ideals, images, myths, stories, symbols, rites, and writings that nourish living faith, hope, and loving consonance in regard to the transcendent mystery as understood in that tradition.

Specific form traditions may develop on the basis of a specific faith tradition. Within such specific form traditions, the corresponding faith tradition functions as their necessary, lifegiving, inspiring, and controlling presuppositions. The content of faith traditions is subjected to rational explicitations, explanations, and justifications in terms of contemporary cultures and experiences. These may develop into self-consistent, rational systems of an ontological or theological nature. They give rise to belief systems to be distinguished from faith traditions, form traditions, and subsequent form systems.

Form traditions, unlike faith traditions, are primarily concerned with the empirical-experiential facets and the practical effectiveness of customs, styles, exercises, communications, spiritualities, methods, directives, and so on. These ways of faith implementation have been developed and handed over in the packages of form traditions by generations committed to the same religious or ideological faith tradition. They may give rise to form systems of a common or personal nature.

Two Sources of Traditional Form Directives
The two sources of traditional form directives are faith and formational implementation experiences. Form directives are disclosed partly in answer to the presuppositional specific beliefs regarding the nature and meaning of the mystery and its epiphanies as held in the tradition concerned. What distinguishes a form tradition from a faith tradition is the fact that its practical attempts to implementation of that faith develop in dialogue with the demands of everyday life in the world. This dialogue extends itself to other form traditions and to the formational expressions, findings and insights of the arts and sciences that affect one's society.

Philosophical and theological disciplines about ultimate causes as understood in the light of faith traditions are not as such the primary concern of the students of form traditions. They are used by such students as necessary, auxiliary tools. They enable them to better understand the religious or ideological faith base of the form tradition they are investigating.

A form tradition is more flexible and open to change than the foundational faith tradition that is its presupposition. The practical form tradition, because of the twofold source of its directives, must somehow change with changes occurring in factual and theoretical knowledge of the exact nature and demands of human life formation. Yet change in formation praxis should not betray the foundational faith presuppositions of which this form tradition is an implementary expression. In the course of a profound change in the human understanding of formation, however, certain formulations of faith traditions may come into question. It is possible that certain faith formulations were less nuanced than they could be at present. Because of insufficient precision, these formulations may not have excluded the possibility that adherents of the tradition have mistakenly mixed with the foundational faith tradition certain nonessential accretions. They may have misunderstood some timebound formulations as if they expressed the very essence of the lasting foundational faith presuppositions. Formation scientists cannot solve such problems of the underlying faith tradition itself on the basis of their own expertise. They may pose such problems and then refer them to philosophers or theologians, who are experts in the faith questions of their own tradition.

Ultimate Thought in Faith Traditions, Proximate Thought in Formation Traditions

Up to the eighteenth century, ultimate thinking of a mainly philosophical and theological nature prevailed in Western traditions. It focused attention on the basic presuppositions of faith and form traditions. Proximate thinking focuses attention not on the ultimate but on the proximate causes of experienced and observed facts and events. It gives rise not to ultimate disciplines, such as philosophy and theology, but to proximate disciplines, such as medicine, education, anthropology, sociology, physics, psychology. In the realm of tradition, proximate thinking is primarily relevant not to the faith tradition but to the proliferation of its corresponding form traditions.

Proximate thinking can be either specific or integrational. When specific, it concentrates on specific form traditions as specific. When integrational, it is concerned with what formation directives various specific traditions may have in common. Integrational proximate thinking focuses attention not primarily on ultimate causes as philosophies and theologies do. Neither is its main interest in particular proximate causes of a specific region of facts or experiences that are the object of particular proximate sciences. Its primary attention is centered on the potential and actual integration of facts and experiences and their proximate causes into an open-ended coherent body of proximate knowledge that can apply to many specific formation traditions. It tries to develop open-ended syntheses of such common insights to make them serve all human formation.

In the period of prevalently ultimate thinking, masters of form traditions were compelled to think also proximately. Proximate life formation demanded an understanding of the proximate causes and conditions of the problems of people who tried to live by the wisdom of their form tradition. The masters of proximate traditional formation had thus to develop also a way of thought that was mainly proximate. They had to connect presuppositional thought about ultimate causes with reflection on proximate causes in service of the practice of proximate spiritual life formation. Hence instead of calling them theologians or philosophers, they were called spiritual masters in many traditions. These masters of formation integrated into their unfolding form traditions the then available knowledge of concrete form structures, fields, effects, dynamics, and conditions. Because of the absence of well-developed proximate social, human, clinical, and educational sciences, the concrete, factual knowledge available was scant, tenuous, and not scientifically validated. It often took the form of anecdotal observations.

Cooperation of Proximate Sciences
and Formation Traditions via Formation Science

Presently formation scientists and practitioners can profit from the accelerating explosion and expansion of proximate scientific knowledge. The art and discipline of proximate observation and reflection have been refined in numerous proximate sciences. In principle, it has now become possible for form traditions to refine and validate their transcendence oriented customs, exercises, methods, and symbols by dialogue with the new knowledge gathered by the empirical and experiential arts and sciences. This natural extension of the age-old dialogue between the revealed aspects of a formation tradition and the new insights gained by observation of the dynamics of generic human transcendent formation have been delayed by various factors. The main ones are mutual overreaction of proximate sciences and form traditions, fragmentation of the proximate sciences, form traditional as well as proximate science imperialism.

Overreaction of Modern Sciences

The past dominance of religious form traditions evoked an overreaction against them in newly independent proximate thinkers and scientists. They rejected or ignored the necessary function of form traditions in the past, present, and future history of humanity. A number of proximate scientists may have ignored or underestimated the crucial role of the traditional foundational formation triad of faith, hope, and loving consonance as inspired and nourished by classical formation traditions. They overlooked the formative role of traditional myths, symbols, rites, and writings. Neither may they have appreciated their rational elaborations by corresponding philosophical and theological disciplines, which rationally sustain, deepen, and highlight that foundational formation triad.

Overreaction of Formation Traditions

Certain representatives of form traditions, in turn, may have overreacted against the rejection or neglect of their traditions by proponents of the proximate social and educational sciences. Such overreaction of form traditions was especially strong when their adherents felt, rightly or wrongly, that the faith presuppositions of their traditions were at stake. Such presuppositions can neither be proved nor disproved by the methods of the proximate social sciences.

This overreaction of a form tradition may have deepened when some sophisticated adherents of their own tradition in imprudent zeal advocated the promotion of the necessarily fragmented view of only one or the other proximate social science or, worse still, of only one specialization within such a science. These well-meaning but unwise adherents may have tried to link their form tradition with an exclusive dialogue with only one piece of fragmentary scientific knowledge. Such piecemeal information does not represent all available proximate knowledge of formation, critically appraised, complemented, and cautiously reformulated in compatibility with the foundationals of one's tradition.

Fragmentary Nature of Modern Science

The proximate sciences and disciplines such as, for instance, the field of education, are by their very nature proliferating in increasingly specialized sciences and subdisciplines whose approach is more and more fragmentary, i.e., each one focuses exclusively on one aspect of reality. This made it impossible for each form tradition *as a whole* to conduct an effective, critical, creative dialogue with *all* relevant proximate formation insights *as aspects* of an emergent potential science of relevant formation insights. Undue generalizations based on the findings of only one or a few proximate social sciences made the dialogue suspect in the eyes of the guardians of transcendent or quasi-transcendent form traditions. The proliferating proximate sciences and disciplines are in need of a foundational, synthesizing proximate science. If this integration would be pursued in light of the relevance of such arts, sciences, and disciplines for effective transcendent human formation, the results could provide humanity with a unified field theory of generic transcendent formation. In my opinion, representatives of our auxiliary social, clinical, and educational sciences, arts, and disciplines have not yet critically focused on the mutually complementary integration of their findings in terms of their relevance for the consonant formation of life and world. The possibility of a dialogue of form traditions with the findings of the proximate sciences, in their mutually corrective and complementary totality, depends on efforts made in this direction.

Urgency of Integration

The form traditions cannot keep waiting indefinitely for such integration. During this waiting time their adherents are exposed to the fragmentary insights of the social and educational sciences, arts and disciplines. These affect their sociohistorical sources of life formation, especially the popularizing media and educational institutions. The adherents of classical transcendent faith and formation traditions may become increasingly confused by such unintegrated pressures and persuasions. In the end they themselves may engage in an amateurish way in a deceptive integration of popularized fragmentary social, therapeutic, and educational insights with their form tradition. Building their life's formation on such tenuously integrated foundations can spell disaster for themselves, their families, or anybody in their care.

Both the lack of integration of the relevant findings of the social, clinical, and educational sciences and disciplines as well as the confusion of adherents of the form traditions seem to point to the urgent need for dedicated scholars who become experts in both their own form tradition and in the development of an integrative generic science of transcendent human formation.

Imperialism of Specific Form Traditions

Some form traditions may have raised the expectation that the world population as a whole would convert to their tenets. Other traditions may have believed that all cultures could be coerced to accept their form directives. Such traditions may have anticipated that world peace among various populations and their segments could be attained by conversion or coercion. In that view a universal agreement would be obtainable in a relatively simple way.

For example, some representatives of the Islamic form tradition may have anticipated that the whole world by conversion or coercion could be made the followers of the prophet. Some Buddhists may have been encouraged in the same direction by a growing interest in their tradition among new followers in Western countries. Certain Christians may have dreamt about a repeat of the glorious thirteenth century, when a tiny part of the world, seen as the whole world, was guided by a unified Christian tradition. Certain humanists may have high hopes for the humanist tradition, and Marxists for the socialist tradition. It has only gradually dawned on people that planet earth will have to bear with many and varied traditions. No one tradition will be able to convince or coerce all others to establish world peace and unity in its own exclusive image alone.

Historical studies make it evident that the imperialism of form traditions has contributed to wars, violent revolutions, persecutions, and social injustice. Rulers play on the defensive imperialistic feelings of the adherents of such traditions to enlist them in their cause. At present the human race is in danger of destroying itself in nuclear conflict. This threat heightens the interest of enlightened representatives of many traditions finally to cooperate in the development of a unified transnational and transcultural science of generic transcendent formation, which, I believe, may compel a world-saving dialogue. It would diminish the war and conflict potential in traditions that may be enlisted to promote bellicose rulers.

Since I celebrated in Europe the end of World War II, my hope has been that world peace could be fostered by a unified generic science of distinctively human formation on which reasonable people of good will in various form traditions could in principle agree. Such agreement, in service of world peace and justice, would be increasingly affirmed if a generic formation science would contain not only the common wisdom of such traditions, but would become more cogent and convincing by the validation of some of its empirical-experimental tenets by proximate arts, sciences, and disciplines. My vision is that this universal foundational science develop in such a way that it can be articulated uniquely in each and all consonant transcendent form traditions without diminishing their own unique complementarity, rooted in their own faith traditions. Any attempt to level forcefully or to eliminate all the form traditions of the world population will destroy perhaps our last chance for social peace and justice. The survival of our planet may be at stake.

Insufficiency of Formation Science, Absolute Necessity of Specific Formation Traditions

Some people may assume that an integrative generic science of foundational human formation by itself alone could be convincing enough to motivate people to abide by its tenets. They may conclude falsely that only such a science should dominate the formation of all world populations. Integrative scientists could, in principle, develop a theoretical frame of reference that would do justice to the elementary foundations and dynamics of the formation of person and society. They could make it theoretically compelling but not compelling for life. First of all, it would be difficult for them, if not impossible, to construe such a theory without utilization of the wisdom of the existing form traditions as a source of important hypothetical leads in their research. More important, however, is the fact that without faith, hope, and loving consonance, it would be impossible for the majority of people to try to implement more or less regularly the directives proposed by a science of formation. The foundational formation triad of faith, hope, and consonance is rooted in abandonment to the formation mystery. Because form traditions are grounded in faith traditions, they facilitate this triad considerably. Faith traditions are ways of relating via this triad to the transcendent mystery. They give to the human heart what no formation science as such can ever give. No proximate science can exactly identify and demonstrate the ultimate meaning of the formation processes in the universe. What is needed is mutually respectful cooperation of the science of formation and the classic form traditions that nourish in people faith, hope, and loving consonance.

To say that formation science can substitute for the specific transcendent formation traditions would be tantamount to saying that the universally intended prerevelational philosophy of Aquinas in the thirteenth century could take the place of the scripture, tradition, and doctrinal theology of the Catholic Church. Just as he denied this power to his philosophy, I deny the same in regard to my formation science.

CHAPTER 28

Carriers of Form Traditions

C hildren are formed by formation communities replete with form traditions. During their initial formation, children adopt the directives of these tradition carriers without fully grasping their meaning. This adoption generates in them certain dispositions. Later in life more of the formative meaning of these dispositions may be disclosed. This may happen in the light of acquired or infused formation wisdom. Such wisdom is evoked by the daily experience of people who try to implement a tradition in everyday life. The sheer experience of life stimulates formative reflection. It leads to a gradual assimilation of personal directives that have been adopted in childhood. The roots of form traditions have been preserved in memory, imagination, and anticipation. This preservation is not primarily an intellectual feat. It is far more a question of the heart, of feeling, and imagination, of symbolism as well as of their reverberations in one's neuroform of life.

Credibility of Form Traditions

The role of the community in *initial* formation is superseded by its role in *ongoing* formation. Traditional formation will continue only if it is somehow expressed at times by ourselves or by others. Otherwise it may lose for us its solidity and credibility. It would become shadowy and unreal. The formative power and credibility of traditional texts, symbols, and rituals would dissipate if they were not shared in some measure with a like-minded community. Absence of any communication and the cessation of all public expression of form traditions would leave them open to forgetfulness or to idiosyncratic interpretations. These could not be intersubjectively tested, corrected, complemented, and validated. Subjectivistic interpretation by intraformative powers would make the link with inter- and outer reality tenuous. Therefore, it is my contention that some form of interformative communication is necessary between people who presently strive to stay faithful to their own form traditions in daily life as lived in a pluritraditional society. Vertical interformation with the masters of formation of the past should be complemented by horizontal interformation with those who live the tradition in the present. For example, shared ritual plays a crucial role in the transmission and maintenance of a tradition. It keeps its credibility alive. Ritual facilitates the sharing of a tradition by acting it out together with others in the enhanced experience of a community's memory.

Cyclic and Progressive Form Traditions

Cyclic form traditions are typical of many tribal groups. People may develop a certain pattern of form-giving in worship, weaving, pottery, construction of shelter, ways of hunting, fishing, or initiating the young. Over prolonged periods of their formation history, they tend to repeat the same forms. They may expand and modulate them as well as their underlying dispositions, but rarely do later generations spontaneously reach out for new creations or innovations.

In contrast, progressive form traditions are dynamic. They evidence a creative critical history of formation. Their forward movement can be traced along with their journeys through the centuries. Such advancing traditions are notable for their power of expansion, assimilation, and dialogue without diluting the foundations that assure the maintenance of their community's uniqueness. Their dialogical interaction with people, events, things, new knowledge, and other form traditions gives rise to innovations that enhance and amplify their foundational identity and consistency. This is not to say that some representatives of progressive form traditions may not lose temporarily a balanced view of their tradition. Dialogical openness entails that risk. During certain periods of formation history, even large groups of adherents of a progressive form tradition may be caught up in passing pulsations. These are a fertile breeding ground for dissonant movements within and without their form traditions. The consonance of a progressive form tradition may seem lost momentarily. If the foundational form of the tradition remains strong enough, the seemingly deviant insights of such groups and individuals may be complemented and corrected later by a new communal self-expression of the original form tradition. Their views may be assimilated, with the necessary modulations, into the expanding vision of the progressive yet basically faithful form tradition.

Form Tradition and Initial Disposition Formation

The initial disposition formation of children in the light of consonant form traditions is of crucial importance. This is the founding period of their life. The form traditions communicated by their parents provide them with directives from which they may deduce the main lines of their ongoing disposition formation. The foundations of form traditions may be obscured by parental, segmental-traditional, and cultural accretions. Hence certain form directives instilled early in life may be partly or wholly uncongenial, incompatible, or lacking in compassion. For example, many Hindu families in India may instill in their children a cold disposition of superiority toward Muslims that kills off all compassion. Muslim families may react with similar contradispositions. Something similar happened in many Russian and other European Christian families in regard to Jewish people.

Original deformation by the accretions of a form tradition may be corrected later in life. Yet such reformation may still be shaped in some measure by the dissonant beginnings the tradition had to overcome. Initial deformation may still have an influence on later disposition formation, albeit indirectly. It may shape to some degree one's particular type of reformation. For example, a child formed in a fanatically communist family may later turn into an equally fanatic Christian.

In childhood dissonant dispositions may be initiated by deviant accretions of traditions. They do not necessarily disappear completely after the reformation of one's dispositional life. They may sink into oblivion. Their potency remains latent. They bide their time, ready to reemerge when crisis strikes unexpectedly. For instance, excessive religious guilt dispositions instilled in early life may be overcome in adulthood only to return when its victim, now lonely and old, is struck by a heart attack or other crisis.

Certain religious form traditions hold that reformation can be elevated to transformation by the formation mystery itself. The adherents of such form traditions believe that the elevating and transforming power of the mystery can become so pervasive and powerful that it burns out even the latent dissonant form dispositions left over from childhood.

During the founding period of infancy and childhood, one learns to satisfy, in the light of familial form traditions, the innate striving for maintenance and activation of one's form potency and effectiveness. Achievement in this area is accompanied by agreeable feelings of consonance and self-appreciation. As a result of this experience children begin to appreciate their own unique life form and their emergent secondary dispositional form of life. Form effectiveness makes them feel secure and worthwhile as formative participants in a universe of consonant form traditions. For them that universe is initially scaled down to a formation field embracing mainly the form traditions of family and neighborhood. Under the influence of these form traditions, a more or less constant set of formation dispositions is initiated in this period. This constancy is due to the relative steadiness of the child's conforming reactions and responses to form directives, dispositions, and opportunities presented by the version of form traditions that prevail in its familial surroundings.

Traditional Formation and Formation Anxiety

One factor that motivates such conformity can be formation anxiety. Formation anxiety is a vague, free-floating dread of form impotence. Children often conform to form traditions as exemplified by parents in order to overcome a mounting fear of form impotence. Representatives of form traditions can temper this fear by manifesting genuine faith, hope, and love in regard to the unique life form of the children. Such loving respect for the congenial unfolding of the young will mellow the paralyzing hold of anxious conformity. Confirmation of uniqueness hastens the moment of self-formation and self-disclosure without excessive fear. Self-formation will give way gradually to free, trusting coformation. The assurance of congenial self-unfolding in tune with the essentials of consonant form traditions early in life will dispose one for later mature conformity. The child may be disposed later in life to ratify without fear or resentment a flexible conformity to those routine aspects of social living that do not necessarily detract from the foundational uniqueness of one's life.

Congenial formation in childhood disposes people to a relaxed appraisal of the foundations of their form traditions. It liberates them from the tyranny of empty accretions as well as from the bane of formation anxiety. By the same token, they can freely affirm and honor accretions that prove to be consonant in either a lasting or current way. Congenial formation of children in accordance with the foundations of their form traditions has a special impact on those who, in line with their chosen or ratified form tradition, believe in transformation by the formation mystery itself. They will be more disposed to be open without fear to any inspiration that may lift them beyond worldly or personally dissonant conformities, pulsations, and conventions.

Implications for Initial Disposition Formation

A basic assumption of my personality theory is, therefore, that form tradition plays a significant role in the initial disposition formation of people. Infants and young children learn through conditioning the form traditions of their parents. Young children adopt traditional form directives for their dispositional life without being able to appraise and ratify them personally. Initial formation is prevalently what I call *con*formation. Children conform to the directives of their parents. Gradually such *con*formation may become what I have termed *co*formation, a more free and understanding formation of one's life. It means forming one's life with significant others on the basis of relatively free options for what one appraises as good in one's life direction.

Conformity to parental form traditions in early childhood, if confirmed and appreciated by the parents, generates an agreeable sense of security and consonance, of being in tune with the people, events, and things that comprise one's familial field of life. This feeling is linked with an early sense of form potency and effectiveness. Children experience this potency when they feel form-effective within their families, schools, and neighborhoods. Lack of this experience of personal form-effectiveness threatens, for instance, to destroy the future formation possibilities of whole generations of Afro-American children.

One condition for this feeling of form effectiveness is the firm and gentle structuring of the familial field in the light of consonant form traditions.

The home life must be arranged in a fashion that facilitates childlike effective conformation with some of the elements of the traditions cherished by the family. Children must be able to behave effectively and begin to give form to their lives by performing small chores in conformity with the tradition directives that are cherished by the adults around them. Such effective functioning must be confirmed by warm and loving manifestations of appreciation from the parents or their substitutes. One should be careful to promote as much as possible the foundations of such consonant form traditions and not to overemphasize the importance of the idiosyncratic modulations of the foundations that are peculiar to the parents or their substitutes. Unavoidably, children will initially imitate some parental accretions of traditions. There is no way to circumvent this totally, for there is no other way in that phase of formation to present the foundations outside the way the parents model them. The child lives mainly in its vital senses, feelings, and imagination. Hence it takes form traditions over in their concrete nuanced implementations in the lives of those on whom it totally depends.

Still the parents should try not to overemphasize the significance of their peculiar concretizations of the form traditions. Such mitigation will facilitate the process of congenial self-disclosure, which the children will have to initiate later in life. Also the risk will be less that they will then reject, along with the peculiar parental accretions of the form tradition, also its more fundamental treasures.

Anxiety that one is unable to command parental attention, presence, and support is quieted by conformity and the subsequent reward of confirming approval and appreciation. Without this the child will soon lose the feeling that one can give form to life in a way that enables one to ensure the attention, love, and appreciation of the parents. This experience establishes a first appreciation of one's ability to give form to relationships with others with predictable consequences. Otherwise feelings of relationship-inability and its consequent deformative anxiety, guilt, and insecurity will take over, thus giving rise to dissonant instead of consonant dispositions.

Form Traditions and Form Impotence

Initial conformity to the directives and dispositions fostered by the parents' form traditions can be explained in terms of my universal principles of formation. I hold that a basic tendency of all forms in the universe is to maintain their form and to unfold their being in a way that is consonant with their own form potency. A rose is only a rose insofar as it unfolds its rose-form in congeniality with its essence and in adaptive compatibility with its formation field.

I believe that the child is moved by the same universal dynamic in regard to its given form potency. However, I made it also a leading principle of my personality theory that the typically human form potency, no matter how unique, is always already coformed somehow by traditional coformants. These are changeable but never totally absent. Accepting the reality of one's unique and individual life form implies the acceptance of the reality of its implicit traditional coformants. Implicit acceptance of this reality for children implies that they should be enabled to receive and give form in their relationships with their family in ways approved of by consonant family traditions. They should be helped to experience that such conformity to tradition attracts manifestations of attention, love, confirmation, and appreciation. Otherwise they might experience not only relationship-inability but also form impotence. Prefocally they might feel powerless to be effective in relation to others and hence rejected. This may build a slush fund of hidden rage. Children do not dare to acknowledge such dispositions to themselves. They are afraid to offend traditional standards by their anger and indignation. They fear, moreover, that any show of anger may turn the seemingly all powerful representatives of the form traditions against them. Later in life such denied dispositions of rage may come to the fore again when the original experience of form impotence is relived in memory, imagination, anticipation, or actuality. Rejection of parental form traditions is often due to this buried disposition of powerless rage evoked by the experience of impotence in the face of form traditional demands to which one was unable to respond effectively in childhood.

This initial dissonant disposition of rage may influence all other dispositions that coform one's secondary foundational life form. It may cause persons to strive inordinately after impressive feats of form-giving to life and world. They feel the urge to persuade themselves and others of their potency to gain approval and appreciation. They may nurture an excessive performance disposition in religious and secular practices. They may feel compelled to prove that they can outdo others in perfect fulfillment of the directives of their traditions. Conversely others may try for a lifetime to disprove the form tradition whose parental representatives made them feel ineffective and impotent by their irrational demands or lack of appreciation. The wound of the experience of form impotence in childhood may be so deep that it takes a lifetime to heal, if ever. A feeling of vague distrust of the form traditions concerned and their representatives may never be alleviated completely.

Form Traditions: Conformation and Coformation

In their better moments children try to please their family by conformity to the directives of the form traditions that hold sway in familial life. They like to feel consonant by adoption of like apprehensions, appraisals, choices, and directives as well as by their functional and vital implementations insofar as they can sense them in their manifestations in family members. Such conformity may secure for them expressions of love, appreciation, and confirmation by their parents and others. If so, they experience the agreeable, secure feeling of form potency and form effectiveness. The formation of certain consonant dispositions, such as those of appreciation of form traditions, may be the fruit of such experiences. By adopting the traditional form directives of their parents, children fashion an initial dispositional life form. They adopt these dispositions, for they are approved of or at least tolerated by the dominant familial representatives of these form traditions.

The next experience of form effectiveness in tune with the form traditions of the family is an experience of *co*form effectiveness. It signals the primordial awakening of the experience of a minimum of human formation freedom. The child hesitantly ventures into a first phase of *co*formation that goes beyond mere conformation. This experience nurtures a deeper self-appreciation. It also lays the ground for a potential appreciation of the formation mystery in which one's deepest unique life call and its traditional coformant are rooted. The experience of form ineffectiveness or impotence, on the contrary, would give rise to dispositions of self-depreciation.

Form Traditions and Form Potency Confirmation

The conviction of form potency cannot be engendered by our own isolated selfhood. Others have to give it to us. We need the gift of confirmation by the representatives of humanity's form traditions, at least initially. Without it we cannot believe in our own forming powers and their sustenance by the formation mystery. Family life surrounds children with many traditional form directives and dispositions. These appeal to the inner dynamic need in all of us to give form to life in consonant ways. Children are too small and too inexperienced, their brains are too underdeveloped, to be able to appraise form traditions or to take the initiative in their own formation. They cannot personally appraise the form directives and dispositions presented to them. By imitating formative acts and dispositions of parents, who live by certain form traditions, they can gain parental appreciation and secure the confirmation of their own form potency. If children fail in their attempt to secure form potency confirmation, guilt feelings may overwhelm them. They may feel guilty about their very existence. In accordance with my universal formation law for all appearances in the universe, we exist only insofar as we can maintain and unfold the form we are uniquely called to be. I found that the necessary condition for this maintenance and unfolding in humans is the experience of form potency and form effectiveness. Children must be enabled to express their emergent potencies in effective formative acts and dispositions. This demands, at least initially, confirmation by significant representatives of form traditions.

First Experience of
Traditional Functional Control and of Form Effectiveness

In the early stages of infancy, children are formed mainly in the vital dimension of human life. There is not yet a really significant development of the integrative form structures, such as the core, current, apparent, and actual forms of life. Only their neuroform has developed some conditioned facets. A crucial moment in their development is the challenge to learn some functional form control of the vital dimension during toilet training. Toilet training is ruled by certain form traditions that differ in various societies. Children may be effective in their response to this early challenge by their familial form traditions. Parents and others representing the same tradition may praise them. This experience of form effectiveness extends itself to functional form control of other vital operations, again in tune with familial form traditions. The basis is laid for the emergence of integrative form structures that combine dimensions such as the vital and functional in effective unities.

The experience of form effectiveness may extend itself to an awakening of the possibility of a certain control of the parental representatives of the familial form traditions. The child discovers that it is possible to play on their obvious concern and expectation during this training period. The child feels its power to surprise or disappoint them, to let go or to withhold. Children in this stage begin to engage in some modest measure of minimally free coformation with the parents and the traditional form directives and dispositions they represent.

I see in all of this a small manifestation of a beginning tiny shift from *con-* to *co*formation with the parents and the form traditions represented in their adult dispositions. Ongoing formation widens this freedom of *co*formation with form traditions. It points to the gradual dissolution of sheer conformity to form traditions, a conformity that has not yet attained to the maturity of personal appraisal and ratification. Interestingly enough, the growth in *co*formation gives rise to a new type of *con*formation with form traditions. The essential difference with infant conformity is that mature conformity is freely chosen or ratified. It extends itself mainly to dispositions that, once confirmed, do not require a new appraisal and decision. It replaces blind conformation to form traditions as modulated by the parents. Dispositions are affirmed not merely because the parents said so in the past, but because they are personally appraised as good and as true gifts of one's form tradition.

One's formation history as a whole keeps on developing around the axis of the basic laws of formation dynamics I have formulated, namely, at any and all times the human life form strives to maintain and enhance its sense of form potency and effectiveness in its reception, expression, and donation of form. Dispositions are formed around the victories and failures of this striving.

CHAPTER 29

Dispositional Form; Types of Tradition; Key Situations and Symbols

Empowerment of Dispositions by Formation Traditions

Form traditions, insofar as they are consonant, enable people to initiate and maintain well-appraised dispositions for consonant life formation. They offer directives and dispositions, the benefits of which have been substantiated by the lives of people in many generations. Persons rooted in such traditions experience the silent endorsement of the generations that went before them. They feel inspired by the outstanding initiators of these traditions. The confirmation power of shared form traditions can be compelling. Their adherents may maintain the conviction of shared form potency in the face of rejection and persecution by their contemporaries. People whose sense of form potency is steadily threatened by society and who do not find potency confirmation in living participation in any form tradition may feel deeply insecure. Some of those who miss a sense of sustenance and confirmation by a meaningful form tradition may be tempted to suicide, to commit crime, to join street gangs or engage in terrorism. They feel compelled to evidence to themselves and others their form potency and effectiveness, be it in a dissonant fashion. Others may try to numb their despondency in drug addiction or in a robot-like or overambitious existence.

Certain form traditions, rooted in religious or ideological faith traditions, enable their adherents to maintain a sense of confirmed form potency in spite of apparent failure in the eyes of achievement-oriented societies. The Marxist form tradition confirms the form potency of its imprisoned or persecuted militants. Their form potency may be confirmed by a shared disposition to give form together in history to a brotherhood and sisterhood of all people on this planet. Their shared hope and faith disposes the real believers among them to bring the ultimate sacrifice of their life if the Marxist form tradition would demand this in the struggle for a new world. Muslims may extol the gift of potency to join Allah in glory when dying in a holy war. Their form potency is enhanced by this faith. They feel confirmed in their possibilities by their ultimate source of confirmation. In times of suffering and adversity the Buddhist faith and

277

form tradition may point to the form potency implied in the disposition of detachment from an illusory world leading to Nirvana. The Christian faith and form tradition enables those who suffer to unite their pain and disappointment with the Lord's passion. They abandon themselves to him in physical and psychological suffering, in loss of career, popularity or possessions. Confirmed by him, they share with him his potency and disposition to save humanity through redemptive suffering.

The confirmation power of shared form traditions enables true believers to spot opportunities where many would only perceive misfortune and affliction. An enhanced conviction of their potency to give meaningful form to life under any circumstances makes them appreciate opportunities for beneficial form reception and expression even in the worst thinkable situations.

Three Types of Form Traditions

In previous volumes I distinguished the cosmic, the human (personal-social), and the transhuman epiphanies of the formation mystery. All form traditions can be classified as prevalently concerned with one of these epiphanies. For example, the Buddhist form tradition seems intracosmic. It excels in its reverence for the mystery of macro- and microcosmic formation. The same holds for Taoism. The Confucian form tradition is more inspired by the personal-social epiphany of the formation mystery. Something similar can be said of the metaphysical aspects of certain humanist and socialist form traditions. The monotheistic Hebrew, Christian, and Islamic faith traditions have generated form traditions based on a belief in a transhuman revelation of the formation mystery. This by no means excludes their faith in and concern for the cosmic and personal-social epiphanies of the same formation mystery.

Each of my three types of form traditions elaborates the implications for the art of living of what is seminally inherent in their sustaining faith traditions. Their concern is the practical implementation of their faith traditions in everyday life formation. Hence they contain practical formation insights in regard to consonant living in the light of each one of these three epiphanies. The concentration of each of these three types on a specific epiphany gives rise to potentially relevant insights in the art of living that can be meaningful for all people inside and outside classical form traditions.

I believe that my science of generic human formation can extract the basic wisdom of each of these three types of form traditions. I can look for the universally consonant form dispositions each one of them might cultivate. This effort may clarify and validate the measure of wisdom and effectiveness of the maxims and dispositions proposed by each of these form traditions. They may be complemented and sometimes enriched by corresponding data and insights of the auxiliary social and educational sciences and disciplines. In turn, many practical insights of the science of formation itself, essentially different from the field of education, can enlighten similar insights gained by each of the three types of form traditions. The universalized insights obtained by critical-creative research from one type of form tradition may be helpful for the understanding and enrichment of other types of the same. The latter traditions, in turn, may opt to create more room in their own formation practices for the development of dispositions of presence to the epiphany concentrated upon by still other types.

I also believe that my formation science can facilitate the translation of other form directives and dispositions into one's own form traditions. This can be done by establishing the generic human meaning of such directives and dispositions. I detach such generic meaning from all particular meanings that are typical of only the specific form traditions that developed these directives and dispositions. Once I have found their universal human meaning, it is easier for me to bring it into consonance with my own basic form tradition.

The internationalization of the world has brought the three types of form traditions nearer to one another than ever before in the formation history of humanity. The absence of a critical-creative science of generic transcendent formation sometimes led people of one type of form tradition to adopt the practices and dispositions of another before sufficiently detaching them from their underlying particular faith traditions and from sociohistorical accretions. Such a lack of previous universalization of form directives made it more difficult to integrate them wisely and critically within one's own form tradition. Spontaneous premature adoption failed often to maintain a profound and pure consonance with the faith tradition that gave birth to one's own form tradition. This led to dissonant practices in a number of adherents of such increasingly eclectic form traditions.

Form Traditions as Assimilated Key Situations

Our form tradition is a key situation in our life. A form tradition offers people a key to the understanding of who they are. It clarifies in some measure what I call the secondary founding form, the dispositional form of life. Our particular tradition pyramid explains this secondary founding form insofar as it is initiated, sustained and nourished by certain socio-historical situations. The historical response of the form tradition to these situations keeps reverberating. The situation is frozen into a lasting formation symbol. It makes the form tradition brim over with emotions, dispositions and directives that trigger the wisdom and courage, or the resentment and rage, accumulated and deepened over decennia, even centuries. For instance, the sociohistorical humiliation of Arab populations by the Crusades and by the colonizing Western powers gave rise in their form traditional pyramid to a fierce tradition of symbolically demonizing Western powers as imposters and Satanic infidels.

Initially only the actual form of life of children may be affected by the form tradition. They reenact the formative acts of their parents. Gradually they develop beyond mere acts of imitation certain dispositions to appear as their parents do in consonance with their form tradition. A conformative apparent life form marks this formation phase, sustained by appearance-dispositions for public conformity. Out of parental or public sight, people may forget about the right appearances.

In the next phase of formation, the less peripheral, yet not core or central, current forms of childhood life emerge. They may dispose children to live in accordance with the directives and favored dispositions of their tradition, even without supervision, when the eyes of the reproaching other are absent. In the meantime their core form or heart may be increasingly touched and moved by their form traditions via their parents. They begin to develop lasting dispositions of the heart. This intraformation, especially on the adolescent and adult level, implies a gradual awakening of the spirit, and therewith the possibility of personal apprehension, appraisal, and modulation of form directives and dispositions in congeniality with one's own unique preformation and in compatibility with one's changing life situations. This transcendent formation of the child can be complemented by public education on the pretranscendent level, a quite different yet necessary addendum.

Maintenance of
Specific Form Traditions in Pluritraditional Societies

A form tradition is usually assimilated within a specific communal situation that symbolizes that tradition, such as an Islamic, Hebrew, Hindu, Christian, family, church, congregation, school, neighborhood. I use the term *situational transposition* to indicate that the subsequent dispositions may begin to give form to other situations as well. I mean situations that are not intimately interwoven with those of a formation community that implements its specific tradition within that community itself. For instance, Christian formation traditions of pioneering families in the United States wisely generated dispositions for Christian education, a pretranscendent education that leaves room for transcendent formation. These dispositions affected profoundly civil life in the small towns and villages, in the early colonies, and in the incipient States after secession from England. Soon the dispositions in question influenced not only their own schools but also the emerging public school systems that by their very nature were not intimately interwoven with the Christian faith and formation tradition.

Adherents of various form traditions may live and labor in situations that do not foster or symbolize their preferred form directives and dispositions. Hence they may feel the need to initiate or maintain some formation situations that express more fully their own traditions. They form support communities that make available, renew, and sustain their specific sources of faith, hope, and consonance. These must help them to keep alive the wisdom and discipline of concrete everyday life formation developed by their own form tradition. One basic type of community nourishes primarily the faith tradition in which one's form tradition is rooted. A most obvious example of this kind of faith community is churches, temples, synagogues, chapels, revival tents, and other kinds of preaching and prayer spaces.

Another type of community is the formation community, which concerns itself mainly with the more practical aspects of the art and discipline of concrete everyday living of the faith outside such sacred spaces in the profane world. This bridge community sustains the personal-social and empirical-experiential implications and implementations of one's faith formation. It does so in the light of one's faith tradition and in dialogue with the general wisdom of human life formation that is available in one's contemporary society.

The nature of a supportive formation community changes with the temporal conditions of a form tradition. When a culture and a form tradition are identical, as in a theocratic state, as, for example, in Ancient Egypt, the culture itself may serve as a support community for one's form tradition. Such has been the case in medieval Christianity, in the Israel of the faithful Hebrew kings, and in Islamic, Buddhist, and Hindu cultures of the present or the recent past.

Pluriformational societies cannot offer proximate guidelines for the formation of dispositions in tune with each one's own form tradition. No one form tradition is legally dominant. Many people are not in touch with any classical form tradition. Many are animated by their faith tradition, but it is not sufficiently complemented by a well worked-out, finely nuanced, regularly updated art and discipline of everyday effective living in the light of this tradition. Hence the problem of keeping one's faith tradition effective in everyday life formation is obvious.

One response to this formation need is a proliferation of secular-humanistic formation centers, workshops, weekend retreats, or gurus and cults that offer an amalgamation of sometimes valuable, sometimes exotic suggestions for wholesome psychological and biophysical living. The existing faith traditions may not offer their own practical life formation centers. A number of their adherents may frequent the widely advertised pluralistic, eclectic centers to fill this lacuna in their confused life formation. The result may be an increasing dissonance between their own faith tradition and their style of life formation. They may become alienated from their faith.

The faith tradition in a pluritraditional society can respond to this need by fostering a critical-creative integration of its classical form tradition with the compatible formation insights made available by other form traditions, arts, sciences, and disciplines. Experts well formed in this integrational wisdom of living can be used in formation centers and other support communities to fill the need for formation in the light of one's own form tradition. These centers could do for the adherents of a faith tradition what the monolithic form traditional cultures did for their predecessors in the past.

Cultural Compatibility without Compromise

Supportive formation centers should give their participants the conviction that they can be effective in society in many compatible ways without betraying the foundationals of their particular faith and form tradition. This is an initial step in the process of cultural compatibility without compromise. Representatives of the Jewish form tradition, for instance, started their own health and fitness centers to help their people to implement the ideal of Hebrew physical, psychological, and spiritual effectiveness in the typical American world of attractive masculine or feminine appearance and of respect for strong stamina in business life and athletics. The Protestant formation tradition did something similar by the establishment of Y.M.C.A. facilities and later their own counseling centers.

One means of sustaining and deepening one's transcendent presence in the culture is to celebrate together the ideals and symbols of one's tradition. These point to the mystery that goes beyond yet includes and illumines the limited projects of one's personal and social life. At the same time the mystery is related to the concrete formation events one meets in everyday existence. One important function of form traditional centers is to enable their adherents to interiorize the transcendent symbols of their faith tradition.

Transcendent Imagination, Memory, Anticipation, and Form Traditional Symbols

Transcendent imagination is the modality that enables one to experience, create, or innovate symbols of transcendent meanings communicated by one's form tradition. *Transcendent memory* is the capacity to let such symbols live on in one's ongoing life formation, to recall them together with others in one's traditional community of shared memory, to relate them to corresponding formation events. *Transcendent anticipation* is an imaginative-intuitive readiness to apprehend alone or with other members of a tradition-community new transcendent symbols regarding the mystery of formation in relation to anticipated formation events.

Transcendent symbols are thus creations of *transcendent* imagination, memory, and anticipation. They foster the attunement of one's life to the formation mystery and its epiphanies. Mandalas and myths, rituals and archaic sacred words are examples of transcendent images and symbols. They point to what in principle cannot be fully known. The great form traditions hand such transcendent symbols over from generation to generation. To benefit from this treasure, a transcendent memory is important. It enables one to bring the mythical symbols back to awareness in their transcendent meaning and to be nourished by them accordingly. The classical masters and rites of a form tradition are able to evoke the great mythical symbols of their tradition, to bring them to life again, to link them inspirationally with the concrete formation events and desirable dispositions in the lives of their readers and listeners, or of the participants in formative rituals. Such writings and rituals are the living transcendent memory of a form tradition and its sustaining community of memory. Formative reading or ritual participation leads to a revitalization of the sources of faith, hope, and consonance represented by these symbols.

Form Traditions
Rooted in Revealed Transcendent Ideals and Symbols

Certain form traditions hold that the formation mystery itself, in a transhuman epiphany, revealed certain transcendent ideals and symbols. These traditions believe that the mystery also elevated the formation history of a chosen people and of certain historical events to powerful symbols of revealed and infused faith, hope, and love and their objects. Such transhuman creations, believed in by certain form traditions as their axiomatic ground, do not have their source in the arts or sciences or the generic science of formation, or any other science or philosophy. They are prior to any scientific or philosophical investigation. Not only the transhuman symbols of the revelation-traditions, but the transcendent symbols of the mystery of formation in all form traditions are prescientific.

The science of formation may utilize such symbolic visions metaphorically in its integrating generic presuppositions. It does so in a way that does not contradict established scientific data. Seeming contradictions are often solved by a reconsideration of the data and their formulation. As long as the symbols are about the formation mystery as a whole and the data about observable particular facts, apparent contradictions can often be reconciled. As a matter of fact, a theoretical integrational type of science may utilize compatible symbols of the whole of formation and its mysterious ground. It needs them, as it does all-encompassing presuppositions, to maintain its superordinate, integrational role in regard to the immense variety of partial contributions of the auxiliary social and educational arts, sciences, and disciplines.

Participation in Symbols by Believers —
A Source of Ongoing Life of Tradition

Vital for any form tradition is the aliveness of the formative faith experience in its adherents. Then the symbols, rites, and texts of a tradition come to life for them. The more one shares in a tradition by means of meditation, reflection, contemplative dwelling, and implementary functioning, the more traditional symbols gain in meaning. One begins to experience them as significant pointers, to the mystery of formation itself. Ritual points to the mystery as celebrated in a tradition. The formative aspects of rituals are a creation of the transcendent imagination of the initial participants in a tradition. Because of its early effectiveness, their ritual has been elevated to a repeated rite. The ritual formatively lived opens its participants to "the more than" that it commemorates. It points to the mystery it presents. Preoccupation with ritualistic precision alone could keep the mind focused on formal details. It might bypass unspoken aspects, symbolic acts, pointers and pauses that leave room for the transcendent intuition, imagination, memory, and anticipation of the participants. Rituals as lived experience do not necessarily imply that all participants maintain a focal consciousness during the celebration. Some of them may be absorbed in the participative contemplation that a ritual may evoke by its presentation of the mystery. The more one lives a ritual the less focal its details become. People who perform rituals in a rigid, anxious manner may manifest a knowledge of ritual formalities in painstaking detail. Yet they may be unable to let themselves be absorbed in the ritual.

Interformation and
Dispositional Formation in the Light of Traditions

Human formation is interformation. Initial interformation is marked by the domination of parents who act mainly as interformative agents and by the submissiveness of children who act mainly as interformative recipients. Parents committed to a specific form tradition may mix their exemplification and communication of that tradition with personal and sociohistorical accretions embedded in the structure of their own dispositions. Such idiosyncratic and passing formation factors may prevail over the foundations of the tradition in the disposition formation of the parents and children.

Our primary foundational life form is the preformed unique life direction we are called to disclose and realize during our formation history. It is the uniqueness of our embodied life call. Its tentative disclosure and realization gradually leads to a flexible constellation of dispositions to give and receive form in specific ways. This tissue of dispositions gives rise, as it were, to a secondary foundational, empirical life form. I say "empirical" because unlike the primary foundational life form it is more fully available to experience, at least in principle. I call it "foundational" because it is the foundation of the everyday empirical actualization of our life. I call it "secondary" foundation because it follows the first foundational life form; ideally it should be formed, reformed, and transformed in congeniality with the disclosures of this primordial form. In practice, it can be totally or partially dissonant in relation to this primary image of what our unique life might be like if fully disclosed.

This dispositional foundation of the empirical life may be uncongenial with the primary, preformed unique foundation or pregiven image of a child's life. The forming power of parental idiosyncrasies and socio-historical accretions may have contributed to this uncongeniality of the child's dispositions. They may have obscured the liberating power of the foundations of their form tradition. These foundations are liberating in that they tend to release the inner, unique preformed image or direction of each person's life insofar as that is possible in the particular moment and situation of disclosure.

Ongoing life formation is, among other things, a struggle to release one's spirit, as mediator of the primary life form or image, from the shackles of uncongenial coercive dispositions. An important means to overcome uncongenial coercive dispositions, due, among other things, to dissonant accretions of form traditions, is to deepen oneself in the foundations of the consonant form tradition and its undergirding faith tradition to which one is committed.

Fallacy of Tradition-Free Formation

The foundations of classical form traditions have gained over the centuries a status that transcends our particular familial and sociohistorical situations. The formulations of many of their foundationals have been purified from passing pulsations by successive generations in their appraisal and reappraisal, formulation and reformulation. They have been tested out in recurrent attempts by many populations to implement them in their formation.

During formative periods of contestation of one's initial formation, one may be imbued with the mistaken notion that one can unfold one's life consonantly in total independence. One denies the inescapability of vertical and horizontal interformation. The wisdom of foundational form traditions may be resisted. Careful observation reveals that believers in autarkic self-actualization soon become the naive or credulous victims of their own insufficiently appraised needs and of current sociohistorical pulsations. A priori rejection of the foundational wisdom of all form traditions makes it impossible to find a viewpoint from which one can critically and creatively appraise the passing pulsations of one's own cultural period.

Contemporary pulsations that are popular carry the force of environmental confirmation of one's vital functional impulses and compulsions. They can be far more inhibitive of one's unique unfolding than the temporally distant and disinterested foundations of one's form tradition. The latter have a quality of transtemporality and universality. They have withstood the test of time. They can confirm one's deeper, transcendent form potency, which is unique and rooted in one's hidden calling by the mystery. The temporal and local additions to or subtractions from a tradition may be as powerful as the sociohistorical pulsations that called them forth. Temporal pulsations, influential only in a passing generation, may become quasi-traditional pulsations in their own right. Such emergent passing cultural pulsations may enrich or contaminate our traditions.

Archaic Wisdom of Human Formation

The history of form traditions reaches as far back as the history of humanity. The unfolding of distinct cultures led to the development of distinctly formulated form traditions. These were preceded by what may be called an archaic wisdom of human formation. Its insights were more lived than focally formulated. If this wisdom was expressed, it was in oral fables, myths, rituals, and other symbols. Conceptual written systems of formation were unknown during that vast archaic period of the initial formation of humanity and its emergent field of presence and action. This archaic wisdom could, therefore, not be called a form tradition in the sense this term acquired later in history. The initial formation insights of humanity were closely linked with the basic human predicament. The universality of this predicament explains the fact that similar remnants of archaic formation wisdom can be found in form traditions that emerged later as well-formulated, diverse systems of human life formation. Some of their similarities suggest the existence of a kind of early formation insight that was implicitly universal and foundational.

While this wisdom as a whole is not identical with any particular form tradition, some of it can be traced in many classical styles of human formation. I take this implicit universality of archaic formation wisdom into account in my effort to develop the basic generic science of human formation. This explains my interest in myths, symbols, rituals, and rites in their archaic emergence. Such archaic wisdom, when traced foundationally, often has to be purified from later accretions that restrict and hide its original intent. It has to be restored to its initial meaning. Only then may it reflect some of the original intuitions into basic human formation.

Distinctions and Relationships between Form and Faith Traditions

Basic form traditions, as I have shown repeatedly, are usually rooted in religious or ideological faith traditions or belief systems. As a matter of fact, no human system of thought, even scientific thought, is possible without some implicit faith in axioms or presuppositions and in some ultimate meaning of life. Such beliefs sustain the existence and the sense of meaningfulness of the scientists concerned and their specific type of involvement. Faith traditions refer to propositions that cannot be directly validated by means of empirical scientific methods or analytical logic. Such propositions are not necessarily irrational or antirational. While they cannot be proven compellingly to the functional mind, it may be possible to show that they are neither at odds with human reason.

A form tradition, unlike a faith tradition in which it is rooted, is not primarily about the ultimate stands toward reality expressed in that faith tradition. A basic form tradition is primarily about the art and discipline of giving and receiving form in the light of the ultimate stands of the faith tradition concerned. A form tradition, therefore, does not specialize primordially in innovative doctrinal statements and explanations regarding its underlying faith tradition. It leaves that to the authorities and the philosophers or theologians of the faith tradition concerned. Doctrinal innovation or explanation is beyond the expertise of formation scientists.

The form tradition may give rise, however, to what I call seminal-doctrinal statements. These are not expressions of doctrine, but they do contain the *seed* of such expressions that can be watered and tended by professional theologians or philosophers of the faith tradition. Dealing with practical formation issues in the light of a faith tradition, the corresponding form tradition only points to concrete solutions to everyday problems of effective living. Formation solutions are primordially practical. Yet they may unwittingly contain suggestions for further theological or philosophical reflection. Such pointers by formation experts may be followed up by theological or philosophical experts of the corresponding faith tradition.

Conversely, anything in a faith tradition, like the sayings of the Bible, the Koran, the Sutras, can be an ultimate source of formation for the acts and dispositions of those who believe in them. Faith propositions contain the seeds for form directives and dispositions. These can be elaborated and nuanced by formation directors and scientists. Such directives and dispositions translate the principles of faith into a practical style of life.

The form tradition assists people more specifically than the faith tradition in the task of implementation of faith directives in acts and dispositions. The sources of the faith tradition themselves contain some specific form directives. But most of them are the fruit of elaboration by the form tradition. Usually formation practices are developed afterward, during the formation history of the tradition, by experiential experts and masters in the concrete life formation of the adherents of a faith tradition. Examples of specific form tradition practices are the art of archery, flower arrangement, or Zazen meditation in the Buddhist form tradition or the method of hesychastic prayer in the Eastern Orthodox tradition. Most of these form directives and subsequent dispositions are not directly revealed or precisely described in the faith sources of the form tradition. Neither are they invented or initially elaborated by its theologians or philosophers. They originated in the course of practical formation experience.

Formation scientists are not necessarily adherents of a particular form tradition they examine. Nevertheless, they can study the form effectiveness of its recommended directives, dispositions, and exercises. Leaving the theological issues to other experts, they ask how a particular formation practice affects concretely the disposition formation of people and the human formation of their fields of life. They may suggest improvements in the effective communication and implementation of a formation practice. Such practical suggestions in service of effective everyday life formation should not distort or diminish the faith content implicit in a formational directive, disposition, or exercise. They should serve the formative effectiveness of the faith application while preserving respectfully the faith content itself. They should assist people in living their undistorted faith more congenially, compatibly, compassionately, joyously, and effectively in the light of self-awareness and of consonant contemporary knowledge of life and world formation.

Focal Conceptual and Prefocal
Symbolic Interconscious Life of Formation Traditions

A form tradition is not limited to clearly focused conceptual formulations. Much of it is alive in the interconscious symbols, customs, and rituals of people. Periodically this living awareness of certain aspects of the form tradition may become latent. The symbols are maintained, but their deeper meaning is no longer assimilated. Their enshrined wisdom lies dormant. Changing formation situations within its formation field may challenge a community to resurrect the latent wisdom of the past. This wisdom may then come to life again. The reflection such a challenge evokes may open people to the deeper meaning of their routinized customs and symbols. A germinal form tradition for a great part may be latent in the interconsciousness of a society during long periods of time. New circumstances may foster the awakening of dormant meanings of a form tradition in the minds and hearts of its adherents. I observed such awakening in suffering people hiding with me in the last year of World War II in Holland. The diaries of Anne Frank and Etty Hillesum gave a lasting voice to the resurrection of the dormant wisdom of Jewish traditions experienced by so many around me at that time.

Tradition is thus not constricted to clear formulations, available to the focal interconsciousness of a community. A great part of it is alive or dormant in the prefocal interconsciousness of the community of memory formed by a tradition. This interconsciousness, focal and prefocal, is, as it were, a consciousness that has been exteriorized in customs, images, symbols, and rituals. Hence people can in various measures participate in these externalized expressions.

Other manifestations of consciousness are identified in my formation theory as, respectively, focal, pre-, infra-, and transconscious. My construct of interconsciousness is related to all of them, but it is only formatively alive insofar as the adherents of the form tradition participate in it. Different members do so in different ways and measures. Such means of individual conscious participation may be focal, pre-, infra-, and transconscious. It is not mainly a question of intellectual learning. Both faith and form traditions may live on in simple, less educated people. Meanwhile more sophisticated adherents may have lost contact with these treasures. The *anawim* may be the last refuge of a dying tradition.

If a uniform tradition dies or is destroyed in a community that lives by this one tradition, the culture it sustains will die too. Its participants may lose all initiative until they find another coherent configuration of meaningful formation symbols and form directives. Such a disclosure may enable them to form a new animating interconsciousness in which all can share. A tragic example of the loss of a uniform tradition and therewith of culture, dignity, initiative, and creativity can be found in the history of certain tribes of American Indians. It is a crime of social injustice to diminish or destroy violently the conditions for the survival of a faith and form tradition of a population. If changes in human history make it impossible to maintain their traditions, they should be helped to complement them by more consonant form traditions. As far as possible the basic wisdom of the residues of their own traditions should be integrated into their new style of life formation.

Formative Power of Tradition

The preservation of formation wisdom by a tradition happens in the very act of receiving, expressing, and giving form in life. People receive form from salient aspects of life and world that are symbolically enhanced as meaningful by their form tradition. Once these symbols are appropriated inwardly, they inspire people to express them somehow in lifestyle and appearance. They affect the way in which they give form to their surroundings, to their tools and utensils, their residences and cities, to art and nature. These innovative expressions preserve the tradition in a living way while enriching and deepening its directives and dispositions for present and coming generations. The great tribes of American Indians preserved their formation wisdom by symbolic acts, dances, ceremonies, by initiation, hunting, and fishing rituals. In their symbolic, ritual reenactment of creation they gave form to their life and world. By their style of transcendent engagement in nature they received form abundantly and developed corresponding dispositions. In this way they preserved their form tradition effectively. Foreign conquerors destroyed the conditions for this type of life and world formation. They undermined the sense of form potency and effectiveness in the Indians. The conviction that they were able to give form to nature was the basic condition for the courageous continuation of an effective manner of human form reception, expression, and donation in a resistant world. To kill that conviction is to kill a culture. To maintain that conviction and tradition, even when conquered, is to be victorious.

While a form tradition is mostly alive in people on a prefocal level, as embedded in the unique constellation of their form dispositions, it can be lifted to the level of focal consciousness. Focal conscientization enables the adherents of a form tradition to exteriorize the lived directives and dispositions verbally or otherwise. This makes them available to personal and shared reflection and subsequent formulation. Before such externalization people may live form directives and dispositions mainly prereflectively. They are less able to appraise and articulate them explicitly. Helpful in this regard is the formative reading of the masters of one's oral or written form tradition. So is reflection on the formative meaning of traditional symbols, rituals, and liturgies. By means of such reflections, done privately or in common, the form directives and dispositions implied in these expressions can be made explicit.

Focalizing of Traditions by Reflection, Appraisal, Verbal Symbolization, Foundational Tracing

Form traditions may be much more available to focal consciousness in advanced cultures. Pretranscendent education in such cultures gives people the skills to engage in an organized common effort of making explicit what is implicit also in their transcendent customs, dispositions, movements, and motivations. In such cultures the participants in form traditions will attempt to make explicit in critical-creative formulations the transcendent experiences they are living implicitly in their dispositions and in their daily style of life. To lift the implicit tradition to the level of focal consciousness can enrich and deepen the understanding of its treasures. The means for such focalizing are reflection, appraisal, verbal symbolizations, and foundational tracing. I shall consider each of these tools.

Reflection can enrich and deepen one's understanding and appreciation of one's form tradition, its directives and dispositions. It enables the mind to gain access to what is lived prereflectively and to explain and sustain it rationally and practically. It enriches the focal imagination, memory, and anticipation nourished by such reflection. If reflection is engaged in systematically by successive generations of critical-creative participants, it may disclose little by little the wealth of consonant form directives and nuanced dispositions developed by the form tradition over the centuries. Not all of these directives are lived and utilized in all periods of a formation history. Systematic reflection may be able to disclose and formulate form directives and dispositions that otherwise may be neglected periodically.

Appraisal by our focal mind can purify the foundational form directives and dispositions from their sociohistorical accretions. Often they are not clearly distinguished from the foundations when these are lived in the prereflective region of consciousness. Some of these accretions may have become harmful instead of helpful in present formation situations. They may cling like barnacles to our ship of life, slowing its course. One typical advantage of this conscientization of a form tradition is its explicit *verbal symbolization*. Verbal symbols offer a powerful means of a clear and explicit transmission of a form tradition to a population. Such verbal transmission in a critical-creative way seems crucial in advanced pluritraditional cultures where most traditions tend to be transmitted by verbal symbols that complete and reinforce the nonverbal communication. People in such cultures, especially school children and students, are continuously exposed to explicitly verbalized views of cultural and other form traditions different from their own. They are, moreover, imbued with the well-formulated findings of a variety of arts, sciences, and disciplines perhaps in expressions contaminated by their underlying belief systems. The form directives implicit in their communications may lead to a confusing, syncretistic view of desirable dispositions in contemporary life. A systematic verbalization of our own form tradition will enable us to integrate consonantly within a master scheme the relevant formation contributions of other traditions.

Bringing prereflective tradition to the level of reflection is enhanced by the method of *foundational tracing*. This method enables the students of a particular form tradition to trace the foundational themes of formation insofar as they have been verbalized and recorded in the writings of the masters of the tradition under study. The students investigate critically which common themes can be identified in those writings; how they may have been enriched, deepened, or distorted by sociohistorical influences on various authors over the centuries; how they compare with the findings of the generic science of foundational formation. They ask themselves if this particular form tradition can be articulated in terms of the generic science. If so, to what degree? What reformation would be necessary? Can we suggest certain refinements in the expression of the particular form tradition? Are certain insights of the science helpful for the enhancement of the form effectiveness and the overall consonance of the form directives of a particular form tradition?

Ecumenical and
Transecumenical Dialogue between Form Traditions

Diverse form traditions share by their formative nature some similar concerns for effective responses to contemporary challenges posed by the same sociohistorical formation fields they share. Hence the ecumenical dialogue between form traditions can be mutually enriching. Such dialogue between the experts of form traditions may enliven and enlighten also the different type of ecumenical dialogue by theologians or ideological philosophers on related issues in their corresponding faith traditions. The lack of distinction between faith and form tradition, before the emergence of formation science, may have delayed the development of a basic dimension of ecumenical dialogue. This new type of dialogue about the practical life dimension in the contemporary formation field may prove to be crucial for the liveliness of the ecumenical enterprise as a whole. It may infuse new life in the theological dialogue between experts in the related faith traditions. Something similar would apply to the transecumenical dialogue with non-Christian faith and form traditions.

I believe, therefore, that the science of formation, as I envision it, should zero in on the foundations of each form tradition. In this way we may foster in their adherents and in those of our own tradition a basic self-awareness. Such conscientization facilitates the ecumenical and transecumenical dialogue, directly in the form tradition, indirectly in the faith tradition. By concentrating on the foundations, one does not get lost in idle discussions of countless sociohistorical accretions of each tradition. I believe that one concrete result of this effort can be a mutual formational concern. Colleges, graduate schools, high schools, elementary schools, and other educational institutions might establish integrative formation departments. These could become a cherished complement of their educational efforts, while remaining essentially different from the primarily pretranscendent orientation of the field of public education.

CHAPTER 30

Common and Specific Formation Traditions: Their Interformation and Articulation

I f we articulate the wisdom of a specific formation tradition in the light of generic formation science we should do so without impinging on its sustaining faith tradition. In such articulation we should also take into account that each tradition develops a language of its own. This language differs from the language of the common tradition of a society as well as from that of other specific traditions and from the metalanguage of the science. For example, the languages of Marxist theorists, Greek Orthodox monks, and Islamic emirs will differ from each other and from the common language in a pluritraditional society.

The public form tradition of a society may be studied from specialized pretranscendent perspectives by researchers and scholars of various social, clinical, and educational sciences. Each of these sciences, too, brings its own language to this research and to the formulation of its findings. For instance, different scientific formulations will be offered by students of such disciplines as anthropology, psychology, sociology, medicine, education, art history, and comparative religion. Their insights will be couched in terms of their own pretranscendent scientific languages. A similar difference in language applies to adherents of different formation traditions. By contrast, people not committed to any of these different traditions as basic for their own life will not experience this lingual commonality. For they do not share intimately a same specific community of memory. They may participate in the surface traditions that direct the common facets of social life. Over and above this, they may be swayed by selected aspects and words of traditions of other people. Such aspects and verbal expressions happen to attract them or find their way to them randomly through education, the media, friends, colleagues, and acquaintances. Without a basic sufficiently structured tradition of their own, it is difficult to integrate these new ways into their personal tradition pyramid. They miss the catalytic power of a specific tradition and language to which one is committed. Commitment to a specific tradition acts as a catalytic agent. It initiates processes of conciliation with other traditions in one's internalized form tradition pyramid of which one's basic form tradition is the ground floor.

As I have tried to show in previous chapters on my concept of the "form tradition pyramid," in the course of time the base tradition may be changed in many of its accidentals and lingual expressions but not in its essentials. For these essentials of the basic form tradition are rooted in the foundationals of the underlying faith tradition. If the base does not hold, the pyramid as a whole tends to disintegrate. Of course, commitment to another specific form tradition may provide a new launching pad for pyramid reintegration.

Secularization of Remnants of Religious Traditions

As I have insisted throughout this book, directives of specific traditions may give rise also to certain form directives in the commonly shared tradition of a society. Persons immersed in these common remnants may be in no way committed to the traditions from which they sprang in the first place. Accordingly, they will give a different neutral or secular meaning to directives that have infiltrated the common form tradition. For example, in accordance with the Dutch common form tradition, almost all children celebrate on the sixth of December the feast of Saint Nicholas, a canonized bishop of the Roman Catholic Church. Many children and their parents are not committed to this faith tradition. They celebrate the feast in a secular fashion. For them it means a joyous occasion of gift giving, with the saint being demoted to a kind of Santa Claus figure. Something similar applies to the common Swedish feast of light in honor of Saint Lucia.

Professional and Vocational Form Traditions

The population of a contemporary society is divided in many professional and vocational formation segments. Examples of such segments are farmers and craftsmen, business persons and executives, technicians and mechanics, doctors and lawyers, administrators and politicians, police personnel, the military, factory workers and cab drivers, homemakers and career men and women. People in these occupations give form to their own professional or vocational segmental traditions. Each occupational tradition, to the degree that it is internalized, becomes one of the significant layers of one's tradition pyramid. One's segmental tradition may influence also one's style of participation in the common form tradition of a pluritraditional society.

In some instances aspects of one's segmental way of life infiltrate the common form tradition itself, coforming it in a lasting fashion. For example, in the course of the history of formation of the French public lifestyle, certain forms of the courtesy tradition of the royal court — a definite segment of the population — were imitated by other segments. Appreciation of some forms of courtly *politesse* became part of the French form tradition.

In a similar fashion some directives of other segmental traditions can become ingredients of the common tradition. For instance, business men and women in the United States may contribute to the always unfolding common American tradition remnants of a style of appraisal that can somehow be traced to their functional commercial outlook on life. In the same way, facets of the free-floating ideological tradition of individualistic capitalism or of military patriotism can leave sediments in the overall American tradition of preferences and appreciations.

Social Sciences as Segmental Traditions

Among the segmental traditions that impact on public life, the tradition of the social sciences is growing in influence. The focus of their research as well as of their methodologies enables these sciences to examine systematically other segmental traditions. Their approach implies theoretical reflection on the data gathered by such research. Indirectly they may influence the course of formation of such investigated segments by communicating to them the outcomes of their scientific experiments and endeavors. From the viewpoint of formation science, we would maintain a cautious stance in our appraisal of their results. All scientific social research and theorizing is based on prescientific assumptions rooted in the implicit tradition of the science or school concerned. Such a tradition can indirectly influence the unfolding of either other segmental traditions or the common tradition of a society. One of the main protections against undue interference is focal awareness of the prescientific presuppositions of a human, social, clinical, educational science or discipline and/or its schools.

The sciences in question provide us with insights that can be significant for the appraisal and improvement of our various form traditions. Such findings can be utilized while protecting one's basic traditional assumptions from contamination by scientific-segmental assumptions, some of which may be incompatible with one's own traditional identity. Conversely, nonscientific traditions provide necessary sources of data for scientists and scholars who themselves represent in a special way the scientific traditional segment of society.

The new science I am still in the process of initiating in this *summa* of transcendent or distinctively human formation is formation science. In this science I try to give form to a coherent system of fundamental transcendent directives. This purpose is pursued by a critical-creative openness to and an exploration of an increasing number of traditions. One must be open to the common form directives of societies in the past and present, of specific religious and ideological form directives, of segmental directives, and of form directives proposed or implicitly suggested by the arts, sciences and disciplines of the pretranscendent life, especially the social, clinical, and educational branches. I propose as a never-finished task of formation scientists to examine all such directives as manifested in present and past societies and communities.

My science, like all others, has its own prescientific assumptions. Therefore, I go to great lengths to elaborate the prescientific assumptions at the root of my formation anthropology. This may set a precedent for the social, clinical, and educational sciences of the pretranscendent life and their proliferating schools of thought. They, too, may clarify under which assumptions they operate. This approach, if more generally implemented, may help to overcome the illusion of absolute scientific objectivity of all aspects of scientific data selection, theoretical reflection, and formulation.

Appraisal of Traditional Form Directives

Throughout this volume I have tried to explain the plurality and power of form traditions to which we are exposed in contemporary society. They carry the accumulated wisdom, experience, and knowledge of generations. But they also contain deformative dissonant directives. Each of us is faced with everyday formation events. To deal with them effectively and wisely, we can draw upon the traditions available to us. We should do so in ways that are consonant with our basic tradition as well as with our life call and situation. The consonant choice and implementation of formation directives depends in great measure on the right dispositions of our core form, heart, or character. We should develop dispositions of wise appraisal of traditional directives. It is for this reason that I want to propose six different aspects of this appraisal process. Insight into these aspects of appraisal can guide us in our options and implementations. It can really make a difference in the way we live our own life and influence present and future generations:

1. In the light of transcendent traditions, appraise and appreciate opportunities for transcendent formation in everyday formation events.

2. Be guided by these traditions as well as by growth in insight into your own life call, life situation, formation history, and experience. This will facilitate consonant apprehension, appraisal, and implementation. Ask how can I implement effectively and optimally formative responses to opportunities for growth?

3. Appraise how such directives of implementation should be modulated to adapt them to the particularity of each uniquely situated formation event.

4. Appraise the basic congeniality of both *content-directives* and *implementation-directives*. Are they congenial or consonant with the foundationals of the belief system that sustains the religious

or ideological form tradition to which you are committed as the basis of your own formation pyramid? Are they also consonant with compatible directives of other traditions that you were able to integrate wisely without compromise into your personal form traditional pyramid?

5. In the course of projected or executed implementations, appraise, in the light of formation traditions, which *competency directives* should be tried out or which new ones should be acquired in service of the optimally effective implementation of both content and implementation directives.

6. Appraise, in response to attempts at implementation, new questions as they emerge that might expand, refine, complement, or correct the traditional form traditions and directives now operative in your life.

Tradition and the Inherent Inquiry Dynamic

My advice to ask the right questions about traditional directives needs some elaboration. Inherent in the human life form is a dynamic potency for questioning. Initially this potency is prescientific; it is a dynamic tendency that keeps form traditions alive and unfolding. From infancy to death, we are inclined to question ourselves and our field of life as well as the traditions that give form to them. The ongoing processes of formation and reformation are bound up with this tendency to ask questions. We want to find out about the forms and dynamics that appear in our life and world. We question in order to discover how to give consonant form to our mind and heart, to our everyday existence, its dynamics and conditions for growth in distinctive humanness.

Formational inquiry, as well as the informational type of questioning that is subordinated to it, is an essential part of the process of formational appraisal. This process guides the critical-creative unfolding of the formation traditions by which we live. Questioning also accompanies the unique-individual implementation of traditional wisdom in our own life. Keen and persistent inquiry can be a source of new appreciative apprehensions. Hence the inherent dynamic of inquiry, when not suppressed, generates ever new questions.

What keeps this dynamic going is an awareness that continual appraisal of both our form traditional pyramid and of our new answers to inquiries is never complete. Neither we nor our predecessors or descendents will have all the answers. In fact, answers, such as they are, usually give rise to more questions. Therefore, the dynamic of formative inquiry will always be operative in humanity during its formation journey and the creation and expansion of its traditions.

In our own life, the ongoing process of formation gives rise to spon-

taneous questions about our own formative or deformative experiences
and the contemporary relevance to them of the form traditions by which
we live. Answers to these questions should be confirmed in dialogue with
knowledgeable, mature, and sincere adherents. They should also be in
consonance with the legitimate authorities of our traditions. Then our
questions may serve the unfolding of our traditions more than we realize. Briefly, prescientific formative inquiry keeps form traditions open,
dynamic, adaptive, and progressive. Each of us is called to play a role in
this process, no matter how modest.

Society-Wide Interformation of Reforming Questions and Answers

The effects of the dynamic of inquiry on our specific form traditions apply also to the public tradition we share with most people in our society.
In this regard, the process of questioning is a society-wide matter of interformation. How does this happen? First of all, the common form tradition
in a society is often compelled to find new answers to events that challenge
society as a whole. For example, the defeat of Japan and the subsequent
occupation of a humiliated and impoverished country generated new questions about the common form of life. Some old traditional forms had to be
dropped, such as veneration of the emperor as a divinity. Military power
had to be replaced by growth in economic power — a growth that could
also assuage the sting of defeat and humiliation.

Initially, only a limited number of people engage in such acts of new
form expression and donation. Then others, participating in the same field,
begin to interform with the new adaptations. Empirically they may find
out for themselves that the new ways are effective. This puts their own
common traditional patterns into question. They begin personally to imitate new ways of carrying on the common tradition. Gradually imitation
of and adaptation to the attempts of the tradition pioneers become part of
their own life. They now appreciate and accept the new attunements that
enhance the common ways.

This process of reformation of a form tradition is supported by mutual
transmission. We transmit to each other our appraisals of the renewal of
the common tradition. This twofold operation of formative imitation and
formative mutual transmission enriches and renews the common tradition
constantly.

A similar process applies also to the unfolding of the special traditions
to which we adhere. Imitation may be our first response to form traditional
acts of others that disclose new possibilities of traditional form reception
and expression. When we look back on the imitations we attempted, new
appreciative apprehensions may emerge regarding the formational and
reformational powers of our specific traditions.

A new traditional interformation is thus initiated by the dynamic of inquiry, by tentative imitation of the pioneering responses of others, and

by subsequent spontaneous appraisal of its effects on our life and of its consonance with the foundationals of the form tradition to which we are committed. These three acts of the initial process of tradition reform and expansion are complemented, as I have just shown, by a fourth one, the act of transmission. In mutual interforming communication, we transmit to each other the fruits of apprehensions and appraisals. New experiences were generated in us by our exploratory imitations of the few pioneers who risked the outreach of our form tradition into the virgin territory of new adaptive responses. We verbalize for one another our appraisals of our experiences of these probing imitations. We put into words our mutual confirmation of new responses and directives that seem to work well. We then submit the tentatively added new directives to the scientific, scholarly, and authoritative appraisals of formation science, of the articulation experts of the tradition concerned, and of the acknowledged ultimate authorities that protect it.

Such, respectively, prescientific, scientific, scholarly, and authoritative processes of updating form traditions historically go on continuously. The reason is that the detailed implementation of a form tradition in actual personal and social life is always faced with at least minor changes occurring in an ever-changing society. An effective form-giving tradition has to take into account such modifications. Therefore, a living tradition is not static but dynamic. It grows from current form to current form. This process should not lose consonance with the basics of the form tradition and the foundationals of its sustaining faith tradition.

Disposition of Identity-Protection

Tradition-consonance is protected by a specific disposition, which I have named the "identity-protection disposition." It disposes us to protect the basic identity of our tradition when expanding and reforming its directives. For example, people rooted in the Japanese form tradition are disposed to look differently on the meaning of life and labor, recreation and work, than people rooted in an Anglo-Saxon form tradition. The process of economic Westernization may change the Japanese formation field, necessitating an adaptation of its form traditions. At first glance this change may seem to suggest a giving up of the basic Japanese mindset. A closer look will reveal, however, that the Japanese way of apprehending and appraising such Western forms is kept alive. Even if it may appear temporarily lost, it will still be restored sooner or later because of the survival of the fundamental form traditional identity-protection disposition.

This identity disposition operates spontaneously, albeit prefocally, in the adherents of a tradition. It is one of their several prescientific appraisal dispositions. Therefore, it operates differently than appraisal dispositions that are scientific. To understand the difference, let us reflect for a moment on scientific appraisal dispositions.

One of the purposes of my science is to apprehend and appraise generic transcendent and quasi-transcendent formation directives in their empirical-experiential facets. Its scientists, scholars, and practitioners are disposed to appraise which transcendent directives of formation can be established scientifically as probably basic and effective for many, if not all, populations in many formation fields. Their quest is to determine such generic directives by means of systematic research of human nature as formational. They examine the expressions of formational human nature in present formation traditions as well as in classical historical ones.

If this is the scientific appraisal disposition, what characterizes a prescientific appraisal disposition? How is this disposition lived prereflectively by participants in common and specific traditions? What purpose does this prescientific disposition serve? It serves as an immediate prefocal protection against any perceived threat to the basic identity of the tradition to which one is committed. This disposition warns us immediately and prefocally of any threat to our traditional identity. When we are confronted with the changing situations of everyday life, it operates like a built-in radar system that picks up relevant signs of threatening changes in our environment.

Historical Form Traditional Directives of Implementation

We are not only able to identify many of our original form traditional identity directives; we can also see that they are complemented over the years by a host of adaptive implementation directives. These have been developed in confrontation with a rich variety of historical situations and challenges. Such directives of implementation provide us with a storehouse of traditional formation wisdom. They give us significant clues, hints, or pointers to possible ways of giving form effectively to our faith tradition in our own life situation. We would do well to take their wisdom into account. Often we may find that certain historical implementation directives are no longer fully in tune with contemporary demands for effective implementation of faith directives. Some of these traditional directives of implementation may still only function as inchoate, abridged form directives. We have to complement them in response to the differences between their and our historical situation. We must appraise their relative importance to the immediate demands of our present-day predicament and modulate them in this light.

Many traditional directives of implementation are communicated by symbols, parables, stories, proverbs, fables, legends, fairy tales, and myths handed over from generation to generation. They carry a wisdom that should be taken seriously. They may contain keys to basic facets of the traditional response to be given to new formation questions emerging in our life. They may point us in the right direction. But we cannot always deduce from them directly by formal logic what the exact response of the form tradition should be here and now. The concrete historical situation faced by a tradition is always somewhat different from the situation out of which the wisdom of the form traditional symbol, story, myth, or proverb emerged.

Therefore, the language of a common or specific formation tradition should be essentially different from the exact, abstract, theoretical language of generic formation science. Our everyday form traditional life direction is concerned with the effectiveness of our immediate compatible formative presence to distinct actual formation events in their particular appearance. The everyday language of a living form tradition must serve the compatibility of our faith implementation with current situations. Hence our everyday lived tradition and its language must remain sufficiently fluid, subtle, open, and adaptable. Only then can it give rise to the pointing and suggestive quality of adaptable yet faith-consonant form directives. This flexibility leaves room for adaptive appraisals that allow in turn for modulations of the form tradition in the light of new particular facets of present-day events.

Having presented these findings regarding formation tradition and interformation, I would like to turn now to the scientific articulation of specific form traditions in ways that protect their self-acknowledged identity.

Identity-Protection of Form Traditions
by Respectful Articulations by Formation Scientists

Formation science is the strictly human science of the empirical-experiential vicissitudes of the transcendence dynamic. As such it can attain only scientific probabilities. It can study human formation only insofar as it is open to scientific empirical-experiential reason. History demonstrates, however, that distinctively human formation takes place via religious or ideological transcendent formation traditions whose treasures of directives are richer than what only science can disclose to us. Such rich and profound traditions integrate their transscientific faith directives with empirical-experiential practices that accommodate such directives. These empirical practices and expressions are partially or totally open to scientific inquiry. Hence the scientific articulation of such form traditions must restrict itself necessarily to those aspects that are not transscientific or that can be considered from the viewpoint of empirical implications. Form traditional articulation is not concerned with faith convictions as such. Its primary concern is with the effectiveness of the formational expressions, communications, applications, and consequences of transcendent or quasi-transcendent belief systems for the whole of our personal and social life.

The subject matter of form traditional articulation is the formationally effective expression of a particular religious or ideological form tradition. To be used as a subject matter for my science such expressions must fulfill certain conditions. For example, symbolic expressions of mourning in indigenous African form traditions can be a subject matter for articulation if such conditions are present.

To be eligible for articulation research, the expression of a formation tradition must:

1. Manifest a sufficient probability of general formational relevance for a significant number of adherents of the tradition concerned;

2. Be accessible to the methodology of objective form traditional articulation;

3. Manifest sufficient probability of basic compatibility between the provisional articulations of the particular form tradition by students of formation and the authoritative fundamental formulations of its legitimate authorities.

An example of the need for compatibility of our research with the grounds of the tradition we investigate can be found in the articulation of the Freudian tradition. Formation scientists who articulate the orthodox Freudian formation tradition cannot objectively do justice to it — as specifically Freudian — when their provisional articulations are incompatible with the underlying Freudian ideology. This ideological identity is established by the consensus of the acknowledged ideological philosophers of the orthodox Freudian ideological tradition. The same is exemplified in, for example, the Adlerian, Jungian, Eriksonian, Rogerian, and Maslowian faith and form traditions as expressed by their true believers. This does not mean that the formation scientist engaged in articulation research of a particular form tradition has to agree personally with the content of its researched facets or its underlying religious or ideological faith tradition. For example, formation scientists who happen to be personally committed to one of the Christian faith traditions may articulate objectively a Jewish, Islamic, Hindu, humanistic, Freudian, Jungian, Eriksonian, Rogerian, or Marxist faith and form tradition without personally agreeing with all its presuppositions.

One of the objectives of form traditional articulation is to make available to the adherents of the form tradition in question, as well as to their underlying faith tradition, provisional hypothetical insights. These may help them to apprehend the possible implications for their form tradition of analogous relevant findings in formation science. This presupposes, however, that the articulation has been guided by honest and wise accommodation.

The articulation of a particular form tradition by formation experts is accommodating if the experts are guided in principle by the intention to clarify that tradition in its own self-expression and direction. For example, formation experts may suggest, in the light of their expertise in distinctively human formation, that an aggressive war mentality in some Islamic form traditions seems counterproductive from the viewpoint of a global, distinctively human life formation in the nuclear age. They must accommodate, however, the sayings of the Koran regarding holy war, as expressed in these form traditions. This may prevent incompatibility of their hypothetical articulation with the basics of the Islamic faith tradition.

Accommodation implies my "if-then" proposition in which I propose the following articulation rule: *If* and to the degree that the findings of formation science can be made compatible with a particular formation tradition and *if* the resulting version can enhance the effectiveness of both the traditional formation of the adherents and their participation in the global distinctively human formation of our race, *then* this provisional articulation could be advised as desirable pending final judgment by the legitimate authorities of the particular tradition concerned.

The provisional hypothetical articulations of a formation tradition are probable in the sense that they may prove or not prove to accommodate the form tradition concerned. The intended clarification must be compatible with the foundational tenets of its underlying faith tradition as presently interpreted by its legitimate authorities or by the consensus of its professional theologians or ideological philosophers insofar as this consensus is neither confirmed nor rejected by these authorities.

Accordingly, the scientific articulation of any form tradition remains in principle open to the possibility that it may be cancelled, reformed, confirmed, or elevated to either higher probability or transscientific certainty. Such appraisal is performed, explicitly or implicitly, by the legitimate authorities of the tradition. They may do so in dialogue with the professional theologians or philosophical ideologists of the faith tradition that underlies its form traditional expression. A formation scientist may choose to participate as an adherent of a specific faith and form tradition in the transscientific dialogue of this specific tradition with formation science. He or she shifts from the scientific to the transscientific attitude. The dialogue is approached, as it were, from the inside out. In pending chapters I shall allude once again to this complementary approach as exemplified analogously in the discipline of philosophy by philosophers such as Augustine, Aquinas, Pascal, Kierkegaard, and Ricoeur.

CHAPTER 31

Interformation and Articulation
of Traditions

Implicit and Explicit Structuring of Form Traditions

Research and observation reveal that we can live the traditional structures of our formation in an implicit or explicit way. Implicit abiding by customs prevails in uniform societies. They are uniform when they are wholly identified with one specific tradition, such as the Jewish, Christian, Buddhist, Islamic, or tribal. An exclusive tradition shapes from the beginning to the end the field in which the life of its participants unfolds. Persisting conflict with the only known tradition will be more the exception than the rule. Usually problems can be solved on the basis of historical solutions invented and implemented by the tradition itself over many generations.

Pluritraditional societies are permeated by a variety of traditions. In these societies the implicit structures of any specific tradition are less exclusive even for their own adherents. Directives of other traditions that are operative in the same society may infiltrate one's own basic traditional style of life.

At this moment of history, most societies are becoming pluritraditional. We live in a time of upheaval of the dynamic formation history of humanity. We observe an accelerated transition from unitraditional to multitraditional societies, even in Far Eastern and African countries. In the past, people may have lived their own traditions in a nonfocal way. As a result a rational understanding of the meaning of their own tradition may not be available to them at this moment of crisis. This leaves them more vulnerable to incompatible directives popularized by other mushrooming traditions.

As the pace of discovery of other past and present form traditions accelerates, new problems arise. Scientific data unknown before, archeological and historical findings, literary and artistic creations multiply almost daily. Under the impact of popularized media and mass education, people may begin to grope for clarification of these new, potential directives in terms of their own familiar traditions. They may not yet be able to appraise wisely their compatibility with their own basic traditions. Hence the ne-

304

cessity to provide people with the intellectual tools that can enable them to articulate explicitly their own tradition is obvious. Articulation can be more effective when it is done first of all from the viewpoint of a generic understanding of human nature as formational. This generic appraisal of unfamiliar form traditions should be complemented by a specific appraisal from the perspective of human nature as seen in the light of one's own specific form tradition. This approach is analogous to what Thomas Aquinas did in the thirteenth century in relation to the confusion of philosophies about human nature. As I argued earlier, the fast-approaching first century of the third millennium must find us ready to accomplish something similar for formation traditions and their pretranscendent appraisal by clinical, social, and educational disciplines. My modest mission is to do the spade work for the building to be erected.

One aspect that form traditions share is their dependency — for the very effectiveness of their guidelines — on a reasonable and realistic consonance with the make-up of human-nature-as-formational. Every person on earth shares the same nature. This truism inspired me since the end of World War II not only to respect the basic doctrinal theology of transcendent formation in my own tradition but also to devise a prerevelational system of understanding of the constitution, potencies, dynamics, and conditions of human formation in general. In the last year of the war, I experienced the clash of implicitly lived traditions wherever I turned. The devastation I witnessed led to my determination to develop not only a Christian foundational anthropology of human formation as lived in my own tradition but also an empirical-experiential science and anthropology of the universal make-up of human life as formational.

In the midst of this crisis, I developed my construct of a form traditional pyramid. It served as a diagram of how I saw different traditions operating in a sequential order of influence in various people hiding with me in the countryside. What complicates things for any specific tradition is that its adherents are also participants in a pluritraditional society. Usually they have already assimilated implicitly some directives of other traditions before they are fully formed by those of their own. Hence there is an increasing need to help adherents of specific traditions to cope with formation questions evoked by other popularized form traditions. These questions can no longer remain implicit; they must become explicit.

Form Traditions as Interforming; Formational Sedimentation

Most societies today are pluritraditional. Their culture is influenced by remnants of various significant form traditions that are operative within their appraisals and customs. Observation of such influences suggests some degree of interformation between them. For example, the Shinto, Buddhist, and Confucian form traditions, insofar as they are *formation* and not merely *faith* traditions, shape interformatively certain facets of the Japanese lifestyle.

The interformation of various form traditions within the same field contributes to the ongoing emergence of a common formation tradition. For example, certain traditional forms of life are common to most French men and women. Other forms are common to most Germans, still others to Mexicans or Scots. Analysis of such common traditions discloses a certain influence of remnants of past or present religious or ideological faith and form traditions during the formation history of a population.

A common form tradition is a shared empirical-experiential style of giving, expressing, and receiving form in a shared field. This style has emerged during centuries of shared history within that particular ambiance. The common style of form reception and expression is in part a result of the successive responses of participants in a society to historical challenges and changes. Secondly, it is in part a result of particular religious or ideological traditions. During significant periods of the history of a society, certain religious or ideological traditions influenced the responses of people to the challenges and changes with which they were confronted. This influence may be continued through what I call *formational sedimentation*. I invented this new construct to indicate that the sediments or silt of past particular traditions are still active or formational in specific as well as common traditions today. For example, certain aspects of Taoism and Confucianism are still implicit in the Chinese common tradition, even in their present socialist society. Certain communitarian aspects of the Marxian form tradition may be absorbed in their common Chinese tradition, modulating it in some measure. Conversely, the Marxian tradition may be modulated by the common Chinese tradition of the past.

Infiltration by New Traditions

A religious or ideological tradition may try to infiltrate a society where it is still unknown. This tradition can only become meaningful and effective for a significant number of people in that society if it interforms, without compromise of its own foundations, with the existing common tradition. Evidently it should interform with consonant facets of the common tradition only insofar as they are in some measure compatible with its own foundational faith tenets. A rationale for such interformation of a new specific tradition with the common tradition is as follows.

The majority of participants in a society can communicate neither with one another nor with people of other traditions without the common tradition with which all participants in that society are familiar. That tradition functions as their everyday frame of reference. It is the main means of communication for the majority of people. Hence a new tradition cannot be communicated to the people at large without sufficient interformative dialogue with the only tradition common to all of them. For example, the sixteenth century interformative dialogue of Christian missioners with the common Far Eastern traditions was prematurely cut off. This made wide understanding and acceptance of Christianity in Asia a problem to this day. Later missioners may have imposed on people of the East as basic their own faith tradition although it was already dressed in alien European form traditions.

Traditional interformation facilitates the building of bridges between a newly introduced tradition and the already existing common tradition. Such interformation modulates both the existing common tradition and the new one. For example, the Islamic form tradition is lived differently in Iran, Turkey, and Nigeria. The source of the differences is the interformation of the Islamic form tradition with the common traditions existing in these societies. Conversely, their common tradition will be modulated in some measure by a strong Islamic presence in the midst of their society.

Formation fields are dynamic, not static. Human forms of life continuously coform their shared formation tradition. They are faced with ever new challenges and changes. Their responses to them modulate the shared common tradition of form reception and expression.

A religious or ideological tradition may wish to participate effectively in the ongoing formation of a common tradition. To achieve this requires a continual modulation of the form tradition without compromising the foundations of its sustaining faith tradition. Such interformation keeps a particular tradition in tune with compatible changes in the common tradition. It would also enable the adherents of a particular tradition to challenge the dissonant facets of the changing common tradition. Only by interformation can a new specific tradition radiate its own unique contributions into this common tradition.

Hence there is a need for continual critical articulation of specific form traditions in our pluritraditional, ever-changing societies. For example, the faith foundations of the Gospel find new formational expressions that are due in part to the common tradition of each new society where they are implemented. Potential articulations, unseen previously, of both the Gospel and of the consonant common tradition of the new field of its implementation are disclosed. Our understanding of both is thereby enriched.

Formative Culture and Formation Tradition

Culture, formatively speaking, is the fabric of institutionalized expressions of the common form tradition of a society. This common tradition contains sediments of coforming particular traditions. Culture as formative animates the general modes of form reception and expression in a shared field. For example, Japanese culture is a fabric of institutionalized expressions of a common form tradition. Initially this tradition was shaped in great measure by *Bushido*, the unwritten code of directives for form reception and expression. In the past, this set of directive symbols guided and animated the lives and conduct of the nobles (the Samurai). Gradually, it was transposed into the common ways of the people. This implicit or "lived" set of form directives was coformed by popularized sediments of Shinto, Buddhist, and Confucian form traditions and their directives.

Scientific Generic and Tradition-Perspectival Articulation

My new science is concerned with common and specific transcendent formation traditions. Some formation scientists specialize in the articulation of these traditions. They articulate them in the first place from the universal point of view of this science. This approach is justified insofar as specific form traditions necessarily imply considerations of the generic transcendence dynamic inherent in all human life. This is the scientific articulation. Specialists in formation science may then complete this first generic type of articulation by applying its findings, concepts, and constructs to the observable empirical-experiential facets of a specific form tradition as seen in the light of empirical-experiential reason only. This scientific traditional-perspectival articulation should be distinguished from the postscientific, doctrinal-formational, traditional-perspectival articulation. This doctrinal articulation starts out from the *radix*, or root, of the specific tradition itself. This radical articulation completes and, if necessary, corrects the first specific scientific articulation. It bases itself on the acknowledged formation sources and on the basic doctrinal formational theology or ideological formational philosophy intrinsic to the specific form tradition itself. It articulates them from the faith perspective itself of the tradition. This goes beyond what science can demonstrate by its own methods. It is thus a transscientific approach to tradition articulation. Ideally this transscientific articulation should be kept in constant dialogue with the scientific articulation. This dialogue is in essence what makes the doctrinal articulation of a formation tradition dialectical versus a merely didactical approach. This applies as well to ideological doctrinal as to religious doctrinal formation traditions.

Transscientific Approach to Transcendent Form Traditions

The transscientific or doctrinal traditional-perspectival approach consists of several factors, including:

1. The study in depth of the transcendent communications of the acknowledged scriptures, masters, and methods of a classical formation tradition. These cannot be subjected exclusively to the methodologies of either the human or the positive sciences because of their origin in faith in either religious revelation or in ideological intuitive axioms.

2. The study in depth of the formational spiritual doctrines and formation theologies or philosophies insofar as they are practically relevant to and implied in these transscientific communications about distinctively human formation. These are formational communications by the acknowledged doctrinal formational theologies and doctrinal ideological philosophies. As such they are not primarily about the underlying faith traditions in all their speculative complexities. They are mainly about their impact on the subsequent formation traditions.

3. The comparative study of the possible relationships between these formational transscientific communications about practical spiritual formation and those aspects of the practice of spiritual formation that can be subjected to the methodologies of either the human or positive sciences.

4. The integration of the results of this comparative dialogue between faith and formation science within a comprehensive theory and effective practice of a particular form tradition.

We can compare the comprehensive theory of a particular form tradition with that of the science of formation. We will see then that the science extends itself, in principle, to those aspects of spiritual formation that a significant number of adherents of particular formation traditions can hypothetically share. In contrast, students who specialize in the transscientific approach will usually focus their main attention on one particular formation tradition such as the Christian, the Judaic, the Islamic, the Hindu, the Buddhist, the Freudian, the Eriksonian, the Jungian, the Marxian, the Lacanian, to name a few. They will only touch on other formation traditions insofar as they can shed some light on the particular tradition they are researching.

Spiral Aspects of the Dialectical Approach to Traditions

I prefer to think of my dialectical approach as more spiral than linear. It implies a spiraling back-and-forth movement. I may clarify the faith-rooted formation tradition from the perspective of the faith in question insofar as it is more directly relevant to formation. Then I spiral back to what the scientific articulation has disclosed about the meanings and dynamics of human formation in general. I examine the consonances and apparent dissonances between my tradition-specific and my scientific-generic articulation of the same formation tradition. Returning again to the tradition-specific articulation, I reformulate this articulation in a way that takes into account the compatible aspects of the scientific-generic articulation, albeit in the scholarly or popular language of the specific form tradition itself.

This process of integrating the two articulations of a particular form tradition may in turn bring me back again to the basic scientific-generic articulation of formational human nature as such from whence my research efforts began. The latter may have to be reformulated, expanded, corrected, or enriched because of newly gained insights that are relevant to basic generic human formation. These new contributions to our understanding of the universal formational nature of human life are the fruits of this critical-creative dialectic with particular form traditions. In this spiraling back and forth, the basic scientific-generic as well as the scientific-perspectival and the doctrinal-perspectival articulations gain in depth, clarity, and mutual consonance.

History of Articulation Research

The dialectics of tradition articulation are intricate and demanding. To execute them well and wisely is crucial for the effectiveness of both formation science and the articulated form tradition. For most people this science only proves to be useful insofar as it can be articulated in terms of their own formation tradition. Similarly, Augustine's, Aquinas's, Kierkegaard's, or Ricoeur's philosophies interest most Christian traditions only insofar as they can clarify their own faith tradition.

It took many years personally for me to find the right person to assist in this momentous task of articulation, one who was ready and willing to sacrifice personal agendas to make the dialectical articulation of the science a life mission, giving whatever time and energy might be necessary to lay the groundwork for this enterprise and to exemplify it in actual works of Christian articulation. Superior ability in dialectical-Christian articulation would demand a close examination and even a coediting of my own seminal works in the science of formation and its scientific articulation.

In the beginning stages of development of the science in Holland, I found significant help in my cooperation with the Belgian educator and initiator of the Dutch Life Schools for Young Adults, Ms. Maria Schouwenaars, whom I hosted later as a guest lecturer at Duquesne University. Her approach, excellent as it was in the field of education, did not prepare her for a lifetime specialization in the scholarly articulation of the Christian tradition in the light of formation science and of implicit doctrinal formational foundations. She was more intuitive than scientific, not specialized in the study of the acknowledged spiritual masters of Christian formation and already committed in terms of her time and energy to another mission in her life. It was only in the American period of my continuing research in this new science and in basic doctrinal, formation-specific theology that I found the person with the appropriate background in Prof. Dr. Susan Muto. She felt called to make her life's work the pursuit of the Christian articulation of formation science. Because for me as a Christian this specific articulation has been the crucial and final aim of my work, I consider her, as a coauthor and colleague of mine for over twenty-five years, in some sense the co-originator of the field of formative spirituality as a whole. For this field encompasses both formation science and all its specific articulations and, for me especially, the Christian. Its most recent expression is in a book we coauthored entitled *Commitment: Key to Christian Maturity* (1989) and its accompanying workbook and study guide (1990). Another outstanding example of the same is found in Muto's latest book, *John of the Cross for Today: The Ascent* (1990). In addition to these texts I would also recommend by her as exemplary of the work of Christian articulation: *Blessings That Make Us Be: A Formative Approach to Living the Beatitudes* (Rpt. 1990); and *Renewed at Each Awakening: The Formative Power of Sacred Words* (1979). My own volumes, *The Vowed Life: The Woman at the Well* (1976), *Looking for Jesus* (1978), and its sequel, *The Mystery of Transforming Love* (1982) are also significant in this regard. Perhaps the most important recent contribution to this phase of scientific development is the six-part video series Dr. Muto and I have written and facilitated on the theme, *Becoming Spiritually Mature* (1991). These books and some related video and audio resources are listed in the bibliography of this volume. Taken together they illustrate, I trust, the initial efforts being made in the area of articulation research. They also forecast how much remains to be done by myself and my eminent colleague in this area of research in the years to come. I think here especially of the forthcoming volumes in this series in which I hope to deal systematically with the doctrinal-formational dialogue of Christian formation traditions with formation science.

CHAPTER 32

The Generic Scientific
and the Tradition Specific
Approaches to Human Formation
in Different Denominations

I n the previous chapter I appraised the transscientific facets of traditions. I explained that such facets cannot be examined adequately by means of the methods of the social, clinical, human, and educational sciences alone. In this regard, I include among them my own science of formation. My conclusion was that my science, too, as science, covers only one basic dimension of the field of formation traditions, namely, that which is open to examination by human reason. I developed this idea by way of analogy to Thomas Aquinas's development of a universal philosophy of nature insofar as it could be understood by empirical-experiential human reason not yet illumined by special revelation.

The difference between his approach and mine is that he spoke mainly about philosophical human reason while I speak mainly about its empirical-experiential complement, empirical-experiential reason. He considered it part of his life's mission to appraise critically, to correct, complement and integrate, the relevant contributions of the philosophical disciplines of his age. I see it as part of my mission to raise some questions and suggest some theoretical principles and methods that may point to a similar concern in regard to the empirical-experiential facets of the universal transcendence dynamic and its numerous metamorphoses on both transcendent and pretranscendent levels of life. This implies a critical consultation of the sciences that did not exist in his time. I extend similar questions to other formation traditions. I hope to awaken a passionate concern among men and women who come after me for this desperately needed enterprise that has been delayed far too long.

As this volume draws to a close, I want to restate my conviction that it is high time to adapt the dialectical approach of Aquinas in philosophy to the findings of the social, human, clinical, and educational sciences that

312

can be made relevant to a well-integrated transcendent-pretranscendent formation of human life.

Aquinas's primordial aim in the development of his universal philosophy of human nature was to serve the Christian faith tradition and its theology. Similarly, my aim has been to point to the possibility of a generic empirical-experiential science of human-nature-as-formational in the hope that this science can serve all formation traditions, and, for me personally, especially the Christian one.

Later Thomistic scholars maintain a methodological distinction between Thomistic universal philosophy and his tradition-specific theology. I analogously maintain a distinction between my science of generic distinctively human formation and the specific discipline of Christian formation. Like Thomas himself, who initiated this new approach to philosophy and theology, I, too, feel obliged to point out the similarities and differences between formation science and the formative spirituality of specific traditions such as the Christian. I want to point out, however, how both the approach of formation science and the approaches to its articulation can complement each other in the overall academic and practical discipline of formative spirituality without confusing or losing their essential distinction. Analogously, Thomistic philosophy and theology can be united in one system without denial of their basic distinction.

Scientific and Transscientific Facets of Formative Spirituality

One of my main concerns is to point to the boundaries as well as to the connections between the scientific and transscientific facets of the discipline of formative spirituality as utilized by religious denominations. Formative spirituality, understood as a scholarly discipline, comprehends formation science as well as its scientific and doctrinal articulations in transcendent formation traditions. In the previous chapter, I referred already to the different bases of formation science and of either its scientific or doctrinal-dialogical articulation in transcendent formation traditions. I discussed the dialectics between these approaches and their subsequent systematic developments.

These distinctions seem to me of utmost importance in the contemporary confusion between social, clinical, and educational sciences or disciplines and some forms of pastoral theory and practice in various denominations. This confusion may even be greater than that experienced in the thirteenth century between philosophies and theologies due to the reemergence of divergent philosophies at that time. Often the statements of social, clinical, and educational sciences or disciplines are insufficiently appraised from the unique doctrinal viewpoint of the Christian formation tradition. What compounds this problem is the lack of a general frame of reference like Aquinas created to assist his contemporaries in the critical appraisal of philosophies and their philosophical life directives. The harm done to the Christian formation tradition by similar confusions in the realm of the social sciences, especially when popularized by the media, ought not to be underestimated. As I said earlier, this chapter will be concerned with the implications of the articulation of the Christian formation tradition. I want to stress, however, that adherents of other form traditions, too, should be encouraged in the application of the principles of formation science in service of the scholarly articulation of their own form traditions. In service of this discussion I shall have to repeat at times in summary fashion the main principles dealt with earlier.

Formative Spirituality and Formation Science

Formative spirituality is both an art and an academic discipline. Its focus is on the spiritual formation of humanity and the transcendent formation traditions that emerge in the history of this formation. Formative spirituality is a dialectical discipline. It cultivates a systematic dialogue between two main coformants: (1) the scientifically researchable facets of spiritual life formation, and (2) the transscientifically experienced and expressed facets of the same formation as well as their scholarly theoretical elaboration and practical application.

Researching the scientifically researchable facets of spiritual life formation gives rise to formation science. This science is the primary coformant of *formative* spirituality. The formal object of formation science is those facets of spiritual life formation that are researchable by its own methods as well as by uniquely adapted and critically complemented methods of the human sciences. We purify these latter methods from aspects that are basically incompatible with the nature and purpose of formation science.

Systematic research of the transscientific facets of spiritual life formation gives rise to the form traditional articulation of formation science. This is the twofold second coformant of formative spirituality. It comprehends the possibility of a scientific and of a doctrinal form traditional articulation. The form traditional articulation complements, corrects, and enlightens the findings of formation science for the adherents of a specific denominational tradition. The formal object of form traditional articulation is those facets of the traditions of spiritual formation that can be related to formation science by both specific scientific and specific doctrinal articulation. Such facets are coformed by religious or ideological faith traditions that cannot be disclosed totally by the methods of empirical science alone. These faith traditions underlie the corresponding form traditions. Hence the complementary use of the doctrinal-formational articulation.

Faith facets of spiritual life formation are transscientific. As such they cannot be researched by the methods of the human sciences. They are researchable, however, by means of historical, hermeneutic, dialogical, and theoretical methods. Such faith facets can be related to corresponding findings of formation science. Conversely, through this dialogical process, formation scientists may become attentive to transscientific facets not noticed before by them. For, formation science itself may not yet have identified and articulated certain scientifically researchable concomitants or extensions of these transscientific aspects.

Analogical Concept of Faith Traditions

The formation traditions by which people live are influenced by faith traditions that can be religious or ideological. The original meaning of the term *faith* is religious. Historically the term refers primarily to religious acts and traditions. We observe similarities between peripheral facets of religious faith convictions, as formatively lived by people, and ideological convictions, as formatively lived by adherents of ideologies. Hence these latter convictions can be called faith in only an analogical sense.

The two types of faith are essentially different. Adherents of either religious or ideological traditions share only certain peripheral, yet *formatively* significant, concomitants of their respective lives of conviction. Unlike religious faith traditions, ideological faith traditions are not rooted in an explicit religious revelation. They are elaborations of the believed-in intuitive assumptions of ideological humanistic thinkers. While such intuitions can be compatible or incompatible with certain facets of a religious faith tradition, their meaning cannot be identical with that of a religious faith conviction rooted in revelation. Faith presuppositions of religious traditions are religious because they are rooted in an explicit religious revelation as transmitted by a specific religious faith tradition.

Denominational Spiritual Formation

The existence of different denominational faith traditions generates different types of spiritual formation traditions or formative spiritualities. The terms *denomination* and *denominational* are used here by me primarily not as theological or doctrinal but as classifying terms.

Each religious denomination, Christian or non-Christian, is identifiable by a basic unifying faith and formation tradition. The latter is usually diversified in a number of subordinated formation traditions. The emergence of such formation traditions within each denomination depends not only on the underlying faith and uniform basic formation tradition. The multiplication of formation traditions is mainly due to the concrete demands of the implementation of a faith tradition and corresponding basic form tradition in a wide variety of historical as well as actual formation fields. Each form tradition that emerges in a denomination should be fundamentally compatible with the foundational tenets of its sustaining, unifying denominational faith tradition as well as with the foundations of its universal denominational formation tradition. They should be taken into account implicitly or explicitly. For example, the numerous formation traditions of Roman Catholic religious communities should be basically compatible with *the* foundational Roman Catholic faith and formation tradition.

Each denominational faith and formation tradition is basically one in its foundations. It differs in the manifold ways in which its adherents implement these foundations in their lives in accordance with the compatible directives of the distinct formation field in which they have to give practical form to their life-with-others within shared environments. The ongoing formational differentiation of the foundations of the faith and formation tradition within the same denomination is due to the concrete life formation of denominational adherents insofar as they are simultaneously members of a pluritraditional society changing over time.

Many facets of the pluritraditional field and our effective responses to it are *not* supernaturally revealed. Many other people who share our situations of work and play do not adhere to our own specific denomination yet a number of their responses can be in some aspects compatible with the responses of our own specific faith and formation tradition. Conversely, adherents of denominations themselves can initiate attempts to integrate their faith and formation responses with effective responses of other people not belonging to their own denomination. They can only do so insofar as these other responses are compatible with the foundations of their own religious traditions. For example, certain secular responses to social injustice can be integrated with certain denominational faith and formation responses to the same problems albeit rooted in different motivations.

Denominational form traditions have facets that can be explored by formation science. It can help us to explore and explain dynamic factors of human formation that are involved in our attempts to implement faith in our everyday life. Such dynamics can be researched by the methods of the human, social, clinical, and educational sciences or disciplines if and insofar as they are uniquely adapted by formation science to its own formal object.

Certain scientifically researchable facets of the spiritual life as practiced in various denominations appear to be compatible with one another. Their compatibility should be demonstrated. Only then can they can be responsibly synthesized in a discipline of spiritual formation. This discipline will give rise to a more general knowledge of spiritual formation, which may prove applicable to different denominations.

Denominational Traditions
and Transdenominational Formation Science

The study of certain compatibilities between various formation traditions can provide us with insight into a limited number of general formation directives, dynamics, dispositions, and disciplines. Formation science, which integrates these commonalities, cannot replace the depth, richness, truth, authority, and inspiration of a faith-rooted denominational formation tradition. Neither can it substitute for the grace and meaning-laden doctrines, narratives, symbols, rituals, disciplines, and convictions that only faith traditions, as promulgated by their legitimate authorities, can offer.

The limitations of a transdenominational formation science, in comparison with the denominational formation tradition, are obvious. Still, if we explore any denominational form tradition, it is helpful to look at it also from the generic viewpoint of formation science. A preceding or simultaneous study of formation science will increase mutual understanding and appreciation between denominations in regard to the observable concomitants of spiritual formation they may have in common. It can also make adherents of various denominations attentive to facets of the pluritraditional formation field they have to share with one another and with adherents of ideological traditions who are responsible for the same society. They should take such facets into account if they want to implement their own faith tradition in daily life in ways that are effective and reasonably conciliatory without betrayal of one's faith foundations.

Formation science can provide students as well as adherents of denominational traditions with data, theories, methods, and metalingual tools that enhance the quality of their own systematic critical approach to denominational formation practices and disciplines as coformed by their underlying faith traditions.

Form Tradition as Coformed by Faith Tradition

Different religious faith traditions — as distinguished from their form traditions — may manifest compatible aspects of belief. The appraisal of such compatible faith aspects falls under the formal object of the discipline of dogmatic theology. They are not a primary object of study for either formation science or its form traditional articulation.

Transscientific articulation examines facets of a specific form tradition insofar as it is coformed by a denominational faith tradition. Various factors can be instrumental in this implicit or explicit coformation of a form tradition by a faith tradition. For instance, not only the doctrine but also the formation theology of a denomination is one of these coforming factors. The transscientific exploration of the influence of faith on form traditions implies that researchers take into account corresponding theological factors. They explore such factors only insofar as they are coformants of the facet of formation they are examining. Their primary focus is not on the theological content as such in all its speculative complexities but on its influence on the formation tradition, its effective implementation, its formational communication, and so on.

The formal object of transscientific formation research is formation events, directives, dynamics, dispositions, disciplines, and communications of religious formation traditions from the viewpoint of their coformation by the corresponding faith tradition. Each denomination has a different faith tradition. Hence the point of departure for initial form traditional articulation can only be a specific faith and form tradition. Preferably one may choose as this point of departure one's own religious form tradition, for usually researchers are more familiar with their own tradition than those of others.

When applying the concepts or constructs of formation science, researchers in this area should be cautious not to go beyond their own limited field of competence. Only the legitimate authorities of the denomination concerned, usually in dialogue with their theologians, can ultimately decide whether the probable similarities, hypothesized by formation researchers, are indeed doctrinally and/or theologically compatible with their basic denominational faith and form tradition.

CHAPTER 33

Field of Traditional Communities, Their Outreach to Others, Threefold Approach of Formation Science

I want to begin this final chapter of volume 5 with a closer look at the form traditional communities that foster their tradition within and without their own circle of adherents. From my vantage point such a community is always also faith traditional. No form traditional society can survive when it loses the religious or ideological faith that sustains its vitality. Keeping this in mind, I still look at any faith and form community mainly from the perspective of its formation aspect. For only the formation dimension falls under the formal object that constitutes the science of formation and the basic orientation of its specific scientific and specific doctrinal-formational articulations.

What is a form traditional community? It is a more or less structured society of adherents of a same faith and form tradition. Two main types of form traditional communities should be distinguished. The first one I call the *general*, the second the *particular* faith and formation community.

The *general* community is the all-encompassing, supreme or preeminent, more or less structured society of all adherents. The *particular* community is any particular faith and formation society maintained by a group of adherents in basic consonance with the general community of those who adhere to the same tradition.

For example, in the past period of power of the Leninist-Stalinist ideological faith and form tradition, the Comintern or International Communist Leaders Conference functioned as the general supreme community. Communist national parties and other organizations functioned as particular communist communities. Over and above their national and special objectives they were supposed to stay in consonance with the general communist community. Both types of community were interforming as well as, in this case, tightly structured.

To clarify the main dynamics and structures of a form traditional community I shall use my formation field diagram.

Form Traditional Community and Formation Field Diagram

As an integrating base of formation science, I developed in the first volume of this series my diagram of the formation field. This field represents graphically the fundamental parameters or formation conditions of each human life. We can apply this metaphor of a field of generic basic formation conditions to our personal life as well as to a form traditional community to which we belong. Not only our personal field but also the field in which our form traditional community receives and gives form can be envisaged as coformed by the pre-, inner, inter-, and outerspheres of my diagram (Van Kaam 1983).

A Christian form traditional community, for example, has a sphere of intraformation as unique-communal persons do. This intraform of the community is coconstituted by those who belong to its *inner* realm or inner circle. Yet the community needs also a sphere of interformation. This is the sphere of *interforming* dialogue between this community and other form traditional communities as well as with its own sustaining faith tradition, though the mystery forms it uniquely. Finally a community in search of consonance gives rise to a sphere of interaction of this community of faith with *outer* situations and the wider world insofar as this form traditional community must take into account and care for what transpires there. In turn, this inter- and outersphere of a form traditional community insofar as it is consonant offers to the world and to the situations in which it finds itself — and on which it feeds for its effective implementation — its own wisdom, experience, and means of social and personal improvement.

The opportunities for worldwide interformation between different traditions and their communities have increased more than ever before in history. All kinds of ideologies and religions that in the past were geographically separated from one another are now living in proximity through increased travel possibilities, the omnipresence of the media, and widespread emigrations. Interformation and cooperation of form traditional communities with all people are more necessary than ever. The rise of the pluritraditional society has increased the number of people who are alienated from any spiritual tradition. While we may not be able to attract them to the inner circle of our own community of faith and formation, we may serve the awakening of their inherent transcendence dynamic. Like all of us they are invited by the mystery of transformation to heal and transfigure humanity's wounded life. The pathway to this transfiguration is the cultivation of their transcendent dimension. Adherents of form traditional communities may have examined and tried this path in the light of the transcendent wisdom of their classic traditions. They must be attentive to opportunities to outreach to others who are in the throes of the hesitant awakening of their own transcendence dynamic. Adherents of classic transcendent traditions may make available humbly, wisely, generously, and graciously some of what they learned and experienced on their own journey. They will only give what others ask for. In respect they will not unload on them all faith treasures that they themselves cherish within the intrasphere or inner circle of their own transcendent community.

Participants in a transcendent form traditional community are thus called in some way to serve the intra- as well as the inter- and outerspheres of the community to which they have committed themselves. First is the call to intratransformational presence. One is called to care for the intrasphere or inner circle of one's form traditional community. One may feel invited to a special kind of care for this inner circle by one's own special capabilities and the corresponding inner needs of one's community. The authorities of the community may ask one to be available to the transcendent aspirations or to some of the subordinated sociohistorical, vital, functional, functional-transcendent, or transcendent-functional wants of the inner circle of the faithful.

In contrast, the call to inter- and outer transforming presence is a call to share in the outreach of the community of one's shared tradition to others outside its own family circle.

Not all are called to serve in the same mode and measure each sphere of the form traditional community to which they belong. Many are called by the mystery to be mainly (not exclusively) present to the intrasphere or family circle of their own community. They may be called, for instance, to serve the inner circle of faith and formation as parish priests, ministers, rabbis, imams, theologians, religious, or lay participants in the care for the inner community and its members. They may exercise this family care through works of charity, of formation and education, of teaching, writing, speaking, of parish assistance. This care for the maintenance, growth, and expansion of the inner circle stretches itself out to the teaching of the faith and form tradition of the community to those who manifest explicitly or implicitly a need or desire for such instruction. Implicit interest may be observed in those who live in a disposition of search and curiosity that creates a minimum of receptivity for such teaching. People serving the intraformation of their community may enhance such interest and curiosity.

In contrast, other members of the community, such as ecumenists, missioners, diplomats, teachers in public institutions, artists, actors, writers, and laborers may be called to serve mainly the interformational and outerformational spheres of the formation field of their community either by word or work, and always by their style of life and presence. Among those to be served by this interformation are contemporaries who have lost the experience and understanding of their own transcendence dynamic and of the aspirations it generates. A transcendent faith and formation community must reach out to them, too, through its members called to the work of interformation with those belonging to other traditions. Through the message of their life they should facilitate the awakening of the transcendence dynamic inherent in human nature also in those who may never have disclosed its presence often by no guilt of their own. We call all these forms of care and outreach outside the inner circle of the family of an explicit transcendent faith and formation tradition interformational. For in this encounter not only is some form communicated to them, they also communicate some forms of life to us. We come to appreciate what they tell us as about their wisdom and courage of living. They and we ourselves can leave each encounter richer than we came.

But how can we communicate about the transcendent life with people who do not have any insight or interest in the specific traditional ways in which we feel called to live transcendently? My war experience taught me that one possible aid for them in their awakening could be formation science. I compared it then with the aid that Aquinas's universal human philosophy has been for the philosophically minded who were not or not yet ready for his theology and the revealed faith tradition to which it pointed. How is formation science relevant to the awakening of the dynamic of transcendence?

Relevance of Formation Science
for the Awakening of the Transcendence Dynamic

Formation science implies a formation anthropology and a corresponding scientific empirical-experiential body of knowledge. The science implies, moreover, a consideration of practical applications. Many of these may be formulated in ways that make sense to those who lost or misinterpreted the awareness of their transcendence dynamic. We should try to respond to the kind of openness to the transcendent with which people may be gifted at a certain moment of their history.

Formation science, to be helpful to all people in their transcendent aspirations, needs to go beyond its scientific approach to the empirical-experiential elements of transformation. It must develop also a transcendent formation anthropology. Such an anthropology can help the student of formation science to choose topics of empirical investigation that are relevant to the distinctively human process of transformation. A formation anthropology will also complement the science with those more basic facets of transcendent transformation that cannot be sufficiently disclosed by empirical-experiential methods alone.

Formation science should develop, moreover, postscientific practical approaches such as those of transcendence therapy and formative spiritual direction. The wisdom gathered by spiritual directors of many traditions today and over the centuries is wider and deeper than can be demonstrated by empirical methods alone.

Such pre- and transscientific studies should utilize, whenever possible, the theory and language developed by the science. Otherwise the mutually enriching unity of the discipline of formational spirituality as a consistent system of thought would be endangered.

It is important to realize that a threefold scientific, pre-, and post-scientific approach is typical of also the social and educational sciences and disciplines about pretranscendent human life and development. In these sciences, as in the science of formation, the integrative scientific theory should remain central.

Other human sciences may not be as explicit in the identification and analysis of their pre- and postscientific approaches and of the relationships of those to their central scientific approach. We do not find in all of them the epistemological rigor of thought cultivated by formation science.

Example: Threefold Approach
in Psychology as a Human Science

The term *psychology as a human science* refers to the type of psychology that I initiated and elaborated during my nine years in the psychology department of Duquesne University until the administration allowed me to return full time to the project of formation science, which I had started in Europe before my assignment to Duquesne University in 1954 upon personal invitation by its president. The scientific approaches in human psychological research always imply certain prescientific premises. These are about the nature of human life. Such presuppositions cannot be discovered by merely empirical operations. They are established by an implicit or explicit philosophic approach. The results of this prescientific approach can be critical and explicit or uncritical and implicit. They affect the hypotheses that are submitted for scientific research in psychology as a human science.

The postscientific approach in psychology gives rise to the theoretical expansion of the results of the scientific approach to theoretical hunches about human psychology as a whole. Another form of the postscientific approach is an adaptive application and articulation of its results in such psychological endeavors as psychotherapy, counseling, group dynamics, sensitivity training, industry, and advertising. All detailed applications and articulations cannot be rigorously proven to be scientifically valid. Postscientific methods of valuing the results have to complement the empirical-experimental as well as the empirical-experiential scientific approaches. Psychologists in all three phases of their discipline will refer to the same theoretical concepts and constructs of the school or specialty to which they are committed, only expanding or changing them when necessary.

The reason for the inevitability of the threefold approach in human sciences is that any facet of human life as human, when it is chosen as the formal object of a science, is rooted somehow in human nature. With all the facets of its potential and actual self-expression, human nature is so rich, complex, and finely differentiated that it is impossible to understand it exhaustively by means of strictly empirical-experimental and empirical-experiential approaches alone. Hence every human and social science tends in some additional fashion to become also more than a science. It becomes also a human discipline.

Human and social sciences can give form to hypotheses for empirical testing that are humanly relevant only by implicit or explicit reference to prescientific premises about human nature. For in this nature the facet to be researched is rooted. The same nature has to be taken into account when psychologists ponder the possible postscientific usefulness for human life of the data they collected.

Transpersonal and Transcendent Approaches

Our studies of transcendent transformation are complicated by the emergence of interest in seemingly similar topics in contemporary transpersonal and humanistic psychologies. To gain clarity in this matter, I shall briefly reflect on the differences between their and my approach.

Both the transscientific and scientific approaches of the discipline of transcendent formation traditions are essentially different from the approaches in transpersonal and humanistic psychologies. The object of transcendent formation differs in intention and in extension from the object of any psychology. Psychology as psychology can only research by strictly psychological methods the pretranscendent psychological aspects of any phenomenon and tradition, also the phenomena it calls transpersonal.

We study transcendent and related pretranscendent transformation and tradition by methods that are not strictly psychological or merely transpersonal. We complement this approach by a transpsychological dialogue with classical or potentially classical formation traditions. We take into account phenomena described by such traditions that cannot be sufficiently clarified by merely psychological methods alone.

Another fundamental difference is the prescientific premise of some humanistic psychologies. They seem to assume that mere human potential in and by itself is sufficient to actualize human existence transcendently. In contrast with this existentialistic premise of humanistic psychology and tradition, the discipline of transcendent life formation holds to its own premise. Its assumption is that both the awakening as well as the actualization of the transcendence dynamic relies ultimately on a mystery that transcends merely human potential. The transformation of human life is an event of coformation with that mystery. According to the discipline of transcendent formation, human life to the degree that it is set free from coercive dispositions becomes able either to freely refuse or to freely flow with the transforming power of the radical mystery of formation.

Pretranscendent and Transcendent Life

Transcendent traditions point to ways of spiritual transformation. They see these ways as a response to what I have identified as an inherent transcendence dynamic. They believe that this dynamic is awakened and actualized in some kind of cooperation with a higher power or mystery. They communicate this message in a great variety of metalanguages, each of them developed in dialogue with their own tradition of origin. Transcendent traditions insofar as they are consonant distinguish in some way between what I define as respectively the pretranscendent and transcendent way of life.

Human life is encapsulated in a pretranscendent way to the degree that it cannot see and go beyond a merely or mainly socio-vital-functional or functional-transcendent life. It is a life in some way still subordinated to the quasi-foundational autarkic pride form. This subordination is expressed in self-preoccupied attachments or what I call coercive dispositions. These coercive dispositions engender routinized form directives in our neuro-form that generate in turn robot-like processes of attention, and thought, of appreciation and depreciation, of affect, imagination, memory, anticipation, and action.

Human life is transcendent to the degree that it can see and go beyond a merely or mainly autarkic socio-vital-functional or merely functional-transcendent existence. Transcendence of the autarkic self and its coercive dispositions with their routinized directives does not mean rejection of the socio-vital-functional and functional-transcendent dimensions of human life. The expression of these dimensions should be consonant with the transcendent life orientation as a whole and with each one's unique life call. Then they are fostered and enhanced by the transcendent dimension in light of consonant transcendent formation traditions.

Timeliness of the Emergence
of the Science and Discipline of Transcendent Formation

The time seems ripe for the emergence of the discipline and science of transcendent life formation. This discipline is a response to the fading away of an earlier pervasive traditional wisdom about the transcendent unfolding of human life. The pressure of increasing functionalization of present-day civilization paralyzed spiritual wisdom and practice. The transcendent core of true formation in depth seems often forgotten.

Symptoms of the eclipse of transcendent formation wisdom are many, a few being secularistic human development, contamination of pastoral counseling, rejection of pastoral counseling, less spiritual relevance of the cloistered life, ignorance of spiritual disciplines, reduction to functional activity. I will briefly allude to each of these symptoms.

The classical traditional wisdom of pretranscendent and transcendent formation by the mystery is increasingly replaced by the theories and practices of secularistic formation traditions. An existentialistic tendency to pretranscendent self-actualization and self-development of a person or group dominates also many facets of developmental psychologies. Secularistic developmentalism leads many people to substitute pretranscendent self-development for the essential and existential openness to life formation by a higher power as announced by classical transcendent traditions.

Developmental humanism and existentialistic therapism can become an insufficiently appraised source of pastoral counseling courses and techniques. It may not leave enough room for the wisdom of traditional spiritual direction, for formative counseling, for the inspiration of the classical transcendent formation traditions in which pastoral counselors should resource themselves continuously.

Because of the scarcity of inspirational transformative wisdom in some pastoral counselors, teachers, and preachers, many people in crisis seek the assistance of social workers, psychiatrists, psychologists, and secular counselors not only for the socio-vital-functional facets of their suffering but also for the transpsychological and transdevelopmental facets of their struggles.

Even the cloistered life as lived in various degrees and styles in different faith and formation groupings does not always foster a primordial concern for the transpsychological and transdevelopmental wisdom of formation as treasured in classical faith and formation traditions. This diminishes their vital role in society as centers of spiritual value radiation. Often the lack of transcendent wisdom implies a less profound understanding of the transformative meaning of traditional religious symbols and disciplines. Such ignorance may sometimes tempt people to reject even basic disciplines as no longer relevant in view of our secular psychological and developmental knowledge.

The narrowing of transformative reflection and practice can lead to a merely functional ethicism and to a reduction of prayerful meditation on classical texts to their exclusively intellectualistic analysis. Excellent and necessary professional and social work, too, may be insufficiently inspired by transformation wisdom and practice as communicated by classical formation traditions.

Transcendent Formation,
Human Sciences, and Formation Traditions

Human and social sciences, such as political science, anthropology, sociology, psychology, psychiatry, and education are indispensable sources of information. They give us an insight into the mentality and behavior of contemporary pretranscendent life, its crises and problems, memories, imaginations, and anticipations. Having said this, I must add that the most serious threat to the public effectiveness of transcendent traditions and their wisdom is an emergent tradition in some people of pan-psychologism and pan-developmentalism. Both threaten to enfeeble and reduce traditional transcendent wisdom, knowledge, and practice to mere psychological, transpersonal, educational, or developmental strategies of actualization of merely pretranscendent formation potencies, no matter how high they may be in the hierarchy of these talents.

If social, clinical, and educational sciences and disciplines remain within the realm of the formal object that constitutes their identity, they can excel in the knowledge of the pretranscendent form of life. As such they can be auxiliary to the science and discipline of transcendent life formation. They can clarify for the latter the pretranscendent life of the average contemporary person who gives form to live in a world that is secularistic and silent about the transcendence dynamic of human nature.

The science and discipline of transcendent life formation is concerned with the human life as it is lived here and now. Hence it is necessary to gain insight into the way in which a majority of people live today. Social, educational, and clinical sciences and disciplines tend to reflect the contemporary image of people with whom they are faced and to analyze it in great detail. Without consulting them, it is almost impossible to gain sufficient information about contemporary life and the formation traditions that guide its development.

The average person today, whether or not one belongs to an ideological or religious faith grouping, lives often in an implicit denial of a transcendent mystery that makes itself constantly available to coform one's life graciously. Even people who adhere to a religious tradition may mainly adorn their secularistic strivings with ideological or religious symbols, texts, and phrases. They may not be able to grasp and live their deeper transformative power and meaning.

A compassionate yet well-informed appraisal of the pretranscendent life, both inside and outside contemporary formation traditions, presupposes the understanding of that life within its contemporary field of form traditions. This field of pretranscendent life is in considerable part explained by the social, educational, and clinical sciences or disciplines. The pretranscendent life in turn is constantly reinforced in its unfolding by the popularization of the theories and findings of these sciences and disciplines, which themselves are also based on some of these contemporary traditions.

The appraisal by formation science of the contributions of other human sciences, disciplines, and traditions should be truly formational, not only informational. It should complement, correct, transcend, and critically reformulate the informations and explanations of these sciences, disciplines, and traditions of the pretranscendent in the light of its own knowledge of transcendent formation.

Purpose of Formational Appraisal of Form Traditions

Formational appraisal of form traditions takes place in service of the aim of the science and discipline of spiritual transformation, namely, to assist people in their often implicit search of a way to transcendent living. They may be searching unwittingly for a transcendent path of life or tradition. They look for a way that includes and yet transforms all that is consonant in their present-day existence. They may live their life outside or inside formation traditions to which they may belong by birth and education and whose churches, temples, synagogues, or meeting halls they attend at least functionally and periodically.

One of the premises of formation anthropology is that human life is essentially traditional. To commit oneself to a classical transformation tradition is to gain access to the treasures of transformation wisdom and practice inherent in such tradition. Otherwise one may drift blindly along with a syncretism of remnants of traditions that happen to be current in a secular common tradition and its media.

The option for a form tradition with its underlying faith tradition and sustaining faith community should be guided by criteria to be appraised in the light of the mystery that graces and lights the way of humanity. These criteria for a responsible option are developed by the ethical philosophies and moral theologies of the various ideological and religious faith and form traditions. By themselves alone such criteria are not sufficient for a wholehearted option. The mystery of transformation must move the human heart to see and flow freely with such criteria.

The science and discipline of formation develops mainly criteria for the consonant foundational aspects of transcendent formation in any faith and form tradition insofar as it is consonant. The science and discipline of spiritual formation are not primarily modes of psychotherapy for mentally and emotionally severely disturbed patients. Rather, this approach directs itself first of all to people who live a relatively balanced existence and who, upon awakening to their transcendence dynamic, begin to search for a transcendent transformation of their life. The pretranscendent life form in its potential or actual expressions, conflicts, adaptations, manipulations, and integrations must be the point of departure for researchers and practitioners of any transcendent formation tradition that strives to be relevant to contemporary existence.

Afterword

W here does "traditional formation" fit in my formative science and its Christian articulation? How does it relate to the preceding and to the upcoming volumes in this series? To answer these questions let us look at my work as a whole.

The war made me aware of the need for a program of studies about the unfolding of the human and Christian spirit in people. In many of them I saw the need for more insight in the deeper meaning of human and Christian life. Social, clinical, and educational disciplines, in their popularized forms, began to respond to this interest. All of these disciplines help our understanding of human life. My concern was that a number of people might see the directives offered by these disciplines as highest guidelines for their formation. Human and Christian formation could be brought down to merely developmental principles, particularly when these were made the basic guides of life by those who taught or popularized them. I began to suspect that in the realm of human development and higher formation new kinds of "deadly sins" were in the making. Deadly sins are so named because they can give rise to many other faults that deaden the life of the spirit. The new deadly sins I have in mind are idolizations of such popularized developmental traditions as sociologism, psychologism, therapism, developmentalism, ethicism, spiritualism, gnosticism. Notice well the ending "ism." Disciplines such as sociology, psychology, therapy, human development, ethics, and so on are indispensable sources of information. They acquaint us with our own pretranscendent life and that of our contemporaries. They should be utilized. The ending "ism," however, points to their abuse. It refers to a turning into ends what are necessary means. Our pretranscendent life comprises the means to prepare us for our transcendent life. Once these means are submitted to transcendent life directives they enable us to carry these directives out in our everyday world. We should not worship these means as "works" of salvation.

I felt that a thorough program in human and Christian formation should start out from a framework that is more systematic and comprehensive. It should be a blend of higher formation wisdom and empirical-experiential data. This framework should assist us in the critical appraisal of pretranscendent "isms." Formation science would be a blend of the founda-

329

tionals of formation wisdom and knowledge. The science should also be the basis for a response to the contemporary concern for both pretranscendent development and transcendent formation.

Overreaction to Lack of Spiritual Awareness

Another experience moved me to lay the groundwork for a science of formation and its Christian articulation. The last year of the war I was struck by the fact that a lack of deeper awareness evoked in some people an overreaction. Alarmed pioneers began to search for ways to awaken the powers of transcendence. A number of them would chance on a path that worked well for them and for people whose mentality and temperament they shared. They would be tempted to turn their own particular path into *the* path for all. This tendency could cause divisions among people. Many feel a deep hunger for the lost transcendent dimension of life. They may be attracted to anything that is offered as *the* way, even if it is not in tune with who they are called to be.

One of the outcomes of such a confusion of the whole with a particular spirituality was a distortion of balance. The chosen facet could be doctrinally sound within one's classical formation tradition. Still it could cause a loss of balance. It would be difficult, if not impossible, for such devotees to appraise the limited position of their chosen way. They would not be able to acknowledge its limited place within the whole of the tradition of human and Christian transcendence. They could uphold their particular path of transcendence as the way for all.

Many "awakening movements" boosted such particular paths. They inspired people. They added vital elements to the picture of transcendent human and Christian formation. However, each way can also cloud the full picture of classical human and Christian spirituality. Some of their directives may be excellent but not well balanced. Adopted by followers of classical traditions, they can distort the traditions themselves. It is harmful if a preferential option is treated as if it were the whole of human and Christian spirituality. Instead of being integrated into the whole of human and Christian wisdom and knowledge, it tends to integrate the whole of such classical traditions into itself — as if it were *the* only way for any and all people on the road to transcendence. I began to realize how any exalted movement in the field of human and Christian transcendence could distort the delicate balance of our heritage as a whole.

Postwar Years:
Proliferation of Special Spiritualities

In the years after the war my forebodings proved closer to what would be happening than I could have anticipated. I witnessed an endless procession of spirituality preferences, slogans and programs. Many of them seemed helpful, recommendable, even essential, in themselves. Yet their cult-like proselytizing, their self-exaltation as *the* basic solution of the spiritual anemia of whole populations led to consequences that I feared. They threatened the soundness of human and Christian life. At times the solutions seemed worse than the ailments for which a cure was proposed. I appreciated the particular assistance of such special spiritualities for numbers of people in search of a transcendent life. Often I heard about remedies that seemed like indispensable aids for a first awakening. But many of these movements could have gained in balance and depth by relativizing their function under the canopy of, for instance, a basic, all-embracing vision of a formational Christian spirituality, rooted in scripture, tradition, and doctrine. This vision should be preceded or accompanied by a rational understanding of the given and acquired formational make-up of human nature. The Christian formation vision should be hooked into these natural bases of human formation. They should be worked out not by theological or philosophical reason but by empirical-experiential reason. Formational human nature in its actual formation dynamics and conditions should be taken into account realistically by any basic framework of Christian formation. I called the research in human formation and its outcomes formation science (*vormings wetenschap*).

A more fundamental human and Christian frame of reference would help the devotees of each movement to place their preferences against the background of a wider outlook. This would protect their balance and their respect for the partial pathways of other people.

In later years I saw many ways of the spirit coming and going as movements of the hour: the charismatic path; the path of religious psychologism, of the enneagram, of the Myers-Briggs inventory, of cosmic awe; the path of centering; the spirituality of the masculine or feminine, of marriage encounter, of the cursillo, of social justice; the paths of various other awakening and renewal programs, of ecumenical, biblical, liturgical, and sacramental spirituality; of ethicism; of in- and out-of-the-body experiences; the spiritual paths of followers of Carl Jung, Carl Rogers, Abraham Maslow, Joseph Campbell; the ways of directive and nondirective spirituality; of American Indian spirituality; the Christian Zen path to transcendence; transcendent meditation spirituality; family therapy and numerous twelve-step ways of growth; dream analysis spirituality; the list goes on and on of the attempts still proliferating to satisfy the longing for the "more than." Their passing or still lasting popularity and validity in the realm of formation is a powerful testimony to the hunger for transcendent meaning. Each of them may provide people with a means of entering into the fullness of the wisdom of basic human and Christian life formation.

Empirical-Experiential Formation Traditions

Let us return to the original aim of my project, its mainspring and prime moving force. What is the origin that has been guiding my undertaking as its final cause? This is the cause that moves and directs a venture from the beginning to the end by its overall visionary purpose. My project started as a founding intuition in the last year of the war in Holland. Then it proceeded through laborious efforts of initial expression, theoretical reflection, reality testing, and metalingual formulation. Slowly it grew into a coherent yet open system; a means to foster my original purpose; a framework through which the founding intuition can be realized, expanded, and applied by others who adopt it.

How did this intuition lead not only to a new mode of distinctively human but also of Christian reflection? To explain this let me review briefly the circumstances of its emergence.

The intuition of which I speak came to me in the midst of the stress of the horrible Hunger Winter in Holland (1944–45) when I was involved with the Dutch resistance hiding people from famine and Nazi persecution. The intuition was rooted in a series of experiences, the most notable of which can be summed up as follows.

I was surrounded not only by non-Christians but also by Christians who wanted my support. I realized that each person or small group, while sharing the same faith tradition, for instance, that of a specific Christian denomination, lived by a surprising variety of formation traditions. These were traditions telling them how to live their faith in their everyday life. Many had made one or the other of these form traditions the basis of their life. Counseling them meant that I was faced with two problems. The first was that the formation traditions by which they lived were affected by other traditions. These were traditions lived by people around them in the past or the present. Often this influence had distorted the consonance of their own formation tradition with the faith tradition it was meant to implement in their everyday spiritual life in the world.

The other problem I discovered in the course of our encounters was that some people tried to live, for instance, by a *special* Christian formation tradition that was dissonant with their *foundational* Christian tradition. I called this basic Christian formation tradition *classical*. It embraces the foundational Christian forms of life that adherents of all Christian churches can share in some measure. More especially and finally, this classical tradition comprises the unique expression of these shared Christian forms in the faith and formation tradition of the specific Christian church to which people are committed. I was called upon to help them to purify their Christian form tradition in both of these ways. In other words, they had to purify their style of life formation from dissonant accretions while returning in a clear and strong way to their Christian roots. Only a fully and properly implemented faith could sustain them in the times of terror they had to endure.

Need for a Christian Articulation
of Empirical-Experiential Formation Traditions

Among the many fields of theology I had studied, I found no theological discipline that could help me directly and practically in this task. I realized more and more that no specialty of theology was as yet available that could have helped me to deal with the detailed experiential problems of Christians living and fighting for freedom with me. None of the theologies known to me had specialized primarily in the systematic study of the empirical-experiential aspects of implementary formation traditions.

Out of these and kindred experiences there came the founding intuition to which I previously alluded. I said to myself, if I survive this war I must honor in some way the death of those who were tortured and murdered. In their memory I shall strive to initiate, no matter the cost, a way of formational human and Christian reflection. People needed this to sustain them in the last months or days of life, though it was not readily found. My life task would be to complement speculative philosophy with an empirical-experiential science of formation and its traditions. My subsequent Christian articulation of this science ought then to make explicit the classical Christian formation tradition and its underlying faith tradition. My basic assumption was that the pluriform traditions of Christians should be consonant with the basic formation tradition of Christianity as such, both in its ecumenical and in its denominational foundations.

In due time concepts of formation science could be quoted and used also by professional theologians in various religions and denominations as they have used for centuries concepts of philosophies. Both the Christian articulation of formation science and its use by theologians should point the way to the carrying out of the Christian formation tradition in everyday life and labor.

Elaboration of Formation Science

This founding intuition inspired me to start what would demand a lifetime of elaboration. I was also influenced by dialogues and discussions with nontheistic professionals and university students hiding with me. They made me realize that many of them lived, at least implicitly, by some transcendent formation traditions or, more often, by pretranscendent developmental traditions. Their discussions gave me some insight into the implicit impact of popularized traditions on the formation traditions of Christians. I discovered that non-Christians, too, had valuable insights to offer. They reported on fruitful ideas, experiences, and formulations, some of which I could validate in my formation science and its Christian articulation.

During these discussions I thus became aware of the fact that non-Christians could share with us certain fundamental principles and dynamics of life and world formation. Such foundations could be meaningful to all people because of our shared human nature. Would it, therefore, not be important first of all to find out about human nature *as formational?* Should I not develop a basic, general science of human formation? This question reminded me of the approach of Thomas Aquinas. He preceded his theological formulations with philosophical ones. Then he used these clarifying concepts of non-Christian thinkers as intellectual instruments in the formulation of a theology of the Christian faith tradition. Something similar had been attempted by other Christian philosophers such as, for instance, Augustine, Pascal, Kierkegaard, Tillich, Marcel, Lewis, and Ricoeur.

It became at once clear to me that for my new addition to the wide arena of human and Christian reflection, I must follow a similar path. I should develop a formation science that could also serve my subsequent articulation of Christian formation. This articulation could in turn be used by Christian theologians as they had used the Christian articulations presented by Christian philosophers.

Hence the first four volumes of this series and the related provisional glossaries in the journal I edit, *Studies in Formative Spirituality*, as well as my preceding less systematic publications in Europe and America are about formation science. At the same time I published in a less systematic fashion books, articles, and poems containing seeds for my pending articulation of formation science and of Christian formation traditions.

Working at this project since 1945, I began to realize the immensity of the task before me. Formation science alone would demand years of thought and formulation. At the same time my first concern should be to keep my eye on the Christian articulation of formation science. This formational articulation would be as distinguished from theology as the Christian articulation of philosophy by Christian philosophers is different from professional theology.

Institute of Formative Spirituality

My work in Europe in the area of formation was interrupted by an appointment by my community as a teacher of psychology in the psychology department of Duquesne University. This was a new field for me. It demanded graduate studies in other universities that led to my obtaining a Ph.D. in psychology in 1958 from Case Western Reserve University in Cleveland, Ohio. The title of my dissertation was "The Experience of Really Feeling Understood by a Person: A Phenomenological Study of the Necessary and Sufficient Constituents of This Experience as Described by 365 Subjects in Chicago and Pittsburgh."

After gaining my doctoral degree, I organized upon request by the president of Duquesne a new type of program, which I called "psychology as a human science." At the same time I tried to take up my formation studies again by starting to work toward a series of courses in transcendent human and Christian life formation. I could only do so when I made these courses initially a division of the psychology department. I functioned in that department as both a professor and as the initiator of the human science aspect of psychology.

To justify my formation approach as part of a psychology department, I spoke about distinctively human formation as distinguished from typical pretranscendent human development. I had to give this division temporarily the title "Institute of Man" to make it acceptable to psychologists. Later, when this institute became independent, I could give the program a name closer to its meaning. I had coined in Europe the name *Vormings Spiritualiteit* or *Formative Spirituality*. Accordingly I called it temporarily the "Institute of Formative Spirituality."

Study of Christian Formation Traditions
in Service of a Christian Articulation of Formation Science

I made the study of transcendent life formation the heart of the Institute program. Students were first of all initiated in formation science. Similarly theology students in my own tradition are first of all initiated in philosophy. My students in formation science were at the same time initiated in its Christian articulation. In the light of formation insights, they would research the scriptures, the church fathers, the classical masters of formation, the doctrine of the church about spiritual formation, and related textual sources. Specializing in Christian formational articulation would mean not restricting oneself to only theological manuals abstracted from these classics. Nor should students limit themselves to a mere history of spirituality or only to literary textual critique of these masters. They would have to research the classical sources themselves. They should do so in light of their applicability to concrete Christian formation.

My Christian articulation would use the conceptual tools gained from the science of formation. The latter would be taught in different yet related courses. Christian articulation would point to the practical applicability of the Christian formation tradition in everyday life situations.

Limited and sometimes wrong solutions for problems of human development are popularized by the media through talk shows, movies, video cassettes, and popular publications. Often they take their cue from the social, clinical, and educational disciplines about the pretranscendent life. Helpful as these may be, they are not the final word. For the Christian, not these disciplines, but foundational Christian spirituality *as formational* should be the basic. This articulation of formation science is achieved by a comparison of formational concepts with Christian formation pointers in scripture, classical tradition, and doctrine.

Revealing the dynamics of the *formational* application of scripture and the masters, in conformity with church doctrine, should be a crucial part of the research done by both faculty members and students. It would give them a program of Christian formation that could enable them, among other things, to appraise wisely the insights and findings of other formation traditions. It would, moreover, provide them with the knowledge and skill needed to critique disciplines of the pretranscendent life from a Christian viewpoint.

Christian Articulation and
Christian Professional Theology of Formation

What is the difference between the Christian articulation of formation science and a Christian theology of formation? Let us look here at another traditional distinction: between philosophy with its Christian articulation and professional theology. Theology makes use of philosophical concepts and their Christian articulation by philosophers insofar as they are relevant to theology.

In order to clarify this distinction we must first think about Christian philosophers. We must ask ourselves how they are distinguished from non-Christian philosophers. They differ in various ways. For instance, they may point to possible Christian articulations of their philosophical concepts, but they do not claim that they are, therefore, professional theologians. We find such borrowing of philosophical ideas in Thomas Aquinas. He utilized the concepts of such philosophers as Aristotle and Plato. Being a professional theologian himself, he also worked these philosophical clues out theologically. Later scholastic philosophers distinguished themselves explicitly from professional theologians. The church encouraged them to start their own autonomous philosophy departments in seminaries and universities, to grant their own degrees, to start their own publications and learned societies, to develop their own metalanguages.

The same happened to other Christian philosophers. We see Christian articulations of their own philosophical concepts in Hegel, Kierkegaard, Marcel, Ricoeur, Ellul, Strasser, Lewis, and numerous others. Professional theologians may take up these articulations of philosophy in their own way, as St. Thomas did. That does not mean that these philosophers should now be called professional theologians.

The same applies analogously to the empirical-experiential aspect of transcendent life formation. Christian students of transcendent life formation develop a systematic empirical-experiential science about this formation. They may then choose to articulate the possible relevance of the concepts and constructs of this science in relation to Christian life formation. Their suggestions may also move some theologians to use these concepts in a theology of Christian formation. As in Christian philosophy, so, too, this articulation and this borrowing by theologians does not make the formation scientist a professional theologian. If anything it underlines the need to keep formation science and its Christian articulation separate from professional theology as the church demanded for its philosophy departments in seminaries and universities.

We are back to the question: What is the distinction between Christian articulation and the professional theology of formation? First of all, we ought to distinguish between theology in the widest sense and *professional* theology. In the broadest sense, adherents of any religion who are in some way occupied with any of its doctrines and traditions are doing theology. Obviously they would not be called theologians in the same way one could name Karl Rahner, Bernard Häring, or Karl Barth theologians. Children learning their catechism are doing some kind of elementary theology yet they would not be called professional theologians. Neither are Christian philosophers or Christian formation scientists professional theologians. For one thing they limit themselves to possible Christian articulations of their own philosophical and formational concepts and constructs.

Aims of Articulation

What is articulation? According to Webster's dictionary, we find the word *articular* in Medieval English. This term was derived from the Latin *articularis*. It means belonging to the joints or to a joint. The adjective *articulate* comes into English from new Latin. It means jointed, distinct; formed with joints (an *articulate* animal). It can also mean formed by the distinct and intelligent movements of the organs of speech; expressed clearly; distinct (*articulate* speech or utterance). The verb *articulate* means to join; to unite by means of a joint; to utter by intelligent and appropriate movement of the vocal organs. Articulation is, therefore, the act or manner of articulating or being articulated; a joining or juncture, as of the bones; a joint; a part between two joints.

According to the Family Word Finder, *Articulation* has been a part of the international scientific vocabulary since the 1500s. How do we use it in formation science? In both a general and a specific way. General methods of articulation have been introduced by me in formation science to enable its students to identify the general underlying structures, joints, and connections of the formation field they are researching (for more information on this point see volume 4, *Scientific Formation*, 94, 107, 120, 122, 125, 128, 177, 180).

The special articulation I am speaking about here is the Christian articulation of formation science. In this articulation we ask ourselves how the concepts and constructs disclosed by it can be joined to and remain at the same time distinct from similar concepts in Christian formation traditions. For example, how can we join the science's concept of transcendent contemplation with the Christian concepts of contemplation? And in what sense is this concept of the science different from this Christian articulation?

This approach differs from a theological starting point. Professional theologians usually do not start out from a concept or construct of formation science or from a formation event that underlies that concept. Their starting point is biblical revelation, doctrinal teachings, a faith tradition, or statements by other theologians.

Second, the aim of the Christian articulation of formation science is to facilitate for Christians their actual Christian life formation. Its primary aim is not to develop this formational articulation, no matter how systematic in itself, into a full-fledged professional theological treatise. Such a treatise would have to deal in detail with the relationships of this articulation to all aspects of the whole edifice of speculative theological knowledge. This enormous task can be undertaken by theologians who may, with proper reference, borrow and translate these Christian articulations of formation science in their own theological metalanguage.

Where do Christian articulators of formation science find Christian concepts of formation? These can be found in such Christian classical writings as the Bible, the desert and Church Fathers, the spiritual masters insofar as they touch on empirical-experiential Christian life formation. Professional theologians, on the contrary, usually do not limit themselves to the empirical-experiential aspects of Christian life formation when they consult the same sources.

It can happen that formation scientists as articulators step beyond these boundaries. They may dip into other aspects that are more or less related to the field of professional theology. Our colleagues in Christian philosophy often do the same. At times I find myself on this detour because of my interest in theology. Yet such side trips in another professional field are still guided by the interest and concern of formation science. Therefore, such a bypass in itself does not make philosophical or formational articulators professional theologians. Neither do they have the authority of professional theology. Their unique authority is, first of all, in the field of the empirical- experiential aspect of transcendent human formation. They do so on the basis of related concepts that they find in the writings of classical Christian masters of formation.

Preparation for the Christian Articulation of Formation Science

The research and teaching of the science of human formation took all my time and energy. Another person had to be found who was willing to assist me in gathering the formational wisdom of the classical and potentially classical Christian formation traditions. In preparation for my proposed more systematic Christian articulation of formation science, I had developed the method of formational theme tracing. Its purpose was to trace in the scriptures and in the classical masters of formation traditions the foundational themes of a Christian transcendent life formation. I could draw on these themes for my foundational Christian articulation of formation science. I wanted this selection and formulation to be done in the light of relevant concepts and constructs culled from my servant science of formation. If other basic themes would be discovered they should give rise to added concepts and constructs in my science.

The work I set out to do had to evolve in analogy to that done by Thomas Aquinas. He found the basic themes for his speculative and speculative-practical theology by tracing them in scripture, in doctrine, and in theologians who preceded him. He examined them in the light of his servant philosophy of human nature. I realized that I in the realm of Christian articulation would not be able to do this work as systematically as it deserved before having developed sufficiently my science of formation. Yet I felt that it would be crucial for the students that a preliminary preparation and version of this emergent Christian articulation of transcendent human formation would be at the heart of the program from the beginning. Otherwise they might be tempted to mistake the servant science as more important than its Christian articulation. Therefore, I insisted that they would be formed simultaneously by a six-semester cycle of courses in the Christian classics of spiritual formation as seen in the light of the findings of the science of formation. Gradually this range of formational theme tracing should be absorbed into the emerging body of an empirical-experiential Christian articulation of formation.

I found in Professor Susan Muto, Ph.D., a scholarly, persevering person, willing to devote her life and energy to teaching and developing this course cycle. She would work with me to lay the groundwork for what would be a comprehensive Christian articulation of formation science. The six-semester sequence she initiated revolved around the Christian classical formation tradition as touched upon by masters of formation. This tradition stood for different Christian formation traditions insofar as they proved to be consonant with the ever-evolving basics of Christian formation as such

Dr. Muto annotated and attended all of my courses in the science of formation and assisted me in the editing of my books and glossaries. This enabled her to offer the six-semester cycle in the light of the concepts and constructs developed in both formation science and its provisional articulation in Christian formative spirituality.

Transition from Formation Science
to Its Systematic Christian Articulation

I am now at the point of moving toward a more systematic formulation of a Christian articulation of formation science. This volume and the next one will be a transition from formation science as such to its articulation in Christian formation. The transition, however, to a more systematic

Christian articulation has to make sense to those who study my series on the science of formation. The bridge between the two can be found in the term *formation tradition*. It is one of the key terms both formation science and its Christian articulation have in common. To move wholeheartedly into Christian formation traditions as a true believer demands the gift of Christian faith. This cannot be the result of unaided human reason alone. Many scholars may stay in formation science. Some of them may articulate Christian form traditions only scientifically, from the outside as it were. Others complement this with a transscientific Christian articulation. Their endeavor can be compared to the work of Christian philosophers. A number of them may study the Christian faith tradition yet they may keep evolving and perfecting their philosophies of human nature as professors or students.

My next book, volume 6, will still be a transition volume. I have to say there more about the generic transcendent power and meaning of form traditions in all human formation. Only then can I do justice to its role in Christian formation in a way that makes sense to human reason while going beyond it through reason as illumined by the Christian faith and formation tradition. In volume 6 I also have to show in a generic way the role of formation phases as distinguished from the pretranscendent developmental life cycle construct in, for example, the Eriksonian faith and development tradition. Only after that can I show differences and similarities between the Christian formation phases and developmental life cycle stages. I hope to end that transitional sixth volume with a generic anthropology of transcendent human formation. This anthropology is touched upon in many places in all volumes and glossaries. It should be briefly summarized and where necessary complemented. Only then can I enter into the Christian formation anthropology. This anthropology will underlie my systematic Christian articulation of formation science.

Dialogue with Everyday Christian Existence

In the meantime the preparations for the Christian articulation of empirical-experiential formation are in progress. Because it is about the praxis of the implementation of faith in everyday life and world by Christians, it cannot be done in the seclusion of academia alone. It must unfold in dialogue with Christians in the midst of life. A solution to this problem was offered to us by Dr. George Armstrong Kelly IV, an eminent professor of the philosophy of history and religion at Johns Hopkins University. An outstanding teacher, scholar, and author and a deeply committed Episcopalian, Dr. Kelly studied my project with deep interest. He felt that he had been called and graced to create the means for us to develop, in dialogue with various faith groups, the intended Christian articulation and field validation of formation science.

Professor Muto and I had already founded and established the Epiphany

Association as a nonprofit ecumenical center for research, publication, and resource development in the field of lay formation and spiritual ecumenism to facilitate this aspect of my work.

Professor Kelly enjoyed a great prestige in the academic world as a scholar and writer. He was also a man of means in spite of his simple style of life. This enabled him to set free for this research and publication a beautiful home owned by his family, the Kelly house, an old but superbly preserved Victorian mansion in Pittsburgh. He encouraged Professor Muto in 1988 that it was time to relinquish her tenure as a full professor and director of the Institute at Duquesne University. He encouraged her to follow her call to devote herself full time to the preparation of the empirical-experiential phase of our work in specifically Christian formation and spiritual ecumenism. He did this at the last meeting we enjoyed with him before his untimely death at the age of fifty-four.

Always thoughtful and concerned about the six-semester cycle at the heart of the program at the institute, he and I both felt that Professor Muto could continue to make herself available to teach cycle courses as an adjunct professor whenever and wherever the need arose. These academic contacts at Duquesne, the University of Notre Dame, the Pittsburgh Theological Seminary, Louvain University, and other centers together with our preparation of textual, audio, and video resources for the laity in Christian formation are an excellent preparation for a Christian empirical-experiential articulation of formation science.

Bibliography

Books

Agus, Jacob B. *Dialogue and Tradition: The Challenges of Contemporary Judeo-Christian Thought*. New York: Abelard Schuman, 1971.

Argyris, C. *Personality and Organization: The Conflict between System and Individual*. New York: Harper Torchbooks, 1970.

Aronoff, Joel. *Psychological Needs and Cultural Systems: A Case-Study*. Princeton, N.J.: Van Nostrand, 1967.

Asch, Solomon. *Social Psychology*. Englewood Cliffs, N.J.: Prentice Hall, 1959.

Ashley Montagu, M. F. *Anthropology and Human Nature*. New York: McGraw-Hill 1957.

——, ed. *Culture and the Evolution of Man*. New York: Oxford University Press, 1962.

Bachelard, Gaston. *La formation de l'esprit scientifique: Contribution à une psychanalyse de la connaissance objective*. Paris: Vrin, 1957.

Bakan, D. *Sigmund Freud and the Jewish Mystical Tradition*. Princeton, N.J.: Van Nostrand, 1958.

Barbour, Ian G. *Myths, Models and Paradigms*. New York: Harper & Row, 1974.

Barnett, H. G. *Innovation, The Basis of Cultural Change*. New York: McGraw-Hill, 1953.

Barnouw, Victor. *Culture and Personality*. Homewood, Ill.: Dorsey Press, 1964.

Bastide, Roger. *Sociologie et psychanalyse*. Paris: P.U.F., 1950.

——. *Les grands thèmes moraux de la civilisation occidentale*. Paris: Bordas, 1958.

Baudouin, Charles. *De l'instinct a l'esprit, précis de psychologie analytique*. Paris: Desclée de Brouwer, Les Etudes Carmelitaires, 1950.

Becker, Ernest. *The Structure of Evil: An Essay on the Unification of the Science of Man*. New York: Braziller, 1968.

——. *The Denial of Death*. New York: Macmillan, 1973.

Benedict, Ruth. *Patterns of Culture*. New York: Mentor Books, 1952.

Berger, Peter L., and Thomas Luckmann. *The Social Construction of Reality: A Treatise in the Sociology of Knowledge*. New York: Doubleday, 1967.

Berman, Harold J. *Law and Revolution: The Formation of the Western Legal Tradition*. Cambridge, Mass.: Harvard University Press, 1983.

Blondel, C. *Introduction a la psychologie collective*. Paris: Armand Collin, 1952.

Brown, Norman O. *Life against Death: The Psychoanalytical Meaning of History*. Middletown, Conn.: Wesleyan University Press, 1959.

Buytendijk, F. J. J. *Traité de psychologie animale*. Paris: P.U.F., 1952.

Cassirer, Ernst. *An Essay on Man: An Introduction to a Philosophy of Human Culture*. New York: Doubleday Anchor Books, 1953.

Claparede, ed. *L'éducation fonctionnelle*. Neuchâtel: Delachaux et Niestle, 1958.

Cobb, John. *Christ in a Pluralistic Age*. Philadelphia: Westminster Press, 1975.

Conger, C. P. *The Ideologies of Religion*. New York: Round Table Press, 1940.

Coward, Harold. *Pluralism: Challenge to World Religions*. Maryknoll, N.Y.: Orbis Books, 1985.

Cronin, Vincent. *A Pearl to India: The Life of Roberto de Nobili*. London: Darton, Longman and Todd, Libra Books, 1966.

Dillard, Annie. *An American Childhood*. New York: Harper & Row, 1987.

Dilley, Frank B. *Metaphysics and Religious Language*. New York: Columbia University Press, 1964.

Dole, Gertrude E., and Robert L. Carneiro. *Essays in the Science of Culture in Honor of Leslie A. White*. New York: Thomas Y. Crowell, 1960.

Dufrenne, Mikel. *La personnalité de base, un concept sociologique*. Paris: P.U.F., 1953.

Dunne, Tad. *Lonergan and Spirituality: Towards a Spiritual Integration*. Chicago: Loyola University Press, 1985.

Durkheim, Emile. *Les formes élémentaires de la vie religieuse*. Paris: P.U.F., 1960.

Eliade, Mircea. *The Sacred and the Profane: The Nature of Religion*. Trans. Willard R. Trask. New York: Harcourt, Brace and World, 1959.

———. *From Primitives to Zen: A Thematic Sourcebook on the History of Religions*. New York: Harper & Row, 1967.

Elias, Norbert. *Über der Prozess der Zivilisation, Soziogenetischen und Psychogenetischen Untersuchungen*. Basel: Haus zum Falken, 1939.

Erikson, Erik H. *Young Man Luther: A Study in Psychoanalysis and History*. New York: Norton, 1958.

———. *Identity and the Life Cycle*. New York: International Universities Press, 1959.

Ey, Henri. *La conscience*. Paris: P.U.F., 1963.

———, dir. *L'inconscient (6e colloque de Bonneval)*. Paris: Desclée de Brouwer, 1966.

Feldman, A. Bronson. *The Unconscious in History*. New York: Philosophical Library, 1959.

Filiozat, Jean. *Inde, nation de traditions*. Paris: Horizons de France, 1961.

Fitzpatrick, Joseph P. *One Church, Many Cultures*. Kansas City, Mo.: Sheed and Ward, 1987.

Freud, Sigmund. *Civilization and Its Discontents*. Vol. 21 of the *Standard Edition*. Ed. and trans. J. Strachey. London: Hogarth Press and the Institute of Psycho-Analysis, 59–145.

———. *Psychoanalysis and Faith: Dialogues with the Reverend Oskar Pfister*. New York: Basic Books, 1963.

———. *Three Essays on the Theory of Sexuality*. Vol. 7 of the *Standard Edition*. Ed. and trans. J. Strachey. London: Hogarth Press and the Institute of Psycho-Analysis, 125–43.

Fromm, Erich. *Beyond the Chains of Illusion: My Encounter with Marx and Freud*. New York: Simon and Schuster, 1962.

———. *The Dogma of Christ and Other Essays on Religion, Psychology and Culture*. New York: Holt, Rinehart and Winston, 1963.

———. *Psychoanalysis and Religion*. New York: Bantam Books, 1967.

Gehlen, Arnold. *Anthropologische Forschung, zur Selbstbegegnung und Selbstentdeckung des Menschen*. Hamburg: Rowohlt, Rororo, 1961.

Gilbert, Alphonse. *You Have Laid Your Hand on Me: A Message of Francis Libermann for Our Time*. Rome: Spiritan Research and Animation Centre, 1983.

Gillin, John, ed. *For a Science of Social Man: Convergences in Anthropology, Psychology and Human Behavior*. Symposium of the Anthropological Society of Washington. Washington, 1962.

Guardini, Romano. *Das Ende der Neuzeit.* Basel: Hess Verlag, 1950.

———. *Welt und Person.* Würzburg: Werkbund-Verlag, 1950.

———. *Pascal for Our Time.* New York: Herder and Herder, 1966.

Gurvitch, Georges, and others. *Traité de sociologie.* Paris: P.U.F., 1958.

Gusdorf, Georges. *Mythe et métaphysique.* Paris: Flammarion, 1953.

Habermas, Jürgen. *Erkenntnis und Interesse.* Frankfurt a.M.: Suhrkamp, 1968.

Halbwachs, Maurice. *La mémoire collective.* Paris: P.U.F., 1950.

Haring, Douglas G. *Personal Character and Cultural Milieu.* Syracuse, N.Y.: Syracuse University Press, 1956.

Hasegawa, Nyozekan. *The Japanese Character: A Cultural Profile.* Trans. John Bester. Palo Alto, Calif.: Kodansha International, 1966.

Helminiak, Daniel. *The Same Jesus: A Contemporary Christology.* Chicago: Loyola University Press, 1986.

Heschel, Abraham. *Man Is Not Alone: A Philosophy of Religion.* New York: Harper & Row, 1951.

———. *The Insecurity of Freedom: Essays in Applied Religion.* New York: Farrar, Straus and Giroux, 1966.

Honigmann, John J. *Culture and Personality.* New York: Harper, 1954.

Hsu, Francis L. K. *Psychological Anthropology: Approaches to Culture and Personality.* Homewood, Ill.: Dorsey Press, 1961.

Huizinga, J. *Geschonden wereld, een beschouwing over de kansen op herstel van onze beschaving.* Haarlem: Tjeenk Willink, 1945.

Hymes, Dell H., ed. *Language in Culture and Society: A Reader in Linguistics and Anthropology.* New York: Harper & Row, 1964.

James, William. *The Varieties of Religious Experience: A Study in Human Nature.* London: Longmans, 1952.

Jayatilleke, K. N. *The Buddhist Attitude to Other Religions.* Kandy, Sri Lanka: Buddhist Publication Society, 1975.

Kierkegaard, Søren. *The Concept of Dread.* Trans. Walter Lowrie. Princeton, N.J.: Princeton University Press, 1957.

Kluckhohn, Richard, ed. *Culture and Behavior: The Collected Essays of Clyde Kluckhohn.* Free Press of Glencoe, 1962.

Koch, Sigmund. *Psychology: A Study of a Science.* Study II. Empirical Substructures and Relations with Other Sciences. Vol. 6 of *Investigations of Man as Socius: Their Place in Psychology and the Social Sciences.* New York: McGraw-Hill, 1963.

Kroeber, A. L. *The Nature of Culture.* Chicago: University of Chicago Press, 1952.

Lee, Dorothy. *Freedom and Culture.* New York: Prentice-Hall, 1959.

Lévi-Strauss, Claude. *Anthropologie structurale.* Paris: Plon, 1958.

Lévy-Bruhl. *La mentalité primitive.* Paris: P.U.F., 1947.

Malinowski, Bronislaw. *A Scientific Theory of Culture and Other Essays.* New York: Oxford University Press, Galaxy Books, 1960.

Marcuse, Herbert. *Eros and Civilization.* New York: Vintage Books, 1962.

Mead, George Herbert. *Mind, Self and Society.* Ed. Charles W. Morris. Chicago: University of Chicago Press, 1934, 1974.

Mead, Margaret. *Anthropology: A Human Science.* New York: Van Nostrand, 1964.

Mendel, Gerard. *La révolte contre le père, une introduction à la socio-psychanalyse.* Paris: Payot, 1969.

Moles, Abraham A. *Sociodynamique de la culture.* Paris-Den Haag: Mouton, 1967.

Mumford, Lewis. *The Condition of Man.* New York: Harcourt, Brace and Co., 1944.

Murphy, Charles M. *At Home on Earth: Foundations for a Catholic Ethic of the Environment.* New York: Crossroad, 1989.

Muto, Susan A. *Renewed at Each Awakening: The Formative Power of Sacred Words.* Denville, N.J.: Dimension Books, 1979.

———, and Adrian van Kaam. *The Emergent Self.* Denville, N.J.: Dimension Books, 1968.

———, and Adrian van Kaam. *The Participant Self.* Denville, N.J.: Dimension Books, 1969.

———, and Adrian van Kaam. *Commitment: Key to Christian Maturity.* Mahwah, N.J.: Paulist Press, 1989.

———, and Adrian van Kaam. *Commitment: Key to Christian Maturity, A Workbook and Study Guide.* Mahwah, N.J.: Paulist Press, 1991.

Niebuhr, Reinhold. *The Nature and Destiny of Man.* New York: Scribner and Sons, 1941.

O'Brien, Conor Cruise. *God Land: Reflections on Religion and Nationalism.* Cambridge, Mass.: Harvard University Press, 1988.

Otto, Rudolf. *The Idea of the Holy.* New York: Galaxy Books, 1958.

Pfister, Otto. *Die Frömmigkeit des Grafen Ludwig von Zinzendorf.* Leipzig-Vienna, 1925.

Ricoeur, Paul. *The Symbolism of Evil.* Boston: Beacon Press, 1969.

Rieff, Philip. *The Triumph of the Therapeutic: Uses of Faith after Freud.* New York: Harper & Row, 1966.

Rubinstein, R. L. *The Religious Imagination.* New York: Bobbs-Merrill, 1968.

Schimmel, Annemarie. *Mystical Dimensions of Islam.* Chapel Hill: University of North Carolina Press, 1975.

Schiwy, Gunther. *Der französische Strukturalismus.* Hamburg: Rowohlt, Rororo, 1969.

Schneider, Herbert W. *The Puritan Mind.* University of Michigan Press, 1958.

Schumacher, E. F. *Small Is Beautiful: Economics as if People Mattered.* New York: Harper & Row, 1973.

Sève, Lucien. *Marxisme et theorie de la personnalité.* Paris: Editions sociales, 1969.

Shapiro, Harry L., ed. *Man, Culture and Society.* New York: Oxford University Press, Galaxy Books, 1960.

Shea, John. *Stories of Faith.* Chicago: Thomas More Press, 1980.

Smith, Wilfred Cantwell. *The Faith of Other Men.* New York: Harper & Row, 1972.

Stock, M. *Freud: A Thomistic Appraisal.* Washington D.C.: Thomist Press, 1963.

Szasz, Thomas. *The Myth of Psychotherapy.* Garden City N.Y.: Doubleday/Anchor, 1978.

Thompson, Norma H., ed. *Religious Pluralism and Religious Education.* Birmingham, Ala.: Religious Education Press, 1988.

Thornton, E. M. *The Freudian Fallacy.* Garden City, N.Y.: Doubleday/Dial, 1983.

Tillich, Paul. *The Courage To Be.* New Haven: Yale University Press, 1952.

———. *Christianity and the Encounter of the World Religions.* New York: Columbia University Press, 1963.

———. *The Protestant Era.* Chicago: Phoenix, 1963.

Toynbee, Arnold. *A Historian's Approach to Religion.* London: Oxford University Press, 1956.

Tracy, David. *Plurality and Ambiguity.* San Francisco: Harper & Row, 1987.

Troeltsch, Ernst. *Der Historismus und Seine Probleme.* Tübingen: C. B. Mohr, 1972.

van Kaam, Adrian. *The Art of Existential Counseling.* Denville, N.J.: Dimension Books, 1966.

———. *On Being Involved: The Rhythm of Involvement and Detachment in Daily Life.* Denville, N.J.: Dimension Books, 1970.

————. *On Being Yourself: Reflections on Originality and Spirituality.* Denville, N.J.: Dimension Books, 1972.

————. *In Search of Spiritual Identity.* Denville, N.J.: Dimension Books, 1975.

————. *The Dynamics of Spiritual Self Direction.* Denville, N.J.: Dimension Books, 1976.

————. *The Transcendent Self: The Formative Spirituality of Middle, Early and Later Years of Life.* Denville, N.J.: Dimension Books, 1979.

————. *Religion and Personality.* Denville, N.J.: Dimension Books, 1980.

————. *Living Creatively.* Denville, N.J.: Dimension Books, 1981.

————. *Foundations for Personality Study: An Adrian van Kaam Reader.* Denville, N.J.: Dimension Books, 1983.

————. *Fundamental Formation.* Science of Formative Spirituality 1. New York: Crossroad, 1983.

————. *A Light to the Gentiles.* Lanham, Md.: University Press of America, 1984.

————. *Human Formation.* Science of Formative Spirituality 2. New York: Crossroad, 1985.

————. *Formation of the Human Heart.* Science of Formative Spirituality 3. New York: Crossroad, 1986.

————. *Scientific Formation.* Science of Formative Spirituality 4. New York: Crossroad, 1987.

————, and K. Healy. *The Demon and The Dove: Personality Growth Through Literature.* Lanham, Md.: University Press of America, 1982.

Vitz, Paul. *Sigmund Freud's Christian Unconscious.* New York: Guilford Press, 1988.

Weber, Max. *The Protestant Ethic and the Spirit of Capitalism.* London: George Allen & Unwin, 1930.

White, Leslie A. *The Science of Culture.* New York: Farrar, Straus and Cudahy, 1949.

————. *The Evolution of Culture: The Development of Civilization to the Fall of Rome.* New York: McGraw-Hill, 1959.

Whitson, Robley E. *The Coming Convergence of World Religions.* New York: Newman, 1971.

Zilboorg, Gregory. *Psychoanalysis and Religion.* London: Allen and Unwin, 1967.

Articles

Abbott, W. M., ed. "Declaration on the Relationship of the Church to Non-Christian Religions." *The Documents of Vatican II.* New York: Guild Press, 1966.

Allport, Gordon B. "The Historical Background of Modern Social Psychology." In Gardner Lindzey, *Handbook of Social Psychology.* Cambridge, Mass.: Addison-Wesley, 1954, 1:3–56.

Barden, Garrett. "II. The Symbolic Mentality." *Philosophical Studies* 15 (1966): 28–57.

Bateson, Gregory. "Cultural Determinants of Personality." *Personality and Behavioral Disorders* 2. Ed. J. McV. Hunt. New York: Ronald Press, 1944, 714–33.

Blanquart, P. "Le structuralism en France." Supplément de *La vie spirituelle* 83 (1967): 559–74.

Cafargna, Albert Carl. "A Formal Analysis of Definitions of 'Culture.'" *Essays in the Science of Culture in Honor of Leslie A. White.* Ed. Gertrude E. Dole and Robert L. Carneiro. New York: Thomas Y. Crowell, 1960, 111–32.

Cattell, R. B. "The Principal Cultural Patterns Discoverable in the Syntal Dimensions of Existing Nations." *Journal of Social Psychology* 32 (1950): 215–53.

Cattell, R. B., H. Breul, and H. Hartman Parker. "An Attempt at a More Refined Definition of the Cultural Dimensions of Syntality in Modern Nations." *American Sociological Review* 17 (1952): 403–21.

Chavez-Garcia, Sylvia, and Daniel A. Helminiak. "Sexuality and Spirituality: Friends Not Foes." *Journal of Pastoral Care* 32 (1985): 151–63.

Coward, Harold. "A Critical Analysis of Raimundo Panikkar's Approach to Inter-Religious Dialogue." *Cross-Events* 29 (1979): 183–90.

Devereux, George. "Charismatic Leadership and Crisis." *Psychoanalysis and the Social Sciences*. Ed. W. Munsterberger and S. Axeldrad, 1955, 4:145–57.

Ferenczi, Sandor. "The Ontogenesis of the Interest in Money." *Sex in Psychoanalysis*. New York: Dover Publications, 1956, 269–79.

Fischer, J. L. "Art Styles as Cognitive Maps." *American Anthropologist* 63 (1961): 79–93.

Haring, Douglas G. "Is Culture Definable?" *American Sociological Review* 14 (1949): 26–32.

Henry, Jules. "The Inner Experience of Culture." *Psychiatry, Journal for the Study of Interpersonal Processes* 14 (1951): 87–103.

Hermès (Receuils de textes et d'études), n. 6. *Le vide, Expérience spirituelle en Occident et en Orient*. Paris 16^2, 48 rue Cortambert, 1969.

Jones, Owen. "Joseph Campbell and the Power of Myth." *Intercollegiate Review* 25, no. 1 (Fall 1989).

Lacan, Jacques. "Fonction et champ de la parole et du langage en psychanalyse, Rapport du congrès de Rome 1953." *Ecrits*. Paris: Seuil, 1966, 237–322.

Muto, Susan A. "Caring for the Minister or Caregiver." *Network Papers* 39 (1990).

Piryns, E. D. "The Church and Interreligious Dialogue: Present and Future." *Japan Missionary Bulletin* 4 (1978).

Radcliffe Brown, A. R. "White's View on a Science of Culture." *American Anthropologist* 51 (1949): 503–12.

Rahner, Karl. "Natural Science and Reasonable Faith." *Theological Investigations 1*. New York: Crossroad, 1988, 16–55.

Reich, Wilhelm. "L'application de la psychanalyse a la recherche historique." *L'homme et la societé*. Revue internationale de recherches et de syntheses sociologiques, 11 (January–March 1969): 7–17.

Straus, Erwin. "The Miser." *Patterns of the Life-World*. Ed. J. M. Edie. Evanston, Ill.: Northwestern University Press, 1970.

Swales, P. J. "Ce que Freud n'a pas dit." *La sexualité d'ou vient l'Orient: Ou va l'Occident?* Ed. A. Verdiglione. Paris: Belfond, 1984.

Troeltsch, Ernst. "The Place of Christianity Among the World Religions." *Christianity and Other Religions*. Ed. John Hick and Brian Hebblethwaite. Glasgow: Fount, 1980, 11–31.

van Kaam, Adrian. "Transcendence Therapy." *Handbook of Innovative Psychotherapies*. Ed. Raymond J. Corsini. New York: John Wiley and Sons, 1981.

———. "Erosion and Depletion of Social Presence in the Helping Professions — A Formative Perspective." *Studies in Formative Spirituality* 9 (1988).

———. "Formative Spirituality." *Dictionary of Pastoral Care and Counseling*. Nashville: Abingdon Press, 1990.

Vitz, P. C. "The Psychology of Atheism." *Truth* 1:29–36.

———. "Sigmund Freud's Attraction to Christianity: Biographical Evidence." *Psychoanalysis and Contemporary Thought* 6:73–183.

———, and J. Gartner. "Christianity and Psychoanalysis, Part 1: Jesus as the Anti-Oedipus." *Journal of Psychology and Theology* 12, 4–14.

————, and J. Gartner. "Christianity and Psychoanalysis, Part 2: "Jesus as Transformer of the Super-Ego." *Journal of Psychology and Theology* 12, 82–90.

Waardenburg, Jacques. "World Religions as Seen in the Light of Islam." *Islam: Past Influence and Present Challenge.* Ed. A. Welch and P. Cachia. Edinburgh: Edinburgh University Press, 1979.

White, Leslie A. "The Concept of Culture." *American Anthropologist* 61 (1959): 227–252.

Video

van Kaam, Adrian and Susan A. Muto. "Becoming Spiritually Mature." Part 1: "Know Our Source." Pittsburgh, Pa.: Epiphany Association, 1990.

————, and Susan A. Muto. "Becoming Spiritually Mature." Part 2: "Open Our Heart." Pittsburgh, Pa.: Epiphany Association, 1990.

————, and Susan A. Muto. "Becoming Spiritually Mature." Part 3: "Listen to Life." Pittsburgh, Pa.: Epiphany Association, 1990.

————, and Susan A. Muto. "Becoming Spiritually Mature." Part 4: Say Yes Always." Pittsburgh, Pa.: Epiphany Association, 1990.

————, and Susan A. Muto. "Becoming Spiritually Mature." Part 5: "Mirror the Mystery." Pittsburgh, Pa.: Epiphany Association, 1990.

————, and Susan A. Muto. "Becoming Spiritually Mature." Part 6: Flow with Grace." Pittsburgh, Pa.: Epiphany Association, 1990.

Audio

Muto, Susan A., and Adrian van Kaam. "Commitment: Key to Christian Maturity." Mahwah, N.J.: Paulist Press, 1991.

Index

accretions: accidental, 261; of form traditions, 271
actual life form, 3, 280
adaptation: *see:* adjustment
adjustment, 115
affectivity, 94, 98
affinity: horizons of the field, 88
affirmation: 217; of eros, 180
alcoholism, 204
anality: anal disposition, 223; anal eroticism, 226; anal formation phase, 223, 233
analogy: analogical form potency, 157
anger: intraconscious, 177
anthropology: 9; of formation, 79; of formation science, 181; presuppositions, 22
anticipation, 282
anti-Semitism, 7
anxiety, 90, 148
apartheid, 72, 135
apparent form, 54, 280
appeal: modes, 153
appraisal: 43, 290; capacity, 251; confrontational, 66, 146; dispositions, 109, 132; of directives, 53; of failure, 253; of form tradition, 328; process, 296
appreciation: 170; appreciative abandonment, 240; -depreciation questions, 168; directives, 115; in-depth, 228; of disclosure, 165

Aquinas, Thomas, 103, 130, 180, 190, 305
Aristotle, 17
articulation: dialectics, 310; radical, 308; research, 311; reverse, 82; transscientific, 308
aspiration: and inspiration directives, 111; for fulfillment, 224
atheism: 3, 256; atheistic tradition, 132
attachment strivings, 148
attention: attentiveness dispositions, 218; strategic reduction, 89
Augustine, 69
autarky: formational autonomy, 44; as self-actualization, 285; as quasi-foundational form of life, 52
autism, 191
autonomic nervous system, 52

behaviorism, 28
belief system, 24, 48
Benedict of Nursia, 178
Bonhoeffer, Dietrich, 69
Buddhism: faith tradition, 30; form tradition, 278

call: efficacy, 216; failing 250; of life, 83, 247
Calvinism: faith tradition, 229, 230; formation tradition, 54
Campbell, Joseph, 80